New Horizons in Sephardic Studies

SUNY Series in Anthropology and Judaic Studies
Edited by Walter P. Zenner

New Horizons
in
Sephardic Studies

EDITED BY

Yedida K. Stillman

and

George K. Zucker

STATE UNIVERSITY OF NEW YORK PRESS

Published by
State University of New York Press, Albany

© 1993 State University of New York

For information, address State University of New York
Press, State University Plaza, Albany, N.Y., 12246

Production by Cathleen Collins
Marketing by Bernadette LaManna

Library of Congress Cataloging in Publication Data

New horizons in Sephardic studies / edited by Yedida K. Stillman and
    George K. Zucker.
        p.   cm. — (SUNY series in anthropology and Judaic studies)
    ISBN 0-7914-1401-9 (acid-free). — ISBN 0-7914-1402-7 (pbk. : acid-free)
    1. Sephardim—History. 2. Jews—History. 3. Ladino philology.
    4. Sephardim—Folklore. 5. Jews—Folklore.   I. Stillman, Yedida
    Kalfon, 1946– .   II. Zucker, George K., 1939– .   III. Series.
    DS134.N48   1992
    909'.04924—dc20   92-13578
                                                                       CIP

10 9 8 7 6 5 4 3 2 1

Contents

PART THREE
Ethnography and Folklore

Preface

New Horizons in Sephardic Studies is, as the title implies, a look at some of the latest research in the field—a panoramic view in which the essentially interdisciplinary nature of Sephardic studies cannot be overlooked. Although the editors have attempted to divide the contents into the areas of history and philosophy, language and literature, and ethnography and folklore, even those divisions indicate the impossibility of aligning a chapter in the field of Sephardic studies with a single academic discipline. The contents of the chapters do not allow them to be neatly categorized, even under these multiple headings.

Look, for example, at the contribution entitled "Camilo Castelo Branco and the Portuguese Inquisition" by Shepard. Does it belong in the section on literature, divorced from the history which is the context in which the literary work is developed? Mota's chapter on the anti-Semitic poetry of Alfonso Alvarez Villasandino gives us an insider's view of the social dynamics of sixteenth-century Spain and the plight of the *converso*, one which is every bit as revealing as the image in the late Stephen Gilman's *The Spain of Fernando de Rojas*. In its view of Spanish society, Shmuel Trigano's chapter on social linkage during the thirteenth century could be placed next to Carlos Mota's.

Is not the wedding song in the chapter by Cohen also a literary phenomenon? And the proverbs in the chapter by Lévy and Zumwalt are as much items of folk literature as are the folktales in the chapter by Haboucha. Perhaps no title is as revealing of the connection of areas as is "Literature as a Source for the History of Libyan Jewry During the Ottoman Period" by Simon.

The reader will also find here some new insights into matters historical, linguistic, and ethnographic dealing with Sephardic studies in its broadest definition. A new set of criteria for contemporary Jewish historiography is offered, illustrated by the case of the Venetian ghetto in the fifteenth and early sixteenth centuries (Genot-Bismuth), as well as a new perspective on the stages of the history of the New Christians' arrival in South America (Uchmany) and of their settlement in the Spanish colonies there (Gini de Barnatán).

The editors would like to express their heartfelt gratitude to the Lucius N. Littauer Foundation, who generously made publication of these proceedings possible. Also, because this international and interdisciplinary collection would have been impossible without the impetus of a conference held in 1987 on the campus of SUNY-Binghamton, for their help in permitting its realization, we would like to thank the editors' two home institutions, SUNY-Binghamton and the University of Northern Iowa, as well as the Lucius N. Littauer Foundation; Iowa Electric Power & Light; the Foundation for the Advancement of Sephardic Studies & Culture, Inc.; the Broome County Jewish Federation; SWANA, Suny-Binghamton; Mr. Jack R. Newman; S. Levy Incorporated; and the Jewish Student Union of SUNY-Binghamton. As you can see, the feeling that such a conference was needed as a spur to Sephardic studies activity in the United States went well beyond academia—and this collection further supports that idea.

For translations at the conference, we are indebted to Marilyn Gaddis Rose, who did double duty as both coordinator of translators and as a translator herself. Among the corps of translators were A. Preus, C. Coates, R. Cassel, M. Hayman, R. Norton and J.A. Long. To them—as well as to Deborah Mitchell, Susan Savitch, Gail Kupferman, and Dita Rimer—go the thanks of the conference participants, who were impressed by how smoothly everything ran. It would not have been as pleasant a conference without the help of these valiant people, and the editors are grateful for their participation, participation that resulted in this collection.

Special thanks for their invaluable help in completing this manuscript go to several colleagues at the University of Northern Iowa. It was the good will and artistic talent of Jan Harken, secretary of the Department of Modern Languages, that produced camera-ready copies of the two figures in the text. For their yeoman work in verifying sources, dates, and publishers through the Donald O. Rod Library at the University of Northern Iowa, we are grateful to Barbara Allen, Ed Wagner, and Barbara Weeg.

The editorial board for this collection (in addition to the editors), consisted of Professors Sandra Cypess, Samuel Morell, and Norman A. Stillman, all of SUNY-Binghamton, and David Gitlitz, now at the University of Rhode Island. They have invested much effort in selecting and organizing the material in this volume. Any errors remaining are solely the fault of the editors.

PART ONE

History and Philosophy

Introduction by Norman A. Stillman

The study of Sephardic history and thought has its origins at the very beginning of the modern academic discipline of Judaic studies in nineteenth-century Germany with the *Wissenschaft des Judentums* movement. The founding fathers of the field—Leopold Zunz, Moritz Steinschneider, Abraham Geiger, Salomon Munk, and Heinrich Graetz—all viewed the Jewish experience in Islamic Spain and in the early and more enlightened kingdoms of the *Reconquista* as one of the high points of diaspora history. It was they who created the notion of "the Golden Age of Spain," an idea borrowed from classical literary history. They were particularly impressed by the rich and original literature in poetry and philosophy produced by Andalusian Jews. They were also struck by the Sephardim's high degree of cultural assimilation (a consummation they devoutly wished for European Jewry in their own day). The *Wissenschaft des Judentums* scholars were classicists by predilection, and they had little interest in Sephardic history and thought after the Expulsion. Whereas Graetz devotes nearly an entire volume of his monumental *History of the Jews* to the medieval Islamic period and several chapters to the period in Christian Spain, only two full chapters and small parts of one or two others deal with Sephardim in the centuries that followed, and much of this is devoted to the Sephardim of Holland.

The *Wissenschaft des Judentums* school set the pattern of research in Sephardic history and thought for several generations. Over the past three decades, however, scholars have been turning their attention to the later periods and to broader regions of the Sephardic world such as North Africa and the Eastern Mediterranean that had hitherto been, if not totally ignored, little studied. A primary impetus for this new direction of scholarship was the mass exodus of

1

the Jewish populations from much of the Muslim world following the establishment of the State of Israel. With the sudden dissolution of most traditional Sephardic communities, a need was felt for a salvage operation to learn as much as possible about these Jewish cultures before they disappeared in the Israeli melting pot or assimilated into the culture of their host countries, particularly France, which also received large numbers of Sephardic émigrés. (Not surprisingly, Israel and France have become the two leading centers of Sephardic studies.) A good deal of this early 'salvage' work was ethnographic and consisted of collecting folklore, oral histories, or objects of material culture. Later, however, scholarly attention came to have a more historical focus.

The study of Sephardic history and thought over the past three decades has been very much influenced by the ethnographic anthropological, and sociological work of the preceding decade, as well as by the new trends in social-scientific history—what has been dubbed "the new history." (By the same token, some of the work of anthropologists and ethnographers—for example, Harvey Goldberg, Shlomo Deshen, or Laurence Loeb—has become decidedly historical.) This interdisciplinary, social-scientific historical approach is particularly evident in the papers in this section by Shmuel Trigano on social bonding and strategies in thirteenth-century Jewish society and Daniel Schroeter on the complex inter-relation between the Jewish quarter (*mellah*) and the larger Morrocan city of which it was a part. It is also taken into account and commented upon in Jacqueline Genot-Bismuth's critique of some of the presuppositions of contem-porary Jewish historiography in which the society of the sixteenth and early seventeenth-century Venetian ghetto is taken as a case study. Another example of the interdisciplinary approach may be found in Rachel Simon's paper which examines the way in which indigenous literature and especially oral literature may be used as source for the history of Libyan Jewry in late Ottoman time.

Not all Sephardic historical studies, of course, are of the new social-science variety. A great deal of significant work continues to be done in humanistic style of historical writing. Eva Alexandra Uchmany's paper on *cristianos nuevos* and *marranos* in Spanish America takes up the traditional historical concern with periodization and is concerned with archival and chronicle sources. Likewise, Matilde Gini de Barnatán's vignettes of Latin American marranism in the Rio de la Plata during the seventeenth century and Pier Cesare Ioly Zorattini's overview of the Sephardic and Marrano community in Ferrara, Italy, in the sixteenth century employ similar traditional sources and methodologies.

The two chapters in this section that deal with the history of thought also reflect the two poles of methodological approach—namely, that of the humanities and that of social science. In his study of the concept of beauty in Yehudah Abrabanel's *Dialoghi d'Amore* Ze'ev Levy traces the classical philsophical roots of Abrabanel's attempt to merge Jewish religious conceptions with Renaissance Platonism, while at the same time placing him as a pioneer of Jewish aesthetics on the threshold of modern Jewish intellectual history. Zvi Zohar, on the other hand, looks at the thought of Yitzhak Dayyan, a little-known rabbi in Aleppo, Syria, during the 1920s, who while decrying the abandonment of traditonal Jewish studies for modern intellectual pursuits shows that he himself was not at all immune to modern cultural influences. Zohar's discussion of Rabbi Dayyan's thought is presented as a mirror of contemporary social change more than as a study of intellectual history *stricto sensu.*

While by no means covering all areas, the chapters in Part I reflect the geographical, temporal, and disciplinary diversity that characterizes present-day research in Sephardic history and thought and, indeed, Sephardic studies in general.

ONE

Sephardic Settlement in Ferrara under the House of Este

Pier Cesare Ioly Zorattini

The expulsion edict issued by the Catholic Monarchs in 1492 marked the end of the longstanding legal existence of Judaism in Spanish territory. Jews were forced to choose between the dramatic alternatives of exile and conversion.[1] Emigration to Italy[2] was an important aspect of the complex mosaic of the Sephardic diaspora in the Mediterranean area. Ferrara not only attracted many settlers, but also acted as a transit center for Jews and New Christians from the Iberian Peninsula[3] on their way to Ancona[4] and Venice.[5] On November 20, 1492, Ercole II sent a letter patent, via the lawyer Corrado Stanga, the Este resident in Genoa, to a group of Jewish refugees[6] granting them permission to settle in Ferrara and its district. They were also given a series of privileges, ranging from the right to practice medicine freely (under condition that permission to treat Christians be gained from the Pope), to the right of "arendare et condure ad ufficio datii et gabelle" (that is, to levy duties and tolls), or to run pharmacies and even practice other trades, with substantial tax exemptions. The Duke also granted the new immigrants "all the privileges and immunities granted to the other Jews in the city except the right to practice usury."[7]

These privileges were confirmed by the Duke in another letter of February 1, 1493, in which he granted the requests of an additional 21 families to settle in his dukedom in Ferrara, "quod possint ac eis liceat omnes et singulas eorum familias conducere et conduci facere habitandum in hac nostra urbe Ferrariae et in quibuscumque aliis urbibus, terris et locis nostris."[8] This letter lists the 21 heads of family, including a woman. Of these, six were involved in trade. There were also 'Rabi Santo Abenamias', very probably Shem Tov ben Nahmias, another physician-rabbi, a tax contractor or 'datiero', five 'artisans' and six people of unknown profession.[9] The presence of two rabbis among the immigrants guaranteed the ritual autonomy of the Sephardic group from the outset. By the early years of the sixteenth century, the group had its own *yeshiva*, run by Mosé Navarro.

It is interesting to note that, while the Sephardic refugees established their own synagogue immediately, the same cannot by said for the Ashkenazi who arrived in Ferrara at approximately the same time. It seems, in fact, that the latter used the Italian synagogue at least until 1532, when they succeded in establishing a separate community and gained the authorization to open a synagogue which followed Ashkenazi ritual, on condition that they use an existing building and not erect a new one.[10] This state of affairs, then, continued until civilian life was shattered by the earthquake of 1571. Evidence of the disaster can be found in the first part of Rabbi Azariah min ha-Adumim or de Rossi's *Me'or Einayim 'Light of the Eyes'*; that is to say, the *Kol Elohim 'Voice of the Lord'*.[11] In the wake of this cataclysm, the Italian and Ashkenazi Jews decided to unite in a single 'Università'. However, despite Shulvass's observations, it is by no means clear if the two groups used the same oratory for their religious services.[12]

In the late fifteenth century, the first New Christians, popularly known as 'Marranos',[13] came from the Iberian Peninsula to join the original community of Sephardic Jews. This group also appeared in contemporary Christian sources, as, for example, the Ariosto necromancer Master Iachelina who "is, to tell the truth, a Jew by origin, of those thrown out of Castile."[14] It should be noted that the term 'New Christians' is ambiguous, as it was not always used to denote the *Conversos*; it could also refer to those Sephardic Jews who had not been baptised.[15] The presence of Marranos is, though, indirectly attested in a famous Jewish chronicle of the time, the *Emeq ha-bakha 'The Wailing Valley'* by the physician and rabbi Yosef ha-Kohen. In referring to the privileges granted by Duke Ercole to the Jews to induce them to come and settle in his lands, the author alluded to the fact that many of them had already been circumcised. Since this practice was strictly forbidden in the Iberian Peninsula, we must assume that the group included numerous New Christians who took advantage of the hospitality of the Este city to follow their ancestral religious practices again without much risk.[16]

In 1550, the very year in which the Republic of Venice renewed its ban on Marranos,[17] Ercole II of Este decided, to the contrary, to grant a general decree of safe-conduct to the "Portuguese and Spanish Jewish Nation" in which he assured the Jews that they would suffer "no harm" even if, for some reason, they had used Christian names and denied their Jewishness, "per qual si sia stato rispetto havessero detto non essere ebrei et servitisi del nome christiano." This statement essentially offered the New Christians the opportunity to declare themselves Jews and to resume their ancestral religious practices, if they so desired.[18] Therefore, it comes as no surprise that years later, in 1570, several Jews from Ferrara, who had fallen into the clutches of the Venetian Inquisition, defended themselves against the charge of being Marranos by maintaining that, since they were from Ferrara, they had always been Jews and had never been baptized. Such cases include those of Abram Righetto alias Abraham Benvenisti, arrested and tried by the Venetian Holy Office in 1570,[19] and a certain Moisé Salim, who managed to get himself released from the Cremona jail in 1573 by being able to show that he was "hebreo vero et non Marrano."[20]

The Sephardic community in Ferrara in the sixteenth century, as we have seen, was made up of Spanish Jews and New Christians, mostly of Portuguese origin, who were to become the majority. A significant presence of Marranos in the first half of the sixteenth century was even to be found at the University of Ferrara. In 1540, Duke Ercole II offered a chair of medicine there to the renowned physician João Rodrigo da Castelo Branco, better known as Amato Lusitano (1511–1568), a member of the Chabib family, baptised in 1497. He was to hold the post until 1547, when he transferred to Ancona.[21]

The most prestigious family of Sephardic Jews to move to Ferrara in the sixteenth century were the Abravanels, forced to emigrate from the Kingdom of Naples after the ban imposed in 1541.[22] Don Shemuel, son of the Philosopher Yitzchaq, counselor to the Catholic Monarchs,[23] and his second wife, Bienvenida, who had enjoyed immense favor and privileges at the court of the Viceroy of Naples, Don Pedro de Toledo,[24] soon became a focal point for the Sephardic diaspora in Ferrara, thanks to their wealth. In their home they maintained not only a rabbi, as was the custom among wealthy families, but they also boasted a private synagogue.[25] Their high social position enabled them to keep in contact with the courts of Italy. Doña Bienvenida had been lady companion to Eleonora of Toledo, the future Duchess of Florence who, it seems, actually called her *mãe* 'mother'.[26]

The widows of Francisco and Diego Mendes, the sisters Beatriz, or Gracia, and Brianda de Luna, also lived in Ferrara for some time. Beatriz was there briefly in 1549, before moving, via Venice, to Constantinople.[27] Brianda, on the other hand, came to Ferrara in the autumn of 1555, after having been banned from Venice on September 13 for having asked the Council of Ten openly for the right to live with her daughter in the ghetto as a Jew.[28] Brianda and her entourage stayed in Ferrara until about 1558 when, responding to the repeated requests of the Ottoman court, Ercole II allowed them to leave the Este state, provided that they give up all claims to large loans granted to the Duke himself.[29]

We can describe, however summarily, the physiognomy of the group of Portuguese Marranos who lived in Ferrara following the granting of privileges by Ercole II. The proceedings of the Lisbon Inquisition against a picaresque adventurer, the Portuguese Marrano Annrique Nunez, alias Abraham Benvenisti and more popularly known as Righetto (who had been tried by the Holy Office of Venice in 1570 for the crime of Judaism[30]) gives that information. At his trial, begun in 1576, Righetto, in contrast to his caution during the Venice proceedings, turned informer and provided a detailed list of the New Christians whom he

had known between 1550 and 1561 who had returned to the Jewish religion in
Ferrara. The list is of great interest for two reasons: first, it refers to the oldest
period of Marrano settlement in Ferrara,[31] and second, in addition to a double
list of Ferrara Marrano names (Christian and Jewish), it clarifies family relations
and the occupations the people professed to practice. According to the list, some
forty Portuguese heads of families had reverted to Judaism. Most of them were
merchants, but there were also goldsmiths and silversmiths, a jeweler, two
shopkeepers, a physician, a not clearly defined 'licenciado', a bookseller and even
an astronomer. Most were married to converted Jewish women, following the
tradition in Marrano circles. The list tells us, for example, the Jewish name of
one of Gracia Mendes' agents, the doctor and merchant Duarte Gomez, or David
Zaboca, who, with his colleague Agostinho Enriches, was charged with Judaism
three times in Venice—twice before the Inquisition and once before the Avogaria
di Comun—but always managed to be absolved as a good Catholic.[32]

But of those people mentioned by Abram Righetto, the most important are
Francisco Mendez Vesinho alias Esdras Vezinho and Gabriel Annriquez alias
Yosef Saralvo. The former, who according to Righetto,[33] "entende da astrologia
e da ley," is clearly the astronomer Esdras Vezinho, son of the renowned Yosef
Vezinho, physician and scientist at the court of João II of Portugal. Esdras, as
stated in another accusation (of November 1580) against the Ferrara Marranos
brought by the New Christian Lopo Luiz, lived with his wife and his son Andrea
in via Gattamarcia, the Ferrara street where the Portuguese Jewish synagogue
was to be found.[34]

Gabriel Annriquez (Yosef Saralvo) is one of the most notable figures in the
history of the Portuguese Jewish diaspora in Italy. A native of Lisbon, Saralvo
moved to Ferrara about 1545. He seems to have lived in via dei Sabbioni, where
he practiced his trade as a goldsmith and a silversmith. Not only had he openly
reembraced Judaism, but he had begun, fervently, to reconvert New Christians,
acting as a secret circumciser. Within a few years, at least according to Estevão
Nogueira (Stefano Noghera), another informer on the New Christians to the
Venice Holy Office in 1579, Saralvo was supposed to have circumcised six or
seven hundred boys in Ferrara and Venice.[35] Toward the end of 1581, for reasons
we cannot yet document but which traditional historiography attributes to the
pressures exercised by the Church on Duke Alfonso following active communication with the Portuguese Inquisition courts, Saralvo was arrested in Ferrara
and extradited to Rome, where he was sentenced to be burned alive in Campo
dei Fiori as an unrepentant and persistent apostate.[36] But the courage with which
he faced his fate was to leave a deep impression among the Jews of the Marrano
diaspora, who hailed him as a martyr for centuries.[37]

Ferrara was one of the most active Italian centers for the Jewish re-education
of New Christians from the Iberian Peninsula until the devolution of the Este
dukedom to the Church in January 1598. It is, therefore, no surprise that it was
also "the cradle of the Marrano book production."[38] The hospitality of the House

of Este had as one of its most significant outcomes the brief, but important, publishing activity which flourished towards mid-century, promoted by the Spaniard Jerónimo de Vargas, alias Yom Tob ben Levi Athias, and by the Portuguese Duarte Pinel, alias Abraham Usque. Between 1551 and 1558 they published about ten volumes, among which were seven liturgical texts in Ladino, two texts in Portuguese and an ancient Spanish philosophical work.[39] Of these works, it is worth noting the *Biblia en lengua Española traduzida palabra por palabra de la verdad Hebrayca por muy excelentes letrados, vista y examinada por el oficio de la Inquisicion*, which appeared in two versions—one for the Jews and one for the Christians, both submitted to, and approved by, the Inquisition and edited with the privilege of the "ylustrissimo Señor Duque de Ferrara."[40] Interesting is the fact that, while the version for Christians is dedicated to Duke Ercole, the Jewish version is dedicated to "Doña Gracia Nassi," now considered to be the undisputed patron of the Marrano diaspora. The differences between the two editions are also clear in the colophon; in fact, in the Christian version, the Christian names of the two printers, Duarte Pinel and Jerónimo de Vargas, appear, while in the Jewish version they are replaced by their Jewish equivalents, Abraham Usque and Yom Tob Athias.

Among other works printed by the Ferrara Marrano press, two classics of sixteenth-century Portuguese literature are worth recalling: the *Consolaçam as tribulaçõens de Israel* by Shemuel Usque[41] and the *História de Menina y Moça* by Bernardim Ribeiro.[42] The *Consolaçam* which was placed on the *Index librorum prohibitorum* by the Spanish Inquisition in Madrid in 1640,[43] was also dedicated to Doña Gracia Nassi, who had always come, as a "justa dona," to the aid of her brother Jews when they were in trouble.[44]

It is not clear why the Ladino-Portuguese press in Ferrara had to close down. A series of events which affected Jews and Marranos in Italy must have had an influence, even though Ferrara was not directly involved. The confiscation and destruction of the Talmud decreed by Pope Julius III in 1553 led to the calling of a Jewish synod in Ferrara in 1554, at which it was decided to subject the Jewish press to preventive censorship.[45] The tragic end of the Ancona Marranos in 1556 through inquisitorial repression ordered by Paolo IV and, finally, the institution of the ghetto, again the work of Paolo IV, with the bull *Cum nimis absurdum*,[46] contributed to rendering the climate of control on the part of the Counter-Reformation Church more oppressive to Italian Jews. Abraham Usque was still able to publish in Ferrara an elegy in Hebrew in honor of the martyrs of Ancona, but Cardinal Ghislieri ordered the Duke of Este to confiscate the work, destroy it, and severely punish its author.[47] In spite of this, Usque continued to publish in Hebrew until 1558, but the times were changing and he finally ceased activity.

The devolution of the Este dukedom to the Church (since Duke Alfonso had no direct male heir) meant crisis not only for the Sephardic community, but also for the rest of the Jews in Ferrara. In 1598, as power changed hands, a large group of Jews, including many Sephardim, left Ferrara to follow don Cesare to the new seat of Modena and Reggio. Even those who remained behind must have felt nostalgia for the House of Este. What Moisé Alatino wrote to the ducal counsellor Laderchi in February 1598 is significant. After the departure of the Estes from Ferrara, he seemed "to be in another country and in another world," in the hands of capricious fate, "where there is a constant flow of innovation."[48]

Nevertheless Jews, including some Sephardic Jews, continued to live in Ferrara after the city had passed to Church hands. The golden age, however, had disappeared, even though the eighteenth century saw a considerable recovery of entrepreneurial activity on the part of some local Jewish families.[49]

The Jews were to maintain—and they still maintain—their centuries-old settlement, but were subject to restrictions and were relegated, beginning in 1626, to a ghetto which was to last until the arrival of French troops in 1797.[50] In 1826, the ghetto was re-established,[51] to be finally abolished when Ferrara became a part of the Kingdom of Italy.[52]

Evidence of the continuous presence of Sephardic families was a Sephardic *Beth ha-Keneset*—the so-called "Spanish Levantine School"—which was destroyed by the Nazis in 1944. Today, the only monument that reminds us of the great Sephardic Jewish tradition in Ferrara is a tiny cemetary in via del Pavone, closed to burials, in which four *mazevot* are preserved, all pertaining to members of the Saralvo family.[53]

NOTES

1. Within the extensive bibliography, special mention should be made of the classic study of Y. Baer, *A History of the Jews in Christian Spain*, 2 vols. (Philadelphia: The Jewish Publication Society of America, 1971) II, pp. 44ff.; and the collection of documentary sources, *Documentos acerca de la expulsión de los judíos*, edición preparada y anotada por Luis Suárez Fernández (Valladolid: Biblioteca "Reyes Católicos", 1964).

2. For an introductory bibliography on the Sephardic diaspora and the phenomenon of Marranism, see *Actas del primer simposio de estudios sefardíes (Madrid 1-6 de junio de 1964)*, edición a cargo de I. M. Hassán con la colaboración de M. Teresa Rubiato y E. Romero (Madrid: Instituto "Arias Montano," 1970); G. Nahon, "Les Marranes espagnols et portugais et les Communautés juives, issues du Marranisme dans l'historiographie récente (1960–1975)," *Revue des Etudes Juives*, CXXXVI (1977), pp. 297–367.

3. L. Modona, "Les exilés d'Espagne à Ferrare en 1493," *Revue des Etudes Juives*, XV (1887), pp. 117–121.

4. V. Bonazzoli, "Ebrei italiani, portoghesi, levantini sulla piazza commerciale di Ancona intorno alla metà del Cinquecento," in *Gli Ebrei e Venezia, secoli XIV-XVIII. Atti del Convegno internazionale organizzato dall' Istituto di storia della società e dello stato veneziano della Fondazione G. Cini, Venezia, 5-10 giugno 1983*, ed. G. Cozzi (Milano: Edizioni di Comunità, 1987), pp. 727–770: 733–734.

5. Many Jews and New Christians, particularly from the Iberian Peninsula, lived in Ferrara before moving to Venice. See, for example, the agents of the widows Mendes, Licentiato Costa, Agostinho Enriches and Duarte Gomez. See also *Processi del S. Uffizio di Venezia contro Ebrei e Giudaizzanti (1548-1560)*, a cura di P. C. Ioly Zorattini (Firenze: Olschki, 1980), pp. 225-247, 251-263; *Processi del S. Uffizio...(1561-1570)*, a cura di P. C. Ioly Zorattini (Firenze: Olschki, 1982), pp. 67-96.

6. C. Brizzolari, *Gli Ebrei nella storia di Genova* (Genova: Sabatelli, 1971), p. 77.

7. D. Kaufmann, "Contributions à l'histoire des Juifs en Italie," *Revue des Etudes Juives*, XX (1890), pp. 34-72: 55.

8. L. Modona, pp. 118-119.

9. Loc. cit., pp. 120-121.

10. A. Pesaro, *Memorie Storiche sulla Comunità Israelitica Ferrarese* (Ferrara: Tipografia rist. anast.: Bologna, Forni, 1967), pp. 16-19: 19. The ban on erecting new buildings for synagogues dated back before 415 A.D. See V. Colorni, *Gli ebrei nel sistema del diritto comune fino alla prima emancipazione* (Milano: Giuffrè, 1956), pp. 47-48.

11. On the Ferrara earthquakes, 1570 to 1574, see E. Guidoboni, "Rita di calamità: terremoti a Ferrara nel 1570-1574," *Quaderni Storici*, n.s., 55 XIX, I (1984), pp. 107-135. For the testimony of Azaria de Rossi, see N. Shalem, "Una fonte ebraica poco nota sul terremoto di Ferrara del 1570," *Rivista Geografica Italiana*, XLV (1938), pp. 66-76.

12. M. Shulvass, *The Jews in the World of the Renaissance* (Leiden & Chicago: Brill and Spertus College of Judaica Press, 1973) p. 57. Shulvass bases this assertion on A. Pesaro, *Memorie Storiche*, 31, from which, however, it does not emerge that the two groups used the same synagogue to perform their rites, but that they simply met in the Italian synagogue to found the new community.

13. On the use of this term, see A. Farinelli, *Marrano: Storia di un vituperio* (Genève: Olschki, 1925).

14. L. Ariosto, "Il Negromante," *Opere*, ed. A. Seroni (Milano: Mursia, 1966), p. 1062.

15. The "Diario ferrarese dall'anno 1409 sino al 1502," ed. G. Pardi, in *Rerum Italicarum Scriptores*, t. XXIV, parte VII (Bologna: Zanichelli, 1828-1833) 135 mentions the baptism of numerous 'Marani et Marane' that took place during Lent of 1494.

16. Yosef ha-Kohen, *Emek ha-bakha*, estudio preliminar, traducción y notas por P. L. Tello (Madrid-Barcelona: Instituto Arias Montano, 1964), p. 190.

17. D. Kaufmann, "Bie Vertreibung der Marranen aus Venedig im Jahre 1550," *Jewish Quarterly Review*, V.S. XIII (1900), pp. 520-532; idem, "A Contribution to the History of the Venetian Jews," *Jewish Quarterly Review*, V.S., II (1890), pp. 207-305.

18. A. Balletti, *Gli Ebrei e gli Estensi* (Reggio Emilia: Anonima Tipografica Italiana, 1930, rist. anast. Bologna: Forni, 1969), p. 77.

19. On Righetto, see *Processi del S. Uffizio di Venezia contro Ebrei e Giudaizzanti (1570-1572)*, ed. P. C. Ioly Zorattini (Firenze: Olschki, 1984).

20. R. Segre, "Gli Ebrei lombardi nell'età spagnola: Storia di un'espulsione," *Memorie dell'Accademia delle Scienze di Torino, Classe di Scienze Naturali, Storiche e Filologiche*, #28 (Torino: Accademia delle Scienze, 1973), p. 61, nota 1.

21. M. Malavolti, *Medici Marrani in Italia nel XVI e XVII secolo* (Roma: Istituto di Storia della Medicina dell'Università di Roma, 1968), pp. 18-24.

22. For the history of the Jews in the Kingdom of Naples at the time of their expulsion, see the recent study by V. Bonazzoli, "Gli Ebrei nel regno di Napoli all'epoca della loro espulsione, I parte: il periodo aragonese (1456-1499)," *Archivo Storico Italiano*, CXXXVII (1981), pp. 179-287.

23. On Yitzchaq Abravanel, see, among others, the study of B. Netanyahu, *Don Isaac Abravanel, Statesman and Philosopher* (Philadelphia: The Jewish Publication Society of America, 1968).

24. A. Milano, "Abrabanel," *Encyclopedia Judaica*, II.

25. Pesaro, *Memorie storiche*, 22; idem, *Appendice alle Memorie storiche sulla comunità Israelitica Ferrarese* (Ferrara: Tipografia Sociale, 1879, rist. anast. Bologna: Forni, 1967), p. 14.

26. M. Kayserling, *História dos Judeus em Portugal* (São Paulo: Livraria Pioneira Editôra, 1971), p. 224.

27. P. Grunebaum Ballin, *Joseph Naci duc de Naxos* (Paris-La Haye: Mouton, 1968), p. 48.

28. *Processi del S. Uffizio. . .(1548-1560)*, pp. 349-351.

29. Grunebaum Ballin, p. 75.

30. *Processi del S. Uffizio. . .(1570-1572)*.

31. Loc. cit. 271ff. The other two lists of Marranos resident in Ferrara have been edited or indicated respectively by C. Roth, "I marrani in Italia: Nuovi documenti," *La Rassegna mensile di Israel*, VIII (1933-1934), pp. 419-443, and by E. A. Uchmany, "Entre el judaísmo y el cristianismo: un judío italiano ante la Inquisición de la Nueva España," in *Proceedings of the Eighth World Congress of Jewish Studies, Division B: The History of the Jewish People* (Jerusalem: World Union of Jewish Studies, 1982), pp. 55-60.

32. *Processi del S. Uffizio. . .(1548-1560)*, p. 57.

33. *Processi del S. Uffizio. . .(1570-1572)*, p. 32 and n. 272, 273, 275, 277. On his family, see C. Roth, "A Note on the Astronomers of the Vecinho Family," *Gleanings: Essays in Jewish History, Letters and Art* (New York: Hermon Press, 1967), pp. 175-177.

34. Roth, *I marrani in Italia*, p. 436.

35. *Processi del S. Uffizio di Venezia. . .(1571-1580)*, ed. P. C. Ioly Zorattini (Firenze: Olschki, 1985), p. 142.

36. C. Roth, "Joseph Saralvo: A Marrano Martyr at Rome," *Festschrift zu Simon Dubnows siebzigsten Geburstag* (Berlin: Jüdischer Verlag, 1930), pp. 180–186: 182–183.

37. Loc. cit. 184–185

38. C. Roth, "The Marrano Press at Ferrara, 1552–1555," *The Modern Language Review*, XXXVIII (1943), pp. 307–317: 307.

39. Ibid.

40. Kayserling, op. cit., p. 50. On the Ferrara Bible, see the recent study by H. V. Séphiha, *Le Ladino, Judéo-espagnol calque. Deutéronome. Versions de Constantinople (1547) et de Ferrare (1553). Edition, étude linguistique et lexique* (Paris: Centre de Recherches Hispaniques, 1973).

41. Kayserling, op. cit., p. 129. On Shemuel Usque, see M. A. Cohen, "Usque, Samuel," in *Encyclopedia Judaica*, 16, coll., pp. 21–22.

42. On Bernardim Ribeiro, see K. R. Scholberg, "Ribeiro, Bernardim," in *Encyclopedia Judaica*, 14, col. 151. See also the recent study by H. Macedo, *Do significado oculto da Menina e moça* (São Paulo: Morães, 1977).

43. C. Roth, "The Marrano Press at Ferrara," pp. 313–314.

44. Usque, *Consolaçam as tribulaçõens de Israel*, x. 52 r. and v.

45. On the burning of the Talmud, see K. R. Stow, "The Burning of Talmud in 1553 in the Light of Sixteenth Century Catholic Attitudes toward the Talmud," *Bibliothèque d'Humanisme et Renaissance*, XXXIV (1972), pp. 435–459; P. F. Grendler, *The Roman Inquisition and the Venetian Press, 1540–1605* (Princeton: Princeton Univ. Press, 1977), pp. 92–93. On the Jewish synod in Ferrara, see L. Finkelstein, *Jewish Self-Government in the Middle Ages* (New York: Ph. Feldheim, 1964), pp. 92–93.

46. K. R. Stow, *Catholic Thought and Papal Jewry Policy, 1555–1593* (New York: The Jewish Theological Seminary of America, 1977).

47. Roth, "The Marrano Press at Ferrara," p. 316.

48. Balletti, *Gli Ebrei e gli Estensi*, p. 79.

49. W. Angelini, *Gli Ebrei a Ferrara nel Settecento. I Coen e altri mercanti nel rapporto con le pubbliche autorità* (Urbino: Argalia, 1973).

50. Pesaro, *Memorie Storiche*, p. 37ff.

51. Loc. cit., p. 79.

52. Loc. cit., p. 103ff.

53. P. C. Ioly Zorattini, "I cimiteri sefarditi di Ferrara," *Annali di Ca' Foscari.*

TWO

The Università Degli Hebrei and the Nationi of the Venice Ghetto (1516–1630): A Reconsideration of Some Presuppositions of Contemporary Jewish Historiography

Jacqueline Genot-Bismuth
French text translated by Marilyn Gaddis Rose
Italian citations translated by Serafina Clarke

F irst of all, why such a formulation? My intention in proposing this subject is not to focus interest on the history of Venetian Jews. On the contrary, through a case I consider exemplary, I invite you to reflect epistemologically on what is generally meant by 'Jewish history.' It has become a discipline in itself, without there ever having been any theoretical critical elaboration since this so-called "discipline" was imposed as such by what could be called the force and inertia of things. As for my subject, I prefer to call it, more adequately in my opinion, 'Jewish historiography.' We should no doubt substitute the more properly critical concept of 'history of the Jews' to put into play this cultural revolution which will finally retrieve the history of Jewish societies from the dangers and derivatives of ideological militancy, whatever its tendency or horizon.

I shall not insist on the fact that on several occasions[1] a fair number of us have already shown our skepticism vis-à-vis an approach which pleads the principle of ethno-cultural autarchy of diasporic societies, at least up to their emancipation. This type of epistemological autarchy would justify the study of Jewish societies in isolation (the sacrosanct 'communities,' a grab bag concept, the obligatory obsequious language of that nearly historiographic cult) and abstract them from their complex constitutive articulation with the surrounding host societies in which Jewish societies are an undisputed part and with which, objectively, they have a parasitic relationship. Therefore, it is unrealistic and intellectually flawed to neglect to investigate the entire picture of inevitable phenomena of acculturation in the name of the assimilation phobia which characterizes the identity myth.

Overall, modern Jewish historiography is marked by a number of salient traits. Immediately evident is Judeocentricity and 'community' taken as a worldbase. The effects deriving from this choice lead inevitably to the practice of micro-history in which the criterion of parceling remains purely descriptive of the dispersion of the nuclei of the diasporic population. It never attempts a synthesis which would integrate group circulation networks to population transfers which constitute, nevertheless, its unifying and signifying framework. Finally the still nearly general division solely by results, the exclusive consideration of the 'fact' in the still traditional sense of positive history, accounts for the near nonexistence of social history in the Braudel or Duby sense.[2] The phenomenon appears all the more aggravated since it is institutionally legitimized in the Israeli academic world, which, of course, carries a decisive weight given the existence of departments of Jewish history, separate from the instruction and research entities of history in general.

The ensemble of these presuppositions, never directly formulated to be sure and remaining implicit, leads history called 'Jewish' to be doubly atomized: on the plane of geographic fragmentation on the one hand and on the temporal plane, of short or brief duration on the other. All of which leads to a history, today quite dated, which conceives of duration only as an overaccumulation of times of narrative or 'evenemential' history. This history, an addition to the dust layer of micro-histories, is naturally antithetic to history of mean and long durations[3] and is related more to the spirit of traditional chroniclers than to the orientations and methods of contemporary history. Such a practice ignores the global dimension of societies and rejects internal social dialectics evolving over the long term as outside its purview. An additional danger is the separation of the realities which it presumes to take into consideration from the extra-Jewish context in which such realities are inserted but with which they necessarily maintain functional relations objectively indispensable for the historian. The significant risk is that of effacing the equally essential perception of the dialectic resulting from the interaction of this micro-society with the macro-society that shelters and rejects it, by turns tolerates and excludes it, in its turn finally the parasite, presenting us with the impossibility of achieving historical understanding of a phenomenon (however singular) of problematic interethnic relations which are, however, the essential key of a history literally more than twenty centuries old. And that ends by again accumulating compulsively a list of infinite sums of punctual, 'factual' data, of undeniable value to be sure, and which are nonetheless the historian's indispensable raw material. At the same time, it radically deprives us of the means of reconstructing the code systems which would allow us to interpret coherently and would enable us to assure an otherwise fertile development of them, and additionally of the general environment more actively useful to historians. We historians of Jewish material today are brought to crucial self-criticism, for lack of which our marginalization will accelerate, closing upon us the ghetto gate of thought in one of those "well-enclosed gardens"[4] where Braudel refused to relegate history.

From this point onward the risk becomes much greater of seeing the special ideology of the historian manipulate his mind at leisure. This is what Braudel denounced most pertinently nearly thirty years ago as "the traditional arrangements fraction...living and deeply unified history. The historical narrative is not a method or the objective method par excellence, but rather a philosophy of history itself."[5] If I may be permitted a hint of provocation, I must confess that very little separates for example the chronicler of *Shevet Yehuda* from the present-day individual historians of the Israeli school, too often exclusively focused on a pointed perception of persecution phenomena or an artificial investigation of a radical consciousness. The relevance of a certain philosophy of history thus becomes noteworthy soley from its choice of paths and selection of perspectives. This, for example, is the origin of an instructive and symptomatic debate heard after a paper at the last World Congress of Jewish Studies, (Jerusalem, August 1985), which created the appearance of a tendency among certain historians to justify the legitimacy of a 'Zionist historiography' (an expression used in informal Congress discussions as well). This essentially ambiguous militancy which strangely recalls the mindset of a Michelet, Augustin Thierry, or Fustel de Coulanges, and which is far from constituting a consensus among historians in the field, can, however, lead to indisputably exemplary enterprises such as the publication of the archives of the Spanish Inquisition,[6] thus putting into the hands of researchers from different horizons the means of reaching syntheses which will undoubtedly be more finely shaded, but it will be no less the sign of an immaturity that we must of necessity transcend.

My thesis, quite the opposite, is to try to demonstrate by means of a specific case how these presuppositions lead in reality to cutting off the means of doing history *qua* history, as long as it is understood that the stakes make it worthwhile. As George Duby says: "To understand the ordering of societies and...to discern the forces which make them evolve...this can only go forward with the elaboration of new questionnaires, a rereading of documents and the exploitation of new sources, like a reconnaissance and prospecting of new fields of investigation."[7]

Now it happens that being engaged myself in a cultural approach to the historical phenomena of Judaism which owes much to Duby's history of ideologies or Goff's history of mentalities,[8] I have had occasion to concern myself for several years with the phenomenon of the Expulsion of the Jews from Spain, a circumscribed case that appears to me to be the very example of an event that can acquire its dimensions and impact only after a long time span and through the analysis of the organic dialectic among minority Jewish societies in the plural and dominant encompassing societies, as much Christian as Islamic.[9] Because how can it not be perceived that this case concerned a critical moment for putting into motion that veritable nebula that constitutes the Jewish diasporic world at least since the disaster of seventy. This world's fluid contours nevertheless cover the dilated dimensions of what, since Braudel, we have called the Mediterranean world. Space in expansion, paradoxial key of the closure, slow time exceeding centuries, significant crucible of a specific and exceptionally short history, convulsively, periodically riddled by expulsions, with precipitous departures, provisional havens and precariousness inevitably accepted—the routine of a bothersome but so often necessary people. It is this slow time, nearly immobile in that nebulous rhythm of life which compels the historian to trace his understanding and knowledge back several centuries.

This perspective of wide horizons naturally led me to integrate Italy, the Ottoman world, and finally the Mediterranean world so dear to Braudel. Was that space, traversed by the fluid diasporic macro-society, not also the sole stable reality of the temporary micro-societies apparently animated by a perpetual circling movement?[10] Venice became one of the focal points of this inquiry, given its obviously decisive role in that world economy. Now it happens that Iberian Jews, abruptly compelled to mobility just as massive as it was concentrated in the Mediterranean space, contributed a new dynamic network which catalyzed its general evolution because this movement coincided with an exceptional moment of general redistribution, a reshuffling of the cards. This extraordinary convergence of chance happenings thus conferred on the Jews (and in spite of themselves, so to speak), a decisive role out of proportion to the relative weakness of their global demography,[11] a role which put into motion the unification of dispersed Jewish societies. The technological and military affirmation of Ottoman power, at least until Lepanto, is certainly one of the perceptible symptoms of this movement as recognized by contemporaries.

For proof we have this testimony of a *Marrano* who escaped from Spain to Italy, subsequently becoming an important businessman in the Venetian system of commerce at Candia (Iraklion) between 1603 and 1625. A valuable chronicler of Iberian Jewish historiographic traditions, Immanuel Aboav wrote the following at the beginning of the seventeenth century:

> Many of these exiles went to the Levant. They were welcomed by the House of Ottoman, all its successive kings being amazed that the Spaniards, known to be circumspect, should have expelled such people from their kingdoms. Rather, Sultan Bayazit and Sultan Soleiman received them very well and the arrival of these Hebrew was very pleasing to them, as well as to their heirs, seeing of what great use and benefit their stay was to the Ottoman States.[12]

It is precisely at Venice, between the beginning of the sixteenth century and the great plague of 1630, where we best see the catalyzing effect of the broad-gauged changes that the Mediterranean world economy was then experiencing.[13] The Jews of Venice entered the lagoon in 1502 and mark the general changes linked among other things to the appearance of the modern notion of the state, granting primacy to the logic of economics and gaining bit by bit a new space for political autonomy vis-à-vis imperialist pretentions of the theological power of the Church, a survival of the former order. We should undoubtedly add decisively the shock of Mediterranean hegemonies which are going to have as a lasting effect the irreversible Venetian retreat and the expansion of Ottoman control over the markets of the Levant.

It is undoubtedly the Jewish case where this very slow process, which will lead in the long run to the total secularization of European societies, is best measured, just as the depth of the transformation of mentalities leading to the crisis of Venetian capitalism is measured. This crisis was caused by the Ottoman expansion into the eastern Mediterranean and Adriatic, an expansion which only really resumes the old policy of Byzantium, Venice's rival. It happens that on this plane—affected earlier than the others by the new factor but affected also by its particular mentality as a merchant state—Venice was simply ahead of the rest. The history of its Jewish policy is, as we shall see, the most eloquent indicator.

I shall leave to one side Calimani's recent work[14] where this amateur historian, staying within the logic of narrative history to which all compilers are unfailingly condemned, lacked the tools for encompassing the phenomenon, while having, we must concede, an unerring intuition for the changes occurring. The merit of his book, honestly carried out, is that it constitutes an accessible exposé of facts for the uninitiated; still the book must be used with some caution. However, since the specialists know these facts,[15] I will not review them except to signal the decisive moments in the history of the three *nationi* which in the end compose what Venetian authorities called the *Università degli Hebrei*, and the Venetian rabbi Leon de Modena, *qahal gadol*.

1516: The *natione todescha* ("German nation") is assigned residence in the peripheral quarter called the Ghetto Novo (old founderies). The founding nucleus is composed of Italian Jews whose ancestors emigrated from Germany, from whence their name *ashkenazi*, in the Venetian language *todeschi*. They have been titulars of a *condotta* in Venice since 1502[16] which strictly limits their activity to banking loans on securities and pawns, with interest severely limited and controlled.

1541: The magistracy of the *Pregadi* ("Provosts," members of the Senate of the Venetian Republic) recognizes the specific identity of a second Jewish "nation" in Venice: the *Levantini*, in granting them a distinct new quarter, the so-called "Ghetto Vecchio," and a special *condotta* granting them the privilege of practicing trade on the Venice square.

These "Levantines" are, in fact, merchants who are Portuguese or
Spanish in origin, who emigrated first into Ottoman territory and
became Turkish subjects.[17] This is the *natione levantina* ("Levantine
nation").

1589: The *Cinque Savi alla mercanzia* (the Venetian Board of Trade)
recognize a group of *Marrano* merchants represented by Daniel Rodriga
as having its own identity and grant it commercial privilege which,
according to Raird, fewer than ten percent of the Venetians themselves
enjoyed.[18] This is the *natione ponentina* ("the Occidentals").

This evolution constitutes a century-long cycle schematically punctuated by
a ternary rhythm. We thus find again the schema of the century-long tendency
articulated in intercycles.

Now, still symmetrical at the level of the century-long tendency of the same
period, Venice experiences a profound structural crisis which jeopardizes its place
in the Mediterranean world economy following the fall of Constantinople[19] and
the opening of the "Spanish Atlantic," to quote Pierre Chaunu.[20] Three peaks
likewise mark the curve of the crisis and constitute the acute phases:

1499–1503: First conflict with the Turks and decisive loss of Modon and
Coron, trading posts assuring the markets of the Peloponnesus.[21]

1537–1540: Second confrontation with the Turks at the time of Soliman's
expansionist policy. The effect of the outcome was to accelerate the
Venetian retreat from the Levantine markets. With the ruinous loss
of Nauplia and Malvoisia came the collapse of the last economic
positions of the Peloponnesus and a part of those of Morea.[22]

1564–1573: Third confrontation which seals the failure of the military
option,[23] after that of the diplomatic option, and completes the eviction
process with the catastrophic loss of Cyprus.[24] Venice keeps (but for
how long?) only Corfu and its outposts in Dalmatia and Albania.
Moreover, Venice is ruined by a century of war, despite the spectacular
victory at Lepanto which, as Braudel has shown, had no real
significance or impact.[25]

Thus, not only were the coffers of the Republic emptied, but worse, Venice
lost the means essential for re-establishing economic health.[26] If we now juxtapose
the two series of facts just mentioned, we note a remarkable setting:

First Crisis: *condotta* of the *Todeschi* (1502–1503), then severe revision of
the *condotta* conditions (1516)[27]

Second Crisis: commercial concessions for the *Levantini* (June 2, 1541)
who undertake to return to Venice the profits of the access to markets
henceforth under Turkish control[28]

> Third Crisis: slow negotiations which finally end in the granting of
> privileges to the Ponentines on specific economic proposals made by
> their leader and negotiated on an almost equal footing with the *Cinque
> Savi alla mercanzia* (1574–June 27, 1589)[29]

The convergence is too striking to require comment.

However, parallel to the crisis which saw the collapse of the Republic in the
Mediterranean world economy, a second decisive drama was being played out
within Christianity. This was the centuries-old iron arm policy then entering
its final phase, having put Venice in opposition on grounds of ideological
independence (a kind of insular mentality) to the Holy See and the Curia
Romana. It is the exasperation of the tendency proper to Venetian particularism
that the singularity of the Venetian patriarchate illustrates so well.

The "secular tendency" present here also, although no longer a function of
economic or social circumstances, appears in reverse and works, to the contrary,
in favor of Venice. Two significant dates, in fact, symbolize the materialization
of the process:

> February 25, 1510: black day when the Republic's representative to Rome
> is forced to a public act of contrition and confesses submission to Julius
> II at the end of the wars of the League of Combrai[30]
>
> 1606–1616: resounding failure of the excommunication of the Senate of
> the Republic decreed by Paul V, with the countereffect of the
> affirmation of the Venetian theology of Paolo Sarpi[31]

Perhaps it would be well to recall two important postions taken by Paolo
Sarpi resisting Roman power. The first, significantly, claims political autonomy
vis-à-vis the temporal pretensions of the Pope and argues against the relevance
in the Interdiction (irrelevant according to Sarpi) in replying in the name of the
Republic to Paul V's Epistle: "The princes," Sarpi declared, "by divine right that
no human power can abrogate have authority to rule in the temporal domain
within their jurisdiction. Nothing justifies the admonitions of Your Holiness
because the subjects discussed are not spiritual but temporal."[32]

The second, dating from December 1616, denies the Venetian Inquisition
any rights over the *Marranos* apropos the case of a Portuguese *Marrano*, Simon
Gomez, refugee in Venice:

> To cross examine him about events which took place in other dominions
> would be undermining the privileges which have been conceded to that
> *natione* by the Republic for very righteous and necessary reasons for many
> decades now, as has been done elsewhere for that *natione* by other
> religious princes. These privileges cannot be abused without breaking
> a promise, and we are very sure that they are righteous.[33]

Here are three more peaks on the curve, three acute phases in the crisis:

1502–1516: Franciscan propaganda against the Senate policy concerning Jews and pawn shops;[34]

1545–1554: Pressure of the Council of Trente[35] and the Counter-Reformation;

1606: Crisis of the Interdiction against Venice.

A new observation of the coordination of the two series:

1516: Closure in the Ghetto. It appears at the time as a concession to Franciscan pressure after many dilatory maneuvers of the Council of X, opposed to the _Avogadori di comun_, partisans of expulsion. This is an "attenuated" measure, a palliative to the expulsion demanded.[36]

1547–1550: Reluctant acceptance of a Venetian Inquisition, confined however to the Terra Ferma (1547); banishment of the _Marranos_ (1550); campaign against Jewish books and the Talmud (episode of the crisis of the Venetian Hebrew printing establishment); rare _Marrano_ trials with seventy cases of a negotiated total of 1,560 (can this figure be correct?) and no death sentence, compared to fourteen Protestants or Anabaptists condemned to death.[37]

1606–1610: apparent reversal of the policy symbolized by Paolo Sarpi and expressed in the Senate at the time of the debate over the eventual liberalization of the rights of _cittadinanza_ (summer 1610). Liberal patricians Nicolo Contarini and Nicolo and Antonio Dona defended the policy in these terms: _li esteri benchè di diverso religione e costumi non sono mai stati aborridi da questo stado e stata amesso il fondego dei Todeschi Turchi Ebrei e marani_ (although the foreigners are of a different religion and have different customs, they have never been hated by this state, the German, Turkish, Jewish and Marrano exchanges have been permitted).

Thus this double secular tendency seems to be the key system of the history of the Venetian Jewish nation in the first hundred years of its existence. This is because everything happens as if the progressive loss of direct control of markets and strategic routes in the Levant had in brief pushed Venetian authorities to realize that through the new diaspora of the 'Spanish' _(Sefaradi)_ having its own Mediterranean networks, planted both in Christendom and in Ottoman lands, Venice could find a positive alternative solution, assuring its survival by accessing indirectly the economic zone henceforth controlled by the Sultan. It is no longer a case of refloating public finances by the limited expedient of taxing the _condotta_, of decompressing the danger of impoverished classes by assuring service from the 'banks of the poor,' but indeed of turning toward the Piazza of Venice a part of the benefits of the lost Levantine market by branching out, so to speak, via the prosperous Hispano-Marrano commerce, and in attaching parasitically to its networks.[38] In this respect the success of Spalato (present-day Split), conceived and carried out by Daniel Rodriga and Ponentine businessmen, is the most spectacular proof. Was not the knight of *Marrano* industry to win the popular title of "inventor of the scala [merchant port network]?"[39] The motivation was, moreover, clear in the minds of the actors themselves, since it could already be read in the accounts of the *Levantini condotta* of 1541: *"E data que la maggior parte delle merci che vengono dalla Romania alta e bassa è condotta ed è nelle mani degli hebrei levantini mercanti e viandanti etc.* (It is understood that most of the merchandise which comes from upper and lower Rumania is conducted by and is in the hands of the Jewish Levantine merchants and travellers). Thus, on the Venetian side, harsh economic realities in a Christian state confronted brutally with the necessities for its survival took precedence over the old theological mentality which commended perception and treatment of the Jewish problem, slowly emptying of their content the old juridial formulae, which persisted until the end of the seventeenth century, but with only the value of a few vestiges. Born of these realities, the pragmatism of the Senate and especially the Council of X State Policy ended globally (not, to be sure, without some sudden checks which were not genuine backward turns but which appear retrospectively like occasional tactics)[40] in a veritable weaving of Jewish minorities into the very texture of the city. From Franciscan propaganda at the beginning of the century, a belated medieval phenomenon, to the finally triumphant positions of Paolo Sarpi, much progress had been made. If ignorance of the logic of the immediate Venetian environment makes the history of Venetian Jewish societies literally incomprehensible and makes obvious the essentially absurd character of studying them in the absolute, detached from their host milieu, at the same time ignorance of the geopolitical dimension in which Venice and its minorities are integrated like Russian dolls, jointly affected by its fate, hides a decisive series of causes. Thus, to use only this one example, the logic of the Mediterranean world economy must, in repercussion, produce its effects well inside the far-from-sealed ghetto walls, in a dialectic of relationships among *nationi*. Because if the 'Todeschi,' with their medieval and increasingly unadaptable *condotta* whose anachronism propelled them to ruin with the collapse of the agreed-upon interest rates and the skyrocketing climb of the annual 'patent' subject to Senate demand, succeeded finally in redressing and reconverting commerce, they owe it to the 'Levantini' and the 'Ponentini' who opened the way for them. Indeed, in 1594, the *Cattaver*— their specific tutelary authority decreed by the *Pregadi*, on March 24, 1516—finally allowed them to practice large-scale international commerce at the end of a tenacious struggle lasting several decades, and recognized the statute of respectability of merchants connected with *grande negotio* (large-scale business) of very important Italian families who had arrived from Mestra in 1502 (i.e., the Luzzato or Calimani families). The seventeenth century, when the Ghettos underwent metamorphosis, was also when both Ponentine power and their social model promoted integration into the surrounding civilization with regard to manners, lifestyles, and arts as well as economics and trades. Thus we see the appearance of the profession of *sanser* in the Ghetto, a kind of business agent holding a license from Venetian authorities, as indicated by documentation for the year 1590: beside a dozen Christian *sansari*, we note the names of Simon and Moses, sons of a physician Giuseppe de Dattolis. Even architecture reveals the penchant for integration of the 'Spanish,' since it is Baldassare Longhena who received the commission for the Scola Spagnola at the very moment San Giorgio dei Greci and the mosque of the Fondago dei Turchi were being built (1561). Those whom the Venetians would call from the seventeenth century onward *"gli hebrei qui abitano in questa citta* (the Jews who live in this city)"—the genuinely 'Venetian Jews,'—are thus caught up in a secular circumstance all the more favorable to them, despite numerous checks. The Venetian Patricians who controlled the Senate, smitten with extreme collegiality and obsessed with the risks of plutocracy, could find only advantages in exploiting an economically dynamic minority struck by permanent and undisputed constitutive political limitation. This concurrence of circumstances was to lead in the long run to their eventual integration in the counterpart Venetian society. This was the trump opening played by Simone Luzzato in a pressing address to the Senate, his *Discorso circa il stato de gl'Hebrei et in particolare dimoranti nell'indita città di Venezia,* printed in Venice in 1638:

> The Jewish nation is subject to, submissive, and compliant with the authority of its prince, which it can be said, has been placed of its own accord in the center of the diligent and industrious in very rigorous observation of and correspondence with the laws and payments which it owes the public. . . according to the felicitous ruling of the Republic. . . which did not want to ever allow the practice of relieving poverty with money to be exercised, unless the *natione* were entirely submissive and subject, completely free from any seditious or ambitious thought.[41]

Finally, even the psychosis of a Judeo-Turkish plot which took hold of the Venetians at the worst of the Cyprus crisis, and in part under the effect of the disturbing game of the 'Duke of Naxos,' will in the end have been only a dangerous but ephemeral episode.[42] In a more general fashion, the Jews seem to have been conscious from the dawn of the sixteenth century onward of the singularity of the Venetian regime and of its essentially progressive character from their own point of view. Thus Isaac Abravanel celebrated in the Republic of Venice a collegial regime of officials elected for terms:

> In our days we see numerous nations governed by officers (*soterim*) or governors (*moslim*) chosen for a term with a three-month mandate without any rising to a royalty above his peers. They have at their disposition an elective mandate of a limited order and exercise an absolute power over the people, they have full authority in time of war and no

other power could be tolerated, they are pitiless on this chapter both with respect to their own people and to their own nation. If one of them is guilty of any fault whatsoever, they [sic] are immediately replaced and suitably punished so that they will never again act in contempt of the law. . . It is thus today in the Republic of Venice, sovereign among nations (*goyim*), queen of States; the Republic of Florence, jewel among countries; the Republic of Genoa, powerful and proud, of Lucca, Siena, Bologna, and other republics having no king except the elected chiefs (*manhigim nivharim*) for the set periods which I have mentioned.[43]

But Immanuel Aboav attributed to the Venetian regime especially the merits of clairvoyance both with regard to the "usefulness of the Jews" and to the "madness" of doing without their services, the madness of Ferdinand the Catholic:

> *Fue reprehendido el Rey Catolico de todos los Principes Christianos, y particularmente del Senado de Venecia, como narra Marco Antonio Sabelico; de que una gente tan util assi al publico, como a privado, la vuiessen desterrado sin ningun genero de pretexto* The Catholic King was criticized by all Christian Princes and especially the Venetian Senate, as Marco Antonio Sabelico tells, for wanting to exile a people so useful to the public and to private persons without any kind of pretext.[44]

Therefore, at the end of a century of Venetian policy making regarding Jews, it was believed that the fate of diasporic societies were not only tributary to, but almost unified with the great stakes of Mediterranean geopolitics, and Venice was regarded with deliberate sympathy which was not exclusively self-interest but which denoted the emergence of a kind of Venetian patriotism, specific to the *nationi* of the Ghettos which gained something from being guests, even if in transit.

Consider this notion so specifically Venetian of *natione*, key element in the history of Venetian Judaism. We have here in effect a model taken from general Venetian history applied to the Jews, at first accommodated before being integrated into their own cultural schemas by one of the affirmative acculturation processes described by Nathan Wachtel.[45] The notion of *natione* is peculiar to a merchant republic accustomed from early times to negotiating with other States for the privileges of extraterritoriality and concessions of a commercial nature. Thus Venice had begun to construct its network of "colonies" in the eastern Mediterranean in the wake of the Crusade. A treaty signed in 1124 with the Frankish Kingdom of Jerusalem, a kind of a framework-accord of "nationality" granted Venice a closed "Venetian street" with gates in any city of the kingdom, with its church, bakery, public bath, and exemption from tolls and customs. In certain cases that accord could produce transformation into "Venetian walled cities" in all or part of the conquered city-markets. For example Tripoli was declared "Venetian" in 1099, and a third of Tyre was transferred to Venetian "nationality" in July 1123 and so remained until Saladin retook the city. Acra sheltered a prosperous Venetian quarter, and Candia was even organized on the Venetian model with six *sestieri* and a doge. Later in 1264 the Republic was to obtain from Michael Paléologue a veritable concession in Constantinople and the Byzantine ports—a *sestier*—accompanied by commercial and customs fiscal advantages, the whole operation placed under the jurisdiction of a *bailo* constituting veritably autonomous rule. The fall of Constantinople, following a long negotiation lasting an entire year, permitted Venice to keep the *sestier* and *bailo* there but with loss of territorial and commercial advantages. Venice also had a 'national' concession at Alexandria which assured it a presence on the Egyptian markets for a long time.[46] But the principle the Republic cited in demanding recognition from other States could be applied in Venice itself to the benefit of other 'nations' according to the well understood commercial principle of reciprocity. This is how, in 1313, 'national' concessions were granted to the *todeschi*, a group of merchants from Flanders and Germany who built their Fondego, and later to the Turks themselves who had a license to open a mosque in theirs and in which they could barricade themselves at the height of the tense confrontation between the Sultan and the Republic. Among the other *nationi* welcomed and recognized as such could still be counted the *Greci*, the *Sclavoni*, the *Albanesi*, and the *Armeni*. It was thus in a familiar framework that Venice conceived the welcome of its Jews when the moment came. The assignment of quarters as well as successively developed economic functions to the *Hebrei chiamati todeschi*, *Hebrei mercanti levantini*, and then finally *Hebrei ponentini* stems in some ways from customary Venetian common law.[47] And the division of Venice Jews into *nationi*, at least until 1589, is more the result of a convergence of chiefly external factors than the expression of a concerted community will which would find its justification in the antagonisms and divisions within Judaism at the time.[48] In fact, the diversification of Venetian Jewish society (or, rather, societies in the plural), is more the result of the integration into Venetian history than the product of the traditional rivalry between *Ashkenazim* and *Sefaradim*. The etnic pluralism of the Ghetto was more likely to oppose Jews long in residence (jealous of their privileges), and newcomers (resented as intruders), as Yiddish speakers and Hispanophones because the so-called *Todeschi*, speaking Italian and Venetian dialects, were long-time Venetians and received quite unwillingly the recent immigrants from Eastern Europe who began to venture out in the sixteenth century, constituting the only Yiddish speakers in Venice.[49] As for the Levantini and Ponentini—more or less Ottomanized Spanish and Portuguese—their Spanish and Portuguese, in contact with Turkish, had begun to develop into what would be Ladino. However, the consciousness—or will—to belong to the same *natione*[50] only emerges little by little under external pressures. In fact, it is the Senate which—in granting the privilege of installation to the Ponentine *Marrano* merchants headed by Daniel Rodriga (and thus avoiding the polemic terms

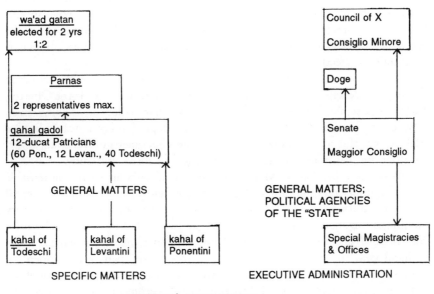

UNIVERSITÀ DEGLI HEBREI

spagnoli, marrani, or *christiani nuovi,* weighted with diplomatic complications for Venice—uses for the first time in the protocol of July 27, 1589, the encompassing notion of *l'Università degli Hebrei,* conceived as a king of federation of colleges. And we must wait until the seventeenth century to have *natione* translate a much vaster consciousness of belonging when Simone Luzzato writes in his *Discorso:* "Nello Stato del Signor Turcho era la principale stanza della Natione Hebraica (after the State of the Turkish Lord [Venice] was the principal sojourn of the Hebrew Nation)," and he frequently employs the expression *hebreo di natione.* The very adoption of a word that Boccaccio was already using[51] designated a group of individuals bound by the same language, history, civilization, and common interests, although a clear consciousness of this division of the patrimony was not part of the connotations of the word until after the eighteenth century. In fact, it appears that in real symbiosis with general Venetian society, despite the closure, Venetian Judaism naturally adopted political or sociological categories for its microcosm, whether institutions or social realities. The admiration of Venetian collegial power, of Isaac Abravanel (installed in 1503 at the Rialto where he would die five years later), had to some extent prepared minds because how could the organigram of powers of the *Università degli Hebrei,*[52] established in the seventeenth century, not call forth a striking echo of the Venetian model?

What Leon de Modena lamented, because collegiality extended to religious powers, was that Venice had no Head Rabbi, and the highly secular nature of

Venetian Jewish society aroused his ire: "Here in Venice, a large city, though not by the excellent quality of our *Bet Din* because we cannot distinguish any, but by the quantity of people who crowd into the *Qahal Gadol* where the *Ashkenazim, Sefaradim*, Levantines and Italians are prevented from conflict by their mutual affection..."[53]

Among charitable and cultural institutions, expecially during the sixteenth century, the development of associations and confraternities inside the Ghettos, and their general movement to surrounding Venetian society are striking. Even a typically Venetian term such as *scola* will be adopted in both areas.[54] But we shall reserve this matter, as well as the specific phenomena of Venetian Jewish acculturation generally during this period, for a subsequent study.

We can see, therefore, to what point the general environment is indispensable for an accurate interpretation of historical data, even if the history is internal and community-oriented such as the Venetian Jewish societies. Such a history illiminates the absence of unified spiritual authority and the lack of rabbinical control which characterize Venetian Judaism. This phenomenon, which goes hand in hand with the increasingly determined will on the part of the Ponentine merchant oligarchy during the seventeenth century to reduce the control of the rabbi in Ghetto government and to affirm lay government,[55] reflects a general Venetian state of mind. Such a climate could only attract opulent *Marranos* whose return to Judaism was more sociological than spiritual. The Venetian case permits us to perceive, I trust, to what point the long view, like the dialectic of the encompassing world economy, is capable of opening a particularly fertile and methodologically renewed, if not innovative, perspective to the history of Jewish societies of the Mediterranean diaspora.

NOTES

1. Notably in the Jerusalem meetings organized by the Center for Research on North African Jews, cf. *Colloque international Maghreb-Mashreq*, Jerusalem, April 9–12, 1984.

2. Fernand Braudel, "Sur une conception de l'histoire sociale," *Ecrits sur l'Histoire* (Paris: Flammarion, 1969), pp. 175–191; Georges Duby, "Histoire sociale et idéologies des Sociétés," *Faire de l'Histoire* I (Paris, 1973), pp. 147–168. With the exception of great breakthroughs such as those of Baron, Goitein, or Ravid, the study of economic, demographic, or social phenomena of diasporic societies has been deplorably isolated and unsystematic. The general rule is still all too likely to be atomized monographs, too impressionistic for the analytic data to be truly useful for the needed syntheses which we will eventually have. Generally speaking, 'Jewish history' still stays too close to 'commemorative' history of the beginning of the century (Braudel, p. 101) or the historicizing history of Henry Berr.

3. See Braudel, *Ecrits sur l'Histoire*. See also the stimulating reflections in "Journées Fernand Braudel": *Une Leçon d'histoire de Fernand Braudel, Châteauvallon Journées Fernand Braudel* 18, 19, 20, October 1985 (Paris, 1986).

4. *Ecrits*, p. 13.

5. *Ecrits*, p. 13. See also this essential passage, p. 22: "Life, world history, all the individual histories are presented to us in the guise of a series of events: understand that dramatic acts have always been brief...a décor...often these are very scant images offered us of the past and human sweat, the chronicle, traditional history, narrative history so dear to Ranke...gleams but no light; facts but no humanity. Bear in mind that this history-narration always pretends to tell things as they really took place...In reality it is presented as an interpretation with a sly manner like an authentic philosophy of history." From whence the necessity of an arrangement which reintegrates a history of short time periods in the much longer time frame of the history of societies and civilizations.

6. See Haim Beinart, *Records of the Trials of the Spanish Inquisition at Ciudad Real* (Jerusalem: Israel National Academy of Sciences and Humanities, 1974–81), 3 vols., a work of immense importance.

7. "Histoire sociale," p. 147.

8. "Les Mentalités une histoire ambiguë," *Faire de l'Histoire* III, 76–94.

9. "Censure idéologique et discours chiffré: le *Sefer hayasar*, oeuvre d'un exilé espagnol réfugié à Naples," *REJ*, CXL (3–4), July–December, 1981, 433–51; *Sefer hayasar (Libro Retto), Reproduction de l'edition de Venise (1625) avec Introduction et notes*, Publications de l'Université de la Sorbonne Nouvelle, Paris III, Paris, 1986, 2 vols. published; "La Mythe de l'Orient dans l'eschatologie des Juifs d'Espagne à l'époque des conversions forcées et de l'Expulsion" (to appear in the *Actes du Colloque Maghreb-Mashreq*); "Recherche sur la fonction de la prière individuelle en milieu marrane aux alentours de 1492; prière et salut," *Prière, Mystique et Judaïsme (Strasbourg, 1984)*, Paris, 1987.

10. In what could be called the diasporic system, Venice played the role of a turntable, since it is found also as one of the essential network poles of the *Marrano* evasion (either through Morocco or through the Ottoman Empire), as well as the network center for the sale of the printed Hebrew book, both in the Mediterranean basin and in central and eastern Europe.

11. Thus, according to Ravid's estimates, the Jews in Venice were only seven hundred in 1516 and 1424 in 1536. They fell to 1043 in 1581, to climb to five thousand in 1630, on the eve of the great plague, when the total population of Venice was one hundred fifty thousand. Therefore, they oscillated from 0.6% to 3.3% maximum. By way of camparison, Paolo Sarpi figured there were ten thousand Protestant refugees and twelve thousand Greek Orthodox in Venice in 1606.

12. Muchos destos desterrados passaron á Levante; los quales fueron acariciados de la casa Othomana, maravillandosse todos los Reyes sucessores della, de que los Españoles que hazen profession de prudentes, echassen de sus Reynos

tal gente. Antes Sultan Bayazit y Sultan Soleiman, los recibieron muy bien, y les fue gratissima la venida de dichos Hebreos y ansi lo hizieron todos sus sucessores, viendo de quan grande utilidad y beneficio les era la estancia de ellos en sus Estados. *Homologia o Discursos Legales*, Amsterdam, 1629, p. 295.

13. The close correlation between the fate of Venice and that of its Jewish population was clearly perceived by Shelomo Simonsohn, *History of the Jews of the Duchy of Mantua* (New York: Ktav Publishing House, 1977).

14. Riccardo Calimani, *Storia del Ghetto di Venezia* (Milan, 1985). A publishing success undoubtedly due in part to the personality of the author, descendant of one of the Mestra families entering Venice in 1502. There is an abundant bibliography (pp. 478–499), despite some omissions. Still, the curiously global references presented without critical rigor is deplorable, preventing necessary verification.

15. See especially Benjamin Ravid's numerous works.

16. Expelled from Venice by the Senate in 1426, the Venetian Jews took refuge in Mestra, acquired by Venice in 1336. From there they continued to exercise their 'Venetian' banking activities by constant daily commuting since they had been forbidden to stay overnight. The insecurity following the wars of the League of Cambrai was the indirect cause of their return since, when renewing their Mestra *condotta*, they obtained the right of refuge in the city: "Tante volte quante a loro piasera . . . et etiam per apura de guerra possino vegnir a stare e habitari senza alcun contradition" (text of the *condotta* of 1502–1503: as many times as pleased them . . . and when we are fearful of war they can come to stay and live without any opposition). The first *Condotta* for the *banchieri* of Mestra with authorization to conduct business on the Venice piazza was accorded by the Senate to Jews of German origin; Venetian authorities, already refusing interference by the Holy See, had sidestepped the pontifical licensing system. See Leon Poliakov, *Les Banchieri Juifs et le Saint Siège du XIIIe au XVIIe Siècle* (Paris, 1965), esp. 271–281, 'Le Cas singulier de Venise.'

17. The *Levantini*, exploiting this fact, tried for a long time to be exempted from the fiscal servitude of the *condotta* which involved a division of banking charges to the point where in 1596 the suits in the Ghetto were to distinguish between *Levantini* who were established citizens of Venice, subject to common servitudes, and "Levantini viandanti sottoposti al Signor Turco" (*Levantini travelers subject to the Turkish lord*).

18. Benjamin Ravid, "The First Charter of the Jewish Merchants of Venice, 1589," *Association for Jewish Studies Review*, I (1976): p. 187–222.

19. Following the concessions Michael Paléologue made to Venice in the Treaty of 1264, Venetian merchants had received free access to reside, do business, travel, and organize throughout Byzantine territory. Venice had at its disposition Venetian *sestieri* in the principal ports and an autonomous government in Constantinople even under the authority of *a bailo*. The fall of Constantinople reopened the matter of the "Venetian system" and, if finally in 1454, at the end

of difficult negotiations, the regime of the *bailo* was kept, Venice on the other hand largely had to give up its territorial and commercial advantages. See John Julius Norwich, *History of Venice* (New York: Knopf, 1982).

20. *Seville et l'Atlantique (1550–1650)* (Paris: A. Colin, 1959); see also Braudel's criticism in *Ecrits*, pp. 135–153. The establishment of the Seville privilege dates precisely from 1504. It will be noted, a significant coincidence, that during the years 1502–1504 the eventually aborted negotiations with King Manuel of Portugal took place. These were to permit Venice to land merchandise at Lisbon. But, in the end, fearing reprisal pillaging in its supply depots at Alexandria and Cairo, Venice preferred to concentrate on studying an opening through the isthmus of Suez, also a failed project. At the same time, Isaac Abravanel was to serve as intermediary in an affair bearing on the spice trade between the Republic and the King of Portugal.

21. But the Peace of Venice offered the islands of Cephalonia and Ithaca in compensation for the loss of ports in the Peloponnesus. The period of calm was to be only relative. On December 21, 1522, Soliman took Rhodes.

22. The indirect effect of a complicated game of diplomatic and espionage intrigues in which were involved Venetian bureaucrats Nicolo and Constantino Cavazza in the pay of Francis I, who was then an ally of the Sultan. Venice lost, besides, a string of islands (Skiros, Patmos, Aegina, Ios, Paros, and Astipalea).

23. Already opposed to war against Soliman, the old Doge Andrea Gritti had seen his motion rejected by the Senate by one vote in 1537.

24. Acquired by Venice in 1488. Famagouste draft of August 1, 1571.

25. Two hundred thirty Turkish ships against two hundred eight in the Christian camp; thirty thousand Turkish dead and two battleships destroyed against eight thousand Christian victims. When the disaster was announced, the Turkish merchants in Venice barricaded themselves in their Fondego. Eleven days later, on October 18, 1571, the galley loaded with Lepanto trophies entered the port. Interpreted as a sign, the victory over the infidel aroused an overflow of anti-Jewish feelings. The Franciscans preached again that not to chase out the Jews was a sin against God.

On the role of the Corfu Jews in the Venetian exchequer, see David Kaufmann, "Contribution à l'histoire des Juifs de Corfou," *REJ*, 32 (1896), 226–235; 33 (1896), 64–76, 219–232; 34 (1897), 263–275.

26. The first signs appeared as early as 1498 with the failures of the Garzoni (Bankruptcy of two hundred thousand ducats) and Lippomano banks. The seriousness of the public financial crisis led to the Senate's adoption of five emergency measures so Draconian that application was resisted (1539). The Republic under attack sought any expedient. From thence the change in tactics vis-à-vis the Jews: no longer threaten them with expulsion, but demand ten thousand ducats in "patente" and a 15 percent rate reduction on loan securities.

27. Proposal of Zaccaria Dolfin on March 20, 1516 at the Collegio concerning the confinement to Ghetto Novo (*sestier* de San Girolano) was immediately voted

by the Senate (130 votes for; 44 against; 8 "non sinceri"). A *Pregadi* decree on March 29 halted the carrying out of the decision and submitted the "natione todescha" to the jurisdiction of the *Cattaver*.

28. The *Pregadi* authorized the extension of Ghetto Vecchio and a second exit towards Canareggio, and the new very quickly signed *condotta*, contrary to the usual practice, stipulated: "*sia data libertà a quel Magistrato che gli parerà di accomodar gli hebrei mercanti levantin viandanti in ghetto. . . non potendo ancora detti mercanti hebrei levantini viandanti far banco, strazzaria, ne esercizio alcuno salvo solamente la semplice mercanzia*" (that freedom be given to the magistrate of their choosing to allow the Jewish Levantine travelling merchants into the ghetto. . . said Jewish Levantine travelling merchants not yet being able to set up banks, "strazzaria," nor practice any except the most simple trade.) These merchants could not live in the city more than four months and could not have their families with them.

29. Of Marrano extraction, this important businessman was known from 1563 on for developing Bosnian wools and silks bought on the Venice Piazza. In 1574 we find him representing Venice in Dalmatia and in Slavic countries. In a memorandum addressed to the Senate three years later, he promoted ambitious assurances: "*Posso largamente promettere non solo di allargare il commercio a questa inclita città, ma assicurare la salvezza del golfo e levare molti impacci che a causa degli usocchi travagliono la Vs Serenità. . . mi offrisco di drizzare nella sua terra di Spalato una ricchissima amplissima scala. . . Da questa importantissima scala capiteranno molte merci in questa città. . . Divertendosi il traffico dalla scala di Ragusa sarà la scala di Spalato un amplissimo aiuto per le ricchezze del Levante il quale tutto intero sarà trasmesso nelle nostra città.*" (I can broadly promise not only to increase commerce to this illustrious city, but also ensure the saving of the gulf and the removal of many inconveniences which because of the Uskoks [Dalmatian pirates] threaten Your Grace. . . I am offering to set up a very rich, very broad 'scala' [merchant port] with your land of Spalato [Split in Dalmatia]. . . Much merchandise will be brought into this city from this very important 'scala'. . . Diverting the traffic of the Ragusan 'scala', the 'scala' of Spalato will be of very great help to the riches of the Levant which will be transferred completely intact to our city.) Two years later came new proposals to the Senate: five thousand ducats of annual income guaranteed to the Republic if it allowed fifty merchants with their families to settle there. The Senate, aware that the proposal, although directly profitable to the city, would nonetheless bring about the ruin of the last remaining international Venetian businessmen, delayed a decision.

30. See Noth, pp. 382–384.

31. Ibid., pp. 471–481.

32. Paolo Sarpi, *Advice Given to the Government of Venice* (London 1693), quoted in Noth, p. 477.

33. L'Inquisir contra lui delle cose avvenute negl'altri Dominii sarebbe un sovvertir li privilegii che per giustissime et necessarie cause sono concessi già molte

decenne d'anni dalla Repubblica como anco altrove da altri prencipi religiosi a quella natione li quali non si possono violare senza mancare della parola et tanto noi stimiano che sie di giustitia.

34.   Traditionally opposed to usury, Franciscans preached the expulsion of the Jews and the opening of pawnshops according to the doctrine of Bernard of Siena. But the formula ran into the opposition of the Council of X, obsessed by the notion of seeing certain Patricians construct a powerful organization. Thus the *Monte di Pietà* question, coming up again at the time of a proposal presented by the *procuratori* of the Hospital of the Incurables. (Thirteen *procuratori* engaged in the financing belonged to Patrician families.) This ended in a radical decision of the Council of X, forbidding the Senate further debate on the matter under penalty of death. The interdiction was not to be raised until 1734. See Poliakov, p. 273. Around 1550 the Dominican Sixtus Medici pronounced in favor of the solution by Jewish banking, the motive being the absence of risk of power.

35.   Inaugural session presided over by Paul IV, December 15, 1545; matter taken up again under Pius IV in January 1563.

36.   The affair had already been discussed by the *Consiglio dei Pregadi* in March 1515 with a proposal from Emo Zorzi (confinement to the Guidecca), but the confrontations had been so sharp that no decision was taken at that time. The Jewish pressure, especially that of Asher Mesulam (Anselmo del Banco), certainly played its part. The latter, with his brother Hayim, was luxuriously established near the Rialto, at Cà Bernardo in the *sestier* of San Polo, and was forced to move to the Ghetto in July 1516.

37.   See the works of Pier Cesare Ioly Zorattini and Yehosu 'a Bloch, "Venetian Printers of Hebrew Books," *Bulletin of the New York Library*, XXX (1932): 3–24. See also Benjamin Ravid, "The Prohibition against Jewish Printing and Publishing in Venice and the Difficulties of Leone Modena," *Studies in Medieval Jewish History and Literature* (Cambridge, MA: Harvard Univ. Press, 1979), pp. 135–153.

38.   The rapid ascent of the Ponentine domination in the Ghetto would confirm in the seventeenth century the wisdom of that choice. Venice attracted large enterprises assured of being at least listened to in the Senate. Thus this project (which in 1622 received the approval of both the *Cinque Savi* and the Senate), coming from businessmen Mose Israel and David Navarro, proposed the development of Ponentine commerce and guaranteed an exportation amounting to ten thousand ducats to Tunis and Algiers via France and Spain. This passage of large-scale Venetian commerce into Jewish hands is also studied in the works of Alberto Tenenti, *Naufrages, corsaires et assurances maritimes à Venise (1592–1609)* (Paris, 1959).

39.   See Simone Luzzato, *Discorso circa il stato de gl'Hebrei et in particolare dimoranti nell'inclita città di Venetia* (Venice, 1638): "*la città di Venezia giamai porrà in oblio la memoria del primo inventore della scala di Spalato che fu hebreo di natione che con i suoi raccordi trasportò il negotio di gran parte di Levante in città giudicata,*

ora detta scala il piu fermo et solido fondamento di traffico ch'abbia la città. (The city of Venice has consigned to oblivion the memory of the first inventor of the Spalatian port, who was Jewish by nationality, who with his connections brought the business dealings of much of the Levant to the city. This port is now seen to be the most firm and solid base of traffic which the city has)."

40. Thus in 1571 an expulsion decision was not carried out at the time of Pius V's anti-Jewish campaign with the bull *Hebraeorum gens.*

41. *La natione Hebrea è per se stessa sommessa soggetta e pieghevole all'ubbidienza del suo Prencipe posta nel centro si può dire della città diligente et industre da per sé in osservare e corrispondere con gran rigore li diritti e pagamenti ch'al pubblico deve...il felicissimo regimento della Repubblica...non ha voluto permettere giamai che la fontione di socorrere con denari la povertà sia praticata se non da Natione affatto rimessa e soggetta, remota assolutamente de qualunque pensiero seditioso o ambitioso.*

42. See the role undoubtedly played by Shelomo Ashkenazi, physician and Venetian subject, successively at the court of Sigismond in Cracow, then at Constantinople, where he seems to have been the secret mediator between the Vizir allied to the guest of the Duke of Naxos and the *bailo* Marc Antonio Barbaro. Named ambassador to Venice by Selim II, he was received with pomp and circumstance in 1574 by the Senate and the Doge Mocenigo.

43. Isaac Abravanel, *Perus 'al nevi 'im rishonim (I Samuel)* (Jerusalem, 1966, reproduced from Leipzig, 1886), II, p. 206a.

44. *Nomologia*, p. 295. Fue reprehendido el Rey Catolico de todos los Principes Christianos, y particularmente del Senado de Venecia, como narra Marco Antonio Sabelico; de que una gente tan util assi al publico, como a privado, la vuiessen desterrado sin ningun genero de pretexto.

45. "L'acculturation," *Faire de l'Histoire* I, 124–145, especially the notion of "integration."

46 For this whole question, see Noth, especially pp. 79, 85, 93–94, 122, 146, 156–159.

47. This was at least the borrowing from Venetian common law a formula destined to resolve the "theological" problem, but it is appropriate to remind ourselves on this point that the Jews were not the only Venetian "infidels" in a Christian state. They shared this condition with Muslim Turks in the Fondego dei Turchi.

48. One of the manifest proofs is the bitterness with which each group, jealous of its identity, wanted to negotiate directly with its own tutelary authority, its statute and rights. And when a semblance of intergroup effort appeared, it was imposed as a condition by the Republican authorities from a concern, above all, for public order, as was the case for the decision of June 27, 1589, where the juridical notion of *Università degli Hebrei* appeared next to that of *natione.* Moreover, it was from the point of view of its own interests that on the occasion of the renewal of the *condotta* for the *Todeschi*, the Senate imposed a unification

of the Jewish population throughout the Italian territories of the Republic placed under the leadership of the *Università*, as the text itself indicates (December 16, 1624): "*Che tutti le hebrei habitanti e che per l'avvenire habiterrano in cadauna Città terra o luogo del stato nostro da terra ferma siano tenuti et debbano tutti et cadauno di loro niuno eccettuato esser compresi nelle gravezze et contribuire alle spese et interessi chi anderanno per il mantenimento delli tre banchi sopradetti di questa Città*. (That all Jewish residents and those who will be living in the foreseeable future in one of the cities, lands or places in our state of 'Terra Ferma' are to be held accountable and each and every one with no exceptions must be included in the taxes and contribute to the costs and interests which go towards the maintenance of the three above-mentioned banks of this city)." And this explicit specification: "*Che tutti quelli dell'Università delli hebrei che pagano tanse siano tenuti ogni quattro nesi esborsar alli banchiere ovvero alli capi et deputati sopra ciò la portione della lora estima affinchè cosi li banchieri come ogn'altro possi consequire il suo pagamento alli tempi debiti* (That all those in the Jewish *Università* who pay taxes are to be held accountable and must pay the bankers or else the heads and deputies above them, a portion of their value every four months in order that the bankers, like anyone else, can make their payments at the official time)." These *capi* are the *parnesim* from Hebrew sources. See following.

49. Among them Rabbi Meir Katzenellbogen who was illustrious in the affair of the *Mishne Tora*, around 1550, putting into unchecked competition the Bragadin and Guistiniani printers. Associated with the Bragadin printing establishment, he solicited from Mose Isserles of Cracow the *herem* of the competing edition (*herem* of August 16, 1550).

50. This particularist mindset of the Jewish societies in Venice was constantly denounced by the rabbis who considered it deplorable. Leone de Modena's diatribes on this point are typical.

51. See *Dizionario etimologica della lingua italiana*, 1987, III, 796.

52. *Universitas* is a medieval juridical term designating all forms of communities and associations e.g., a "university" assembly. The *Universitas* of Paris regrouped in the thirteenth century four "nations" (French, Norman, Picard, and English). See Jacques Verger, *Histoire des Universités en France* (Paris: 1986), pp. 28–29, 37–38.

53. *Še elot utešuvot lezione Yehuda*, 51 (Jerusalem, 1956): 68–69; see also 78: 109–110.

54. See Brian S. Pullan, *La politica sociale della Repubblica di Venezia 1500-1620. I: Les scuole grandi, l'assistenza e le leggi sui poveri* (Rome, 1982).

55. On this point, the study of the texts of the *haskamot* and the *Copie* of the Venetian Hebraic ediction at the end of the sixteenth and seventeenth centuries reveals a fertile area for exploration. See our *Sefer hayasaar, Introduction*, pp. 69–97, and Meir Benayahu, *Haskama uresut bidefuse Venezia* (Copyright, Authorization and Imprimatur for Hebrew Books Printed in Venice) (Jerusalem, 1971).

THREE

On the Concept of Beauty in the Philosophy of Yehudah Abrabanel

Ze'ev Levy

Don Yehudah Abrabanel, the son of Rabbi Yitshak Abrabanel, has been one of the most extraordinary and fascinating personalities in Jewish philosophy on the threshold of modernity. His *Dialoghi d'Amore* has become one of the most celebrated books of Renaissance literature and thought. Despite his personal afflictions—the expulsion from Spain in 1492, the abduction and forced conversion of his son by the King of Portugal (about which he wrote a moving poem: "Complaint on the Times")—he has bequeathed to us one of the most outstanding philosophical books of the epoch. *Dialoghi d'Amore* is one of the chief expressions of Italian Platonism, revived and flourishing at the time. Platonism superseded Aristotelianism, which had been until then the unchallenged authority of scholastic thought. Furthermore, Abrabanel's book also marks a significant encounter between the spirit of the Renaissance and the spirit of Judaism. This aspect comes to its salient affirmation in the reflections on aesthetic issues too, which form the principal topic of this chapter. But if Yitshak Abrabanel may still be considered the latest expression of medievalism in Jewish thought, his son already belongs wholeheartedly to the modern era. The border between old and new thus crosses this famous family of Spanish Jews during one of the most distressing hours of Jewish history.

Although there was a Neoplatonic current in medieval Jewish philosophy, the general trend was toward Aristotelianism, the same as in general philosophy.

This chapter is based on a lecture opening a colloquium on Yehuda Abrabanel's "Dialoghi D'Amore" at Haifa University on January 16, 1984.

There were several reasons for this. First, Aristotle's philosophy did not incorporate mythological elements as did Plato's. It was of a more discursive nature, and therefore more conclusive and decisive than the aporetic tendencies characteristic of many Platonic dialogues. And finally, Aristotelianism was no compatible source for pantheistic or quasi-pantheistic views, although the latter never were entirely alien to Judaism. (Ibn-Gabirol, the greatest Jewish neo-platonist philosopher, whose influence is discernible in Abrabanel's book, is himself a case in point.)

However, with *Dialoghi d'Amore*, all this changed completely. It is perhaps not incidental that the three great Jewish philosophers who exhibited Platonic or neo-Platonic inclinations—Philo, Ibn-Gabirol, and Yehudah Abrabanel—left almost no traces in Jewish thought. The main impact of their work is to be found in general philosophy. This evidently holds also for the philosophy of Spinoza—another descendent of Spanish Jewry and the greatest of all. It is noteworthy that Spinoza drew some of his philosophical inspiration from Abrabanel (whose book he possessed in Spanish translation) as, *inter alia*, the well-known concept of *Amor Dei Intellectualis*.

Abrabanel attempts (especially in the third dialogue of his book) to bring about a merger between Jewish-religious conceptions and Renaissance Platonism. To this purpose he welds together the Jewish concept of love of God with a religious-aesthetic idealization of the world. For the first time in the history of Jewish thought there was a philosopher who awarded space to aesthetic reflections (which had never played an important role in Judaism) and who set out to explicate and define the concept of *beauty*.

Like Spinoza more than a hundred years later, Abrabanel strove toward a unified conception of all being. Under the influence of Ibn-Garirol, and perhaps also of Hasdai Crescas, he considered love to represent a primal drive that penetrates being in different ways—love, desire, friendship, and so on. He underlines explicitly (in the third dialogue again) that, although Plato treated only human love in the *Symposium* (that dialogue, together with *Timaeus*, became a kind of paradigm to most of Abrabanel's theoretical reflections—*vide infra*), he wishes to meditate on love as it reveals itself in the whole of created world. Love constitutes an ontic and cosmic principle, sustaining the world altogether. One cannot overlook, of course, certain Aristotelian motives. Neo-Platonism, from its very beginnings, had absorbed many Aristotelian ideas. In Abrabanel's case, one ought to call attention to Aristotle's assertion that the desire to approach the unmoved mover is the cause of the movement of the spheres. In like manner, Abrabanel explains the force of gravitation as a revelation of love: everything is attracted (in the twofold sense of the word) by earth. Yet, despite certain pantheistic traits, inherited mostly from Ibn-Gabirol, Abrabanel maintains on the whole a transcendental conception of the Godhead conforming with Jewish religious tradition. Therefore he also speaks about love, just like Maimonides, as a desire to come close to God. Notwithstanding the differences between the two philosophers, both identify love of God and knowledge of God, continuing thus a venerable Hebrew linguistic tradition. Love manifests the yearning of the lover to cling to the idea of the beautiful and the good, as it is manifested by the loved one, and to become one with it. There lies the origin of Abrabanel's aforementioned influence on Spinoza's concept of *Amor Dei Intellectualis*.

When twilight settled on Jewish philosophy of the Romance countries—Spain, Italy, and Provence—when Abrabanel and his book faded into almost total oblivion, in the first half of the seventeenth century, *Dialoghi d'Amore* regained its due through the work of the last Jewish philosopher of Spanish-Portuguese descent—Baruch Spinoza. Although Spinoza did not mention Abrabanel by name, it was through him that the latter recovered his well-deserved place in western philosophy in general, and in Jewish philosophy in particular. Modern Spinoza scholarship (e.g., the work of Karl Gebhardt and others) rekindled the interest in Abrabanel's book. At the same time, it helped recent researchers to reassess Spinoza's philosophy and to throw light on its Jewish ingredients.[1]

There are surprisingly many and multifarious subjects discussed in *Dialoghi d'Amore*—the logical relations between the concepts of love, desire, and knowledge; the meanings of *useful* (instrumental), *pleasant*, and *meritable* as criteria for defining love; the good and the beautiful; meditations on the universality of love, its origin and its purpose; man's love of God and God's love of man; lengthy reflections on the symbolic meanings of the gods in Greek mythology (something utterly unprecedented and unparalleled in Jewish thought and literature). From among all these diverse topics I wish to focus on one aspect of Abrabanel's philosophy, namely his *aesthetic* meditations. This will also help us to get a lucid picture of the modes of his philosophizing.

As has been stated, Abrabanel was the first of very few Jewish thinkers to deal systematically with the concept of the beautiful. Jewish thought was always reluctant to engage in aesthetic studies. One of the main reasons was probably the fear that aesthetic contemplation would turn one's attention away from a Jew's chief aim, namely to study the Torah. (There are several statements of this sort in the Talmud.) However, the biblical prohibition—"Do not make for yourselves images of anything in heaven or on earth. . ." (Exodus, 20:4)—did not arrest the development of plastic art and crafts within Judaism, nor did Judaism ever remain completely aloof from aesthetic deliberations. But it is an uncontestable fact that aesthetic reflections hardly ever played any significant role in Jewish thought. It is certainly true that this was also the case in non-Jewish medieval philosophy. All this renders Abrabanel's contributions still more conspicuous. His aesthetic cogitations represented not only a new phenomenon in Jewish thought but became an outstanding feature of Renaissance philosophy as well. The aesthetic dimension of the book certainly was one of the reasons for its startling success at the time.

Abrabanel conceived of art (*arte*) as "craft" and as "art" alike. He described it as the first of five spiritual properties to assure man's happiness. (The four others were understanding, intellect, science, and wisdom.) Since these meditations exerted, on the one hand, a considerable influence on general philosophy, and on the other hand represented the first attempt of a Jewish thinker to interpolate aesthetic notions in his philosophy, let us dwell on them a little more exhaustively.

According to one of his definitions, love reflects knowledge of absent beauty. It is displayed by the desire to give birth to the (not-yet-present) beautiful, to make it resemble its father. This applies to intellectual love no less than to sensual love. Both aspire to eternity:

> The common father of all love is the beautiful, and the common mother is knowledge of the beautiful, together with [consciousness of] its balance. From these two, exactly as from a true father and mother, love and desire are born. Whoever is aware of the absence of the beautiful, desires and loves it at once. So love is engendered by the beautiful which somebody conceives to lack, and therefore he desires it (p. 423).

Love is born from the desire for beauty:

> The loved beautiful is the father who engenders love, while the mother is the knowledge of the lover who gets pregnant by the seed of this beautiful. The seed embodies the structure of the beautiful as conceived by the knowing person who has been impregnated by it, and desires to become one with the beautiful and to reproduce it (*ibid*).

The beautiful itself, however, springs from the form given to matter. Therefore, something beautiful can be found everywhere. Artistic beauty—the beauty of artificial objects—is manifested by "formal grace" ("*grazia formale*") (p. 431).[2] The form which the painter bestows on his painting is born from "the idea in the artist's thought" (p. 423). Therefore, true beauty is nothing material but a truly spiritual achievement. One can perhaps discern here some traces of the religious heritage of Judaism. In classical Jewish thought, man's creation in God's image was interpreted as meaning that he is endowed, unlike all other creatures, with spiritual-intellectual capacity.[3] Sophia, Philo's partner in the dialogues, makes, however, a pertinent remark: "Beauty consists in the relation between the parts and the whole and the appropriateness of the whole to its parts" (p. 426; *a propos*, this had already been the idea of the Pythagorean philosophers). The circle, which she considers the most perfect form, is pleasant to the eye, and displays beauty: "The beauty of the circular form, the most beautiful of all forms, is perfect in itself, and composed of parts" (p. 4429; Aristotle already conceived of the circle as the most perfect form).

But Philo insists that material beauty, conceived by the senses alone, has no inherent value: "Matter which is the element of all inferior bodies, has no form of its own; it is the cause of all imperfection. Only when, under the influence of the spiritual realm, it dons, together with all its parts, a form, it becomes beautiful" (p. 428). He emphasizes his point: "The more a form is capable of erasing material absence-of-form, the more the body becomes beautiful, and *vice versa*: the less it contrives to delete, the less beautiful and perfect the body becomes" (p. 429). This he believes to be one of the reasons why there are people, horses, etc., that are judged to be more beautiful than others of their kind. Retrospectively, this reminds one of Hegel's conception of the dialectic relationship between form and content which formed the base of his aesthetics and philosophy of art. There is, however, a fundamental difference between their two views. While Hegel stressed the changing proportions of the formal-sensual element as against the spiritual-substantial element—form and sense go together—Abrabanel, on the other hand, underlined the contrast between form and the sensual dimension. Briefly, material beauty can be conceived and loved only through the soul and the intellect. It therefore happens quite often that, although different people see the same things, only a few of them are really able to perceive their inherent beauty. Perhaps Abrabanel transferred to the aesthetic plane a view which Maimonides pronounced in regard to the Torah—namely, that philosophically schooled readers can disclose its deeper meaning, whereas simpleminded believers are unable to grasp it. (It is noteworthy that Maimonides also illustrated his distinction between esoteric and exoteric understanding of the Bible by an allegory from the field of art: "Apples of gold in settings of silver"[4]). Love of sensual beauty is the antechamber for higher love; it is no more than a means to achieve spiritual beauty which represents the longed-for end.

In the third dialogue, the concept of beauty turns more and more from an aesthetic concept into a metaphysical one. This occurs once again through the influence of Plato's idea of the beautiful, which Abrabanel attempts to blend with certain notions of Jewish neo-Platonism. In this connection ought to be mentioned an important expression which was very characteristic of scholastic philosophy: *natura naturans et natura naturata*. We are familiar with it chiefly through Spinoza's use of these two terms in the *Ethics*—i.e., in the wake of a philosopher who was one of the inaugurators of modern thought.[5] However, what is interesting in the present context is the following: Abrabanel adopts this expression and uses it in his book, but he also links it with Maimonides' conception of God as the unity of "*intellectus*," "*intelligens*," and "*intelligibile*,"[6] and speaks about "beautifying beauty" and "beautified beauty":

> There are three levels of beauty in the world: the possessor of beauty, beauty itself, and what partakes in it, namely the beautiful that emanates beauty, beauty and emanated beauty. The beautifying beautiful is God himself, beauty is highest wisdom and the first intellectual idea, and beautified beauty is the son of beauty, that is to say the created universe (p. 450).

Abrabanel claims to have discovered the origin of the neo-Platonic idea in
the biblical book of *Canticum Canticorum*. Although in the first two dialogues
of his book he mostly evokes love in its natural forms, he tends to interpret,
as did many philosphers and theologians before him, this book of the Bible
allegorically. His aim is to present God—"How beautiful you are, my love" (Cant.
Cant 1:15)—as "the first creator of beauty." He expressly intends to elucidate the
"merger between supreme beauty [i.e., divine wisdom, *vide supra*] and the supreme
beautiful [i.e., God] from which it has emanated" (p. 454). Beauty thus spreads
all over the universe, and the whole world becomes beautiful, as is written in
Ecclesiastes: "He has made everything beautiful in his time" (3:11). It is quite
interesting again that Abrabanel ascribed to Solomon various ideas that were
borrowed from Greek mythology and philsophy. They show up in *Canticum
Canticorum* and *Ecclesiastes* (of which Solomon was supposed to be the author).
In like manner, Spinoza tried afterwards to find in *Proverbs* (also ascribed to
Solomon, "the wisest of all men") some of his own philosophical ideas. By these
hermeneutic speculations Abrabanel did not, of course, insinuate that there had
been any influence of Greek thought on biblical books (as conjectured by modern
Bible research). He wanted to confirm the contrary—namely, that the books of
the Bible exerted their influence on Greek culture. This was no novel idea in
Jewish thought. One can find it as early as the writings of Maimonides and
Yehudah Halevi.[7]

The aforementioned threefold neo-Platonic terminology is the chief argument
of the third dialogue (more than half of the book), where it appears under various
disguises, sometimes word-by-word as in Maimonides' philosophy. More often,
however, he exchanges the word *intellect* for *beauty*, and sometimes even for
enjoyment. These attempts to weld together general philosophical ideas (mostly
from Plato and neo-Platonism) with ideas to be derived from diverse verses of
the Bible and the Midrash or with major concepts of Jewish medieval philosophy
is a distinctive feature of Abrabanel's philosophy. One can find many interesting—
and sometimes puzzling—examples of this kind in his book.

One such characteristic passage is his attempt to work out a synthesis between
Plato's view in *Timaeus* that the world was created from primeval matter and
the biblical view of *creatio ex nihilo*. While Maimonides refrained from adjusting
the biblical view to Aristotle's conception of the eternity of the world, Abrabanel
had no qualms about combining Plato's conception with the narration in *Genesis*.
But he does not interpret the Bible according to philosophical criteria, as did
Maimonides (and as he does himself on other occasions). On the contrary, he
tries to interpret Plato in such a way as to enable him to adapt Plato's ideas to
the biblical view. In *Timaeus*, Plato described the creation of all things by the
supreme God (the *demiurg*) from primeval unformed matter. Abrabanel adds,
however, that since God was the creator of everything, he also must have created
primeval matter. He employs the Greek word *chaos*—the equivalent of the Hebrew
Tohuwabohu. But God did not create the chaos at a certain definite moment in

time; it emanated from him all the time, eternally, while everything else was created from chaos in time. Chaos has been the "companion of God" from time immemorial, but it was nevertheless created by Him (p. 266). He attributes this arbitrary-seeming theory to Plato:

> The believers in the Torah of Moses hold not merely to the opinion that the world was created in the beginning but that it was created out of nothing in the beginning of time. There are also several philosophers who think so, and among them the divine [sic] Plato; he says in his book *Timaeus* that the world has been made and created by God, and been formed from chaos which is the matter from which all things have come into being (p. 363).

He then accuses Plotinus of having altered Plato's original view, which was akin to the biblical view, to the idea of an ever-existing primary world: "But it seems that Plato's words imply a beginning in time, and so they have been understood by other prominent Platonists" (p. 364). He does not disclose to us who these other Platonists were. The neo-Platonists who absorbed Aristotelian ideas misinterpreted Plato's conception by ascribing to him the false idea of the primacy of the world.

Abrabanel claims to have discovered still another interesting common denominator between Plato's thought and biblical thought by comparing the story of God's creating humans male and female (*Genesis* 1:27) with Aristophanes' amusing story in Plato's *Symposium* (p. 405). He wishes to corroborate once again his thesis that Plato's ideas were inspired by the Bible. The conclusions to be drawn from the two stories are, however, different. According to the Platonic dialogue, the androgyne was separated into two as a punishment for man's insolence toward the gods. The God of the Bible did so out of his concern and love for man, in order to release him from his solitude. Only after having been separated, Adam and Eve committed the crime of eating the forbidden fruit, whereas, according to Plato, man's crime preceded the separation (p. 410).

Perhaps Plato's moral conclusion was not so far from the spirit of Judaism as it appears at first sight. The French Jewish philosopher Emmanuel Lévinas holds the opinion that Plato's myth is not merely a fictitious version of the creation of man and woman but rather expresses a fundamental problem of human existence. Man, by his very nature, is not a perfect being but an imperfect one. This gives birth to his insatiable desire to refill his lack. This had also been Abrabanel's argument in the first dialogue when he dwelt on the logical relations between desire and love. But from the Platonic myth it also follows, according to Lévinas' interpretation, that man's essential deficiency consists of having lost his original second half. He explains this as the loss of one's better *alter ego*. This loss generates man's perpetual yearning, never to be satisfied, for perfection and faultlessness. Man's desire to mend this primitive lack of his nature is therefore not only the will to restore an erstwhile disposition, as had been the moral lesson of Plato's story. Lévinas views it as an expression of man's aspiration—consciously or unconsciously—to find again his *alter ego*—i.e., his better side. While Abrabanel connected the divergent inferences of the two stories with the philosophical issues of good and evil, crime and punishment, divine concern and divine wrath, Lévinas interprets Plato's myth on knowledge of love as the starting point of solipsism in Western philosophy. Being a modern Jewish thinker, his problem is how to harmonize this ontological solipsism with the goodness of the transcendent God. This is one of the fundamental topics of Lévinas' metaphysics and ethics.[8] This, however, transgresses the scope of this chapter.

Abrabanel's meditations on the concept of beauty, as well as the few comparisons between Plato and the Bible, were only random illustrations in order to show how for the first time aesthetic theories became the subject matter of systematic inquiries in Jewish philosophy. Abrabanel was a kind of precursor of Jewish aesthetics, although after him, even in modern times, aesthetic inquiries still remained a stepchild of Jewish philosophy. Very few Jewish thinkers paid attention to aesthetics. Spinoza, notwithstanding his acquaintance with the *Dialoghi*, remained indifferent toward aesthetic issues. Moses Mendelssohn and Hermann Cohen discussed aesthetic theory in their general philosophical writings, but it had no bearing on their Jewish thought. Only one Jewish philosopher in modern times assigned to aesthetics a special place in his philosophy, and judged it by Jewish criteria. That was Franz Rosenzweig. But that once again goes beyond the limits of this chapter.

Therefore, Yehudah Abrabanel can be considered to represent the pioneer of Jewish aesthetics. His book has remained one of the very few philosophical treatises produced by Jewish thought that examined in a systematic manner the concepts of the beautiful and of beauty.

NOTES

1. *Vide* also Menahem Dorman in the exhaustive introduction to his new Hebrew translation of the book which appeared in 1983; Yehudah Abrabanel, *Dialoghi d'Amore*, Byalik Institute, Jerusalem, 1983. (All the following quotations are from this edition.)

2. Two hundred years later this will become the central notion of Friedrich Schiller's aesthetics. *Anmut*; F. Schiller, "Ueber Anmut and Würde", *Schriften zur Philsophie und Kunst*, München 1964, pp. 20–66.

3. See, for example, Moses Maimonides, *Guide of the Perplexed*, Pt. I, Ch. 3, translated by S. Pines, Chicago and London 1963.

4. *Ibid.*, Pt. I, Introduction, pp. 11–12.

5. Baruch Spinoza, *Ethics*, Pt. I, prop. 29, scholium.

6. *Guide of the Perplexed*, Pt. I, Ch. 68.

7. *Guide, ibid.*, Pt. I, Ch. 70, 71; Yehudah Halevi, *Kuzari*, 1st book, Ch. 63, 2nd book, Ch. 66.

8. See his *Totalité et Infini*, Paris 1961.

FOUR

The Conventionalization of Social Bonds and the Strategies of Jewish Society in the Thirteenth Century

Schmuel Trigano
Translated by Roger C. Norton

It is difficult to introduce new historical elements into the study of the controversy aroused by the writings of Maimonides in the Jewish society of Languedoc and in the entire Jewish world during the thirteenth and fourteenth centuries.[1] Many historians have made distinguished contributions. But our aim here is to help develop a new viewpoint in the interpretation of the elements involved and to discover in them a different configuration of the historical event which will make its social logic and sociological structure more apparent. The elements the historian gathers are indeed of great significance for the sociologist, whereas the historian's interpretations are commonly deceiving for the sociologists because they do not grasp more than the appearances of the event—its concrete aspect—that is to say, a controversy and a battle of ideas surrounding the philosophical texts. There is an inability to perceive the social and anthropological dimensions of Jewish history, as if only an ethereal and abstract existence were involved here.

The classical interpretations of this controversy are:

1. The more or less ideological interpretation by Graetz,[2] the Jewish historian of the "Science of Judaism," who sees it as a conflict between obscurantism and reason.

2. Charles Touati's psychological and intellectualizing approach, which
attempts to arrive at an "objective" judgment of the charges against
Maimonides—i.e., to consider them as actual "indictments," in order
to weigh the importance of the matter and finally decide that the
Maimonides controversy revolved around the "status of profane
knowledge within Judaism,"[3] and that the stakes involved were "the
slackening of religious practices and the refusal to understand certain
biblical and talmudic texts in their literal sense."[4]

There are also interpretations which take a more sociological direction but
stop in mid-course. These are:

1. J. Silver's externalizing analysis,[5] whose main thesis postulates
a cause-and-effect relationship between the violence of the controversy and the threat presented by the Church—which from this
time on would be militant and Proselytic—to a Judaism that could
not permit itself the slightest weakness or doubt. The controversy
thus reflected the psychological reaction of a directly endangered
community.
2. The political interpretation of Yitzhak Baer,[6] the great Jewish
historian of Christian Spain, who mentions the political and
religious conflict on which the controversy was based and which
caused a struggle between Nahmanides and the Alconstantini
family, the great Jewish family of courtiers who attempted to draw
the religious and civil authorities of the Jewish community into its
sphere at a time when the interests of the Jews of the court, as well
as those of the highest leaders, coincided with the interests of the
philosophers.

My intention, of course, is not to refute a particular interpretation connected
with any of these theories. Each of them contains a measure of truth. But they
do not seem to grasp the real extent and implications of a conflict which very
definitely concerns social bonds and relations. Their weakness derives from the
very difficulty of their objective—to articulate the philosophical dimension of
the conflict with the social dimension.

Was the conflict in the Jewish society of Languedoc entirely philosophical?
Was the philosophical debate merely a superflous and superficial aspect of the
conflict, as Silver seems to indicate,[7] and also even Baer to a certain degree?[8]
Was it possible for a philosophical conflict to have such a powerful effect? Was
the Jewish community a community of philosophers? Such questions prompted
Silver to say that in fact the conflict was nothing but a conflict of individuals
opposed to other individuals. In any case, all these are very real questions whose
answers necessitate a reconsideration of the sociology of cognition—that is to

say, the processes involved in ideological phenomena—and of the relations between social facts and texts or theories.

This problem is all the more crucial in the case of the Jewish society concerned here—a "textual society," so to speak, centered upon a text as its principle of coherence and legitimation.[9] We may need to refer to what I have called a "sociology of hermeneutics"[10] in order to decipher some of the modalities of the social entity itself by means of observing the different ways it relates to the text— i.e., through its hermeneutic theories and its conflicting interpretations, which for such a society are ways of relating to its self. In this problematic issue we can observe that the philosophical ideology of the Jews is less a matter of 'ideas' that influence society than it is a process of social change as it originates, is formulated, and is reflected in the conceptualizations of Jewish society and history that prevail at a particular time and the process of development of these conceptualizations. It is not the theoretical level that is important here, but rather the theoretical configuration of Jewish philosophical theories (i.e., their organization into conceptual plans, their structure, and their logical framework) in which we can discern the social configuration. The sociology of hermeneutics addresses the ideology of an epoch but is less interested in its particular content than in the general economy of its ideological theory.

A LOGIC OF ALLOGENIZATION OF JEWISH SOCIETY

From an epistemological perspective in which one attempts to discern the social and historical elements within the textual, the structure of Jewish society in Languedoc can be characterized by two essential traits that represent its divided character:

1. The centrality of the biblical text, which seems to give this society its structure, constituting its sociality and weaving the fabric of its social ties in such fashion that its hermeneutic economy determines its configuration, because positions and strategies are determined as a function of the text that serves as the medium of exchange.[11]

2. The polycentric and federative process of social and political action, as, for example, in the practice of excommunication, which has only a localized validity; a decision made by one center of power can annul that of another.[12] Social action and acts of authority seem to require the assent of other authorities (as in the case of the anti-Maimonideans of Montpellier, who required the support of rabbinic decision makers [poskim] from northern France and Aragon) in their excommunication of philosophical studies, for example.

What does Maimonideanism represent for such a society? It is of prime importance to know this, because in our approach the meaning and nature of the texts are not irrelevant to the framework of the conflict, but on the contrary reveal the main axes of social configuration. To attempt to understand Maimonideanism, we may make use of an 'ideal type' constructed in accordance with Max Weber's method and composed of various models:

1. Assimilation of the ideas of the Torah into Greek philosophy on terms of absolute equivalence.
2. Subsequent application of Greek categories to biblical discourse.
3. Allegorization—i.e., the abstract of this discourse in such a way that abstract prisms are applied to a text rich in details and proper names. The biblical text becomes the object of philosophical discourse.
   3a. Abstraction functions as a diacritical schematization of the universal and the particular, culminating in a reabsorption of the particular into the Greek universal, in accordance with which Jewish philosophy defines Hebraism (as language and thought).
   3b. Abstraction also takes the form of a reduction of biblical anthropomorphisms, an overturning of the Hebraic economy of the worldly and corporeal. Logically, the question of resurrection—which for biblical prophecy is the resurrection of the body in this world—focuses this problem and becomes one of the main axes of the controversy.[13]
   3c. If the purpose is to reduce everything in the text that has nothing to do with the 'bodily' and the 'concrete,' allegorization leads either to a detextualizing of the biblical text,[14] or a dehistoricization of the entire biblical text, which as a consequence divorces the Jewish entity from its history, its social being and meaning, and also divorces the divinity from his "proper names"[15]—that is to say, from his presence in history.
   3d. The philosophical allegorization of the text thus imbues it with another logic of meaning and civilization.
   3e. This 'alienation' of the text devolves logically from the principle of philosophical interpretation of anthropomorphisms—the absolute alterity of the divine in respect to language. The principle of alterity reveals itself as a factor or allogenization of self-estrangement of the text.
4. Allogenization of the text has as its consequence the dissociation of the text not only from itself but also from its meaning, existence,

mobility, and its existential depth and Jewish entity. This is a twofold process.

4a. Conventionalization of the text and of the Jewish identity. Since it will from now on be a question of justifying the Jewish reality (text, society, God with proper names), Jewish philosophy will see in all this the effects of a 'convention' between human beings that was artificial, rational, and voluntaristic, and will no longer see its corporeal, linguistic, and historical profundity. The existence of Israel no longer has 'weight' unless it be that of a flat and fabricated 'symbol' divorced from meaning and dimensionality. Even its text will become the product of a convention, a political proceeding.[16] Its meaning is no longer within its self.

4b. The codification of the text into a historically immobile noncreative form, a state of absolute and conventionized rigidity: the *Mishneh Torah* of Maimonides molds the world of the Halakha, mobile in essence, into a rigid abstract form, putting an end to its growth and perpetuating its unyielding dogma.

5. These processes of allogenization represent very directly the irruption of a different logic of civilization into Jewish civilization, operating primarily through minor prisms that are clearly sociological.

THE MINOR PRISMS OF THE CONFLICT

The Cultural Prism

The Maimonidean controversy reveals a cultural conflict affecting relations between North and South, East and West in the Jewish world. Languedoc was at this time the crossroads of that entire world:

From South to North. The Reconquest first introduced the very powerful Jewish-Arab world to the occidental Christian sphere and therefore a closer contact with the Ashkenazi Judaism of the Rhineland and France that was developing in this same period. In addition, the influx of refugees from Spain was revitalizing the Provençal communities. Two Jewish cultural types met in Languedoc—that of the North, focused on the exclusive study of the Talmud and demonstrating considerable cultural creativity on the part of its Tosafists, and that of the South, known for its philosophical preeminence. Exchanges were encouraged between these two poles. From the North came the works of the Tosafists, and from the

South the system of codification of Alfasi and Joseph Ibn Migash. A great debate was initiated in the twelfth century at Lunel concerning the respective merits of both.

From East to West. This current is very old. A disciple (Moshe ben Hanokh) of the Gaon of the Babylonian Talmudic Academy established the first Jewish school of philosophy in Spain at Cordova. The rabbinic authorities of Babylon also played a decisive role in regard to Hebraic law and their influence extended throughout the Jewish world. Also coming from the Middle East (from a Jewish refugee, Maimonides, fleeing persecution by the Almohades) was the *Guide for the Perplexed*, with its entire philosophical perspective—brought to Languedoc probably via the Mediterranean Sea. At Lunel it was translated by the Ibn Tibbons from Arabic into Hebrew, and thus introduced to the entire Jewish world. There was frequent communication from East to West and there were translators (Samuel Ibn Tibbon and Jonathan Hakohen from Lunel) who carried on a substantial correspondence with Maimonides himself concerning their translation. This new perspective had a shock effect upon the relations between the talmudic culture of the Jews of Paris and of Sens, the methods propounded by Rashi (1040–1105), and the school of the Tosafists on the one hand,[17] and the varied academic cultures of Cairo and Bagdad, on the other, cultures where leaders of the Talmudic Academy such as Saadiah Gaon wrote philosophical books, translated the Bible into Arabic, and freely discussed the theory of 'double faith,' which finds equal value in reason and revelation as approaches to truth.

The tension between these two Jewish cultural modalities involved also the nature of their relation to the environment—an open society in Islam and a closed society in the Christian world. An example may serve to explain: Maimonides declared that a Jew who was converted in time of persecution (in Islam) is a *mumar* (apostate), alienating himself by free choice, while Rabbi ben David de Posquières calls such a Jew a *min* (heretic) for being converted to Christianity, whose dogma of the trinity is equivalent to a denial of divine unity.

The Political Prism

The disruption of Judeo-Languedocian social ties is demonstrated in a second dimension of Maimonides' work—the *Mishneh Torah*, the codifiction of the Talmud. It was actually a part of Maimonides' first phase in the sense that, being written in Hebrew and thus not needing translation, it arrived in Languedoc before the *Guide*. And one can say that without the powerful effect of this work and its implications, the *Guide* would undoubtedly never have aroused such a controversy. The *Mishneh Torah* brought to Jewish society a new judicial code of revolutionary import. It substituted for the specific approach of the customary law of the Halakha an abstract, rationalistic, codified approach that had many consequences.

1. Its rationalistic codification stifled the evolvability and creativity of classical jurisprudence. This Code became, as Silver characterizes it, a straitjacket for the rabbinic decision makers.
2. Written in pure Hebrew and not the Aramaic of the Talmud, which few Jews still understood, the Code democratized Jewish law and jurisprudence and opened this complex world to any intellectual.
3. By its very nature, the Code introduced a centralization which had been peculiar to the Middle East, where the gaonate of Babylon had governed for a thousand years. It thus controlled the decision making centers in a Jewish world that had been in essence polycentric.
4. By virtue of its Middle Eastern origins, the Code imposed, regardless of any intention, various specific customs (Sephardic or Middle Eastern) upon the entire diaspora (including the Ashkenazim) at a time when every center of Jewish life had been developing a conscience attuned to its specific locality.[18]

For all of these reasons, the Maimonidean judicial code destroyed the stability of legislative and judicial authority in Hebraic society. It shook the foundations of knowledge that had given the rabbinic decision makers privileges not possessed by the intellectuals nor by political and laic powers in the Jewish world in general. For from this time on, the Code permitted it to disregard the judgment and authority of the decision makers in matters of the Halakha. This was a decisive blow to rabbinic power, most evidently in the Orient, where the gaonate was in conflict with the civil power of the exilarch, the 'Prince of Exile' and was attempting to depose him and assume his powers in order to buttress its own financial resources, for the exilarch had the right to impose taxes. In this controversy, Maimonides sided against the *gaon* of Babylon, Samuel ben Ali (1164–1198), and for the exilarch (whose position dated back to the year 170), David ben Samuel (1195–1240). When the *gaon* claimed that Israel in exile was not bound by any authority derived from national sovereignties, such as the exilarch did in his role as vassal of the caliph, Maimonides defended the exilarch by saying that he "does not have to be a sage." Thus, the Code represented on one hand a menace to the constituted authorities of Jewish society, but it also reflected a conflict of these authorities among themselves in regard to both lay and religious power. Moreover, it is of interest to note that the Code of Maimonides systematized the *Hilkhot Melakhim*, the 'Law of Kings', which is not an important theme in the Talmud and yet which constitutes civil authority in Jewish society. Certain commentators are of the opinion that Maimonides foresaw the imminent restoration of the Jewish state and shaped the contents of his Code in such a way that it would render the exercise of power easier and more rational by giving future Jewish statesmen a kind of pracitcal guide. Did he not define the messianic era as being the end of Israel's political bondage to the "kingdoms of this world" (*shiboud Malkhuyot*)? The political theme is central in Maimonides, as we have shown elsewhere.[19] He even provided a framework for the idea of conventionalizing the text and Hebraic society since this would be an event of a political nature and, with it as the base of political authority for the elite among the sages, the elite and the masses could unite within the same society and under the same principle of power.

But the configuration of the political conflict was not uniquely Middle Eastern, for it seemed equally widespread in Spain (Aragon) and Narbonne. The leader of the *aljama* of Aragon and Saragossa, Bahya Alconstantini (*"rab de la Corte"*), led the counter-excommunication of the anti-Maimonideans of Montpellier in August 1232. But this 'clan chief' of the Maimonideans was himself a large land owner and high dignitary of the court of Jaime I and was involved in a power struggle at the heart of the Jewish community. And Nahmanides, the great Catalan cabbalist who had participated in the famous Disputation of Barcelona, had already opposed the ambitions of the Alconstantini family which, by virtue of its position at court (the center of Jewish political power), was claiming the title of *nasi*, although this title was hereditarily bestowed upon the dynasty of King David. Nevertheless, the king invested them by decree with the supreme rabbinic and judicial authority.[20] The counter-excommunication of the anti-Maimonideans isolated Nahmanides in his own community, which now gave its support to the families Sheshet of Barcelona and Alconstantini as did other famous families who held great influence on the Jews of this region.

Thus, the conflict between civil authority and religious power as exemplified by Nahmanides was taking place at the same time in both Aragon and Babylonia. In Babylonia the religious authority was striving to assume the civil authority of the exilarch, an aim Maimonides opposed. In Spain this situation was reversed: the civil authority was attempting to seize religious authority. This was undoubtedly due to the different political environment. The collapse of the caliphate in Iraq, the schism between East and West, and the creation of independent caliphates in Spain and Egypt had weakened the power of the exilarch as dignitary of the court—all the more so because the divisions within the Islamic empire no longer permitted the Western Jews to view the exilarch as their political sovereign. Although the exilarch was a member of the court, an edict of the caliph Al Mamoun (813–833) authorized all groups of at least ten men to establish a community and choose a religious leader. This allowed the Karaite dissidents to break away from the rabbinate and the exilarch. In Spain there existed, on the other hand, a strong and warlike monarchy which needed its Jewish men of state for the Reconquest and granted its protegés uncontested power over their community.

The Mesopotamian model was repeated at Narbonne, where a *nasi* was prospering who, according to tradition, had come from Babylon and was descended from David. Nevertheless, there was a great difference in the Jewish power in Narbonne because, contrary to the situation in Babylon, the *nasi* coupled the authority of the exilarch with that of the *gaons* as a spiritual and temporal leader who possessed (as in Babylon) a very large fortune in land. Here the conflict unfolded in a different way. In the thirteenth century, the power of the *nasi*, confronted by seigneurial dominance, was diminishing in the community, whereas the power of the Jewish bourgeoisie, the 'parnassim', was increasing. The vicontiel records designated them as *prud'hommes* or *conseils de la juiverie* ('arbitrators' or 'counsellors of the Jews'), and in time they were granted civil authority.[21] In the vicontiel charter of 1217, Aimeri IV drew a distinction between the ten notables representing the community and the "roi juif" (Jewish king), considered a seigneur of the city. Gradually the *nasi* surrendered preeminence to those whom the vicontiel charter of 1269 called the "consuls of the Jews of Narbonne." It no longer mentioned the "Jewish king," who, having lost all civil power, retained only his religious authority, while the consuls gained leadership of the community. This development paralleled the economic evolution that brought the Jews of Narbonne into financial transactions connected with the rise of maritime trade, and had the effect of reducing the value of the rural domains of the *nasi* and forging closer ties (with attendant responsibilities) between the Jews and the new bourgeoisie and the ruling class. It also involved them in the development of the consulate of the inner city as an organ of municipal government, established at the expense of vicontiel authority.

The Social Prism

It is not entirely correct to suggest, as does Silver,[22] that such a radical contrast existed between northern France and the Oriental and Occidental Sephardic world. It is true, of course, that philosophy was a special concern of the Sephardim, but the Sephardic world was by no means as homogeneous as Silver supposes. We see there the very new controversy between philosophy and cabbalism that erupted in Provence and the Spain of the Reconquest, but also the violent conflict between the gaonate of Baghdad and the Karaite dissidence. Similar diversity is found in the Askhenazi world. Although we may observe in it the talmudic predominance of the Tosafists, we must also note the birth of 'pietism' amoung the Hassidim of the Rhineland, who likewise initiated a movement with cabbalistic traits.

We must not neglect the importance of Karaism as an element of the crisis of Jewish society during this epoch. Karaism denied the primacy of the Babylonian gaonate in favor of a doctrine of rationalism and free inquiry that rejected the authority of the Talmud, the oral tradition, and the rabbinate, and also reflected the conflict that was raging at the very center of Jewish leadership.[23] Anan ben David was seeking to attain the position of exilarch, over which the gaonate had gained a powerful influence since the beginning of the ninth century when the exilarch accepted obedience to gaonic authority.

The desire to suppress schism led Saadiah, *gaon* of the Talmudic Academy, to invent Judaic philosophy, so to speak, as a taking up of the karaistic intellectual arms (Reason), in order to use them in the service of rabbinism against this challenge. Thus, Jewish philosophy incorporated the vital energies of Karaism into rabbinism so as to be better able to defeat it. But the consequence was a long lasting upheaval within rabbinism itself, the archetypal godfather of Jewish philosophy.[24] Wherever Jewish philosophy was propagated, it carried with it, implicitly or explicitly, the elements of the conflict between rabbinism and Karaism. These elements were not purely symbolic, for Karaism had originated in Spain and had then taken refuge particularly in Castile, where it was attacked and repressed by Cidelus, or Joseph Ferizuel, the physician of Alfonso VI and *nasi* under Alfonso VI,[25] and Judah Ibn Ezra, tax collector (*almoxariphe*) for the king-emperor Alfonso VII (1147). But, paradoxically the Karaitic doctrine later found a following among the apostate Jews who engaged in controversies over the Talmud. Nicolas Donin and Abner of Burgos, for example, supported its main tenets. Maimonides himself had vehemently opposed Karaism, particularly that in Egypt, which followed in the direct line of Saadiah Gaon, the founder of Jewish philosophy. The social dimension of the conflict over Karaism is clear. In this regard, we may cite Mahler, who regards Karaism as a "Jewish popular reform, a revolt of the lower classes of society against the higher, affluent class composed of the aristocracy of the exilarchs and the *gaonim*, as well as the bourgeoisie of the rich property owners and powerful merchants."[26] However, Mahler goes too far in this directions when he declares that "the soul and substance [of Karaism] are social and economic in nature; religion is nothing but a vehicle and necessary language for it," an affirmation confirmed by the fact that "the totality of the legislative writings (the *Sefer hamitzvot* of Anan ben David) seems oriented toward the lowest strata of society."[27]

The social dimension of the Maimonidean controversy is also clear. We have already seen its economic dimensions as illustrated by the rise of a new commercially oriented bourgeoisie and the decline of the old feudal proprietary order and its connection with rabbinic power. The omnipresence of the social dimension could be observed in the conflict in Aragon between Nahmanides and the Alconstantinis and the Sheshet family of Barcelona, which shows the conflictuality of a Jewish aristocracy that was well placed at the court and dominant in the community, haughty toward the traditional authorities and toward other segments of the Jewish population, who remained hostile to its power and identified more closely with Judaic values. Nahmanides spoke of the arrogance of "the haughty Barcelonians [the family Bar Sheshet] and of the Ishmaelites [the Alconstantini family] of the court."[28] He exposed the errors of these powerful courtiers, describing them as

> men of questionable reputation, full of confusion, guilty of base misdeeds.
> How does our generation differ from the others? In our times the sinners

are encouraged and those suspected of immorality are granted authority and honor. The community is surrendered gratis to men who do not pray, do not bless their food, pay no attention to their bread or wine, and secretly profane the sabbath; they are true Ishmaelites.[29]

In any case, the Jews of the court—for example, Bahya Alconstantini—favored Jewish philosophy and recognized themselves in its attitudes and concepts. They were not lured by the prospect of any elevated contemplation, even if they might receive the accompanying 'glory.' All they wanted was a comfortable rationalization of their uncomfortable situation between the life of the community and the life of the court, between the demands of Judaism and the brilliant life of the palace, the loyalty to their people and the irresistible attraction to the ways and purposes of Spanish aristocracy.

They were fascinated by two results of the deliberations concerning the *Guide*. First, its absolute rationalism led to a rationalization of the precepts of Judaism, making them appear to be only conventions not requiring the categorical obedience that would seem demanded from the Jews of the court, involved in worldly life. Second, the equivalence of Greek truth and Hebrew truth in Jewish philosophy was bound to flatter them and raise their prestige in the eyes of the court, but the equivalence appealed to them particularly because of its universalistic implications, which opened wide the gates of the Jewish quarter and furnished a perfect rationalization of the acceptance of the Jews of the court into the ruling class. Universality served as a rationalization of the 'integration' (or assimilation?) and thus as reinforcement of their social and political power. To them, the great cabbalish Nahmanides (1194–1270) doubtless appeared as an 'obscurantist' fanatically attached to Jewish particularism, incapable of transcending the limits of Jewish existence, and a representative of Judaism who wished to deny them their status, their identity, their existence as members of the ruling class. In this light, we can understand more clearly how dehistoricization, which is an implicit process of philosophical problematics, was able to confirm their concept of the world, just as conventionalization made their daily existence easier. And codification allowed them to make unchallenged use of their power and to claim a religious authority that gave them control over the knowledge of the rabbinic and halakhic class. The process of theoretical allogenization implicit in Jewish philosophy thus went hand in hand with a process of alienation in Jewish society which led to the self-detachment of those who were elite in power and knowledge, and who had arrived not only at the pinnacle of community life, thanks to the court, but also to the pinnacle of the court, thanks to the community and the Jewish historical heritage.

TWO STRATEGIES OF JEWISH HISTORY

In the Maimonidean controversy, we thus see two historical Jewish strategies that crystallized for a long period, confronting each other along the crest of the social and politcal conflict. Their encounter—which coincided with their first appearance, since they were born out of conflict—gave rise to many questions. Their main issue was the definition of the boundaries of Jewish society, the determination of its identity, and its relation to the environment and other people. What were the modalities of this society in regard to the world around, but also to itself? The character of the environment itself was also a definite factor. It was a world characterized by the affirmation of a conquering and powerful Christianity—the Crusades, the persecution of the Cathars, the Reconquest in Spain, the establishment of the Inquisition in Spain, and, as noted by Silver, the change of attitude and strategy of the Church in regard to the Jews.[30] The theological ostracism of the Jews, which had been the primary policy of Christianity, was now being realized also on the concrete social level through the enactment of discriminatory measures by the Lateran Council and the confinement of the Jews in what was to becom the Ghetto. This fact shows that the Church had finally discovered, after thirteen centuries, that the Talmud really existed and that it was an 'oral Torah,' a new revelation which competed with that of the Church and gave the lie to the concept of a fossil Judaism bound to the letter of the law and arrested in its development. In addition, the Church found itself very poorly prepared to combat this revelation because of its ignorance of it. That explains the seizure of Jewish books by the Inquisition in many parts of Europe by order of Pope Gregory IX (1240), which marked a turning point in the history of the Occident, since the Church now opened itself toward the Jews, albeit with great defiance. It is obvious that this moment of self-identification across the boundary was prompted and made possible only by the fact that the communication between them had been strong, and repeated exchanges had produced a certain loss of identity by diminishing the clarity of the dividing line. This is the perspective from which the Maimonidean controversy should be regarded. On this boundary, whose erasure was disturbing the internal economy of Jewish identity, three categories of Jews can be defined—the political elite (regarded in many places as an integral part of the Christian elite), the intellectual elite (which was in permanent and intimate contact with the local elite), and a new category—the apostates. These were the *Malchinim*, who had aggressively defected to the other side (while the elite had remained on a middle ground), and who, far from forgetting the communities from which they came, publicly paraded their knowledge of them and revealed the hitherto unknown interiority of Jewish life in order to use it against them. Examples of such apostates are Nicolas Donin and Pablo Christiani, an opponent of Nahmanides.

This exposure was in itself strong enough to disrupt the internal economy of Jewish society. The apostates questioned the Talmud, while the Jewish philosophers sought to 'domesticate' it, which was tantamount to questioning it. From this perspective, we can better understand the criticism of the *Mishneh Torah* by the great talmudist of Posquières, Rabbi Ben David Rabad. We have already observed the Jewish internal political dimension of this questioning process. But for the political and intellectual elite of Jewish society, Jewish philosophy represented an unexpected formalization of their situation of having to live in two worlds but feeling an irresistible propensity for the outer world. Judaism, especially, in its weightier aspects (history and society), was becoming a burden for them and—considering the growing importance and pressing demands of the kingdoms of the Reconquest—an obstacle to the continuation of their social ascendance and open intellectual interchange with their counterparts. The supposed universalism of Jewish philosophy thus assumed the character of a maximum effort on the part of the Jews toward integration with the society around them (a very particular one, in fact). One can imagine that this strategy had decisive implications. It led to a new relationship between the elite and the masses and to a questioning of which had contributed most to the historicity and sociality of Jewish life, namely, its structure and context.

Indeed, these two questions (which could be called questions of 'social bond') constitute an essential facet of the problematics of Jewish philosophy. In fact, in the framework of a hermeneutic theory in which the biblical text has only a conventional and not a philosophical sense (except insofar as Greek philosophy is concerned), convention as such definitely has a social and political finality. The text is indeed to unite within the same unity of power the elite and the masses, the governing and the governed. The text is, in fact, imparted to the masses by the philosophical elite. Power is granted to the philosopher-king because the masses are there (not by virtue of his intrinsic merits). The masses, the *Hamon heAm*, who by definition are not of the elite, do not have access to true meaning of the text. Therefore, it is necessary to keep in it the illusion—or misapprehension—that there is a 'vulgar' meaning, even when the text in question has a completely different meaning for the philosopher and the elite. Why would the philosopher (who for Maimonides is equivalent to a prophet) maintain his power? Because he alone has the capacity to transmit these two meanings and is alone in mastery of the instrument of this power—namely, allegory, which permits one to say something and something else with the same words. Politics as an allegorical art. An art of poetry?

In such a context, the antinomy of vulgar and universal assumes a different coloration and is no longer to be interpreted in its specifically Jewish setting but in the overlapping one we have noted. The vulgar perspective—closed to the universal and persuaded of the historicity and material reality of the text, especially when it concerns the Jews as a chosen people in the historical context, the resurrection in this world, the concrete messianic promises, etc.—relates to collective Jewish existence in its specificity. On the other hand, the universal perspective—open to the allegory of the text and considering Judaism to be limited and of restricted significance, a parable of humanity—sees the promises of the prophets as simply universal symbols and represents a conception of a Jewish elite integrated into the surrounding elite, ascribing an entirely different meaning to its Judaism (defined by an unescapable bible text), in order to legitimize its own political and ideological choices. The dehistoricization and desocialization of Judaism thus further its assimilation into its surroundings. When this happens, the question of power, of relations between elite and masses, is posed in a completely different way, in completely new terms. Jewish society finds itself broken from within.

But what strategy could be devised to counter the Jewish philosophical strategy? It was initially one that addressed the problem of the Talmud, as demonstrated by the "Hassagot," a critical examination of the *Mishneh Torah* by Rabad from Posquières. This was the first phase of the counter-strategy, perhaps explainable by the fact that the *Mishneh Torah* arrived in Languedoc before the *Guide*. But as the *Guide* became known through its translation into Hebrew, this talmudic strategy proved to be insufficient. Jewish philosophy located the debate on a completely different intellectual level, in a completely different register, and it was necessary to combat it with another kind of discourse and through configuration which would be capable of accepting the challenge of abstraction by reintegrating the fundamental axes of original Jewish thought. This was the cabbala—a movement of ideas and of society that began to systematize and organize this new strategy for a very old intellectual debate. As Scholem confirms,[31] it was essentially in southern France, at Lunel, Arles, Posquières, Narbonne, and Toulouse that the cabbalistic movement originated, before spreading to Burgos, Gerona, and Toledo. The cabbalistic strategy, formulated in ideal-typical traits, may be characterized as follows:

1. It upheld the idea of the universality of the thought of the Torah and its unequivalence to Greek philosophy.

2. This universality enabled cabbalistic thought to compete with Jewish philosophy and construct an intellectual edifice that was conceptually its match. This meant that the phenomenon concerned here did not need to be interpreted in terms of a particular/universalistic polarity in which Jewish particularism opposed an enlightened Jewish universalism. In the internal political controversy among the Jews of Aragon, Nahmanides (who was inimical to the ambitions of the Alconstantini family) had direct communication with the king and influenced his decisions. Similarly, it was Nahmanides who represented Judaism in the disputation of Barcelona. The cabbalistic strategy was in no way a strategy of an ethno-particularistic identity.

3. But cabbalism was nonetheless desirous of preserving, as the fundament of all, the integrity and universality of Hebrew society. 'Integrity' meant the intrinsic coherence of Hebrew society, its systems of authority and legitimacy, the stability of its social bond (which one might, applying a Durkheimian concept, define as the processes of collective ideation that are the fabric of social existence).

The Jewish philosophical movement jeopardized this social bond by conventionalizing it into an abstract voluntarism to such a degree that membership in Jewish society became for the intellectuals an individual, voluntary, rational, and abstract act, while for the 'vulgar' it remained a mode of behavior—

generalized, illusioned, corporeal, and anthropomorphic. The inevitable result was that Jewish society acquired a sectorial finality as a mass provider of charity, an agent for confessionalization of the social bond, a tool of external forces, and so on—because it no longer had a meaning of its own and had lost its depth and bodily substance. It now had to find a *raison d'être*. Its existence did not find in itself its own finality. This state of affairs had arisen no doubt from a particular set of circumstances, but it also devolved from the fact that a text had been the center of this society, which fact predisposed it to such intellectualization of the social bond. Conversely, the cabbalistic strategy opposed the conventionalization of this bond but does not need to be seen as a traditional reaction to another strategy that defined the social bond in terms of reason, contractual obligation, or individualism—as if Jewish society were endeavoring to persevere in a monolithis and undifferentiated traditionality. Such a conclusion would misconstrue the reality of traditional Jewish society, molded as it was by consensualism and held loosely together by an ensemble of pacts and constitutions, the Haskamot[32], which was the basis of Jewish political life. In the cabbalistic strategy, Jewish sociality would, in effect, be preserved if its social bond were not made dependent upon the surrender of Jewish identity to Greek truth. In cabbalistic hermeneutics, meaning does not derive from any agreement of the text with the logos and with Greece, but from openness to its inner side and measuring the intention of the divine scribe, which places it at once at the level of the universal and the cosmic without mediatization by the logos at the level of concept and ideology. A sensitive point of the controversy illustrates the difference between the two strategies—namely, the problem of interpreting the institution of sacrifice. In the philosophical strategy, sacrifice is explained as a function of a historical relativism which considers sacrifice to be a prophylaxis against idolatry among the Jews. Thus, Maimonides very often explains sacrifice as a means to sanctify an idolatrous practice. He viewed the act of situating the Holy of Holies by the setting sun, for example, as the counterpart of idolatrous prostration before the setting sun (See *Guide* III, par. 45). But, in fact, sacrifice has no intrinsic significance in this act: it is merely an instrumental means. Why would the concept need an act in history? In the cabbalistic strategy, such an interpretation "defiles the altar. The function of the altar is not limited to the destruction of evil instincts, but rather, the law of sacrifice permits redemption of the nation's sins."[33] Sacrifice is not a stratagem of sanctification; it is a complete act with cosmic repercussions. The debate over anthropomorphisms was a reflection of the controversy over conventionalization, since anthropomorphisms were for the cabbala not propadeutic instruments of truth or devices to increase the understanding of the masses, but rather real thoughts, to be decipered in their depths. This does not suggest in any way that cabbalistic hermeneutics considered the divine as corporeal. Indeed, it did not raise the question of anthropomorphism at all, at least in such terms.[34] The real question in this controversy had to do with the reactions of a process of alienation of the social bond, which, considering the specificity of Jewish society (centered upon a text), could take the form of hermeneutic disputation. The hermeneutic-social integrity of Jewish society was necessary for its continuance as a historical entity and not a sect or ideological grouping that would be particularistic in comparison with the Greek 'universal.' This is why it was so important to preserve the validity of a text that was in direct harmony with its universal and cosmic meaning. The conventionalistic relativization of the text would open the way to the objectification and reification of Jewish society; conversely, the embracing of its profundity would preserve its quality as a subject functioning within the realm of the universal and historical. This explains the paradox of the strategy of cabbala, which made it appear to be an esoteric, spiritualistic, and mystical body of thought that, at the same time, safeguarded and demonstrated the sociality and historicity of Jewish society. It had to strive for the universal, but to do this it had to remain on the highest level of abstraction. The very nature of cabbalistic thought shows that the strategy which combatted philosophical conventionalism was in no way a particularistic phenomenon. On the contrary, it was a force dedicated to the universal.[35] Thus, the literature and the guiding images of the cabbala stood in conflict with the symbols of established power and leadership of Jewish communities. Baer remarks in regard to the *Zohar*: "Its author, Rabbi Moshe de Leon, was undoubtedly deeply disturbed by the social ills afflicting Jewish society,[36] and, in a great number of passages, the *Zohar* blames Jewish leadership for its accumulation of wealth and its ties to the court...." We have already seen another example of this in the political activities of the great cabbalistic Spaniard, Nahmanides, against the Jews of the court. And the conflict with established power appears to be reflected also in the mysticism of the Rhenish Hassidim with strong social and sociological connotations.[37] The combination of cabbalistic hermeneutics (combatting Jewish philosophy) and criticism of established authority localize very well Jewish philosophy into the problematics of the ruling class.

There was an extremely coherent relationship of all these elements despite their apparent disparity. The idea that these two prisms of Jewish society in the Middle Ages might present two strategies and two general economies of Judaism[38] is not unreasonable, because these two strategies continued long after the thirteenth century. The *Marrano* phenomenon cannot be explained without noting a shifting of the strategy of conventionalization of Judaism. Having become an inconsistent convention, it lost its validity and disappeared, only to be replaced without trouble by another convention (Christian baptism). Marranism could only appear in a society that had become empty and was ready to identify with it and use it from the very first.

THE COLLAPSE OF TRADITIONAL SOCIETY AND THE AUTONOMIZATION OF THE SOCIAL

An interpretation of the Maimonidean controversy as the emergence and confrontation of two strategies is incomplete if it goes no further than to synthesize the diverse sociological elements I have mentioned, because they are actually strokes on a larger canvas. The idea that these two strategies may have had a traceable influence on the subsequent historical process opens new horizons of interpretation. It leads us to a major logic of history which might explain the eruptive violence of the episode and the apparent disproportion between the smallness of the objective, immediate stakes involved (as noted by C. Touati),[39] and the magnitude and repercussions of the dispute that accompanied it. We may repeat a question we have asked previously: Are we in the presence here of a nation of philosophers of such nature that a divergence of theory provokes a social explosion among them? In addressing this question, we can at the same time reconfirm the pertinence of sociological analysis of ideology. It is at once true and false to say that a divergence of theory was at issue in the Maimonidean controversy, because not only was a text involved but also history and the social element. If we consider just the text, it is not a matter of the particular ideas and theories but the particular composition in which they appear, its configuration, its internal principle of economy. Conventionalization is a turning point in the theory of the text, and we must ask: What are the operative forces of conventionalization?

On the other hand, if we consider the role of history, we may say that the controversy does not arise from temporary circumstances but from a process of long duration and great magnitude. It is less a matter of a particular idea than of the structure itself of the Maimonidean discourse, in that it reflects a world structure, and an entire epoch and an entire generation can recognize itself in this controversy: "Maimonides himself, not his subject, is the context of the controversy."[40] The Maimonidean configuration has greater significance with regard to history and society than does the Maimonidean text. What interpretation can be made of this configuration? One certain finding is that conventionalization of the text dominates it, and the Maimonidean theoretical reasons adduced for this conventionalization are interesting and can aid our investigation because they synthesize the content of the controversy over philosophy.

Conventionalization develops when there is a problem of explaining how the biblical text, presumed to be philosophically true (according to the criteria of Greek philosophy), can contain anthropomorphisms so foreign to that philsosphy. The explanation cannot be found in the meaning of the test, since there would be contradictions, but rather in a finalization and instrumentalization (estrangement, objectification, alienation) of the text, which might also be defined as a material relativization of meaning. The text is anthropomorphic for a definite purpose. The anthropomorphisms are fixed and isolated through separation from their meaning. The character of their final, unchanging state and their function as instrumentalities are of particular interest to us, because this finality proves to be sociopolitical in nature. The text is anthropomorphic in order to maintain a mutual relationship of power and authority for the sage and the ignorant, the elite and the masses (specifically, Jewish society). The same text speaks to both the ignorant and the sage, although the latter knows, of course, that the anthropomorphic element is to be interpreted as allegory. Thus society, which includes both the wise and the ignorant, can unite around the text. Our interpretive perspective also tells us that the Jewish philosopher will always be able to feel himself a member of the community and society from which he has also set himself apart. In addition, he will gain from it a particular power, that of governing society, since he is in the category of human beings who are the sole ones to possess the key to the two meanings of the text and are thus able to rule society and maintain political power. In this fashion, the biblical text establishes the power of the elite, and the finality of the text is social.

What then happened to this hermeneutic construct? In order to interpret the biblical text philosophically, the anthropomorphism was isolated by simultaneously isolating its Judaic equation (which had been its function and purpose), by satisfying the exigency of the Greek universal through particularization of the Jewish reality (reducing it, limiting it, attaching it to an external logic) and by restricting the anthropomorphism to Jewish limits. Jewish reality was isolated within the Greek universal. But in this reality, thus separated from its meaning, the social was privileged and set apart. In fact, the specifically Jewish social quality was divorced from Jewish thought, thus rendering it equivalent to Greek thought.[41] And the final effect of the process was political. The Hebraism of the biblical text and the Revelation were only there for the political purpose of governing Jewish society: it had no philosophical meaning. In this fashion, the Hebraic social element found itself singled out and separated for the first time in the Jewish approach to and representation of the text. Isolated from its meaning, objectivized, instrumentalized, and thus made autonomous, it became for the first time an occurrence, an entity, a separate object. This led to its complete politicization. The political was all that remained of the text, since its meaning had been relinquished to the 'universal,' which had, so to speak, functionalized the biblical text. The day of the 'theological-political treatise' had arrived. The Jewish reality was now only a political phenomenon without interiority—dependent solely on its own externality, existing only outside itself (Spinoza's "external cause").

Thus, there were two processes initiated by the Maimonidean movement. First, the unity of the text was broken through conventionalization. Second, in the hermeneutic revolution that the Maimonidean method aroused, the social element was autonomized, causing an expansion of the political arena. The unity and universality of tradition were disrupted, and in this state of division a new social arena appeared under the domination of a comprehensive criterion—the universalization of politics, bereft of meaning, and the creation of the modern political sphere.

The development we have traced offers a scenario of modernity. It can even be said to prefigure the entire modern period, since Maimonidean thought should not be construed as a particular body of thought but rather as a global thought—

the ideological framework of a generation that recognized itself and struggled with itself in this framework. The question had to do with Maimonides, but it was not Maimonides who was in question. In the crisis of interpretation revolving around philosophy, we can see the process of modernity unfolding—the collapse of traditional society and the appearance of a new social arena which a political focus had so autonomized in its relation to authority and to the coherence of tradition that a process of detachment and disintegration was initiated.[42]

Thus the Maimonidean controversy assumed the aspect of a laboratory of modernity. It signaled the moment of breakdown of traditional society and the entire world of tradition and prefigured a new world—the modern one—entirely dominated by the political focus. Allegorism in the interpretation of the biblical text, which was at the heart of the Maimonidean controversy, represented a process of division and disarticulation of Jewish society, very directly indeed (on the theoretical level) for dehistoricization of the representation of Jewish existence, but also (on the theoretical level) the cleavage of Jewish society through the development of two autonomous foci within a single social and intellectual unit. From this viewpoint, we can understand more clearly why the Maimonidean controversy—an eruptive and feverish form of disarticulation of society and tradition—arose from motives that were few in number but of extraordinary importance.

There are, of course, partial explications which were considered and do remain relevant. It is still true that Jewish society is divided in regard to the definition and the validity of its historical role, that the clash between the two strategies occurs, and so on. This can be verified on the basis of Jewish experiences of modernity and the course and effects of the process. But all of these explanations extend only part of the way toward an interpretation that would include them in its comprehension of modern structure and processes.

An approach which is able to discover a profile of modernity at the heart of the Middle Ages raises, of course, various theoretical questions that cast doubt on the classical studies of the Maimonidean controversy and, further, on the global approach of Judaic studies, but also on the classical categories of modern sociology—i.e., its ideas of tradition and modernity, ideas I have considered elsewhere[43] and will not be able to discuss here.

NOTES

1. Two periods of controversy have been noted. I will briefly summarize the historical facts concerning them:

a. 1230–1233. In 1230 a rabbi of Montpellier, Salomon ben Abrahm, and two students, Yona Gerondi and David ben Saul, forbade, under penalty of excommunication, the study of the *Sefer HaMada*, a philosophical introduction to Maimonides' Code and his *Guide for the Perplexed*. The communities of Lunel,

Béziers, and Narbonne replied by excommunicating in turn the rabbi and his disciples. Salomon ben Abraham dispatched Yona Gerondi to the communities of northern France, which he won over to his side. In Aragon, the communities of Saragossa, Huesca, and Calatayud excommunicated Salomon and his disciples in 1232. David Qimhi, Grand Exegetist, made a trip from Narbonne to Spain in order to gain support for the Maimonidean cause from other communities. The rabbis of northern France then retracted their excommunication. Finally, the *Guide* was denounced to the papal legate responsible for representing the Cathar heresy at Montpellier, and in 1232 the *Guide* and the *Sefer HaMada* were publicly burned.

    b. 1301–1306. A controversy arose over alleged excesses in the allegorical interpretation of the Bible. Levi Ben Abraham de Villefranche de Conflent, Menahmen Hamari, and Yedaya Berdersi were defenders of philosophy against the opposition of Abba Mari (Don Astruc de Lunel) at Montpellier, who tried to gain the support of Salomon ben Aderet of Barcelona. The Tibbonides of Montpellier opposed this. In 1305, excommunication was pronounced at Barcelona against those who studied Greek books before the required age. A part of the community of Montpellier was involved in a counter-excommunication. In 1306, the controversy came to an end when Philip IV "The Fair" expelled the Jews from the entire kingdom of France.

    2. H. H. Graetz, *A History of the Jews* (Philadelphia: Jewish Publication Society, 1894), Vol. III, p. 529.

    3. Charles Touati, "La Controverse de 1303–1306 autour des études philosophiques et scientifiques," *Revue des Etudes Juives*, CXXVII (Jan.–Mar. 1968) #1, p. 37.

    4. Ibid., p. 22.

    5. D. J. Silver, *Maimonidean Criticism and the Maimonidean Controversy, 1180–1240* (Leiden: E. J. Brill, 1965).

    6. Yitzhak Baer, *A History of the Jews in Christian Spain* (Philadelphia: Jewish Publication Society, 1978), Vol. I, pp. 105, 143.

    7. Touati, p. 37. "The issue was never Maimonides the man nor Maimonides the philosopher nor the correctness of Maimonides' philosophic system. The issue was survival."

    8. Baer, "Mysticism and Social Reform," *History of the Jews in Christian Spain*, Vol. I, pp. 243–305. By redefining the controversy in political terms, he employs the same reductionism—albeit interestingly—in regard to the cabbala.

    9. See my article, "Comment on écrit l'histoire juive," *Revue Pardès* 1 (Paris: Ed. Lattès, 1985).

    10. See my book, *La Demeure oubliée. Genèse religieuse du politique* (Paris: Ed. Lieu Commun, 1984), Chap. XIII, "Herméneutique et société," p. 331.

    11. Philosophers as well as 'anti-philosophers' (or, as Silver would call them, "Maimonideans vs. anti-Maimonideans") only define themselves with reference to the biblical text although with conflicting meanings.

12. See note 1 in regard to the succession of excommunications and counter excommunications.

13. See Silver, para. 7, "The Resurrection Debate," and the following sentence of Meier Abulafia (*Kitab al Rasail*, Y. Brill [ed.], Paris, 1871, p. 17a): "If the body is not destined to be resurrected, how can the promise of an Israel redeemed be realized?," which demonstrates the social and historical non-metaphysical nature of such a debate.

14. The *Ner Hefetz* of Ibn Tibbon, for example, contains a list of the portions of the Pentateuch which should be understood allegorically. But these are guides (*hanhagot*) for the improvement of social and personal life and do not have to do with history.

15. This develops the theme of the *Kuzari* of Judah Halévi, where the author defines the specificity of the God of Israel by noting the possibility of calling him by a proper name.

16. The text becomes the product of a political conventionalization. See *La Demeure oubliée*, Chap. IV. sect. 3.

17. The school of the Tosafits, which lasted until the end of the thirteenth century, "added" commentaries to Rashi's commentary on the Talmud.

18. The *Sefer haMinhagot* began to appear at this time. See the *Sefer haMinhag* of Abraham ben Nathan ha-Yarhi and the *Sefer haMinhagot* of Asher ben Saul at the beginning of the thirteenth century, through which the various Jewish centers expressed awareness of their own specific character, in opposition to the uniformity of the Maimonidean Code.

19. Cf. *La Demeure oubliée*.

20. Baer, p. 105.

21. A. Grabois, "Les Ecoles de Narbonne au XIIIè siècle (in "Juifs et judaïsme de Languedoc," *Cahiers de Fargeaux* #12 (Ed. Privat, 1977), p. 145.

22. Grabois, p. 136.

23. *La Demeure oubliée*, p. 89.

24. This was a decisive trait that helps to explain the rabbinate's later opposition to the cabbala.

25. Baer, p. 77; and Silver, p. 159.

26. R. Mahler Karaimer, *A Yidish geuleh Bawgung in Mitalter* (New York, 1947).

27. Cited in A. Paul, *Ecrits de Qumran et sectes juives dans les premiers siècles de l'Islam* (Paris: Ed. Letouzey et Ané, 1969), p. 54.

28. Baer, p. 105.

29. Baer, p. 106.

30. Baer, pp. 3, 4.

31. G. Scholem, *Les Origines de la Kabbale* (Paris: Aubier Montaigne, 1966) p. 22.

32. Daniel Elazar, "The Kehillah: from Its Beginnings to the End of the Modern Period," in *Comparative Jewish Politics: Public Life in Israel and the Diaspora* (Israel: Bar Ilan U P, June 83).

33. See Nahmanides Commentary on Lev. 1.1.

34. See *La Demeure oubliée*, 383ff., p. 405, note. 18.

35. We can thus understand why the scholars of the "Science of Judaism," seeking the integration of Jewish politics and culture in the modern Western world, preferred to cultivate an interest in Jewish philosophy, with its idealistic and metaphysical import, and viewed the cabbala as an obscuratism whose identity and origins they perceived to be foreign.

36. See Baer, pp. 261–262, and the chapter "Mysticism and Social Reform."

37. See Baer's artical "L'Orientation socio-religieuse du *Sefer* Hassidim" (in Hebrew) in *Tsion* 3 (1938), pp. 1–50.

38. See my definition in *La Demeure oubliée*, p. 26ff.

39. Touati does not take into account the infinitely greater stakes involved in the controversy and confines himself to its narrower and more immediate implications.

40. See Silver, p. 2.

41. In my opinion, this is the decisive definition, for the dimension of sociality is a criterion profoundly applicable to Jewish thought when compared to Greek thought. The relation to history is a decisive criterion.

42. This process is not limited to Jewish history. It anticipated, prefigured, and to a certain degree laid the foundation for the overall process of Western modernism, notably because of the key figures it has produced—Spinoza, for example. (See *La Demeure oubliée*).

43. See *La Demeure oubliée*, "Avertissement," and Chap. XIII "Herméneutique et société."

FIVE

The Jewish Quarter and the Moroccan City

Daniel Schroeter

The Jewish quarter in Morocco, called the *mellah*[1] was one of the most important features of the Moroccan city. The foundation and development of the *mellahs* in Morocco have been examined in various studies, and from a number of perspectives.[2] The primary focus in these studies has been on the social relationship between the Jews of the *mellah* and the Muslim population, and differing conclusions have been reached. But a crucial aspect of the *mellah* which needs to be further analyzed is the way that the Jewish quarter fit into the wider structure of the Moroccan city, as part of the totality of the urban community. From this perspective, I focus on the *mellah* in precolonial Moroccan cities.

The *mellah* was a distinctive part of the Moroccan city, yet at the same time, it was one of many urban quarters. In the historiography of Arab-Islamic cities of the Middle East and North Africa, the quarter is often considered as the basis of urban society. While it is unquestionable that quarters existed in the city dwellers' conception of urban space, it is not always clear what actually constituted the quarter. Various types of urban divisions were formed because of diverse historical circumstances and based on a number of criteria: tribal, social, religious, sectarian, and professional. But the actual reasons for the foundation of a quarter do not always explain its nature because, in most cities, quarters were ethnically and socially diverse. Although many neighborhoods still bore the name of the specific collectivity who originally settled there—for example, Andalusian quarters in a number of North African cities[3]—new arrivals generally diluted any specific sense of ethnic or social space. Furthermore, quarters were generally not clearly demarcated by wealth or social class. Certainly in Moroccan

cities one could find conglomerations of the opulent houses of the wealthy in
the centers of the *madīna,* and clusters of poor immigrants from the countryside
on the outskirts of the *madīna.* But for the most part, these classes of the
population did not form distinctive quarters,[4] even if some residential neighborhoods were known to contain a higher concentration of a particular social
class or category of the population.

There were, however, crucial exceptions to these generalizations. A number
of quarters within the city did form semi-autonomous units with distinctive types
of social identity and organization. For the most part, the collectivities living
within these quarters can be defined as ethnic groups. These groups shared
distinctive norms while at the same time interacting with the urban structure
as a whole.[5] Ethnic quarters have often been cited as an important element in
Middle Eastern and North African cities,[6] yet the very question of ethnicity in
the urban context as a whole has received little attention.[7] In Morrocco, several
types of ethnic groups who formed distinctive quarters can be identified: blacks
(*abīd*) or descendents of slaves from the Western Sudan, military tribes (*jaysh*
tribes) from specific regions, Christians, renegades, and Jews. In a sense, the
governmental/adminstrative quarters can be included in this category because
of their corporate nature and relative isolation from rest of the town.[8]

If the ethnic quarters constitute a particular type, are there features which
characterize the other residential quarters in Morocco generally? First of all,
quarters are often listed as spatial units for the purpose of administration,
especially with regard to religious endowment property (*ḥubus*).[9] Yet even in this
case, the *ḥubus* adminstration might list its property according to street—*darb.*[10]
The *darb,* often translated as 'quarter,' might be no more than a street containing
a group of relatives, named after the head of the household.[11] In some cases, the
quarter (*hawma,* coll. *hūma*) was considered an administrative unit, often with
a chief (*muqaddam*) who ran its affairs and served as an intermediary with the
government. This was certainly the case in precolonial Fez,[12] Rabat,[13] Marrakesh,[14]
Tetuan,[15] and other cities. At the same time there were perhaps cities without
muqaddams.[16] In some cities, quarters had specific fiscal functions, especially as
units for tax collection.[17] In our present state of research, we can still not determine
to what degree the quarter constituted an administrative unit.

There is some question as to how quarters, generally, constituted a meaningful
social unit. In Salé, for example, Kenneth Brown has shown that the heterogeneous inhabitants of a quarter might interact socially or in the mosque, attend
the same schools, and form lifelong friendships, but such associations were not
structured in a unified sense. Members of the quarter would have ties with other
parts of the city through religious orders, kinship groups, and so on.[18] To what
Kenneth Brown sees as "unstructured," Dale Eickelman assigns a kind of cultural
meaning and informal structure.[19] Eickelman's quarter,[20] based on a set of
affinities, which he calls "closeness" (*qrāba*), is subject to constant fluctuation,
depending on the degree that "big men" have an influence in the quarter, and

those districts where no such individuals exist might not be regarded as quarters. Eikelman is reminded of Ibn Khaldūn of the fourteenth century, where people in distinctive quarters are linked together by a kind of tribal identity, *'aṣabīya*.[21]

Related to the question of what constitutes the urban quarter is how the various quarters made up the city. In the Weberian construct, the Oriental 'city' lacked cohesion because of the absense of corporate identity, and hence did not constitute a political or juridical unit.[22] Scholars in the past have implicitly based their analysis of the Islamic city on the presupposition that the city did not really form a unified community.[23] In the more recent study of Mamluk cities by Ira Lapidus, it has been shown how various crosscutting ties, expecially the *'ulamā'*, glued the city together.[24] If the subject of inquiry is to determine what makes a city 'Islamic,' then these Islamic institutions, overlapping quarter boundaries, play a major role in constituting a sense of community, an urban ethos. This analysis provides us with a more sophisticated understanding of the city than the classical Islamic formula of the *madīna: jāmi'*, *sūq*, and sometimes *ḥammām* (Friday mosque, bazaar, and public bath)—i.e., those Muslim institutions required to make the city a place of civilization (*ḥaḍāra*).

In Morocco, Jews represented the only important non-Muslim group. If one is to define the city as 'Islamic,' then the Jewish community would seem to represent the exception to the rule, a part of the city which would not share the same sense of identity with the rest of urban society. If we are to accept Lapidus' model—that it was the *'ulamā'* that held the city together by cutting across the quarters—then the Jewish community would have a kind of pariah status, clearly demarcated as an 'outcaste' group.[25] Between the fourteenth and the nineteenth centuries, Jews in numerous towns in Morocco were compelled to live within the walled-in confines of their quarters. These *mellahs* became increasingly overcrowded, and as the Jewish population increased in the nineteenth century, the buildings spiralled upwards. The world of the *mellah*, with its filthy, narrow, and dark streets, appeared to foreign observers as another planet.[26] The Jewish quarter, in this sense, was not really part of the Islamic city since those overlapping relations which were so important in forming the identity of the city were absent.

The question of how the Jewish quarter fit into the city as a whole challenges in a sense the concept of the Islamic city. In some cities in Morocco, Jews represented such a numerous and influential minority that they became the dominant element in the economic sector. This was certainly the case for the town of Essaouira, Morocco's principal seaport from the 1760s until the 1880s. Yet in the Muslim concept of 'civilization' (*ḥaḍāra*), the Jews were not a relevant element of the population. In the two traditional histories of the town, Jews are only mentioned incidentally.[27] The stress is on the important *'ulamā,'* and this is for a town which was certainly more noted for its commerce than its learning. Still, the Jews of the town formed part of the wider urban society, and this certainly structured their sense of identity as *Swīrīs*, as being both different and yet sharing certain things with the community as a whole. Despite the 'ghettoization' of the Jews in their *mellah*, ascribing to them a pariah status does not explain very much about everyday Muslim—Jewish relations.[28] It would, perhaps, help to maintain the 'Islamic' type of analysis for the city.

What was unique about the *mellah* quarters in the Morrocan cities? The term 'ghetto' is often applied definitionally to the *mellah*,[29] but was it really a Moroccan counterpart of this European phenomenon? The ghetto was originally the name of a quarter in Venice where the first Jewish settlement was located.[30] In 1516, because of a large influx of Jews, the ghetto became a place of compulsory residence, and eventually the word came to be applied to all those quarters in Europe where Jews were forced to live. These quarters were seen as a kind of refuge, where Jewish identity could be acted out. The Jew who left the ghetto to work often felt like he was entering a foreign milieu. The ghetto was a kind of self-contained unit, with its own institutions and life which semingly had little to do with the rest of the city.[31] The ghetto for the European Jew represented more than a physical isolation, it was also a kind of moral and cultural isolation. The very survival of the Jew as a distinctive ethnic group, with particularistic cultural traits, was dependent on this isolation.[32]

In Islam, there are conflicting notions about whether of not *dhimmīs* should be confined to specific quarters. Some jurists argue that Jews and Christians who buy houses in Muslim quarters should be obligated to resell. It is also argued by some that the social and physical isolation of Jews is necessary, while others contend that, through contact, the Jews would eventually submit to the true religion of Islam.[33] Whatever jural interpretation is given, the physical segregation of Jews is a reflection of the status of a religious minority living under the domination of a religious majority. The Jewish quarter in Morroco, therefore, can be seen both as a means by which the government could protect the Jews while at the same time humiliating them. This is in fact the theory of the *dhimma* pact which defines the relationship of non-Muslims to the state. The ostensive reason for the creation of the *mellahs* in Morroco was to protect the Jews after disturbances broke out following the violation of the accepted boundaries defining the relationship between Muslims and Jews. The establishment of each *mellah* is attributed every time to incidents which often resemble each other in their legendary character.[34]

According to most accounts, the first known Jewish quarter of compulsory residence was founded in Fez in 1438.[35] Disturbances broke out, as the story goes, when the population heard the rumor that Jews had poured wine into the mosque's lamp reservoirs.[36] This led to the confinement of the Jews in the *mellah* which was contiguous to the palatial grounds (*dār al-makhzan*). In the imperial cities of Marrakesh and Meknes, Jewish quarters were established in the sixteenth and seventeenth century respectively.[37] Subsequent Jewish quarters were also called *mellahs*,[38] and similar traditions of incidents involving Jews spilling wine near mosques are recounted.[39] Such was the case in 1807, when Sultan Sulaymān

decreed that Jews who lived together with Muslims should move into *mellahs*—
i.e., they were granted *makhzan* property and ordered to sell their former homes
to Muslims. In most cases, the transfer took about two to three years. The cities
included in the royal decision were Tetuan, Salé, Rabat, Essaouira, and perhaps
others.[40] Each city, however, maintains its own tradition which justified the
decision of Sultan Sulaymān. In Tetuan, for example, the tradition recounts that
the new *mellah* was built by Sultan Sulaymān, because of plans for the recon-
struction of the big mosque of the town. Residents complained that the Jewish
quarter was adjacent to the mosque, and that it was the Jews who heard the
call to prayer of the *mu'adhdhin*.[41] Similar explanations are given to justify the
restriction of Jewish space. In 1864, when the Jews of Essaouira requested to extend
their *mellah* in the *madīna*, the authorities objected because it would have been
in an area inhabited by the Shabānāt tribe and continguous to the latter's mosque.
It was instead proposed that the new *mellah* should be built in an area outside
the gates of the *madīna*.[42] Though the traditions as to why Jews were consigned
to new quarters are varied, the essential principle is that Jews had somehow
violated the private space of Islam.

And yet, there were cities in Morocco where Jews were not confined to
mellahs, but rather lived together with the Muslims and even possessed property
in common. Jews in these cities did tend to be concentrated in specific locations,
but the Jewish quarters had no clearly demarcated boundaries. Such was the
case in Safi,[43] Tangier,[44] and Kasba Tadla.[45] In Demnat, the Jewish quarter was
only clearly demarcated in 1887.[46] Furthermore, even in cities where Jewish
residence was restricted to the *mellah*, this did not mean that Jews could not
move to another city in Morocco, though movement was sometimes restricted
if the Jew owed debts to the *makhzan*. Finally, the Jew in the typical *mellah* of
Morocco could own property, even outside the Jewish quarter. This was not the
case in the typical European ghetto.[47]

The Jewish quarter in Morocco clearly delineated religious space, in the sense
that it was there that Jewish social and religious life, the private life of Judaism
took place. It was not only that the *mellah* was a place of confinement for the
Jews. The *mellah* was off bounds for the Muslims. The government preferred
to regulate the affairs of the *mellah* through Jewish intermediaries. In Islamic
theory, it is the *muḥtasib*—the market provost and upholder of urban morality—
who regulates the affairs of the *dhimmī*. Yet in Jewish literature the *muḥtasib* rarely
appears.[48] In the *mellah* of Morocco, it is the *shaykh al-yahūd* (the *nagīd* in Hebrew),
who as intermediary between *mellah* and *makhzan*, serves as the counterpart to
the *muḥtasib* in the *mellah*.

The separation of Jews in distinctive quarters was also reflected in the internal
organization of the Jewish community. Geertz builds an image of the Jewish
community as being paradoxically both an intergral part of Moroccan society
and yet totally different. The Jews in the *mellah* are characterized by three features:
"hyperorganization, thoroughgoing plutocracy, and intense piety.[49] This contrasts

with the more fluctuating diffuse social organization of the city as a whole. Yet these rigidly defined institutional structures were probably more characteristic of the colonial era, or of the decades leading up to the protectorate when the Jewish communities had been transformed by the encounter with the colonial regime and European Jewish organizations. The foreign consulates and European Jewish organizations needed structures through which they could channel their influence. In the traditional communities of Morocco, communal institutions were more informal and subject to fluctuation. The functions of the various religious officials and bodies were not clearly defined. The relative power of certain community leaders in the *mellah* depended more on their informal attributes than their institutional roles.[50] In some communities—often in the small *mellahs*— the *shaykh al-yahūd* (*nagīd* in Hebrew), the chief mediator between the government and the community, was the all-powerful leader, whereas in other communities he was simply the *mellah* counterpart to the *muqaddam*—and in some respects, the *muḥtasib*—of the quarter, acting as the policeman of the *mellah* but ultimately subservient to the merchant elite oligarchy and religious judges (*dayyānīm*).[51] The extent of their power and jurisdiction depended on their personal influence and local circumstances. Unlike in the classic Sephardic model of communal organization, in which the general council of elders, the *ma'amad* (also refered to as the *junta*), constituted a kind of permanent civic body within the Jewish community, in Morocco it was generally only convened on specific occasions.[52] Only with the growth of foreign influence did the *ma'amad* begin to take on the form of a permanent community council.[53] The numerous voluntary sodalities of the *mellah* also developed under the influence or auspices of foreign organizations, responding to the corporate nature of Western urban structures.[54] From the late nineteenth century, Jewish social organization in the cities began to emulate more and more the world of the European ghetto, ironically at the time when the latter was disappearing.[55]

In the traditional Jewish quarter, therefore, social structure more closely resembled urban society as a whole. This does not mean that the Jewish quarter was not a distinct manifestation of religious differentiation.[56] The *mellah* was certainly the place where distinctive cultural traits were expressed. Social boundaries which separated the Jews from Muslims were expressed geographically by the *mellah*. But at the same time, Jews were an integral part of the city. The social identity of the Jews as an ethnic group was formed according to their interaction with the Muslim population in the city as a whole. This interaction adjusted to the changing political and economic circmstances in which the Jews played a part.[57]

If we examine the Moroccan city in the period prior to foreign domination, boundaries between the Jewish and Muslim community reflected—or, in a sense, magnified—permanent divisions in the wider urban structure. This can be domonstrated by the fact that Islamic law clearly recognized the division between the private, residential sector and the public sector. This was represented spatially by a contrast between an intricate, narrow web of alleyways and *culs de sac*, and the wide open thoroughfares where the bazaar and Friday mosques were found.[58] At nightfall, the residents of the city left the public sectors of the town. The gates to the residential quarters were shut and guarded.[59] Nineteenth century travelers often remarked how the gates to the *mellahs* were shut at night and placed under guard. Perhaps what these observers had in mind was the European ghetto, where movement in and out of the ghetto was carefully regulated. The *mellah*, in a sense, was one of many quarters whose gates were shut at night. Thus, except during the month of Ramadān and on other special occasions such as the popular celebrations of the religious fraternities, the public sectors of the city, the bazaar, became devoid of humans at night. The shutting of both the internal and external gates of the city was marked in many places by the firing of the city cannons at dusk. The residents by then had moved out of the business world of the market, of the profane world of daytime activities, to the sacred and private world of the quarter. This Durkheimian type of division between the sacred and profane realms was therefore expressed both in terms of space and time, and the Jewish quarter of Morocco fits well into this overall pattern.[60] During the day, Jews freely moved about the public sectors of the city. Indeed, many of the shops in the bazaar and the *funduqs*, either belonging to the *ḥubus* or the *makhzan*, were rented by the Jews.[61] But at night, the Jews would shut their shops in the *madīna* and return to their private residences, like all other inhabitants of the town. Jews were able to maintain their distinctiveness precisely because the division between the world of family and religion and the world of business was so clearly demarcated in the wider urban context.

There was probably no quarter as closely guarded at night as the *qaṣba* of the ruling class. In its distinction from the rest of the city, the *qaṣba* was much like the *mellah*.[62] Yet paradoxically, the elite of the *qaṣba* was the model for the Islamic urban ethos.[63] It was they who endowed the city with its monuments—mosques, markets, and baths—which constituted the institutions popularly associated to the city. And yet, at the same time, the ruling classes of the population in some ways mirrored the Jews. As with the *mellah*, the ruling classes often had their distinctive quarter, a *qaṣba* in the city, surrounded by high walls. In fact, in some of the major cities of Morocco, the *qaṣba* was contiguous to the *mellah*. Unlike the residential quarters of the *madīna*, the spatial boundaries separating both *qaṣba* and *mellah* from the rest of the population were clearly delineated. Equally important was the fact that the identity of both the ruling classes of the *qaṣba* and the Jews of the *mellah* was distinct from the other inhabitants of the city. Therefore, both *qaṣba* and *mellah* were segregated from the rest of the urban population, the former because of its social class and political rank and the latter because of its religion.[64]

The *qaṣba* generally contained the palace ground (*dār al-makhzan*) where the rulers resided and which contained the royal esplanade (*mashwar*). It might also house lesser government officials, a military garrison (usually within an inner subsection), and the commercial and international sector. "New Fez" (*Fās al-Jadīd*), for example, was built outside the old city walls in the thirteenth century for this purpose.[65] Both Marrakesh and Essaouira had a distinctive *qaṣba* separated from the rest of the city by formidable walls.[66] During times of urban unrest, both *qaṣba* and *mellah* served as a place of refuge, and the authorities would be responsible for protecting the residents of both quarters.[67] In Essaouira, the *qaṣba* contained government authorities, royal merchants (*tujjār as-Sultān*), and Europeans. A new *qaṣba* was built in the 1860s to meet the demands of a growing foreign community. Essaouira was somewhat unique in that, for the elite social class transcended normal ethnic boundaries. The Jewish and Muslim 'bourgeoisie' held interests in common and distinguished themselves from the rest of the population. Jews were really part of the urban elite and played an active role in urban politics, exercising influence over local government because of their ties with both the Sultan and rural leaders.[68] Yet the Jewish residents of the *qaṣba* of Essaouria were just as distinct from the Jewish population of the mellah as the governing class was distinct from the Muslims of the *madīna*.[69]

In a sense, the spatial distinctiveness of *qaṣba* and *mellah* gave territorial expression to three distinctive orders of society: government, commerce, and military. The *qaṣba* physically represented government, with its citadel surrounding the *dār al-makhzan*. The *mellah* contained a segment of the population which was heavily concentrated in commerce. The social distinctiveness of Jews, expressed spatially in the city, permitted them to specialize as intermediaries between town and country and between the ruling classes and foreigners, since they themselves were not competing with the Muslims for social status or political power.[70]

There was also a third type of residential quarter which was clearly demarcated from the rest of the city: the *qaṣba* of the military recruits. Moroccan rulers historically recruited their armies from certain tribes, who were granted in return the rights to certain lands which they held in usufruct.[71] Contingents of these so-called *jaysh* tribes were sometimes settled in the cities, where they resided in separate citadels (also called *qaṣbas*) separate from the *madīna*. These quarters often formed distinctive social units, since their residents identified themselves with their specific tribal or regional origin and maintained a different culture.[72] There were also military recruits with distinctive racial identities. The most notable example were the *'abīd* (also known as *'abīd al-Bukhār* and *Bawākhir*). The *'abīd* were descended from slaves brought from the Western Sudan, recruited by Mawlāy Ismā'īl at the end of the seventeenth century from laborers (*ḥaraṭīn*) of southern towns and oases, from the descendents of the Sa'adian army in Marrakesh, and from urban slaves. They were originally settled in a quarter in Meknes, contiguous to the palace and the *mellah*. Mawlāy Ismā'īl and later Sultans also settled the *'abīd* in specific quarters in Marrakesh, Fez, Meknes, Rabat, Salé, Tetuan, Essaouira, and other Moroccan cities. Even after they lost their importance as a separate military force following a rebellion in 1778,[73] they continued to maintain a distinct identity expressed geographically in the cities where they had settled. For example, a quarter of *'abīd* was noted in Essaouira in the second decade of the nineteenth century, which was partitioned by a wall and shut by gates at night.[74] Another type of quarter in Moroccan cities was formed by Christian renegades (*'ulūj*), who often formed specific units in the Sharifian army as engineers and experts in artillery.[75] They also maintained a distinctive racial identity and resided in specific urban quarters.

Government, military, and commerce represented three orders in urban society which were often expressed in territorial terms. While this division explains in part the distinctiveness of ethnic quarters and the citadels of the ruling class, this does not mean that the residents in each type of quarter performed only the tasks associated with these three orders. There were certainly numerous Jews in other professions. The soldiers as well could hardly subsist on their military salaries and often were also artisans and traders. But because each group was recognized as fulfilling distinctive professional roles in society, this was manifested spatially in the formation of clearly delineated quarters. These residential quarters were far less fluid that the *hawmas*, quarters in the *madīna* which contained a much wider cross-section of the urban community.

CONCLUSION

What made the *mellah* distinctive from the other quarters in town was its religious differentiation. It was the one type of quarter in the Moroccan city that contained a non-Muslim religious group, apart from periodic quarters formed to confine Christian captives. And yet, in its very distinctiveness, it mirrored other quarters. Like other urban residential quarters, it was the place for the private life of religion and family. As in other residential quarters of the *medīna*, in the *mellah* you could find a cross-section of the Jewish population, both rich and poor.[76] The *mellah*, like the *ḥawma*, contained the more recent arrivals who were generally the poorest.[77] Thus the Jewish community mirrored the Muslim community in another way. Jewish religious institutions tied together the community which was differentiated by wealth and status.

The *mellah* of Morocco formed an integral part of the city above all because it contained a segment of the population that concentrated in economic functions on which the very existence of urban life depended. Long-distance trade was an essential factor for the life of the major cities of Morocco. The smaller-size cities also depended on regional commercial networks. In both cases, the Jews played a key role as middlemen, and therefore performed a crucial role in urban life. The *sūq*, perhaps the most characteristic feature of Middle Eastern and North African cities,[78] was permeated with Jews.

The reasons for the creation of *mellahs* can be seen as an effort to both protect the Jews and, at the same time, segregate the only major non-Muslim group in Morocco. The specific reasons for the confinement of Jews to clearly demarcated districts had to do with diverse factors on which one can only speculate. One major cause was probably the influx of Spanish and Portuguese Jews from the fourteenth through the sixteenth centuries. This created an element of competition between Jews and Muslims for urban residential habitations, and this was often expressed in terms of the Jews' violating the religious space connected to mosques. Furthermore, it was the responsibility of the government to protect the Jew as *dhimmī*, and during times of rural unrest, attacks against Jews threatened the social order. The *mellah* of Morocco served the purpose of maintaining those boundaries required by both Muslims and Jews if they were to live together within the confines of the city. While they kept their distinctive traits, both formed parts of the total urban community.

NOTES

I would like to thank Henry Munson, Jr. for his critical remarks on this paper.

1. This is the French spelling for the term, found in most of the literature. In Arabic, it is transliterated as *mellāh, millāh, mallāh*. On the origins of the term, see E, s.v. "*Mellāh*," M. Goudefroy-Demombynes, "Marocain *Mellāh*," *Journal Asiatique*, 11ᵉ série, 3 (1914): pp. 651–658.

2. The most complete studies of the foundation of the *mellahs* of Morocco are by David Corcos, "Les Juifs du Maroc et leurs mellahs," in his *Studies in the History of the Jews of Morocco* (Jersualem: 1976), pp. 64–130; and 'Abd al-'Azīz al Khamlīshī, "Hawal musā'ala binā' al-millāhāt bi-l-mudun al-maghribiyya," *Dār an-Niyāba* Vol. 4 (Spring 1987): pp. 21–28, vol. 5 (Summer/Fall, 1988): pp. 30–41.

3. Ahmed Abdesselem, "La semantique sociale de la ville d'après les auteurs tunisiens du XVIIIᵉ et XIXᵉ siècles," in Abdelwahab Bouhdiba and Dominique Chevallier, *La ville arabe dans l'Islam* (Tunis, 1982), p. 52; Roger le Tourneau, *Fès avant le protectorat* (Casablanca, 1949), p. 82; *idem, Les villes musulmanes de l'Afrique du Nord* (Algiers: 1957), p. 19.

4. Kenneth L. Brown, *People of Salé* (Manchester, 1976), p. 35.

5. For a discussion on ethnicity in the city, see Abner Cohen (ed.), *Urban Ethnicity* (London, 1974), pp. ix–xxiv.

6. Lucette Valensi, *Le Maghreb avant la prise d'Alger* (Paris, 1969) p. 52; André Raymond, *Grandes villes arabes à l'époque ottomane* (Paris, 1985), pp. 174–5.

7. See Lucette Valensi, "La Tour de Babel: groupes ethniques au moyen-orient et en Afrique du Nord," *Annales ESC* 41, 4 (1986).

8. The ruling elite in Moroccan cities were in fact often strangers to the town. See F. Stambouli and A. Zghal, "Urban Life in Pre-Colonial North Africa," *British Journal of Sociology*, 27, 1 (1976): p. 4.

9. Brown, *People*, pp. 35–7.

10. For example, for Essaouira in a list of *ḥubus* compiled in 1913. Biblio-thèque Générale, archives (unclassified). In Essaouira, the *ḥubus* register contains

at least 72 *darbs*. Thomas K. Park, "Administration and the Economy: Morocco 1880 to 1980. The Case of Essaouira," Ph.D. dissertation, (University of Wisconsin, 1983), p. 79.

11. Lawrence Rosen, "Social Identity and Points of Attachment: Approaches to Social Organization," in Clifford Geertz, Hildred Geertz, and Lawrence Rosen, *Meaning and Order in Moroccan Society* (Cambridge: Cambridge University Press, 1979), pp. 62–63.

12. Roger Le Tourneau, *Fès avant le protectorat* (Casablanca, 1949), p. 219; Norman Cigar, "Société et vie politique à Fès sous les premiers 'Alawites (ca 1660/1830)," *Hespéris-Tamuda*, 18 (1978–79): p. 114.

13. Abdallāh as-Suwwīsī, *Tārīkh Ribāt al-Fath* (Rabat, 1979), p. 152.

14. Jean-Louis Miège, *Une mission française à Marrakech en 1882* (Aix-en-Provence, 1968), p. 124.

15. Muhammad Dā'ūd, *Tārīkh Titwān*, Vol. 3 (Tetuan, 1962), p. 287.

16. For example, in Salé. Brown *People*, p. 37. I have found no evidence of quarter chiefs in nineteenth-century Essaouira.

17. This was the case in Fez. See Cigar, "Société," p. 114; and Tetuan, see Dā'ūd, *Tārīkh*, Vol. 3, pp. 286–7.

18. Brown, *People*, p. 37.

19. Dale F. Eickelman, "Is There an Islamic City? The Making of a Quarter in a Moroccan Town," *IJMES* 5 (1974).

20. Based on his study of the Moroccan town of Boujad. Idem, *Moroccan Islam* (Austin, 1976).

21. In the quarter, *'asabīya* manifests itself by rallying around a notable when central authority is weak, and the quarter becomes autonomous. See Ali Oumlil, "Ibn Khaldūn et la société urbaine," in *La ville arabe dans l'Islam* (University of Texas Press), pp. 43–44.

22. Weber juxtaposes Oriental cities with Western cities to demonstrate an ideal type of Western city, based on autonomous urban communes. Max Weber, *Economy and Society* (Berkeley, University of California Press, 1978), p. 1226ff. For a discussion of Weber and the city, see Bryan S. Turner, *Weber and Islam* (London: Routledge and Kegan Paul, 1974), pp. 93–106.

23. G. E. von Grunebaum, *Islam: Essays in the Nature and Growth of a Cultural Community* (Menasha, Wisconsin: 1955), p. 154. See the discussion of Brown, *People*, p. 211.

24. Ira M. Lapidus, *Muslim Cities in the Later Middle Ages*, 2nd ed. (Cambridge: Harvard University Press, 1984), pp. 113–115.

25. See Gideon Sjoberg, *The Preindustrial City* (Glencoe, Ill.: Free Press, 1960), pp. 133–7. Drawing from Sjoberg and Weber, this type of analysis has been applied to the Jewish community of Shiraz. Laurence D. Loeb, *Outcaste: Jewish Life in Southern Iran* (New York: Gordon and Breach, 1977), pp. 2–4.

26. Le Tourneau, *Fès*, p. 102. Gaston Deverdun, *Marrakech des origines à 1912*, Vol. 1, (Rabat: 1959), p. 496. See, as a typical example, the description of

the *mellah* of Essaouira by Joseph Thomson, *Travels in the Atlas and Southern Morocco* (London, 1889), pp. 69–70. It should be borne in mind that the streets of other quarters of the city may have been equally dark and windy. But often, foreigners would not have access to the Muslim residential parts of the *madīna*.

27. Ahmad b. al-Hājj, *ash-Shamūs al-munīra fī akhbār madīnat aṣ-Ṣawīra* (Rabat, 1935); Muḥammad b. Sa'īd aṣ-Ṣiddīqī, *Īqāz as-Sarīra li-ta'rīkh aṣ-Ṣawīra* (Casablanca, n.d. [1961]).

28. The Moroccan Jew as pariah is ambiguously rejected by Geertz. Clifford Geertz, "Suq. The Bazaar Economy in Sefrou," in Clifford Geertz, Hildred Geertz, and Lawrence Rosen, *Meaning and Order in Moroccan Society*, p. 164.

29. H. Z. Hirschberg, "The Jewish Quarter in Muslim and Berber Areas," *Judaism*, 17 (1969): 412–413.

30. On the ghetto of Venice, see Brian Pullan, *The Jews of Europe and the Inquisition of Venice, 1550–1670* (Totowa, New Jersey: Barnes and Noble, 1983), p. 155ff.

31. Jacob Katz, *Exclusiveness and Tolerance* (New York: 1983), pp. 132–133.

32. Louis Wirth, *The Ghetto*, second edition (Chicago: University of Chicago Press, 1956), pp. 286–289.

33. Antoine Fattal, *Le Statut légal des non-musulmans en pays d'Islam* (Beirut, 1958), p. 93. G. Vajda, "Un traité maghrébin 'adversus judaeos': Ahkām ahl al-dimma du šayḫ Muhammad b. 'Abd al-Karīm al-Magīlī," in *Etudes d'orientalisme dediées à la mémoire de Lévi-Provencal*, Vol. 2 (Paris, 1962), p. 808; al-Wansharīsī, *al-Mi'yār al-Maghrib*, trans. by Emile Amar, "La pierre de touche des fétwas," *Archives Morocaines* 12 (1908), pp. 231–32. al-Wansharīsī was born in Tlemcen in 1430-1, and died in Fez in 1508. This book is a type of literature known as *nawāzil*, a collection of *fatwas*. The book of al-Wansharīsī is a collection of *fatwas* from Andalusia, Ifrīqiyya, and the Maghreb.

34. al-Khamlīshī (1987): p. 25.

35. The name *mellah* is derived from the part of the town where the Jewish quarter was established in *Fās al-Jadīd*. See Note 1.

36. Norman A. Stillman, *The Jews of Arab Lands* (Philadelphia: Jewish Publication Society, 1979), pp. 79–81. One account suggests that a Jewish quarter was founded in 1276. On the various accounts on the creation of the *mellah* of Fez, see al-Khamlīshī (1987): p. 221.

37. On the foundation of the *mellahs* of Marrakesh and Meknes, see Corcos, pp. 81–87; al-Khamlīshī (1987): p. 23.

38. It seems that in the twentieth century, most Jewish residential quarters were called *mellahs*, regardless of whether or not they actually constituted a geographically well-defined, walled-in part of the city. Hundreds of *"mellahs"* have been enumerated in a study undertaken in the early fifties by Pierre Flamand, *Les communautés israélites du Sud-Marocain* (Casablanca, n.d.).

39. K. L. Brown, "Mellah and Madina: A Moroccan City and its Jewish Quarter (Salé ca. 1880–1930)" in *Studies in Judaism and Islam*. (Jerusalem, 1981), p. 255.

40. Dawid 'Ōbadiya, *Qehīlạt Sefrū*. Vol. 1, p. 103–4; Dā'ūd, *Tārīkh*, Vol. 3, pp. 238–39; Public Record Office (London), F.O., 174/13, Mogador, 1 July 1807, Gwyn to Green; Corcos, pp. 99–107, 120–121; Jacques Caillé, *La ville de Rabat jusqu'au protectorat français* (Paris: 1949): 323–324. The Sultan's order for Ragbat and Salé is reported by a contemporary observor: Muhammad b. 'Abd as-Salām ad-Du'ayyif, *Tārīkh ad-Du'ayyif*, ed. by Aḥmad al-'Amārī (Rabat, 1986), p. 344.

41. Dā'ūd, vol. 3, pp. 238–39.

42. Corcos Papers (Jerusalem), 14 Ramaḍān 1280, Bū 'Ashrīn to Abraham and Jacob Corcos.

43. A.I.U., Maroc VII B, Mogador, 15 November 1900, Bensimhon.

44. Charles Didier, *Promenade au Maroc* (Paris, 1844), p. 16.

45. A.I.U., Maroc VII B, Kasba Tadla, 28 June 1935, Botbol.

46. Ahmed Toufiq, "Les juifs dans la société marocaine au 19ᵉ siecle: l'exemple des juifs de Demnate," in *Juifs du Maroc: identité et dialogue* (Grenoble, 1980), 154–159; al-Khamlīshī (1988): 30–36.

47. Pullan, p. 158.

48. Hirschberg, pp. 412–414.

49. Geertz, "Suq," pp. 164–65.

50. Shlomo Deshen, *Ṣībūr ve-yeḥīdīm be-Marrōqō* (Tel Aviv, 1983), pp. 49, 60, 65, 90.

51. A.I.U., France XV F 26, Mogador, Annual Report 1892–93, Benchimol. A.I.U., Maroc XXXIII E 582, Mogador 23 July 1896, 22 May 1908 Benchimol.

52. Deshen, pp. 42–45. A somewhat more static view of the *ma 'amad* is given in the study of Haïm Zafrani, *Les Juifs du Maroc: Vie sociale économique et religieuse* (Paris, 1972) pp. 105–6.

53. The Alliance directors in Essaouira would complain about the absence of a permanent *junta*. A.I.U., Maroc XXXIV E 584, 18 February 1875, Benchimol; A.I.U., Maroc VII B, 5 March 1879, Bensimhon; A.I.U., Maroc XXXIV E 585, 25 August 1880, Benoliel. Over a decade later, the same complaints are heard. A.I.U., Maroc XXXIV E 594, 6 February 1897, 5 February 1898, Bitol.

54. Such sodalities began to proliferate in Essaouira already in the 1870s since Western influence began to be felt in the town at an early date. Among the societies established were Ḥebrat '*Ōz we-Hadar*, a society to establish a girls' school for the poor and orphans; *Hebrat Meshibōt Nefesh*, a society to help the sick in need; *Hebrat Marbīṣei Torah*, for organizing the Talmud-Torah schools and to provide education for deprived children; a local branch of the Alliance Israélite Universelle; and a branch of the Anglo-Jewish Association (*Agūdat Aḥīm*). A.I.U., Maroc XXXIV E 584, 21 January 1875, 27 May 1875, 19 July 1877, Benchimol; A.I.U., Maroc III B 14, 21 January 1875, Daniel d'Abraham Cohen; 14 May 1882, Judah L. Yuly; *Times of Morocco*, 28 February 1891, 28 March 1891, 20 June 1891; *Annual Report of the Anglo-Jewish Association*, Vol. 21 (1891–92): p. 15. The various sodalities of the town are described by Ya'īsh Halewī, *ha-Ṣefīra*, 18 (1891): p. 311.

55. The world of the *mellah* is eloquently depicted in a recent book of stories by Bouganim Ami, *Récits du Mellah* (Paris, 1981).

56. See Lawrence Rosen, *Bargaining for Reality: The Construction of Social Relations in a Muslim Community* (Chicago: University of Chicago Press, 1984), pp. 151–2.

57. Here I am drawing from ideas of Rosen (*ibid.*), Cohen (see Note 6), and Frederik Barth (ed.), *Ethnic Groups and Boundaries* (Boston: 1969), pp. 9–16. Rosen, however, does not see ethnicity as an essential deteminant factor in the individual's "construction" of social relations which involves a wide-range cognition of choice. This theory goes a long way in explaining how *some* forms of relations between Muslims and Jews are negotiable, but as Lucette Valensi has pointed out, it does not explain how many aspects of relationship are structured by specific social practices connected to religious affiliation ("La tour de Babel," p. 829).

58. Raymond, pp. 172–74.

59. Besim Selim Hakim, *Arabic-Islamic Cities: Building and Planning Principles* (London: KPI, 1986), p. 63.

60. Emile Durkheim, *The Elementary Forms of the Religious Life* (New York: Macmillan, 1965), pp. 52–55. This division of time and space has also been analyzed by Abraham L. Udovitch and Lucette Valensi, *The Last Arab Jews: The communities of Jerba, Tunisia* (London, 1984), pp. 63–65.

61. Evidence of this can be found in the various *makhzan* and *habous* registers. Tenants of *makhzan* property, are listed in the registers, in which a high proportion are Jews. *al-Khizānat al-Ḥasaniyya* (Rabat), K[80] (Revenue from *makhzan* property in various cities, 1291–1302/1875–1885); K[93] (Lists of *makhzan* property in various cities, 1296–1297/1878–1880); Bibliothéque Générale (Rabat), there are various registers of *ḥubus* property. It has been shown that the renters of the most valuable *ḥubus* property were Jews. Park, pp. 491–494.

62. A *qaṣba* can be defined as a quarter attached to the ramparts encircling the *madīna*. It constitutes a kind of citadel, and in a physical sense it is relatively independent. Hakim, p. 57. See also the comments of Stambouli and Zghal, pp. 4–5.

63. See Sjoberg, pp. 224–28.

64. The close relationship between the "court Jew" and the ruler in seventeenth century Central Europe seems like an interesting analogy. Both were isolated from the rest of the society (though for different reasons), which gave them mutual interests. Selma Stern, *The Court Jew*, 2nd ed. (New Brunswick, NJ: 1985), p. 12.

65. Le Tourneau, *Fès*, p. 67.

66. Jean Louis Miège, *Une mission française à Marrakech en 1882*, p. 123; James Riley, *An Authentic Narrative of the Loss of the American Brig Commerce* (New York, 1817), p. 421.

67. E.g., When skirmishes broke out between Jews and Muslims in Essaouira, the authorities escorted the Jews in the *medīna* to the *mellah*, and ordered the gates of the *mellah* shut and guarded. Similarly, guards were posted at the gate of the *mellah* of Marrakesh. A.I.U., Maroc III C D, 24 July 1891, Yomtob Dayan to D. Serusi; 28 July 1891, 29 July 1891, D. Haym.

68. The involvement of the Jews of the *qaṣba* in urban politics is examined in detail in my, *Merchants of Essaouira: Urban Society and Imperialism in Southwestern Morocco, 1844–1886* (Cambridge, forthcoming).

69. On this separation between the Jews of the *qaṣba* and *mellah*, see an article of Ya'īsh Halewī in *ha-Ṣefīra*, 18 (1891): p. 733.

70. It has been argued that Moroccan Jews were politically neutral since they were outside the normal sociological pool. Rosen, *Bargaining for Reality*, p. 152. This did not prevent Jews from exercising political influence. In the case of Essaouira, social class in some contexts was an important indicator of differentiation.

71. Magali Morsy, "Moulay Isma'il et l'armée de métier," *Revue d'Histoire Moderne et Contemporaine* 14 (1967): p. 99.

72. For Fez, see Le Tourneau, *Fès*, p. 187. On the Ūdāya quarter of Rabat, see as-Suwwīsī, pp. 65–73; and Janet L. Abu-Lughod, *Rabat: Urban Apartheid in Morrocco* (Princeton: Princeton University Press, 1980), p. 92.

73. Ramón Lourido Díaz, *Marruecos en la segunda mitad del siglo XVIII* (Madrid, 1978), pp. 158–74.

74. Riley, p. 421.

75. Morsy, pp. 104–7, 109–11.

76. For Fez, see Le Tourneau, *Fès*, pp. 103–4; for Demnat, see Aḥmad at-Tawfīq, *al-Mujtama' al-maghribī fī al-qarn at-tāsi' 'ashr: Īnūltān (1850–1912)* (Rabat, 1978), Vol. 1, p. 308. Even in Essaouira, with its rich Jews in the *qaṣba*, the population of the *mellah* was differentiated by wealth and status. Daniel Hirsch, "Rapport sur les écoles et les communautés du Maroc," *Bulletin de l'Alliance Israélite Universelle*, 1ᵉ sem. (1873): p. 142.

77. A.I.U., Maroc XXXIII E 582, 19 December 1906, Loubaton. In Essaouira, the poor Jews were mostly newcomers from the Sous. A.I.U., France XV F 26, Annual Report, 1910–11, Loubaton.

78. See Geertz, pp. 123–24. It has been argued that the bazaar was the one major innovation of the Middle Eastern and North African city in Islamic times. Eugen Wirth, "Villes islamiques, villes arabes, villes orientales? Une problematique face au changement," in *La ville arabe dans l'Islam*, pp. 197–198.

SIX

Literature as a Source for the History of Libyan Jewry During the Ottoman Period

Rachel Simon

The traditional approach to historical research used mainly those sources that tended to report on events and beliefs and was also based on documents which were part of the event. As a result, traditional historical writing was based mainly on official documents (i.e., declarations of war, peace agreements, decisions and announcements of leaders, laws and regulations, etc.). In addition, much use was made of official reports by ambassadors, consuls and other agents, official chronicles, and biographies. There is no doubt that these materials are of vital importance for historical research and provide the backbone for the major processes and political events. Nevertheless, their deficiency is that they *a priori* intended to declare or report important issues, but they hardly describe, and often ignore completely, the social, economic, and cultural context in which affairs of paramount concern develop. Without a thorough knowledge and understanding of the society under discussion, it is impossible to analyze correctly the political processes it undergoes. As a result, one should not be content with knowing the events that occurred and the personalities that shaped them; it is essential to be acquainted with the manners of life, beliefs, and ideas of the various components of the society under review.

Contemporary historical research can make use of complementary works in other fields (e.g., sociology, anthropology, economics, religion, ideology, etc.), visits to the sites of the occurrences, photographs, music, and so on. Research of former periods might be supplemented by substitutes which provide some insight into the social, economic, and cultural situation. The special characteristics of a given society are reflected, to a certain extent, in its culture. Cultural work, and especially literary work, can provide much information concerning the social composition of a population, its mode of habitation, its family life, its women, relations among various components of its population and their relationship with the authorities, and its socioeconomic structure. In addition, cultural work can also reflect ideas, beliefs and yearnings. As with other sources, one should not take things literally: there are often anachronisms, erroneous interpretations of events and situations, concealed facts, and doubtful additions, exaggerations, and distortions due to either lack of knowledge or deliberate falsification. Literary sources are of little value for describing specific events and personalities, but they are useful in order to draw a better picture of the manners, attitudes, and beliefs of a society.

Due to the geographical situation in Libya during the Ottoman period and the status of the Jewish community there, the information on Libyan Jewry that can be derived from traditional sources is scant. Libya was a remote border region of the Ottoman Empire and lacked economic, political, and religious importance (up to the period when European powers threatened it from all sides). Furthermore, the Jewish community of Libya was small, isolated, and spread throughout the inhabited parts of the country. During the late nineteenth century,[1] amid a Muslim population of some one to one and a half million, approximately 20,000 Jews lived in Libya. It is true that there are both Ottoman and consular reports on Libya as well as travelers' books, but they are few and poor in comparison to those concerning more central Ottoman regions. In Libya itself, historical writing hardly developed.[2] As a result, information concerning Libya is scarce and scanty, particularly regarding the Jewish community. External observers, Europeans as well as Ottomans, took interest in it only when something extraordinary happened and rarely related anything about its daily life. Thus, in addition to the general reasons for the importance of literary sources already mentioned, their use for the historical research of Libyan Jewry is indispensable, due to the paucity of alternative data. The following examination focuses on two literary sources—poetry and folktales—aiming to point out the information that can be derived from them, as well as the pitfalls that are hidden in them.

POETRY

Communal events found their expression in poetry: the more important the affair, the greater the echo it had and the preservation of the composition which reflected it. Thus, for example, two calamities from which the Jews of Tripoli were rescued were immortalized through poems that described the events and were recited during special commemorative festivals celebrated ever since.

In 1705, the community of Tripoli was rescued from the tyranny of the Bey of Tunis, Ibrahim al-Sharif who, following his quarrel with the Governor of Tripoli, besieged the town and caused more suffering among both the urban and rural populations in the vicinity of Tripoli. In memory of the expulsion of the Tunisians, Purim al-Sharif has been celebrated ever since on 23 Tevet. In addition, a commemorative poem, "Mi Kamokha" was composed by R. Shabtay Tayyar, whose father was witness to the affair. Another poem by the same name, composed by R. Abraham Khalfon, described the rescue of the community in 1795 following quarrels between the ruling dynasty of Libya at the time, Qaramanli, and an Algerian pirate, 'Ali Gurji (nicknamed Burgul). The latter took over Tripoli and ruled there tyrannically, severely hurting the population, especially the Jews. In memory of his expulsion Purim Burgul was celebrated on 29 Tevet, and the aforementioned poem was composed.

Both poems emphasize dramatically the injuries inflicted on the Tripolitanians in general, and the Jews in particular, by foreign elements who were opponents of the legitimate rulers. Details on the foreign offensive as well as on the local defense, in which the Jews had also participated, are included. Although there are other sources describing these events, the two poems focus on the implications of these calamities for the Jews and the miraculous rescue, whereas other sources hardly mention the Jews and how they felt.

FOLKTALES

Compared with poetry, Jewish Libyan folktales are a better reflection of numerous aspects of the daily life of the community. In contrast to heroic poetry, which commemorates dramatic events, folk literature reflects daily routine interwoven in an artistic structure. The intention of the storyteller was often to teach a lesson, while keeping his audience spellbound and entertained. Consequently, the didactic element is often wrapped in a fascinating tale, in which details from remote and enchanting places and periods are interlaced with details from the immediate and well-known environment. Since the main purpose of the storyteller was not to give a detailed and precise report of the vicinity, but to use well-known (or, at times, magical) elements in order to deliver his message, which contained abstract ideas, values, morals, and lessons, he did not feel bound to provide full and accurate facts. The literary framework serves a didactic purpose and lends it greater credibility by providing a well-known background. Transmitting information, however, is not the main aim of the teller. Moreover, since many stories were retold over the ages, many factual inaccuracies occurred which were not noticed by the new generation, which even added its own contemporary details and commentaries. As a result, folk literature includes detailed descriptions of the society, but these are at times distorted and anachronistic.

The following exploration of Jewish Libyan folk literature is based on published material.[3] The analysis is done in two ways: (1) through the examination of two stories in full, emphasizing communal life as reflected in them; and (2) through the presentation of information on some chosen issues relating to the community from the folk literature and how these details complement information from other sources.

The story, "Thanks to Charity"[4] is set in the late Ottoman period. It provides many details on economic life in Tripolitania—the commercial activities in the markets in Tripoli and its vicinity as well as the relations between these different groups. Details are provided also for food items and dressing customs. In comparison to contemporary reports, however, the prices quoted for various items seem to be quite cheap. The Italian penetration into Libya is described here in negative terms: The Italians are referred to as "spies," inciting against the legitimate Ottoman regime. The inclusion of Italian officers in the caravan seems to be anachronistic. The bad security conditions in the countryside are emphasized by the contempt shown by robbers toward Ottoman officers without any fear of government retaliation. The economic activities of the Jews are also described, with special emphasis on commerce, gold- and silversmithery, and cooking. With regards to work with precious stones and metals, it is stated that this profession was monopolized by the Jews, some of whom reached a very high artistic standard in the field. Furthermore, the cooks in the taverns in the markets in Tripoli and its vicinity were usually Jews who were renowned for the high quality of their dishes, which were desired by both Jews and gentiles alike. This story was not composed in order to describe the social and economic life in Tripolitania, but to demonstrate the moral expressed by the Jewish goldsmith who was saved from the robbers' attack ("Cast your bread upon the waters, for thou shalt find it after many days" [Ecclesiastes 11.1]). It does, however, provide us with a wealth of detailed information on markets and caravans unobtainable from most other sources. It also demonstrates the special atmosphere of those places and the feelings of the participants. Since many Jews were peddlers who spent extended periods on the road exposed to numerous dangers, this story provides a unique opportunity to penetrate into the feelings of members of a caravan during a frightening, although common, incident.

The story, "Thanks to R. Shalom 'Ajib"[5] reflects the relations between Jews, the Muslim neighborhood, and the Ottoman regime in Tripoli. In it, the poverty of the majority of the Jewish population of Tripoli is mentioned, and one occupation is emphasized—moneylending. Due to the deteriorated economic position of the Ottoman Empire during the nineteenth century, the government often delayed the payment of salaries to its officials in the administrative and security branches. This regular habit was especially common in remote regions such as Libya. As a result, these officials were in need of loans to keep them going until they received their salaries. This function of moneylending was usually filled by Jews, since many of them were merchants who accumulated substantial sums of money. From this story, however, it seems that even poorer Jews took part in this occupation. The story also shows the great commotion connected with the celebration of the circumcision feast among the Muslims, including poor ones. The secret which the policeman revealed to the Jewish moneylender in order to receive a loan on preferable terms, reflects a common habit in the Ottoman Empire: due to high inflation and the impoverished state treasury, it was customary to frequently devaluate the currency. This was done by invalidating a certain coin, collecting it all over the country and melting and re-minting it with a smaller portion of the expensive metal or in a smaller size altogether.[6] Another aspect of the socioeconomic situation reflected here is the provision of vital products. It was customary in Muslim towns for the authorities to be responsible for the regular supply at fixed prices of vital products, including grains and oil.[7] This practice was of special importance in government centers due to the apprehension that a shortage might cause civil disturbances. It is for this reason that when the governor of Tripoli heard about the shortage of wheat and oil, he immediately took steps to answer the needs of the population by bringing supplies from the army stores, and only afterward searched for the reason for the shortage and ordered a deterrent verdict. Manners and customs of the population, as well as Jewish-Muslim relations, are also reflected in this story. Thus, for example, the high esteem of 'saints,' Jewish and Muslim alike, by both communities, is reflected in the influence on the governor of Jewish holy men who appeard in his dream. Jewish-Muslim relations are reflected both in the economic field (in this case, moneylending) as well as in the easy access the Jewish woman peddler, Mascudah, had among the Muslim population of Tripoli, including the ruling class, personified by the governor's mother, who was ready to intervene before her son in favor of the Jews.

The examination of Jewish Libyan folk literature according to subject matter also shows the wealth of information that might be derived from this source.

THE ORGANIZATION OF THE JEWISH COMMUNITY

The community was headed by rich dignitaries who had close connections with the authorities. Rabbis are also mentioned as leaders.[8] The folk literature does not distinguish between the changes in the leadership during the Ottoman period, nor does it provide explanations for these changes of the relations between the temporal and spiritual leadership. The heads of the Jewish community were responsible before the Ottoman authorities for collecting the taxes of the community: a fixed sum was imposed on the community as a whole by the government, and the heads of the community divided it among the breadwinners according to their economic status.[9] The community sometimes helped the individual in his profession.[10] There is, however, only minimal mention in these stories of the numerous welfare and educational projects which were operated by the community.[11] On the other hand, there is much reference to feasts around tombs, death anniversaries, and miracles of holy men.[12]

THE PROFESSIONS OF THE JEWS

The most common fields of occupation of the Jews of Libya were commerce, finances, and handicrafts. Another characteristic of the community was that a large majority of its members were very poor. This situation is reflected in the folk literature. Thus, many of the stories deal with peddlers,[13] and there are detailed descriptions of their way of life, merchandise, and feelings. Some of the peddlers wandered for long periods between the villages in the countryside and developed cordial relations with the settled Muslim population. The peddlers both bought and sold goods: they purchased from the farmers fresh agricultural products (fruit, vegetables, beef, sheep, milk, and cheese) and sold villagers manufactured goods and haberdashery (oil, salt, spices, cosmetics, cloth, wool, buttons, and needles). The peddlers carried their wares on their backs and were sometimes aided by donkeys. At times peddlers and merchants also carried expensive goods such as jewelry and embroidery with them.

Other professisons frequently mentioned in the folktales are silver- and goldsmithery, as well as embroidery interwoven with silver and gold threads and precious stones.[14] These occupations were almost exclusively in Jewish hands. The various craftsmen were organized in guilds according to trade, regardless of their religious affiliation. In those professions where Jews were the majority (and at times even gained exclusivity), the guilds were headed by Jewish inspectors (*amin*). This situation was characteristic among the silver- and goldsmiths and the embroiderers. The *amins* in these latter professions were responsible for the quality of the product and for the stamping of the customs sign and the karat on them. Furthermore, they could determine who made the product and summon him for an inquiry when necessary.[15] Many Jews were moneylenders, and some of them were even from the lower economic strata.[16] There were taverns attached to the markets which sold food in addition to coffee and wine, and many had Jewish cooks. These taverns were usually regarded as licentious; nevertheless, according to some folktales, Jewish men frequented them, sometimes even accompanied by their wives.[17] This situation (which started to develop during the Italian period) seems anachronistic compared to the Ottoman period, when Jewish urban women were usually confined to their homes. A profession mentioned as one practiced by Jewish women was that of cosmetics, mainly for brides.[18] Among other Jewish occupations described in the folk literature are the digging and selling of sand to be used for cleaning floors and for laundry,[19] carpentry, [20] and even fishing.[21]

JEWISH-MUSLIM RELATIONS

Intercommunal relations are usually mentioned in the folk literature as cordial, but severe plotting by the authorities and the Muslim population against the Jews are also described. The house of Qaramanli which ruled over Libya from

1711–1835 is mentioned as generally favorable toward the Jews. The most prominent exception among them was Yusaf Pasha (1795–1835), but even in his days not all was black. The stories attributed Yusaf's negative approach toward the Jews to his bad temper and financial distress, which forced him to levy heavy fines upon the Jews.[22]

As a rule, the Muslim population is described as treating Jews with justice and honor. The villagers protected the peddlers who came by, as well as the Jews who lived in the countryside among them, from those plotting against their property.[23] Besides good neighborly relations, however, there were also occasions of hostility, degradation, and contempt.[24]

Generally speaking, it might be concluded that due to the strong interdependence between the two groups, despite the feelings of seniority and mastery of the Muslims, the latter realized the indispensability of the services which the Jews provided, and as a result the hostility shown by the Muslims toward the Jews was at times more influenced by economic reasons than by religious differences. Thus, for example, was the case with Muslim robbers who attacked all property holders in the caravan without distinction and did not hesitate to murder even Turkish and Italian officers, although through this act they could have infuriated the authorities.[25] The Jews usually kept a low profile when animosity was shown toward them, but there were also times when the Jews protected their dignity and arranged for self-defense, even sometimes challenging the Muslims. The description of these occurrences shows, however, that this was not characteristic Jewish behavior in Ottoman Libya.[26]

The extended Jewish-Muslim coexistence in both urban and rural areas in Libya brought about numerous similar customs, as well as holy places, saints, and sacred objects venerated by both groups.[27] Usually, as long as there was a considerable Jewish population in a given place, Jewish holy places (e.g., tombs, synagogues, and so on) were not endangered. Accordingly, as the Jewish population in the hinterlands dwindled, many Jewish holy places were occupied by Muslims, mainly due to religious reasons, but also on economic grounds (i.e., the scarcity of living and agricultural areas). There were, however, also Jewish holy places that were seized by Muslims in areas still densely populated by Jews. The most conspicuous example of this was the tomb of the sixteenth-century Jewish sage, R. Shim'on Lavi', in Tripoli, known by the Muslims as the tomb of "Ibn al-Imam." During the Italian period, a long time after the tomb was seized by the Muslims, the Jews decided against accepting the offer put forward by the Italian regime to return the tomb to Jewish custody. This decision was taken in order not to worsen Jewish-Muslim relations.[28]

CONCLUSION

The examples from the two literary types—poetry and folk literature—point out the importance of their use for historical research in general and for the history of the Jews in Ottoman Libya in particular. In these examples, only the main themes were described, and it should be noted that these sources include many minute details which enable one to draw a comprehensive picture of the life of the Jewish community of Libya and of its relations with the gentile environment. Consequently, it is also an important source for gaining knowledge of the Libyan Muslim majority, despite the Jewish origin of the source. The primary importance of this source is that it provides insight into everyday life, feelings, beliefs, and views of the Jewish community, because the latter issues are often lacking in other sources (particularly external, but even internal).

NOTES

1. On the Jewish community of Libya during the late Ottoman period, see: R. Simon, "The Jews of Libya and their Gentile Environment in the Late Ottoman Period," *Pe'amim* 3 (1979), pp. 4–36 (in Hebrew).

2. Among the rare exceptions is Mordecai Ha-Cohen, *Higgid Mordecai*, ed. H. E. Goldberg, Jerusalem: 1978 (in Hebrew). This is a history of Libya and its Jews written by a Libyan Jew at the beginning of the twentieth century, based on his own knowledge as well as older manuscripts. A partial translation of this source and commentary is H. E. Goldberg, *The Book of Mordecai: A Study of the Jews of Libya*, Philadelphia: Jewish Publication Society, 1980.

3. D. Noy, *Seventy One Stories of Libyan Jews*, Jerusalem: 1968 (in Hebrew). These stories are from the Israeli Archive of Folk Literature at the University of Haifa.

4. Noy, pp. 85–87.

5. Ibid., pp. 57–59. 'Ajib (1799–1869) was a blind judge (*dayyan*) and the president of the Jewish religious court of law in Tripoli, who was known for his learning and sanctity.

6. H. A. R. Gibb and H. Bowen, *Islamic Society and the West*, vol. 1. *Islamic Society in the Eighteenth Century*, London 1950–1957, Part II, pp. 49–59.

7. Ibid., Part I, pp. 283.

8. Noy, pp. 67, 157–158.

9. Ibid., pp. 102, 157.

10. Ibid., p. 53

11. Ibid., pp. 61, 70, 72, 74–76, 103–104.

12. Ibid., pp. 57, 98, 100–101.

13. Ibid., pp. 39, 55–57, 62, 67, 69, 86, 103.

14. Ibid., pp. 86, 102, 111–112.

15. Ibid., pp. 86, 103, 111–112.

16. Ibid., p. 57.

17. Ibid., pp. 64–65, 69–70, 85–86, 106.

18. Ibid., p. 109.

19. Ibid., p. 62.

20. Ibid., pp. 61, 100, 138 (the last refers to a shoemaker).
21. Ibid., pp. 52–53.
22. Ibid., pp. 102, 107, 157.
23. Ibid., pp. 55, 103.
24. Ibid., pp. 60–61, 66–68.
25. Ibid., pp. 56, 86–87.
26. Ibid., pp. 55, 60–61.
27. Ibid., pp. 97, 101, 158.
28. Ibid., pp. 57, 71.

SEVEN

A "Maskil" in Aleppo: "The Torah of Israel and the People of Israel" by Rabbi Yitzhak Dayyan (Aleppo, 5683/1923)

Zvi Zohar
Translated by Sandra Becker

In the Spring of 1924, an important delegation headed by the president of B'nai B'rith in the Middle East, Dr. Yakir Behar, arrived in Syria. The purpose of the delegation was to establish B'nai B'rith lodges in the Jewish communities of the country's main cities which had recently come under French Mandatory Rule. The delegation was honorably received in Damascus by the elite of the community and fulfilled its task with much ceremony and unrestrained support from the local rabbinic leadership. However, the delegation's experiences in Aleppo were totally different. An action-committee of local rabbis, who called themselves "The *Ohr Torah* Committee" publicized an announcement declaring that rabbinic law prohibits participation of believing Jews in the Order of B'nai B'rith. The members of the committee proclaimed that, in any case, there was no place for the opening of a lodge like this in Aleppo, whose Jewish citizens were faithful to the religion of their fathers. Apparently, the religious leader of the community, the head of the court, Rabbi Ezra Hamwe, was inclined to support this position. The members of the B'nai B'rith delegation turned in alarm to well-known rabbinic authorities, Rabbi Haim Bijarano, the Chief Rabbi of Turkey, and Rabbi Ya'akov Meir, the Sephardic Chief Rabbi of Jerusalem. Both attested

that B'nai B'rith was an exemplary Jewish organization, and that its activities
did not involve any suspicion of religious transgression. Rabbi Bijarano even added
that he himself had been a member of B'nai B'rith for forty-two years.

The leaders of the B'nai B'rith delegation thought that they had thereby
overcome the opposition of the local rabbis, but they were mistaken. The rabbis
of Aleppo sent a telegram to the rabbinical court of the Aleppo expatriate
community in Jerusalem, seeking their *halakhic* opinion. The rabbis of the
Jerusalem court, who had no experience in these kinds of matters, sought advice
from the person whom they considered a senior religious authority—Rabbi
Sonnenfeld, the head of the Ashkenazi *Haredi* community in Jerusalem. Relying
on his ruling, they cabled back to Aleppo that the Torah requires abstention
from activity within the framework of B'nai B'rith, for it asserts: "and she secret
herself and be defiled" (Numbers 5:13), the secrecy of the ceremonies of the order
and its meetings casts upon it a suspicion which cannot be refuted.[1]

It is not my intention here to analyze this interesting incident in detail; I
intend to do that in a separate article. I only wanted to point out a tendency
which came to the fore in this case among the Aleppo rabbinate and which
corresponds to a great extent with what seems to be an image which adhered
to the rabbis of Aleppo, not in small measure as a result of the pride which their
spiritual descendants took in it: the image of a conservative group which advocates
continuity of the traditional lifestyle, and which harbors deep suspicion toward
innovation *per se*, which is seen as threatening the proper Jewish way of life by
its very nature. It is no secret that today many rabbis of the Aleppo Diaspora
take this type of approach. Indeed, when describing early twentieth-century
Aleppo, spokesmen of the community emphasize how much it was a "Holy
Community," which prevented its members from succumbing to modern Jewish
influences which had then already spread to other Eastern communities.[2]

There is, no doubt, a lot of truth in these images of Aleppo. But it is not
the whole truth. Not only were there those in the community who objected
to the rabbinic establishment and held liberal European ideas,[3] but the rabbinic
elite itself was far from monolithic in its opposition to modernity. One of the
personalities who undoubtedly belonged to the elite of the Aleppo rabbinate,
and who nevertheless was open in interesting ways to new ideas and currents
in the Jewish world of his time, was Rabbi Yitzhak Dayyan. It is my intention
in this chapter to present and analyze some of the main elements of his views
as they are expressed in his illuminating essay, "The Torah of Israel and the People
of Israel."

About the man himself not enough is known.[4] But we can learn something
about him from his lineage and from the words of his peers. Introducing the
essay, Rabbi Judah 'Attiyya refers to him as follows: "A dear and beloved rabbi,
a basketful of sweet dates, a descendant of saints and angels, son of our great
Master, fortress of strength, the ultimate authority of our city, saintly head of
the court, His Honor Rabbi Yesha'yah Dayyan of blessed memory, none other

than my great and honorable colleague, rabbi, etc., the honorable Rabbi Yitzhak Dayyan, may his light shine, may he enjoy a long life..."

The Dayyan family was one of the most important and distinguished families in Aleppo, perhaps even *the* most important and distinguished. It was an indigenous Musta'rab family whose genealogical tree goes back to King David himself.[5] Throughout the Middle Ages, the sons of the family held the spiritual leadership of the community, and even when exiles came from Spain who, in other communities, spiritually absorbed the locals and seized leadership of the community, the Dayyan family did not submit to them. Even while sharing the leadership with the newcomers, they continued to guard their ancient primacy. Rabbi Yesha'yah Dayyan (d. 1903) was the head of the Rabbinical Court of the community, and in Aleppo it was the head of the Rabinical Court, not the *Haham Bashi*, who had the highest religious authority. His son Yitzhak, whose views we are examining here, was therefore a descendant of the central rabbinic family in the community, and of the central religious figure of the previous generation, and is himself referred to by his colleagues with considerable respect and honor. His essay, which we discuss here, was printed at the beginning of a book which appeared with the authorization of all the great rabbis of Aleppo in 1924.[6] Thus, Rabbi Yitzhak Dayyan was an accepted and honored personality among the religious intellectual elite in Aleppo at the beginning of the 1920s and his ideational positions (even though it is difficult to know to what extent they were adopted by others in the community) are worthy of serious study.

THE AIMS OF THE ESSAY AND ITS MEANING

"The Torah of Israel and the People of Israel" aims to ground a conception of Jewish education, which includes Jewish and general studies within a framework which gives primacy to Jewish studies including Bible, *Aggadot* of the Talmud and *Midrashim*, history of the Jewish people and (apparently) also Hebrew poetry.

In order to anchor this understanding, the author opens with a chapter discussing the essential connection between the people of Israel and the Torah. After that, he establishes a contrast between the distant past generations—who knew this essential connection and internalized its truth—and the generations of the Diaspora, and especially the present generation, who lost that truth, *even if they do maintain a meticulously religious Jewish lifestyle*. He concludes that the proper understanding of 'Enlightenment' obliges us to bestow upon young Jews a Jewish education which will emphasize the *ideational and ethical messages* which are in the Bible and the *midrashim* of Hazal, as a condition for any possible continuity of the Jewish people.

From this summary it should already be apparent that Rabbi Dayyan does not seem to accept the value of Jewish traditional observance as self-evident, as many persons in Aleppo did—at least according to the community's image held today. Indeed, many other scholars who lived both in his and in preceding generations, also did not regard the value of traditional praxis as self-evident, and searched for the inner spiritual meaning of Torah. However, they found this meaning in the intricate and rich world of kabbalistic thought, a preoccupation which became even dearer to them than halakhic and Talmud study.[7] Rabbi Dayyan, however, was a man of contemplation and philosophy, whose spiritual heroes were "the first wise scholars of Spain." Among these scholars were "Rabbi Saadya Gaon, Rabbi Shmuel Ben Hafni, the author of *Hovot HaLevavot*, Rabbi Yehudah HaLevi of the Kuzari and the poet, Rabbi Abraham Ibn Ezra, Malmonides and others." Throughout his essay, one can recognize that he sees himself as someone trying to follow the path of these rabbis, that of understanding and enlightenment, in order to deal with the problems on his own agenda.

We will begin with a presentation of these dimensions, of understanding and enlightenment, which appear in his article, and that move on to study other aspects of his words.

A RATIONALISTIC APPROACH TO THE INTERPRETATION OF RABBINIC AGGADAH

In explaining Aggadah or Midrash, Rabbi Dayyan openly prefers a rationalistic approach, by means of allegory, over a simplistic approach which does not fit the empirical test. Thus, in his commentary to the Midrash on the verse in Qohelet, "and the almond tree blossoms," which describes the "luz" bone of the spinal column that is in no way susceptible to destruction, and is the kernel around which the future body of each person will form at the time of the resurrection of the dead, he says: "Here we are compelled to say that there is something hidden within this statement, because it is not possible for it to be as literally described. For we see that in the place where the dead are cremated nothing remains except a few ashes . . . and therefore a wonderful hint and a lofty allegory are to be sought in this article" (13).[8] And, one of his major critiques of the proponents of Haskalah in modern times is precisely that they "did not realize all this, and did not penetrate the great conceptual depth of Judaism . . . the spirit of the Bible and the *Midrash* and the grand ideas within them" (30).

EMPHASIS OF THE UNIVERSAL ETHICAL DIMENSION IN THE TORAH OF ISRAEL

When explaining the importance of the study of Judaism for Jewish youth, Rabbi Dayyan emphasizes the universal ethical dimension in Judaism, which will influence the personality of the youth if they learn Jewish subjects in the proper manner. Without these studies, the rabbi fears, "the youth goes out lacking all the good attributes and high morals contained in Judaism, which are crucial to his future and success—because only through these will they become good people, beneficial to themselves, to their people, to others and to civilization" (14).

Therefore, it is important "to plant and instill our ethics in their hearts...and then they will become adults filled with wisdom, successful, good and of benefit to God and his Torah, to their people, to themselves, to others, and to the whole world" (32).

The goal of education is, then, to form a Jew who possesses fine qualities and a high ethical level, whose influence is manifest on the religious, the national, and the universal-human levels.

THE "MISSION OF ISRAEL" TOWARD THE WORLD

In connection with his emphasis of the universal moral dimension in the Torah of Israel, Rabbi Dayyan notes that the Jewish people has a mission toward the whole world:

> Israel "was chosen for a special possession to Himself" to be a priestly kingdom of teachers and instructors to the nations, to teach of G-d's existence and unity. *And one of the purposes for their dispersion among the nations is in order to promulgate and announce the existence and unity of G-d to the whole world.* As they of blessed memory said: "G-d did righteousness with Israel by scattering them among the nations" (26).[9]

Later in the essay, there is a clear exposition of the connection between this matter and the idea of "mission":

> The mission of the people of Israel is to promulgate the unity of G-d and His ways in the world, and they did so and succeeded in this mission. Because the fundamentals of the two religions whose members constitute the majority of the civilized world were taken from the religion of Israel and all of them acknowledge the existence of G-d and his unity (Ibid.).[10]

THE IMPORTANCE OF KNOWING
THE HISTORY OF THE JEWISH PEOPLE

Rabbi Ytzhak Dayyan's relatively open and rational approach finds additional expression in the fact that he absorbed and internalized positions and approaches which were characteristic of intellectual currents prevalent in modern European Jewry. One of the ways we see this is in the importance that Rabbi Dayyan attributes to the fact that the education of every young Jew should include knowledge of Jewish history: "It is incumbent upon us...to educate our children in our spirit, our language, *our history*, our studies (32).[11] And why so much? Because one who does not do this, but rather teaches the youth foreign studies and the history of other nations"[12] causes the youth to go out

> lacking in knowledge of his history and his shining past, which was a light unto the nations, with many following in its light. Lacking in

knowledge of the history of the heroes of Israel and their great Rabbis, who courageously imparted a great and steadfast spirit that enabled Israel to live in exile, and shed pure, clean light on Israel and on the nations . . . (24).

That is to say, one who does not know the history of Israel does not want to or will not be able to perpetuate the wonderful mission of Israel toward the world. Furthermore, knowledge of the history of the people of Israel confirms the special quality of the relation between the people of Israel and its Torah, and makes one conscious of the miraculous nature of the people's very survival despite their troubles and persecutions:

He who is intelligent will perceive the history of the Jews throughout changing times and periods, and realize that of necessity they exist eternally. For they have survived in the world thousands of years, while thousands of great powerful nations were completely destroyed and their memories lost . . . (29)

The reason for this uniqueness of Israel is the Torah. That is what Rabbi Yehoshuah replied to Hadrian[13] and the matter is also proven from a study of the history of the people: "and to understand this we will proceed and examine what is known of the history of Israel, that many large nations rose against them with different weapons and were not able to conquer them . . ." (17). The author cites different examples from the Jewish past, including a positive and sympathetic exposition of the Bar Kochba revolt, and the resulting analysis is:

All who rose against Israel with different weapons of war were not able to destroy its *luz* bone, as is written: no weapon will succeed against them; all of the nations that fought Israel were destroyed and their memories lost, and Israel still lives and exists, and its *luz* bone still bears a spark that will once again be kindled, and become a very large bonfire that shall shed light onto Israel and onto the whole world (18).

We see, therefore, that Israel's eternity is proven by the evidence of Jewish history, and its proof is a foundation for faith that in the future the nation will once again shed light on the whole world and thus fulfill its universal mission.

DIASPORA AND REVIVAL

Historic experience itself also serves to clarify why the people presently lacks awareness of its values and its purpose:

And the reason for this is clear, because this exile of ours has been as long as two thousand years, and we have endured many edicts and decrees and religious persecutions, we forgot the value of the Torah, we lost the wisdom of our Rabbis, and the understanding of our Sages was hidden (21).

In the opinion of Rabbi Dayyan, the exile caused an all-inclusive blurring of the Jewish public's self-perceptions:

> Because this knowledge was forgotten to us completely, because of the length of Israel's Diaspora in distant lands and isles, among other peoples and in other lands every few years anew. They labored under conditions of weighty troubles, dwelling amidst different peoples and observing their corrupt ways. And because of their great poverty, and growing lack of necessities. And therefore we have become absorbed, on the whole, in the persistent and great war for survival.[14] Because of all this, the lofty and exalted Hebrew soul has died in our midst... (22)

The type of language that appears in the last sentence of the quotation—"Hebrew soul"—alludes to another aspect of the conceptual horizons of the author—the national aspect. Indeed, a rereading of the whole last paragraph affirms that before us is a text expressing *negation of exile*: the essence of being in the Diaspora entails almost of necessity the destruction of the "Hebrew soul." In other words, rehabilitation of this soul is dependent on a national revival. And indeed, the national dimension appears prominently in this essay by Rabbi Dayyan.

THE NATIONAL DIMENSION

The national dimension, in the modern European Zionist meaning, is expressed in the essay in several ways. To begin with, the terms "people of Israel" and "nation" appear over and over again in different contexts; the author justifies his call for Jewish education by arguing that it is necessary to ensure the benefit and success of the Jewish people. (This education is also necessary to secure the future of the Torah of Israel and its Jewish lifestyle.) Second, although in one place the author emphasizes that "it was said to Esau: you shall live by the sword," whilst "Israel never prided itself on the sword" (27), he emphasizes elsewhere the dimension of strength in battle as a positive characteristic of figures from the past, in light of whom the youth of the present time should be educated. He describes in a sympathetic manner:

> "The hero Bar Kochba who reigned over Israel, and commanded a large army of many heroes of Israel, and in wondrous courage and great devotion stood up and fought against the powerful Roman conquerers of the world, who ruled over many nations" (13–14). And: "The courageous Hasmoneans...who fought with great devotion in deliberation and strength..." (27).

And, as we have already seen, his recommendation is to educate the youth so that they will know the history of the heroes of Israel (25). In addition, he specifically speaks about the great flaws of the absence of national honor and the absence of self-action for a national revival in the homeland without waiting for miraculous intervention:

> In our midst the feeling of national pride has died. Self-recognition has left us. *The longing and the aspiration for our national homeland has disappeared from us. The sentiment in our midst has so declined that we do not even desire to improve our situation by ourselves. We only hope that others will help us, or for great wonders* (22–23).

Here, both the expectation of national salvation by those of earthly power and the hope for miraculous messianic redemption receive equally negative evaluation by an Aleppo Rabbi who preaches autoemancipation ('to improve our situation by ourselves'). There is no doubt that our author was aquainted with the rhetoric and the slogans of political Zionism and identified with them. It is no wonder, therefore, that his educational demands are formulated appropriately: "Therefore, it is incumbent upon us to make sure that we educate our children in our spirit; if we act not for ourselves, who will act on our behalf?" (24)

BIALIK AND TCHERNIKOVSKI AS SOURCES OF AUTHORITY

The positive attitude of Rabbi Yitzhak Dayyan toward modern Jewish national ideas was not restricted to their political dimension, but also encompassed the important cultural dimension of modern literary creativity in the Hebrew language. It is clear from his essay that he is familiar with modern Hebrew poetry and, even more important, that he in fact places the poets of the 'Golden Age' of Spanish Jewry on par with the great poets of national revival in our time, Bialik and Tchernikovski.

After the first section of the essay, in which the author puts forward his ideas using a philosophical-homiletic approach to sections of *Midrash HaAggada*, he proceeds to ground his argument by quoting from Hebrew poetry.[15] Thus, the devotion of early generations to the Torah is illustrated not only in the *midrashic* story about Papus and Rabbi Akiva, but also through quotations from the poetry of Rabbi Yehudah HaLevy ("When I distance myself from you my death is within my life, and when I cling to you my life is in my death") and of Rabbi Abraham Ibn Ezra. In the paragraph in which he describes and praises that devotion by which Jews of medieval times willingly submitted to death in order to sanctify the Divine Name we read that they said to the murderer, "Ho, headsman, bare the neck."[16] Is this chance usage? Not at all, it turns out. For, after another quotation from the poets of Spain, this time from Rabbi Abraham

Ibn Ezra, the author offers proof of his words concerning the degeneration of national honor amidst those in exile, in the following manner:

> and the national poet calls out bitterly:
> "Surely the people is grass, now do they fade like a blossom.
> Ages of endless wandering, exile too vast for endurance
> Turned all the hearts of them backward, counsel has died from the people,
> Taught of the rod and the lash, can they perceive now their anguish,
> Shame and pain of the spirit—aught but the thrall of the body?
> Have they another care at heart than of the moment,
> Men that are lost in the darkness, deep in the pit of the exile" (23).[17]

Note carefully: Bialik is both 'the national poet' and a source of cultural spiritual 'authority,' functionally parallel to Rabbi Yehudah HaLevy and to Rabbi Ibn Ezra.[18] Bialik appears again, as evidence, in the context of a polemic against intellectuals who abandon Jewish culture in favor of other cultures. However, it seems that the most interesting usage of modern Hebrew poetry can be found in a passage in which the author preaches the importance of educating Jewish children in the use of *tefillin*:

> Israel is obligated to educate their sons in *tefillin* when they begin to enter adulthood, in order to plant in their hearts a seed of high learning, both spiritual and physical, in order that their sons come to realize the value of Israel and its devotion to its God in the past and in the future. And the poet says to his son:
>> You are a Jew, my son, and this is your good fortune and your misfortune.
>> As a shoot from the stem of an ancient people, your pride is over the nations,
>> You are still a child, you will yet grow and know your people's past great deeds.
>> Then you will understand how great will be their works when our sun shall rise, (30).[19]

There is no doubt that the views of Tchernikovski could not, in general, serve to support an obligation of instructing youth in the wearing of *tefillin*. It is apparent, therefore, that Rabbi Dayyan knowingly makes a double distinction— between the views of the poet in their totality and the position reflected in the poem quoted, and between the poet's views and his spiritual 'authority.' In other words, his very status as a Hebrew poet of national renaissance imparts to Tchernikovski spiritual authority which could not be undermined even by views sharply anomalous to a traditional religious perspective. So, too, must we understand the author's attitude toward Bialik, whose relative moderation could not obscure his deep criticism regarding central features of traditional Jewish life.

Rabbi Dayyan thus makes a conscious selective use of the poetry of the modern national Enlightenment. He acknowledges its authority and its value while negating those aspects that are blatantly in opposition to traditional Jewish culture. His polemic against such trends in modern Enlightenment appears explicitly in central paragraphs of the essay with which we are dealing.

CONTROVERSY AGAINST KNOWLEDGE THAT NEGATES THE WORLD OF TRADITION

We have already seen that the author's spiritual heroes were "the first wise scholars of Spain." Rabbi Dayyan then contrasts between these scholars of the 'Golden Age' and scholars of the Modern Period.

> The first intellectuals in the period of the wise men of Spain realized and knew well the depth of the light of Judaism and its glorious power. The Torah and rational knowledge walked among them like twin sisters. And there was a true peace among their spiritual tendencies. And therefore in their wisdom and their intelligence they created a strengthening and a permanence to the Torah and the tradition, and made them intellectually accessible.
>   But the new intellectuals of the past generation did not realize this. They did not penetrate the great depth of Judaism. They did not know that the homeland for the soul of the people, which had developed and been perfected over thousands of years, was created by the spirit of the Bible and the *Midrash*. . . and therefore they strayed a great distance and changed their manner (30).

He accuses these new intellectuals of three evils, whose inner rationale is similar: slander and hatred toward the Jewish spiritual heritage, brazen attacks on the rabbinic leadership of the present and past generations, and the causing of assimilation. It is interesting that there is a common denominator also to Rabbi Dayyan's criticism of these intellectuals' evils: all three of them express estrangement from the national-popular dimension. Thus, for example, regarding their attitude to the spiritual heritage, they did not realize that this heritage was the "homeland of the people's soul which had developed and been perfected over thousands of years." Also, the attack on the rabbis is not appropriate from a national point of view:

> for the rabbis were chosen representatives, who achieved their position without force but were, rather, raised up in pride and glory by virtue of their vast knowledge. . . and their exalted qualities and attributes. . . (31).

That is to say, rabbis are an expression of the popular will, since it was the people who freely appointed them, out of the appreciation of their wisdom and their personalities. Thus, whoever attacks the rabbis is, in fact, attacking the people. A similar disregard for the broad strata of the Jewish people is reflected in these intellectuals' attitude toward traditional Judaism:

> They did not attempt to understand the result and the outcome which would come from their knowledge and their wisdom and their research and their remarks of misgiving...they mixed up the people's hearts and confused their thoughts, and misled them in strong doubts and madness of the mind (31).

This irresponsible attitude towards the public/popular effects of their approach is reflected also in the non-national character of the modern intellectuals' cultural creativity:

> Thus, despite all their knowledge, they did not enrich the spirit of their people. They did not cause the people to acquire and establish living spiritual ideas...and these learned spiritual heroes were of no use to their own people, only to others... (Ibid).

The basis of Rabbi Dayyan's above critique is again national. Among the 'men of Enlightenment' there are indeed brilliant minds—but what is the value of their creation if they do not enrich the Jewish people? And Rabbi Dayyan supports this point by quoting the words of Bialik:

> As the national poet complains in his poem:
> When one of your own sons proves an eagle and grows wings,
> From his nest you cast him forever;
> Even when he soars, sun-thirsty and mighty in space,
> Not to you does he bring down the luminaries;
> Far from you on a mountain peak where he shouts exultant,
> Not even the echo to you descends (31)[20]

THE NATIONAL FUNCTIONS OF THE TORAH

The central importance of the dimension of nationality in the set of arguments put forward by Rabbi Dayyan is also reflected in the reasoning by which he attempts to prove the importance of Jewish education. He claims that the importance of the Torah and its value lie in the benefit that it brings to the people of Israel. This benefit is seen on three levels:

A) The creation of a uniting socio-economic framework for the local Jewish community

It is through Torah that the people of the nation unite and are drawn together in material matters in work and business, and in purchase and acquisition and the like. For their opinions come together through the Torah, and it creates love and harmony between them, to help one another improve their lives and to attain a high position in the life of society and in worldly matters (20).

B) *The creation of a cultural foundation that is shared by all of the Jewish people scattered throughout the world*

The people of the nation that are scattered in distant places and far-away islands...by means of the Torah...become dear and friendly to one another. Even though they never knew each other, when they do meet, they immediately become dear to each other as if they were brothers (Ibid).

C) *The creation of a way that enables the people of Israel to achieve joint spiritual self-actualization*

The Torah coordinates and unites the spiritual thoughts of the nation, that is to say, logic, nature and theology, for one purpose, which is knowledge of Reality as it is, and the knowledge of God and the verification of His unity (Ibid).

It is important to note that the underlying premise in this set of arguments is the Jewish people's will to exist in a healthy and proper manner. The Torah is presented as a means for the realization of this will, more than obligation imposed on the people from 'above' in a manner not connected to its strivings and its will. Indeed, Torah is not even presented as a requirement which the people are obliged to fulfill in the context of a covenant or a treaty with G-d!

In conclusion, then, it is necessary to teach children Torah even before engaging them in general studies, for the good of the Jewish people in general and for the future of the Jewish child in particular:

Education is the great foundation on which Israel is established forever, and consequently it is incumbent upon us to educate our sons in our spirit, to sow and implant in their hearts our morals, our language, our history, our studies, our spirit which is hidden in the Bible and in the *Aggadot* of the Talmud and *Midrashim*. For incorporated in those texts is a pure spirit and a lofty morality, which is like the soul, whereas other disciplines and languages are like the body and the outer clothing. It is consequently incumbent upon us to provide our sons with the needs of the soul before providing them with the needs of the body. Then, they will be able to maintain both, because they will be wise, successful men, who are good and useful... (32).

CONCLUSION:
THE IDEATIONAL WORLD OF RABBI YITZHAK DAYYAN

Rabbi Dayyan wrote the essay we have been analyzing, to support the above proposition, i.e.: For the sake of the Jewish people and for the sake of the children of Israel as individuals, it is important to bestow upon the child a comprehensive Jewish-Hebrew education, and only afterwards a general education. While establishing this emphasis, Rabbi Dayyan reveals to us his outlook on a vareity of themes and subjects: the importance of the moral dimension in the Torah and in the *Midrashim*; ways of interpreting Rabbinic *Aggada*; the significance and importance of Jewish history; the centrality of the national dimension in Jewish consciousness; and much more. All of this is expressed within the general context of Rabbi Dayyan's attempt to explain the proper and true connection between the Torah of Israel and Israel's existence as a nation.

In presenting these views, it is apparent from Rabbi Dayyan's words that he was acquainted with ideas, currents, and opinions known throughout the European Jewish world at the end of the nineteenth century and the beginning of the twentieth, beginning with the radical Enlightenment movement which preached alienation from the particular Jewish inheritance, through these views which spoke of the 'mission' of Israel toward the nations of the world, emphasizing the moral-universal dimension in Judaism; and including the modern Hebrew enlightenment and the ideas of the Jewish national movement encouraging autoemancipation and initiation of return to the land of Israel without waitng for international aid or for heavenly intervention, but rather stressing concepts such as national honor and courage in battle.

In Rabbi Yitzhak Dayyan's words, these ideas and values appear in conjunction. He sharply criticizes the radical enlightenment but expresses himself in a sympathetic manner toward the rest. To what extent can one speak about a solid synthesis of these views in the thought of Rabbi Dayyan, and to what extent do we have before us a sort of eclectic collection which cannot be thought of as a clear, coherent point of view?

There is no doubt that Rabbi Dayyan is not a thinker who has created a new and original systematic synthesis between currents and points of view which were originally considered to be in conflict. But his essay is more than merely a naïve collection of viewpoints. It is clear that he understands and knows much more about the spiritual world of modern European Judaism than what he quotes in his essay. His quotes (as we have seen with regard to his citations on modern Hebrew poetry) are purposely selected, and reflect conscious choice of specific messages that are fitting to his values and to the aims of his writing.

One can say, then, that the essay, "The Torah of Israel and the People of Israel," is a sort of mosaic in which the author selected and synthesized elements which he found desirable—either from classic Jewish sources or from contemporary European Jewish sources—in order to create a composite picture which expresses the message he sought to convey. It is interesting (and unexpected, from my point of view) to find a man with these views amongst the senior Torah scholars of the Aleppo community, a community known as a fortress of conservatism and of opposition to innovation and change.

It is possible that the accepted image of this community, and specifically of its rabbinic leadership, has its source more in a selective memory of the Aleppo Diaspora throughout the world than in firm research. In any case, in light of what we have seen concerning Rabbi Yitzhak Dayyan and his views, it is apparent that only additional research can lead to a less one-sided picture of the spiritual world of this special and interesting community.

NOTES

1. Regarding the whole matter, see *HaMenora*, published by B'nai B'rith in the Middle East. *HaMenora*, Istanbul, Vol. II, #7–8 (July–August 1924), pp. 227–229; #11–12 (November–December), p. 299.

2. For the characterization of the people of Aleppo in this manner, see A. Cohen, "Aleppo: A City of Torah and Wisdom in the Nineteenth Century and in the Beginning of the Twentieth Century," *Ba-Ma'arakha* 253 (1982), pp. 16–17; J. A. Sutton, *Magic Carpet: Aleppo in Flatbush* (New York: Thayer-Jacoby, 1979).

3. As was, for example, David Ben Hillel Silvera; see Gaon, *The Jews of the East in the Land of Israel*, Vol. 2 (Jerusalem: 1938), p. 483.

4. Apart from the article which we discuss, he contributed several "Torah Novellae" to the rabbinic journal *Ha-Me'assef*, edited by Rabbi Ben-Zion Kvainka. Later, he emigrated to the land of Israel, established a community in Bat Yam and was involved in the *Keter* affair. See Amnon Samosh, *HaKeter* (Jerusalem; 1987). Rabbi Dayyan died in 1964 and is buried in Tel Aviv.

5. The family tree was printed at the beginning of *Yashir Moshe* (1879) by Rabbi Moshe Dayyan.

6. Rabbi Yehudah Ben Nissim 'Attiyya, *Minhat Yehudah* (Aleppo, 1924).

7. During the nineteenth century and the beginning of the twentieth century, many works were published by scholars from Aleppo, reflecting their Kabbalistic world. See the list of books by Rabbis of Aleppo, published by Rabbi Ezra Batzri (Jerusalem; 1984). The majority of the tens of scholars from Aleppo, who emigrated to Jerusalem from the 1870s to the 1920s engaged there in matters of *Kabbalah*, and conducted an appropriate way of life. This emerges clearly from an accurate analysis of *L'Kdoshim Asher ha-Aretz* Jerusalem, 1980 (2nd edition). In the literature of praises which glorify the greatest wise men of Aleppo (after their death), the ones who dealt with the *Kabbalah* receive recognition of special magnitude. See, for example, *Fruit of the Tree of the Garden (Pri Etz ha-Gan)*, edited by Rabbi Yaakov Katzin (Jerusalem; 1931).

8. Numbers in parentheses give the page of the quote in the original edition of the essay, which appeared—as noted above—in the book *Minhat Yehuda* (Aleppo, 1924).

9. And he explains the word *with* in the sense of 'by means of.'

10. Similar words are included in the *Mishnah Torah* of the Rambam, *Hillakhot Melakhim*, Chapter 12, end of *halakha* 4, but were censored out of the editions published in Europe. The Rambam does not state, however, that this result was the aim of the Diaspora, but rather that it was the aim of G-d in establishing these two religions.

11. For 'history' Rabbi Dayyan employs the Arabid 'Taarikh' rather than the terms 'Historia' or 'Divrei ha-Yamim' more current in today's Hebrew.

12. The intention here seems to be the course of studies of the "Alliance" schools.

13. The author opens his essay by quoting the allegory that Rabbi Yehoshua told to Hadrian, as it appears in the *Midrash Qohelet Rabah* on the verse "the almond tree blossoms," and explains this allegory at length.

14. It seems that the expression "war for survival" reflects modern European influence.

15. The assumption that 'proof' may be brought by the words of a poem probably reflects influence of Arabic culture, which regards poetry as faithfully reflecting the depth of truth.

16. From "Upon the Slaughter," *Selected Poems of Hayyim Nahman Bialik Translated from Hebrew* (New York: Bloch Publishing Company for Histadruth Ivrith of America, 1948), p. 112.

17. From "Surely the People Is Grass," *Selected Poems of Hayyim Nahman Bialik*, pp. 65–68.

18. Later Rabbi Yitzhak Dayyan also quotes from the poems of Rabbi Moshe Ben Ezra.

19. The quotation is from "Cradle Song" by Saul Tchernikovski.

20. The quote is from "Surely This Too," *Selected Poems of Hayyim Nahman Bialik*, pp. 190–191.

EIGHT

The Periodization of the History of the New Christians and Crypto-Jews in Spanish America

Eva Alexandra Uchmany

INTRODUCTION

The presence of New Christians and Crypto-Jews has been felt on the fourth continent since the preparations for Christopher Columbus's first voyage. The admiral had constant relations with Jews, converts, and New Christians who supported him economically and scientifically. For this and other reasons, some historians began to doubt that the sailor was a native of Genoa, Italy, and started looking for his origins in several places in Spain, especially on the island of Mallorca.

The charts and some of the sailing instruments that Columbus used on his first voyage were, in part, furnished to him by Abraham Zacuto, who applied astronomy to navigation and occasionally taught at the University of Salamanca, and by his disciple Yoseph Vecinho, physician and astronomer of King João II of Portugal. In the Spanish Court, Columbus was supported by the New Christians Diego de Deza and Juan Cabrero.[1] Finally, the man who convinced Isabella of the sailor's undertaking was Luis de Santángel, senior accountant of the kingdom of Aragon, who loaned sixteen thousand ducats to the Queen to finance Columbus's first voyage.

Luis de Santángel was a grandson of Noe Chinillo, whose five sons were driven to Christianity in 1415. The conversion opened to them the doors to the highest positions of the kingdom but at once made them vulnerable to the persecutions of the Holy Office. Indeed, the senior accountant had the opportunity to save his cousin's son from being burned at the stake in 1491, when he was imprisoned by the Inquisition for Judaizing. The father of this young man (both of them were named Luis, a common name among the Santángels) was beheaded, quartered, and thrown into the flames for his participation on the night of October 17, 1485, along with other New Christians, in the murder of Pedro de Arbués, the recently appointed Inquisitor for Aragon. The mastermind of the assassination was Juan de Pedro Sánchez, brother of Gabriel Sánchez, treasurer of the kingdom of Aragon, who was also involved in the conspiracy. It is worthy of mention that the treasurer was married to Albutmunta Gilbert, the only daughter of the beheaded Luis de Santángel.[2] Juan de Pedro saved his life by fleeing to Italy, and Gabriel was helped out of that critical situation by the Catholic king. Fernando, though he expelled the Jews from Spain, was ever willing to avail himself of Hebrews useful to the kingdom.

The Sánchez brothers were connected with the enterprise of Christopher Columbus. The admiral sent the first news from the recently discovered lands to his sponsor, Luis de Santángel, and to the treasurer Gabriel Sánchez. The two letters are of the same tenor. The latter was translated into Latin by the New Christian Leonardo Coscón, whose uncle was also involved in the aforementioned conspiracy. This first description of the New World was published in 1493 in Rome and, with the hekp of Juan de Pedro Sánchez, by then a rich merchant in Vencie, saw nine editions before the end of that century.[3]

THE NEW CHRISTIANS OF SPANISH ORIGIN

This period was divided into four phases. The first one is that of the 'discovery' and dates from the days of the preparation of Columbus's first voyage to the year of 1501.

Several New Christians were present in this historical crossing. Among them was Rodrigo Sánchez de Segovia, a nephew of the treasurer Gabriel Sánchez, who embarked as the fiscal Inspector or *Veedor* of the expedition.[4] The recently baptized Luis de Torres, native of Murcia, who knew Hebrew, Chaldean, and Arabic, was also on board one of the three ships. He and Rodrigo de Jerez were the first Europeans to explore the island of Cuba.[5] Torres first addressed the natives that they met in Hebrew and then in other languages, considering them the ten lost tribes of Israel. There was also the apothecary Maestre Bernal, punished in 1490 for Judaizing.[6] (Master Bernal also accompanied Columbus on his fourth voyage.[7]) Also of Jewish descent were Master Marco, the physician of the fleet, Alonso de la Calle, and Rodrigo de Triana, who was the first to sight the new continent.

Converted Jews and their descendents were also to be found in the admiral's subsequent expeditions. Pedro de las Casas (father of the famous protector of the American Indians, Fray Bartolomé de las Casas) sailed with Columbus on the second voyage.[8] Fray Bartolomé embarked for the Indies for the first time in 1501 with the governor Frey[9] Nicolás de Ovando.

The second phase is that of the 'favorites.' In 1501, the Catholic king excluded New Christians from the American enterprise by means of a decree that no son or grandson of any person punished on charges of heresy could be a Royal Counselor; *Oidor* judge; *Alcalde* magistrate; *Alguacil* officer of justice; *Mayordomo* administrator of royal, ecclesiastic, or civil property; treasurer; or hold any public office or honorable position. They were also prohibited from embarking for the Indies. Finally, the Holy Office forbade them from wearing silk or any fine clothing, adorning themselves with gold and receiving academic degrees.[10] However, the king never applied these sanctions to his favorites. For example, he appointed Juan Sánchez, one of the nephews of Gabriel and Juan de Pedro, as the agent of the treasury of Aragon in Seville. In 1502, King Fernando granted to Juan Sánchez and Alonso Bravo an exclusive contract to be the suppliers of the island Hispaniola, from which the monarch received some forty percent of the profits.[11] Later, Juan was heavily involved in commerce with the pearl island of Cubagua.[12]

The third phase is the legal one, because the Catholic king secularized the sanctions of the law in 1501. In other words, the status of the *inhábiles* or disenfranchised New Christians were compound means of obtaining large sums of money. This was very good business for the crown because the 'reenfranchisement' was done in stages. For example, in 1508 Fernando extracted from the victims in the province of Seville twenty thousand ducats for just the return of their property, confiscated by the Holy Office during their trials. The following year in the same area, he collected eighty thousand ducats. Thanks to these enormous amounts of money, persons who were reconciled by the Inquisition were enabled to hold public offices, except those which included criminal jurisdiction. They were also allowed to traffic with the Indies.[13]

The reenfranchisement of 1509 legalized the residency of those New Christians who already lived in America and at the same time induced many others to enlist in discovery, colonization, administration, and—mainly—trade. As a result, between 1509 and 1518, New Christians took an active part in emerging American life.

Many of the names that appear in the "Padrón" 'tax list' are found in the catalogue of passengers to the Indies,[14] and figure in the Geobiographical Index of forty thousand Spanish settlers in sixteenth-century America[15] and on other lists. Several merchants whom Enrique Otte considers most important in the Caribbean pearl trade between 1517 and 1550 are also mentioned in the "Padrón."[16] One of them, registered under number 286, is Juan de Córdoba, who held important posts in the municipal life of Seville and, in 1519, lent Hernando Cortés a large sum of money which the captain general used for the conquest of the Aztec Empire.[17]

New Christians also took an active part in the administration of the recently discovered territories. We will mention only the most important ones, such as Miguel Pérez de Almazán, the King's secretary[18] and Lope de Conchillos, secretary of the Council of Castile. Both were rewarded for the services with a grant of Indian forced labor which they employed in agriculture, mining, or construction. This grant was first called *repartimiento*, and later *encomienda*. The *encomendero* was obliged to strive for the evangelization of his Indians.

Miguel de Pasamonte, who embraced Christianity a few years before the expulsion of the Jews from Spain, served as clerk for the king's secretary. Later, Miguel Pérez de Almazán posted him as treasurer of the Indies. In 1509, Miguel de Pasamonte was named keeper of Fort Concepción in the gold-bearing area and transferred the treasury to Estaban de Pasamonte, his nephew. The Pasamontes also enjoyed a good *encomienda* and when these resources were depleted they entered the sugar industry.[19]

The Cuban historian Fernando Ortiz points out that the New Christians were the first to capitalize on the sugar in Cuba. The convert Gonzalo de Vellosa initiated this process by constructing the first sugar mill on the island, which was transformed by 1515 into a factory. Finally, another convert, Miguel de Ballester, who came with Columbus on his second voyage, was the first to export this merchandise to Europe.[20]

A large number of New Christians arrived in America in 1514 with the expedition of Pedro Arias de Avila (commonly called Pedrarias Dávila), posted by the king as governor of Castilla de Oro. His grandparents has been baptized in the first half of the fifteenth century. Diego Arias, when he was still a Jew, administered the Royal incomes and, after his conversion, in the last years of the reign of Juan II, became the *Contador Mayor* or Chancellor of the Exchequer of Castile. During the reign of Enrique IV, he carried out a fiscal reform.

Several New Christians who came with Pedrarias enlisted later in other expeditions, as did Gil González de Benavides de Avila, brother of Alonso de Avila, the first procurator of New Spain. Both were nephews of Gil González Benavides de Avila, the royal accountant in Santo Domingo between 1509 and 1511, who was in turn the brother or a cousin of Alonso de Avila, one of Isabella's convert secretaries.[21] Another nephew, and namesake of the Catholic queen's secretary, is registered under number 70 in the previously mentioned "Padrón."

In 1511, the royal accountant transferred his post on Hispaniola to his nephew, Alonso de Avila. In 1514, Fernando dubbed him knight of Santiago and permitted him to outfit an expedition. In 1519, Gil González de Avila set out eagerly in search of a strait between the two oceans and, while he was at it, conquered Costa Rica and Nicaragua. When he arrived at contemporary Honduras in 1524, he clashed with Hernando Cortés's captains, who claimed that region for themselves.

The two brothers, Alonso de Avila and Gil Gonzalez de Benavides, embarked for Mexico with Juan de Grijalbo's fleet in 1517, the first as royal accountant and the second as captain of one of the ships. In 1519, Alonso enrolled himself in Hernando Cortés's expedition as accountant and bookkeeper. In 1520, the conquerer named him *alcalde* or magistrate of the recently founded town of Veracruz and sent him later to Santo Domingo in the capacity of procurator of New Spain. In 1522, Cortés dispatched him to Spain with Motecuhzoma's treasury as his private procurator. In 1527, Alonso de Avila returned to New Spain as one of Francisco de Montejo's captains and took part in the conquest of Yucatan.[22]

In 1537, Friar Juan de Zumárraga, New Spain's first bishop and apostolic Inquisitor, ordered the apprehension of Gonzalo Gómez, *encomendero*, *alcalde*, and businessmen in Michoacán, for "evil words" and for Judaizing. Alonso de Avila found out and immediately warned him. Gómez soon appeared at the home of his friend who, besides giving him some legal advice, entrusted him with the names of the denunciators. A few months later, Alonso himself had to meet with the bishop, since Zumárraga accused him of stepping on a crucifix that he supposedly had under his desk for that reason.[23] At first this appears to be Zumárraga's way of punishing Avila for his indiscretion in the affairs of the Holy Office. In any case, Zumárraga had good reason to be suspicious of the procurator because no Old Christian would help a person questioned in a matter of faith. Indeed, Avila and Gómez together committed great irreverences to the visible symbols of the Church, such as sleeping with their mistresses in a chapel that the *encomendero* had turned into an inn.[24] Both had a certain eclectic approach to religious matters, common among some New Christians, which Alonso's brother, Gil González de Benavides, shared. Gil came to Pánuco in 1522 with Francisco de Garay's expedition. In 1527, he was named *alcalde* of Mexico City, and some few months later he was punished by Friar Domingo de Betanzos for blasphemy,[25] along with other conquistadores and settlers. A good number of them had Jewish ancestors.[26]

The fourth stage of the Spanish period began in 1518, the year when Charles of Habsburg became king of Spain. We call this phase that of the 'forbidden ones,' because the future Emperor changed the Crown's policy toward New Christians. On September 24, 1518, Charles ordered the officers of the *Casa de Contratación* in Seville, who controlled all the traffic to the Indies, to prohibit any person once punished by the Holy Office from embarking for the Crown's overseas domains. The New Christians protested, alleging that free passage to America was a paid-for privilege. The King ordered an investigation into the matter, wishing to know, more than anything else, if all of them had paid their debt to the Crown. While the inquiry lasted, the way to the Indies remained open.[27]

The expansion of Spanish domains in Central and South America, territories inhabited by advanced civilizations, deepened the apostolic zeal of the mendicant orders who felt that the presence of individuals punished by the Holy Office could hinder a genuine evangelization of the Indians. Indeed, the consideration that not only the persons who were reconciled by the Inquisition, but all New Christians, were potential heretics, became a point of view that many Spaniards shared at that time. For this reason, from September 25, 1552, all people of Hebrew origin were forbidden from crossing the Atlantic Ocean. Subsequent dispositions ratified this pragmatic sanction and even broadened it and extended the prohibition to grandchildren and great-great-grandchildren of any Jew.

From the beginning, many disobeyed the prohibitory laws, among others, for two main reasons: first, because the captains feared provocation of quarrels and discord in their armies and did not publish the royal bans,[28] and second, a substantial number of captains themselves had Jewish ancestors. Furthermore, many New Christians who had gained access to American life before 1518 had managed to conceal their origins by changing their profession and personality. They made every effort to appear to their neighbors as Old Christians. Many succeeded, but others did not.

A good number were harassed, and several even paid for their ascendancy with their lives. This was the case of the Alonsos, Hernando and Martín, natives of the province of Huelva—the first from the village of Niebla and the second from Palos. Both embarked in the year 1518 for Cuba. Hernando, a blacksmith by trade, worked under the orders of the famous carpenter, Martín López, in building the brigantines which played so important a role in the conquest of Tenochtitlán, the capital of the Mexican empire. Later, he took part in the pacification of Pánuco. For all these services, he was granted the signory of Actopan as an *encomienda*. From then on, he devoted himself to cattle-raising and mining, and between the years 1524–1528 he managed to be the principal meat supplier for Mexico City. In early autumn of 1528, he was accused of having celebrated Passover in the company of some Crypto-Jews in Cuba, having rebaptized or washed out the holy water poured on the head of a mestizo son that he had and, finally, for forbidding his wife to go to church during her period. In this case, Hernando Alonso confused the synagogue with the church to which he attributed a biblical ordinance. (This was very common among the Crypto-Jews, who were obliged to live a Christian life and, within their consciences, desired to keep Jewish commandments.) Weeks later, he was burned in the first public Auto de Fe celebrated in Mexico City.[29]

His relative, Martín Alonso Alemán, engaged in pearl fishing and trade in the Caribbean and soon amassed a large fortune. In 1527, he was named *regidor* (mayor) of Cubagua, a post that provoked the envy of some Basque fellows who denounced him as being one of those prohibited from living in the Indies. Although he managed to demonstrate that the accusation was false, some inhabitants of the town insisted on reminding him of his ancestors. In December of 1528, he was assassinated by Pedro de Barrionuevo, native of Soria, who was convinced that stabbing to death a descendent of a Jew was not a sin. The Old Christian was never punished for the crime.[30]

In the aforementioned Auto de Fe, Gonzalo de Morales, shopkeeper, was also burned at the stake. His sister has been sacrificed in the same way a few years earlier in Santo Domingo. Their brother Diego also appeared on the stand, chained and with a *mordaza* (gag), a sign that he was punished for blaspheming. Indeed, this was his second charge for this transgression; in the first one, his judges were civil authorities. Nevertheless, he was reconciled together with the aged notary Diego de Ocaña,[31] a relative of Pedro de Ocaña who had been a tailor in Seville[32] but in Santo Domingo went into trade. Another notary, Juan Fernández del Castillo, who boasted of the title of Excellency in Santo Domingo and from 1525 held the same office in Mexico City, was reconciled some few days before in a private Auto de Fe.[33] Juan Fernández, who was imprisoned once again in 1536 due to his skepticism in religious matters,[34] was the son of Alonso del Castillo, mirror trader in Seville, registered under number 73 in the "Padrón."

In fact, it was easier to change faith than to assimilate to the *modus vivendi* of the Old Christians which, in itself, was a form developed over centuries. It was not only a question of faith but a cultural behavior in daily life manifested in the form of greeting, eating, praying, and so on. One could be suspected of having Jewish origins because one did not invoke Christ, the Virgin, or the Saints; because one avoided pork; or because one changed his shirt often or washed his hands many times a day. The life of Diego de Morales, who was arrested and punished by the Inquisition six times between 1525–1560, illustrates more than anything the tragedy of compelled assimilation. This unadaptable man, though he managed to survive, could never escape his destiny. During fifty-eight years of life in Christian garb (he was born into a family that continued to practice Judaism after their conversion) he refused to consume any bacon and affirmed many times that God did not have a son. He was recognized and ostracized wherever he went. In 1558, the Dominican friar Juan de Cárdenas charged him once again with all that he had already been punished for in previous trials. He was the talk of all of Guatemala City, and people pointed him out as a defamed man.[35]

Many others, though they stuffed themselves with pork, were not able to hide their ancestry and, therefore, they considered that the only way to escape the shades of their origins was to become noble. One of the conquerors of Peru, Captain Rodrigo Orgoñoz, chose this way. The son of a poor Jewish cobbler who embraced Christianity on the eve of the expulsion, he appropriated to himself the name of the gentleman Juan de Orgoñoz and enlisted in the Italian wars. Rodrigo showed great bravery and, along with some few Spaniards, captured King Francis I at Pavia in 1525. Years later, he embarked with his brother, Diego Méndez, for the Indies and soon became the right-hand man to Diego Almagro the Elder.

In his actions in America—in Honduras, Peru (where he took part in the conquest of the Imperial City of Cuzco), and in Chile—he amassed a large fortune. For all his deeds, he desired to be distinguished with the knighthood of the Order of Santiago, the patron saint of Spain. To reach this goal, he needed to prove not only Old Christian ancestry, but that nobody in his family had been punished by the Inquisition. In fact, his mother had been. To erase his origins, he begged Juan de Orgoñoz to adopt him as his son, offering him in exchange all his gold.[36] Some nobles used to sell this kind of favor, but Juan de Orgoñoz rejected Rodrigo, who, three years later in 1538, was killed in the battle at Salinas.

The famous protector of the American Indian, Friar Bartolomé de las Casas, appropriated to himself the name of a French noble family from the Canary Islands and signed his name as Casaus. They protested, but the Dominican ignored them.[37] According to Américo Castro, the bishop of Chiapas was "trying out capes."[38] This subterfuge was used by many New Christians who desired to divert the attention of curious and gossipy persons who used to check the names attached to the *sambenitos*[39] on display in cathedrals and churches of the entire Spanish empire.

It happened that an indiscreet man discovered the Jewish ancestors of Cristóbal de Miranda, first dean of the cathedral in Mérida, Yucatan. In fact, the doctor of theology got this post only after having given the Inquisition proof of his "purity of blood." In other words, he demonstrated that, at least over three generations, all his ancestors were Old Christians. Nevertheless, years later, he was recognized as the grandson of Diego López, merchant, and Leonor Rodríguez, both punished by the Holy Office in the port of Santa María near Seville. In the same town, his maternal great-grandparents, Diego Donaire, blanket weaver, and his wife, Isabel García, were burned at the stake. Both were considered by their judges to be the "biggest Judaizers" of that district.[40] After it was known publicly that Miranda descended from Jews and had cheated the Inquisition, the Franciscan, Diego de Landa, bishop of Yucatan, persecuted him dreadfully.

At the same time in Cuzco, Peru, no one bothered Father Joseph de Acosta, the brilliant author of *The Natural and Moral History of the Indies*, who was a grandson of a converted family of merchants from Medina del Campo. This Jesuit breathed more freely in American than he did in Spain, where he was harrassed by Father Claudio Aquaviva, the first anti-Semitic General of the Order, who introduced the Statutes of Purity of Blood into the Society in the last decades of the sixteenth century.[41] (The three former Generals had not only rejected the Statutes, but the successor to Ignacio de Loyola, Father Diego Laínez, was even proud of his Hebrew ancestors.)

From the cases analyzed, it can be inferred that the majority of the converts' descendents wanted to become assimilated into the lifestyle of the Old Christians. This was not an easy task for all the reasons previously mentioned, and mainly because the society that should have absorbed them rejected them. Although some of them went unnoticed and climbed to high positions in Spanish society, many other lives and careers were destroyed.

THE PORTUGUESE ERA

The second period, which we call that of the doubly prohibited because foreigners were generally forbidden to go to the Indies, started around 1560 and ended some hundred and sixty years later. Nevertheless, several Portuguese, among them a few New Christians, got to the Spanish overseas domains before that date, though in official documents they are mentioned mainly from about 1560 on. Their presence provoked the zeal of many Spaniards and especially of the royal officers who continually reported to the Crown about the damages caused by Portuguese navigators who arrived in the Caribbean with slaves and other merchandise that they smuggled in.[42] In fact, many ships bound for Brazil stopped in Santo Domingo, although most of them came legally under the commercial contracts between the Iberian Crowns. Among the administrators of the ships were several New Christians, including Miguel Núñez, the Portuguese king's slave agent in Santo Domingo. His daughter, Guiomar, married Luis de Carvajal y de la Cueva, the future governor of the New Kingdom of León. Carvajal spent, in his youth, seven years in Cabo Verde. His maternal uncle, Francisco de Andrada, also served as a public officer in Guinea. Years later, he arrived in Mexico, changed his life, and became an Augustinian monk.[43] Nevertheless, the majority of New Christians of Portuguese origin rejected assimilation and desired to survive, given the circumstances, as Jews in Christian garb. From here on, we shall call them Crypto-Jews.

The doubly forbidden, or Portuguese era, is divided into three periods. We have called the years from 1560 to 1580 the formative phase, because throughout those years small New Christian communities were set up in Spanish America. As we said, many of the people were Crypto-Jews who came to the fourth continent hoping to evade the tribunals of the Inquisition on the Peninsula. Others were attracted by the discovery of rich silver deposits in New Spain and the region of Potosí, which offered good opportunities to entrepreneurs and merchants. Furthermore, the conquest of the Philippines opened a new route to the East and that meant a wide sphere of action for adventurers. Besides, some New Christians had relatives and friends who were in the service of the Portuguese crown or went on trade to the Lusitanian domains in Southeast Asia.

The Portuguese presence and the abundance of pirates, generally of English origin, who had been harassing the coasts of Spanish America since the middle of the sixteenth century and occasionally got inland, bothered the Crown exceedingly. Complaints sent to the king about the Lusitanians who were suspected in matters of faith and of pirates, heretics, and enemies of everything Catholic, were added to the voices of friars who wrote about the dissolution of morality among the Spanish Americans, including the clergy. Felipe II, who kept watch on both the religious purity and the morality of his subjects, decided to act. He abolished the Primitive or Apostolic Inquisition made up of friars and bishops, which had been on the decline since the fifties, and established, on January 18, 1569, the Holy Office in America. The first Tribunal was introduced in 1570 in Lima, Peru, and the second was set up in 1571 in Mexico City with jurisdiction over the Philippines. In 1610, a third tribunal was formed in the port city of Cartagena de Indias.

The inquisitors set right to work. The publication of the first Edict of Faith in all the churches, through which everyone was exhorted to denounce all the offenders of Catholic norms of life and behavior, resulted in copious accusations and attestations against blasphemers, bigamists, libertine friars, supporters of heretical schemes, Lutherans, Calvinists, and Judaizers. For example, a number of persons were denounced at the tribunal of Lima "for taking the sinew out of lambs' legs" and for other transgressions. Though some of them alleged that they did it so that "the meat would roast better and not as a ceremony of the Law of Moses,"[44] they did not escape punishment. However, the large *Autos de Fe* against Judaizers were carried out in the following phase of the Portuguese period.

The Lusitanians became subjects of the Spanish Crown in 1580, the year when Felipe II became king of Portugal. They did not regain their autonomy until 1640. During the period between 1580 and 1640, which we call the era of the United Crown, the Portuguese abounded in Spain and also in its overseas domains. It is necessary to underscore that the majority of them were not only New Christians, but Crypto-Jews. Several of them had settled temporarily in Jewish quarters in Italy or other places, and from there they went to Spain to seek their fortunes. For example, Juan Rodríguez de Silva had lived in France, Italy, and the Turkish Empire. He married in Salonica, where he left his wife, and traveled once again to Italy, and from there to Spain, where he embarked for the Indies. He escaped from New Spain when the officers of the Inquisition were looking for him. Because of that, he was burned in effigy, as all absent persons were, in the *Auto de Fe* celebrated in Mexico City in 1596. Jorge de Almeyda, Silva's friend, lived in Ferrara until the 1570s, and when life became difficult in the Duchy due to one of the economic crises caused by the wars with the Turks, he left with his family for New Spain. His cousin, Blanca Lorenza, settled in Seville and opened an inn where many Crypto-Jews stopped on their way to and from the Indies; for them, kosher food was served. Almeyda, who fled from Mexico in 1590 after the Holy Office apprehended his wife, niece of the aforementioned governor of the New Kingdom of Leon, had good lawyers and defenders in Madrid who helped him to negotiate the absolution of the penitential garments of the Caravajals. Thanks to his contacts, he even obtained a passport for Ruy Díaz, a Portuguese Jew living in Italy, and his son, Diego Díaz Nieto, born in Ferrara.[45]

Many Crypto-Jews, after having lived in Portugal as Christians and benefiting from maritime and other trade, found it difficult to adjust to the austerity and poverty of the Jewish quarters and ghettos. The bold ones, therefore, with the hope of amassing a true fortune and one day being able to return to Italy, Holland, or another place where they were permitted to freely profess their faith, put themselves in danger since in the Spanish domains the Holy Office lay in wait for them. The religious coercion in Portugal forced them to live as Christians, while in the ghettos they behaved as Jews.

This ability to jump back and forth between societies permitted some of them, occasionally, to amass some wealth. For example, Diego Pérez de Alburquerque, born in Bordeaux and raised in Rouen, France, arrived in New Spain in 1618. He lived in Puebla, Mexico City, and finally settled in the mining center of Zacatecas.[46] Alvaro Méndez, arrested in 1531 in Lima, formerly lived in France and sent money to his relatives in Amsterdam from Peru.[47] Julian Alvarez came to Mexico from Holland. He was tried by the Holy Office in his absence, as he had been lucky enough to escape just at the right time.[48] Luis Franco Rodríguez, resident in Cartagena de Indias, had brothers in Holland, and throughout his whole life he yearned for a comfortable economic situation that would permit him to live with them freely as a Jew.[49] Isabel Núñez, who lived with her husband in Mexico, was a native of France.[50] Her brother, Enrique Núñez Espinosa, resided with his spouse, Doña Mencia de Luna, in Lima; she died after being brutally tortured by the Inquisition in Lima without denouncing anyone.[51]

Several Crypto-Jews lost the ability to put down roots anywhere and wandered from one place to another. This was the case of Baltazar de Araujo, descendent of Abraham Seneor or Senior, *Rabbi Mayor* or Chief Rabbi of Castile, supplier of the armies that conquered Granada and one of Isabella's most loyal advisors. For this reason, after signing the Expulsion Edict on March 31, 1492, the Catholic queen did everything possible to keep her ancient servant. The only way to do it was to compel him to a baptismal font. At the christening, Senior and his family took the surname of Coronel.

When the Inquisitors asked Baltazar in Cartagena de Indias what his name was, he responded that "here he was called Araujo but his surname was Coronel, of the Coronels of Galicia. . ."[52] He also said that he was a native of Bayona. Indeed, one part of the Chief Rabbi's family took refuge in Portugal,[53] and from there some of them, fearing a fall into the hands of the Lusitanian Holy Office, returned to Spain and settled in Galicia. In this kingdom, the tribunal of the Inquisition was not formally introduced until 1562 and only began to function in 1574.[54] The persecution of Judaizers began in the very last years of the sixteenth century.[55] At about that time, Araujo-Coronel's mother embarked with her eight children and other relatives from Flanders. From there she moved to Venice, where she had her sons circumcised and gave them Hebrew names. Baltazar was called Abraham Senior after his illustrious ancestor. They began immediately to study Judaism, a study which they continued in Salonica and Constantinople. Later, Abraham Senior went to live with his brother in Cairo and then moved to Alexandria. Some time later, he desired to visit his native land and returned to Bayona, but out of fear of the Holy Office he returned to his mother's home in Constantinople. Nevertheless, Araujo-Coronel "felt the desire to see the world" and crossed the Balkans one more time, traveled through Italy and Spain, and embarked for America.

Travelers like Coronel-Senior infused new life into the small Crypto-Jewish communities and kept them in constant communication with the intellectual centers of Judaism. Occasionally these men, such as Juan Pacheco de León, who came to Mexico in 1639 from Leghorn, Italy, became the spiritual guides for some groups of their coreligionists.[56] Moreover, all these Jews carried books printed in Ferrara, Venice, or some other cultural center, which found their way together with them to the most remote corners of the Spanish Empire. Manuel de Paz, age thirty-four, imprisoned in Lima in 1634, had one of these Bibles.[57] In 1637, Simón Váez Sevilla was denounced by his 'godfather,' Pedro de Navia, for displaying a Bible on his desk.[58] Many others were charged with the same crime.

One of the main characteristics of the period of the United Crowns was that the majority of the Crypto-Jews tried to fulfill the commandments of the Torah. All of them observed the Sabbath, though the men went to their business places so that they would not be noticed. For the women, it was easier to pretend that they were sewing or embroidering without doing anything. A substantial number of them abstained from eating prohibited foods, although they served bacon and ham when they had visitors. To the extent that circumstances permitted, they celebrated the three major annual holidays, namely *Pesah, Shavuot,* and *Sukkot.* They strictly fasted on the *Great Day of the Lord* or *Yom Hakippurim* and at *Taanit Esther* (The Fast of Esther). Due to the religious oppression in which they lived, Queen Esther was considered as one of the greatest Hebrew heroines because she saved her nation from destruction. Many of them fasted Mondays and Thursdays, days when the Torah is read in the synagogues. On the eves and ends of the fasts, they dined only on Lenten dishes such as vegetables, fruit, fish, eggs, and cheese. On the occasion of these banquets, a small group of friends would gather to discuss the Law of Moses. At *Yom Hakippurim,* after supper they would usually pray all night long. The following day, some would go to the country so that they would not be noticed. At dusk, they would return to their homes to break the fast in the company of family and friends. During these gatherings, it was reiterated that the Law of Moses was the only true faith by which man could be saved. On these occasions, those who had once lived in some Jewish quarter in Europe related their religious experiences of bygone days.

The subject of the Messiah came up in all these meetings, since everyone yearned for a quick redemption of Israel. Some even predicted the date of his arrival. Manuel Díaz, sacrificed at the *Auto de Fe* of the Green Cross, celebrated in Mexico City in December 1596, calculated that the Messiah would appear by the year 1600. During his imprisonment, Manuel dreamed that the Annointed One of the House of David had opened the doors of the Inquisition's secret jails. Seeing himself outside and free, he said to some acquaintances: "Look, God took up His cause. . ."[59] Others believed that the Savior would be born into a Crypto-Jewish family. In 1620, when Juana Enríquez was pregnant with her son Gaspar, it was believed that she would give birth to the Redeemer because she strictly observed the *Mitzvoth* and because Simón Váez, her husband, was descended from the tribe of Levy. When Gaspar did not turn out to be the Messiah, other virtuous women were considered as possible mothers of the Savior. Indeed, every irregular and strange happening was seen as a sign of his impending arrival. Simple as well as educated men believed with all their hearts that God had not forgotten his people. Thanks to this deep faith that is at the same time a futuristic ideology, the suriviors of the *Autos de Fe* of this period, in which family and friends were burned at the stake, had the strength and energy to educate their children in their ancestral creed.

For fear of being discovered, the Crypto-Jews educated their children as Christians from the beginning. They revealed their identity to them and initiated them into Judaism at the age of twelve or thirteen. They generally began the teaching a few weeks before the fast of *Yom Hakippurim*. In this way, the *Bath Mitzvah* or the *Bar Mitzvah*, after fasting for the first time, became members of their small communities. It goes without saying that all this was done in complete secrecy, since the Crypto-Jews were not safe even in the privacy of their own homes because their servants, neighbors, 'godfathers,' and friends spied on them. The periodic readings of the Edicts of Faith exalted the religious feelings of the people in general. They believed that their obligation as Catholics was to denounce everything that smelled of heresy. Consequently, the price that the Crypto-Jews paid for differing from the majority and keeping their being and identity alive was the secret jails, torture, confiscation of property, and other procedures that transformed rich and powerful into poor and helpless, all this if they were not converted into ashes in one of the *Autos de Fe*.

The intense activity of the Holy Office and the *Autos de Fe* that the tribunal celebrated between the years 1585 and 1606 in the viceroyalities of Peru and New Spain almost removed from the American map the small Crypto-Jewish communities that had been settled in the second half of the sixteenth century. A large number were eliminated physically, and many more were sent to the galleys for periods of five to ten years. This meant certain death, since none survived being shackled in their own excrement, eating and drinking the leftovers of the sailors, for more than two years. Those who were saved by some miracle had to start all over again, because all their property had been confiscated.

The destiny of the Crypto-Jews who settled in Spanish America in the first three decades of the seventeenth century was similar to that of their brethren in the sixteenth century. The difference was that, in spite of the economic depression that the Spanish domains suffered in the seventeenth century, a good number of New Christians managed to get rich. Their Lusitanian origin as well as their fortunes provoked envy and jealousy among the royal officials. The governor of Panama, Francisco Valverde Mercado, expressed the feelings of many when he wrote to King Felipe III that "today the traders of the Indies are the Portuguese because they have the contract for supplying slaves...and the dispatch

of the fleets and squadrons on the good journey of which all trade depends...
and...of this nation there have been many Jewish merchants around here who
live within their Law and they, upon getting rich, go to other kingdoms before
they fall into the hands of the Inquisition..." One month later, he advised the
king: "I have knowledge...that many of them have gone to Rome, Venice, Ferrara,
and other places..."[60]

Without doubt, many of those who came did leave, but others remained,
and their fortunes did not wind up in distant kingdoms but in the coffers of
the Holy Office. Among these it is fitting to mention the Peruvian Manuel
Bautista Pérez, miner and merchant and, at the same time, a man of deep
intellectual restlessness who became the spiritual leader of the Crypto-Jews in
Lima. The great and powerful, like the merchant Simón Váez Sevilla,[61] supported
their poor and weak brethren morally and economically.

The third phase of the Portuguese era in the Spanish overseas domains began
more or less in the year 1635. This phase, which lasted fifteen years, we call the
period of the collapse because, from 1635 on, denouncements against Judaizers
were very frequent. They began in Peru through the carelessness of a twenty-
five-year-old fellow recently from Spain, called Antonio de Cordero. He was
arrested in 1634 and during his trial suffered terrible torture. The inquisitors
forced the names of two other coreligionists out of him. The persecutions that
followed exterminated, in a few years, almost all the Peruvian Crypto-Jews. Manuel
Bautista Pérez, in spite of being a great benefactor of the University of San Marcos
in Lima and of several convents, was burned as the "captain of the Jews" in the
Auto de Fe celebrated in 1639 in that city.[62]

In Cartagena de Indias, the Mulatto Diego López took it upon himself to
spy on the Crypto-Jews for years. In 1634, he was arrested as a sorcerer and,
in the process of confessing, denounced all of Blas Pinto's friends and many
others.[63] As a consequence, some of the persons detained in Cartagena de Indias
and Peru testified against their acquaintances in New Spain. Thus, in a private
Auto de Fe held in 1635, two men were absolved of the heresy of Judaism, twelve
were reconciled in person and the beggar Domingo Flores in effigy, as he was
tried after his death.[64] The effigies of six other people whose reputation and
memory were condemned were sent to be burned. Those punished in this Auto
de Fe were mainly small merchants in mining towns and centers like Pachuca.[65]

The destruction of the Crypto-Jewish community of New Spain began in
1641 when Gaspar de Robles, member of the large López-Méndez-Enríquez family,
presented himself in the Holy Office with the purpose of discharging his
conscience. Gaspar resented his uncles and he had on occasions threatened them
with the Inquisition. In the tribunal he confessed that, advised by his relatives,
he had observed the dead Law of Moses from the age of thirteen until he became
fatally ill in his early twenties; he changed his religion after he had been cured
miraculously. He said that he was profoundly penitent and manifested his desire
to live and to die as a Catholic Christian. To demonstrate the sincerity of his

conversion, he accepted the inquisitorial proposition of becoming an informer and spying on his relatives and former coreligionists.[66]

During the course of the year 1642, the secret jails swelled with Judaizers. Nevertheless, the first cases were not decided until 1646. In the *Auto* celebrated on April 16, thirty-eight observers of the Law of Moses were reconciled in person and one, Clara Rivera, a twenty-two-year-old woman, in effigy, because, before expiring in prison, she showed signs of repentance.

On January 17 of the following year, twenty-one Judaizers were exhibited on a stand in the Cathedral of Mexico. In 1648, two *Autos* were carried out, one right after the other. The first was public and was celebrated on March 29 in the patio of the Franciscan monastery. The second was private and was held the next day in a church of the Company of Jesus called *Casa Profesa*. In the first one, seventeen observers of the Law of Moses abjured their errors and were reconciled to the Church. Diego Fernández de Elvas, who died in jail without repenting, was burned in effigy. For the same reason, Simón Rodríguez Núñez was reduced to ashes in person. The next day, twenty-two Judaizers abjured and were reconciled after being punished for heresy with the total confiscation of their properties. A large number were given one to two hundred lashes, in public, in the most important streets of the city. Their crimes were announced by a ban. Men and women were sentenced to be whipped for communicating in the secret jails or for anything that could be understood as disrespect to the officials of the Inquisition and for any transgressions that could be interpreted as social dissolution. Most of the men were sentenced to serve in the galleys, rowing without pay, for five to ten years.[67] In other words, they were condemned to a slow death. While at sea, the galley slaves were spared wearing the *sambenito*, which the condemned were always obliged to wear over their garments.

The last and largest of the *Autos* of this phase took place on April 11, 1649. In this terrible fiesta, between the living and the dead, one hundred and nine Jews were exhibited on the stand. Of those, twenty-two men and seven women abjured and were reconciled in person into the Church; two more were reconciled in effigy. The living were condemned to wear the *sambenito* until death redeemed them from that terrible distinction. They were also sentenced to total or partial confiscation of their property. Some, among them Juana Enríquez, wife of Simón Váez Sevilla, got two hundred lashes in the public streets. Most were condemned to permanent exile from the Indies, the city of Seville, and the town of Madrid, residence of His Majesty's royal court.

Thirteen Jews were sent to be burned at the stake in person. One of them, Tomás Treviño de Sobremonte, who manifested his wish to die as a Jew and refused to take a cross in his hands while being tied to the wooden stake, was consumed alive by the fire. Indeed, if those sentenced to death manifested some signs of repentance, such as confessing (which always meant testifying against other persons) and took a cross in their hands during the celebration of the *Auto* and on their way to the *quemadero* or burning place, the Holy Office was merciful with them: the hangman, before setting fire to the wood they were standing on, strangled them.

Eight fugitives were burned in effity; one of them, Jorge de Montoya, who escaped to the Philippines in 1642 and from there moved to Macao, was arrested and burned at the request of New Spain's Holy Office, by the Inquisition of Goa, in India.[68] Fifty-seven people who had died, ten of them in the secret jails, were burned in effigy along with boxes with their bones exhumed from the different churchs and cemeteries of the city.[69]

The collapse of the Crypto-Jewish communities coincided with serious political crises in Spain. To wit, the rebellion of Catalonia broke out in June 1640, and in November of the same year Portugal's war of independence started. These events caused the fall of Gaspar de Guzmán, Count-Duke of Olivares, chancellor of Felipe IV, whose policy was favorable to the New Christians. The Count-Duke wished to liberate Spain from the oppressive monopoly of the Genoese bankers, and he put competitors up against them in the form of Portuguese financiers, the majority of whom were New Christians and suspect in matters of faith. Don Gaspar also wanted to dispel the Purity of Blood psychosis that prevailed in those times in Spain, and he struggled to overthrow the discriminatory statutes that kept the New Christians from any public dignity.

Such a modern attitude fostered the animadversion of various civil and ecclesiastical groups, including the Inquisition, against Olivares. In fact, this antagonism, together with the happenings in Catalonia and Portugal, caused the fall of the Count-Duke. At the beginning of 1643, Felipe IV dismissed his favorite. This act signified a turning point in the internal and external policies of the kingdom. Felipe IV began to mistrust the Lusitanian businessmen, many of whom had been tried by the Inquisition or belonged to families punished by the Tribunal, although he was still unable to dispense with their services. All of these circumstances added to popular scorn and encouraged harassment and persecution of the New Christians.

The *Autos* celebrated in the viceroyalities also had disastrous economic consequences for many Old Christians. The seizure and confiscation of property carried out in Peru during the years 1639–1640 ruined a large number of businessmen in Lima and other merchants in the vast viceroyalty. Consequently, trade was paralyzed and many were driven to bankruptcy.[70] In New Spain, the confiscations froze out the capital of a good number of Sevillian brokers and, therefore, caused their ruin.[71] The seized property was partially sold at public auction. It should be underscored that the officers of the Inquisition and their families were the first to purchase the most valuable goods much below their real worth. The money was used for current necessities of the Holy Office, including the restoration of buildings. The rest was invested in state bonds on the public debt, called *juros*, which paid their holders an annual revenue of seven percent.

In conclusion, the confiscations on the one hand impeded transactions between the mother country and her colonies and, on the other, changed active capital into passive in Spain and her overseas domains. Finally, the confiscations caused mistrust among the big financiers and entrepreneurs, several of whom fled with their capital to the Low Countries and England, kingdoms that were enemies of Spain.

THE ERA OF DECLINE

This period is divided into two phases. The first includes the second half of the seventeenth century and the first decade of the eighteenth. We call it the 'period of the Epigons of Crypto-Judaism.' The second stage extends from approximately 1710 to the victory of liberal ideas in Spanish America, and we have named it the 'phase of the myths.'

The time of the epigons of Crypto-Judaism began after the expulsion and exile of the majority of those reconciled in the aforementioned *Autos*. For many, it was not easy to abandon the land in which they had lived, both as honorable and prosperous subjects of the Crown and as poor and degraded pariahs. Many had been born on this continent and wished to stay in their country of origin. Others, though they wanted to leave the place of their sufferings, lacked the means necessary to do so. They left the secret jails of the Inquisition with only the ragged clothes on their backs, covered with the *sambenito*. All of them had to beg or seek loans to pay passage to Spain. At the same time, the captains and sailors rejected them and refused to allow them on their ships, believing that having heretics with them could cause some misfortune to befall them on the high seas. But the Holy Office was implacable. On the one hand, it hastened the departure of the hesitant; on the other, it forced the owners of the vessels to obey their orders under penalty of two hundred ducats' fine and excommunication.[72]

Nevertheless, a small group of Crypto-Jews found ways of remaining in these parts of the world. Terrible was their fate if, through misfortune, they were to fall once again into the grasp of the Holy Office. This happened to some of them, including Diego Díaz and Francisco Botello. The first was sentenced in 1643 to permanent exile from the Indies. His wife, Ana Gómez, was burned in the *Auto* carried out in 1649, and he wandered from place to place, both to avoid being discovered and because he had no other place to go. He was arrested for the second time in February 1652, at the age of seventy, and condemned as a relapsed Judaizer.

Francisco Botello also remained behind. He was imprisoned for the first time in 1642. In the year 1648, he was tortured. And in 1649, he was reconciled to the church and sentenced to the total confiscation of his property, two hundred lashes, and permanent exile from the Indies. In 1651, he was apprehended for the second time and condemned—as "a heretic Judaizer. . .wanton, wicked and obstinate in the observance of the dead Law of Moses"—to be burned at the stake.

In the *Auto* celebrated in 1659 in Mexico City, Díaz and Botello walked together to the *quemadero*. While being tied to the stakes, Diego Díaz made signs to Botello exhorting him to face his death with courage. A friar, who tried to convert them to Christianity at the last moment, reprimanded him for doing it. Diego Díaz, who refused to take a cross in his hands, answered him: "Well, father, is it not good that we encourage each other to die for God?"[73]

María de Zárate, Botello's Mexican spouse, was also on the platform. Some weeks before the celebration of the *Auto*, she was tortured terribly, but the inquisitors were not able to get any testimony out of her.[74] Jorge de Espinosa was also on the stand. He had been reconciled in 1639 in Lima and sentenced to two hundred lashes and ten years in the galleys. After enduring the flagellation, he managed to escape the hands of his executioners. He moved to New Spain, changed his name to Jorge Serrano, served in Coatzacoalcos as a municipal standard holder or *alférez*, and also became the *alcalde mayor*'s (judge's) deputy.[75]

Nevertheless, many had better luck and were integrated into Creole society. Several children of the reconciled took refuge in frontier regions that were in the process of being colonized. Others came back some years later with new identities and settled in different sites in the vast territories of the viceroyalties.

The lives of the Muñoz de Alvarado brothers are, to a great extent, characteristic of the tribulations caused by assimilation as experienced by many Creoles of New Christian origin. Diego and Pedro were natives of Popayán, viceroyalty of Peru, modern-day Colombia. Both left there for Bordeaux, France, with their father, who was eager to finish his days as a Jew. Later, they returned to Spain and sailed to Veracruz. In Puebla de los Angeles, they married the García del Corral sisters, descendents of conquerors of New Spain, who brought good dowries to the marriage.

Diego, who was for some years *alcalde* in Puebla, was a merchant and had dealings with the Philippines and Spain, while his younger brother, Pedro, was his agent. In the year 1679, the latter went crazy and during a deep depression, in the presence of some servants, exhorted his children to embrace Judaism. When he recovered his sanity, he began to believe that the Law of Moses was not the true one and that he had lived his whole existence in error. Influenced by some friar, he denounced himself to the Holy Office. As a consequence of his confessions, Diego was arrested, along with the widow of his brother Gabriel, Clara Méndez de Olivera.

The Muñoz de Alvarado brothers had come back to America with the goal of amassing a large fortune and then returning to Europe and settling in some Jewish community, but their Judaism was more nominal than profound. Judaism was the secret that tied them together and made them remember their father and other relatives who were far away. On occasion, they would read the Bible and observe some holidays, but they did not have a Jewish conscience, identified with Spanish culture, and were bound to their families and homes. Due to the teachings of Diego Muñoz, their father, they mistrusted the efficacy of Christianity and believed that the Law of Moses was the correct one and that only by it could man be saved. Their mother, Sebastiana de Alvarado, though she had some Jewish blood, was a descendent of Inca nobility and of one of the the Alvarados who had conquered Peru. She knew about their Jewish leanings, but educated them also as good Christians. Indeed, they had four sisters who were nuns and lived in a monastery in Popayán, and brothers in the Company of Jesus.

At the beginning of 1681, Diego Muñoz de Alvarado sent the huge sum of one hundred thousand pesos to Spain, planning to transfer it to some Jewry. Nevertheless, he lived in Puebla as a devout Catholic, famous for his charity and donations to convents and other institutions. On November 1, 1682, the day he was arrested, he had a bag of scapularies, a cross, and other emblems of Christianity around his neck.[76]

Diego and Pedro lived in two worlds, and the doubts gnawed away at their mental health and drove Pedro, the more sensitive of the two, to madness. In a letter dated September 3, 1681, he wrote to Diego that he had changed his faith and lamented having spent his whole existence in error.[77] In the deepest recesses of his being, Diego was unwilling to change his life. After transferring the money to Spain, he did everything possible to bind himself to the *modus vivendi* of New Spain and even began to attend mass daily.

Once he was inside the secret jails, and the notary of the Tribunal presented the list of his seized possessions, he was a lost man. By canon law, as a heretic he had no right to property. His multiple holdings and the previously mentioned hundred thousand pesos helped cause his being found guilty. The prosecutor of the Inquisition also charged him with having desecrated a holy image of the Virgin. He entered jail sick and suffered terrible pains and ailments during his imprisonment and, though the physician of the Holy Office considered him healthy, he died of his infirmities in November 1683. In the *Auto* that took place in Mexico City on June 21, 1684, he was condemned as an obstinate and relapsed Judaizer, and his exhumed bones were burned with his effigy. As was expected, he was sentenced to total confiscation of his property.[78] His children inherited nothing but their father's *sambenito* which was hung in the Cathedral of Puebla and reminded future generations of the shame of Diego Muñoz de Alvarado. His brother Pedro was reconciled and sentenced also to a total loss of his property.

Many Americans of New Christian origin lived in similar torment. On one hand, they were haunted by the memory of their ancestors and, on the other, they were absorbed by the Hispanic-Catholic culture in the midst of which they lived. As most of them lost all contact with Hebrew intellectual centers, Judaism became something remote and apocalyptic for them, while Christianity was the everyday reality. Their descendents, eager to erase the slightest blemish with respect to their origin, became the most fervent and devout of Catholics.

One of the last Jews sent to a pyre in Spanish America was Fernando de Medina, alias Moisés Gómez, native of Bordeaux, France. He was linked to the tobacco monopoly, the administration of which was still in the hands of the

Portuguese financiers who, as has been noted, were in their majority New Christians. Medina-Gómez arrived in Mexico in 1687 and, in 1691, four years later, he was arrested by the Holy Office. He was a practicing Jew and kept the *mitzvoth* even during the eight long years of his imprisonment. Due to that fact, he was burned alive in a private *Auto de Fe* celebrated on June 14, 1699 in Mexico City.[79] Two other Judaizers were reconciled in the same act.[80]

Pedro Gutiérrez, a traveling merchant, twenty-two years old and a resident of Trujillo, had a better fate. In the year 1700, he was reconciled by the Tribunal of Lima and sentenced to the confiscation of his property and exiled from the Indies. While he was being embarked for Seville, in Portobelo, Panama, he escaped and was picked up by an English ship that took him to Jamaica.[81] It should be noted that Gutiérrez was not the only one to succeed in fleeing from the Spanish domains and going to the islands that were English possessions.[82]

In the phase of the myths, the New Christians were, in general, already assimilated into the life of the Old Christians. Even the term 'New Christian' fell into disuse in the Spanish colonies. Spanish-America became almost free of Jews. The inhabitants, who had never seen a living sample, but attended the religious theatre and walked in the solemn processions during Holy Week, considered the Jew to be a mythical being who personified the concept of evil in history. Indeed, the Jew was identified with the devil and was believed to have a tail and horns. Hence, any manifestation that indicated signs of Judaism was severely reprimanded. For example, in 1788, Josefa de Astudillo, a resident of the port city of Veracruz, was seen with a fan that had the story of Queen Esther painted on it. Her husband, after learning the significance of the design, broke it in pieces and threw it in the garbage. Word came to the local commissary of the Holy Office, which immediately ordered a search of the city's garbage dump and, when some pieces of the fan were found, they were taken in a solemn procession to the patio of the main church and, in a small *Auto de Fe*, thrown into the fire.[83]

Different superstitions were confused with Judaism. For example, in 1799, Esteban de Zerecedo, a resident of Tlacolula, Oaxaca, was suspected of being a Judaizer because of having his body painted.[84] (The accusers did not know that the act of tattooing is prohibited by the Law of Moses.[85]) Manuel Vázquez, *alcalde mayor* of Tampico, was also accused of Judaizing for having a book by Voltaire and for daring to say on one occasion that "in Rome the Pope takes care of the public harlots and supports them himself. . . he also defends the Jews so. . . that they might not be prevented from observing their Law and ceremonies. . ."[86] Men who sympathized with different sects and contemporary ideologies, some of which were totally opposed to the Law of Moses, such as the Molinists, Jansenists, Deists, Atheists, and other *ists* of that time, were also accused of Judaism.

Nevertheless, even in the last decades of the eighteenth century, a vestige of Crypto-Judaism manifested itself in the Franciscan Rafael Gil Rodríguez since, according to the physicians of the Holy Office, the friar had obvious signs of having been circumcised as a youngster. He was condemned as a Judaizer, though from his trial it can be inferred that he had inclinations toward the enlightened ideas of his epoch. He was reconciled in a private *Auto* after spending seven long years in prison.[87]

A few eclectics judged in that period descended from New Christians and the Holy Office made them remember their origin. One of them was Pedro Bazán, Spaniard, accused of "believing in only one God, creator of Heaven and Earth. . ." Bazán used to scoff at Mary's virginity and said on occasions that "the Jews had crucified a man called Jesus. . ." but he was "a hopeless drunk and in no way a son of God. . .and. . .we men are like animals and we are not resurrected."[88] Another eclectic, accused of similar charges, was the French merchant Francisco Moyen, who traded in the Brazil and Río de la Plata region.[89]

A few Jews were found in the troops that the Bourbons sent to America. Among them was José Bruzal, French, first musician of the Crown's Regiment,[90] and others, including physicians, some of whom came to Spain from England and enlisted in the military.

In the second half of the eighteenth century, some Jews arrived from time to time, and even temporarily settled in the Spanish overseas dominions, as did José Salomón, physician, who used to slaughter chickens in a Jewish manner and rigorously supervised his cook's preparations. He boarded a ship that was sailing to the Caribbean islands just a few days before the *acalde* of the Holy Office came to arrest him.[91] Indeed, some Jews who lived in the Dutch and English possessions in the Caribbean, where Jewish communities had existed since the second half of the seventeenth century,[92] had business relations with the Spanish dominions.

Finally, we would like to mention the famous pirates, brothers Jean and Pierre Lafitte, natives of Santo Domingo, stationed on Barataria Island in Louisiana Bay, from where they attacked Spanish ships and territory "to avenge the tortures inflicted on their Jewish ancestors," as Jean wrote in his diary.[93]

CONCLUSIONS

The presence of New Christians in Spanish America can be divided into three large eras: the Spanish, the Portuguese, and the Decline. Each one of these epochs has its own characteristics.

In the first period, the majority of the protagonists were assimilated into Spanish culture. Others were in the process of voluntary or obligatory acculturation. Those who refused to abandon the religion of their ancestors and its customs and traditions were cruelly punished. The Spain of the Catholic monarchs, which transformed religion into the 'reason of state,' did not tolerate dissidents in matters of faith.

The Spanish period was divided into the following four phases: the discovery, the favorites, the legal, and the forbidden. Throughout these four phases, New Christians of Spanish origin participated in the American undertaking as financiers, royal officers, conquerors, and settlers. Relatively few of them were punished by the primitive Inquisition, formed by friars and bishops, though some were relaxed to the secular arm, which meant that they were condemned to be burned at the stake. The Holy Office, as a religious institution, left execution for the civil authorities. It should be underscored that many escaped the rigors of the Holy Office in early colonial times because the friars and first bishops were busy with evangelization of the millions of American Indians and with the foundation of the new Church on the recently discovered fourth continent and had little time left for all the Spanish heretics.

The second epoch, the Portuguese one, was divided into three phases: the formative, the united Crown, and the collapse. The principal characteristic of this era is that nearly the absolute majority of New Christians were practicing Jews because they were driven against their will to the baptismal fonts in the year 1497 by King Manuel of Portugal. The coerced conversion did not make them Christians, but rather Crypto-Jews. They were compelled to change their religion as an organized group along with their rabbis, leaders, and intellectuals. Due to these circumstances and the importance of the family in Jewish society, the baptismal waters did not destroy their spiritual convictions. At the same time, the society that should have absorbed them segregated them and through the centuries they were called 'New Christians of the Hebrew nation' or just 'of the nation.' Indeed, they were hated and discriminated against as Jews, and they were disliked and persecuted as New Christians. For this and other reasons, almost two centuries after being compelled to Christianity, they remained faithful to the religion of their ancestors and considered Judaism their national religion. Their belief, their burning faith in the coming of the Messiah—for whom they waited throughout their lifetime and whose arrival they expected every day in their time—and their religious practices were alive thanks to family education and due to the permanent contacts that they maintained with different intellectual centers of Judaism, such as Ferrara, Venice, Leghorn, Amsterdam, and even Salonica.

The large *Autos de Fe* carried out between 1635 and 1650 almost erased the presence of Crypto-Jews in the Spanish domains. Those who survived the persecutions were expelled from the fourth continent and their properties ended up in the coffers of the Holy Office.

The last era, that of decline, witnessed the epigons of Crypto-Judaism. Indeed, during its first phase, the remnants of the New Christians in America were exterminated. Those who persevered in their faith were burned, and the others became assimilated. A significant number scattered across the immense American spaces and were lost to both Judaism and the Inquisition. Some escaped to the Caribbean islands under Dutch and English rule. In the last phase of this epoch, in the period of the myths, the Holy Office stopped using the term 'New Christians' in Spanish America. The people who were suspected of Judaism throughout the eighteenth century were also accused of other *isms* of their time.

On the popular level, the Jew was considered to symbolize evil, to be the personification of Satan himself. It is worth mentioning that these concepts also prevailed in the first decades of the era of independence, until liberal ideas gained ground and different states issued laws of religious tolerance. The Inquisition formed and manipulated public opinion through the periodic publication of the Edicts of Faith, which were read even in the smallest churches in the vast Spanish domains, and by this means transformed not only the Jews but also the English, Dutch, and other non-Catholics into devils.

Nevertheless, the antagonism of the Holy Office was directed mostly against the English due to their presence in North America and the Caribbean. From the very late seventeenth century, some people from these colonies entered the Spanish dominions. Other Englishmen, mostly physicians among whom there were some Jews, came with the Bourbon regiments in the 1760s. It was with these in mind, in the year 1770, that the Mexican inquisitors wrote to the monarch asking him to prohibit foreigners from going to the Indies. The Holy Tribunal feared that their presence would "undetectably dispel among the majority of the natives the horror and abomination that they have against that nation only because of the idea that they are heretics and enemies of the religion and the Church."[94]

Fortunately, the Holy Office was unable to stop the course of history. Indeed, several Jews collaborated with the insurgents and freedom fighters in their struggle for American independence; some enlisted as soldiers, especially in the countries of South America, and others aided the cause with money, guns, and other equipment.

NOTES

1. Fray Bartolomé de las Casas, *Historia de las Indias* (Mexico: Fondo de Cultura Económica, 1965) Vol. I, p. 156, and Vol. II, p. 325; José Amador de los Ríos, *Historia Social, Política y Religiosa de los Judíos en España y Portugal* (Madrid: Aguilar, 1960) p. 573, Note 3, and p. 756; Manuel Giménez Fernández, "Los restos de Colón en Sevilla," in *Anuario de Estudios Americanos* (1953) X, p. 15; Antonio Domínguez Ortiz, *Los judeoconversos en España y en América* (Madrid: Istmo, 1971) pp. 49–50.

2. "Linage de Santángel" and "Linage del Tesorero Garbiel Sánchez," in the *Libro Verde de Aragón*, in Manuel Serrano y Sanz, *Orígenes de la dominación española en América* (Madrid: Biblioteca de Autores Españoles, 1918) pp. 494–506, and "Sumaria y Memoria de los judíos conversos, habitadores de la ciudad de Zaragoza, que fueron quemados en persona o en estatua o penitenciados por la Inquisición desde 1483–1504," in Amador de los Ríos, op. cit., pp. 1010–1022.

3. "Carta de Cristóbal Colón a Luis de Santángel" and "Carta de Cristóbal Colón al Magnífico señor Gabriel Sánchez, Tesorero de los Serenísimos monarcas...," in Martín Fernández de Naverrete, *Colección de los Viajes y Descubrimientos que hicieron por mar los Españoles*.... Vol. I, (Madrid: Biblioteca de Autores Españoles, 1954), pp. 166–181.

4. Bartolomé de las Casas, op. cit., Vol, I, p. 201.

5. Ibid., pp. 226–227.

6. Antonio Domínguez Ortiz, op. Cit., p. 129.

7. De las Casas, op. cit., Vol. II, p. 314.

8. Claudio Guillén "Un padrón de conversos sevillanos," in *Bulletin Hispanique* 65 (1963), pp. 79–80; Américo Castro, "Fray Bartolomé de las Casas o Casaus," in *Cervantes y los casticismos españoles* (Madrid: Alfaragua, 1974), pp. 190–254.

9. *Frey*: a professing member of one of the Spanish military orders.

10. Domínguez Ortiz, op. cit., p. 50.

11. "Real carta permitiendo al aragonés Juan de Sánchez...llevar mercaderías a la isla Española...," in Fernandez de Navarrete, op. cit., Vol. II, p. 308.

12. Enrique Otte, *Las perlas del Caribe: Nueva Cádiz de Cubagua* (Caracas: Fundación John Boulton, 1977), pp. 72, 75, 403, 417, 422.

13. Claudio Guillén, op. cit., pp. 49–85.

14. Cristóbal Bermúdez Plata, *Catálogo de Pasajeros a Indias durante los siglos XVI, XVII, y XVIII* (Sevilla: Escuela de Estudios Hispanoamericanos, 1964), Vols, I and II.

15. Peter Boyd-Bowman, *Indice Geobiográfico de cuarenta mil pobladores españoles de América en el siglo XVI* (Bogotá: Instituto Caro y Cuervo, 1964), 2 vols.

16. Otte, op. cit., p. 72, and others.

17. Ruth Pike, *Aristócratas y comerciantes, la sociedad sevillana en el siglo XVI* (Barcelona: Ariel, 1978), p. 105; Claudio Guillen, "Un Padrón...," in op. cit., p. 71.

18. Miguel Pérez Almazán's cousin was also deeply involved with the assassination of the Inquisitor Arbués and, therefore, burned alive in 1487 in Zaragoza. Amador de los Ríos, op. cit., pp. 681–683, and "Sumaria y Memoria de los judíos conversos...," ibid.

19. Castro, op. cit., Note 15, pp. 280–281; Otte, op. cit., pp. 211–213, 312; Frank Moya Pons, *Historia Colonial de Santo Domingo* (Santo Domingo: Universidad Católica, 1976), pp. 64, 72–73. And, by the same author, *La Española en el siglo XVI* (Santo Domingo: Universidad Católica, 1973), pp. 24–25.

20. Fernando Ortiz, *Contrapunteo cubano del tabaco y del azúcar* (La Habana, 1963), p. 343; De las Casas, op. cit., Vol. III, pp. 273–275.

21. Amador de los Ríos, op. cit., pp. 623–627.

22. Bernal Díaz del Castillo, *Historia verdadera de la Conquista de la Nueva España* (Mexico: Porrúa, 1960), vol. II, pp. 186–187.

23. "Averiguación hecha por el Santo Oficio en lo de Alonso de Avila, acusado de tener un crucifijo debajo de su escritorio y poner los pies encima, Mexico 1537," Archivo General Nacional, *Inq. Index*, Vol. I.

24. "Proceso de Gonzalo Gómez, vecino de Michoacán, por palabras malsonantes, Mexico 1536," AGN, *Inq.*, Vol. 2, exp. 2.

25. "Proceso contra Gil González de Benavides por blasfemo, Mexico 1527," AGN, *Inq.*, Vol. 1, exp. 9ff. 44–45.

26. Eva A. Uchmany, "De algunos cristianos nuevos en la conquista y colonización de la Nueva España," in *Estudios de Historia Novohispana* VIII (1985), pp. 265–318.

27. Claudio Guillen, *op. cit.*, pp. 63–65.

28. Bernal Díaz del Castillo. op. cit., Vol. II., p. 929.

29. "Diligencias sobre los sambenitos antiguos y la renovación de ellos y la postura de los que se han relaxado y requerido por este Santo Oficio, Mexico 1574," AGN, *Inq.*, Vol. 77, exp. 35.

30. Otte, *Cubagua...*, pp. 198–299.

31. "Diligencias sobre los sambenitos...," in op. cit.; Uchmany, op. cit., ibid.

32. Pedro de Ocaña appears in the "Padrón...," under number 214.

33. "Proceso contra Juan Fernández del Castillo por hacer idolatrar a los indios, Mexico 1528," AGN, *Inq.*, Vol. 40, exp. 3 bis A, 4 folios.

34. "Proceso contra Juan Fernández del Castillo por blasfemo, Mexico 1536," AGN *Inq.*, Vol. 14, exp. 14ff., 118–119.

35. "Proceso contra Diego de Morales por hereje, Guatemala 1558." AGN México, *Inq.*, Vol. 31, exp. 2.; Uchmany, op. cit., ibid.

36. John Hemming, *The Conquest of the Incas* (London: MacMillan, 1970), p. 579, note 231.

37. Guillén, "Un padrón de conversos...," in op. cit., p. 80.

38. Castro, op. cit., p. 197.

39. *Sambenito*: a sackcloth resembling a scapular of the Benedictine order. This garment was worn by penitents on being reconciled to the Church or condemned to the fire for their heresies. It was made of yellow cloth painted with red crosses for the first group and of white or black cloth with painted devils and flames for the condemned impenitent.

40. "Cartas, Testimonios e Informaciones" sobre el Doctor Cristóbal de Miranda, in AGN México 1577, *Inq.*, Vol. 79, exp. 10, Vol. 80, exp. 8, 9, 10, 11, and 21; Vol. 82, exp. 34; Vol. 83, exp. 4; and México 1579 AGN *Inq.*, Vol. 82, exp. 14.

41. Castro, op. cit., p. 195.

42. Marcel Bataillon, "Santo Domingo 'era Portugual,' " in *Historia y sociedad en el mundo de habla española*, ed. Bernardo García Martínez (Mexico: El Colegio de México, 1970), pp. 113–120.

43. "Proceso contra Luis de Carvajal, gobernador del Nuevo Reino de León, por sospechoso en la ley de Moysén." México 1589, AGN, *Inq.*, Riva Palacio Collection, Vol. 22, exp. 3.

44. José Toribio Medina, *Historia del Tribunal de la Inquisición de Lima, 1596-1820*, ed. Marcel Bataillon (Santiago, Chile: Fondo Histórico J. T. Medina, 1956), Vol. I, pp. 175-176.

45. Eva Alexandra Uchmany, *La vida entre el judaísmo y el cristianismo en la Nueva España, 1580-1606*, and *Segundo Proceso del Santo Oficio contra Diego Díaz Nieto por judío judaizante, 1601-1606*, AGN, México, in press.

46. "Proceso criminal del Santo Oficio contra Diego Pérez de Alburquerque, natural de Francia, por judaizante, México 1624," AGN *Inq.*, Vol. 348ff., 167-549.

47. Medina, op. cit., Vol. II. p. 41.

48. "Proceso del Santo Oficio contra Julián de Alvarez Fugitivo, por judaizante, México 1634," AGN, *Inq.*, Vol. 431, exp. 3.

49. Manuel Tejado Fernández, *Aspectos de la vida social en Cartagena de Indias durante el seiscientos* (Sevilla: Escuela de Estudios Hispanoamericanos, 1954), pp. 147-152.

50. "Segundo proceso y causa criminal contra Isabel Núñez, natural de Francia, por judaizante, México 1643," AGN, *Inq.*, Vol. 380, exp. 5.

51. Medina, op. cit., pp. 93-96.

52. 'Testificación de Baltazar de Araujo contra Luis Franco Rodríguez,' in the "Proceso contra Luis Franco Rodrígues," in Tejado Fernández, op. cit., pp. 323-324.

53. Maria José Pimenta Ferro Tavares, *Judeus em Portugal no século XV* (Lisbon: Universidade Nova de Lisboa, 1982-1984).

54. Jaime Contreras, *El Santo Oficio de la Inquisición de Galicia* (Madrid: Akal, 1982), pp. 39-65.

55. José Ramón Onega. *Los judíos en el reino de Galicia* (Madrid: Editora Nacional, 1982), pp. 491-494.

56. "Proceso y causa criminal contra Juan Pacheco de León, alias Salomón Machorro, por judío judaizante, México 1642-1650," AGN, *Inq.*, Vol. 400, exp. 200.

57. Medina, op. cit., Vol. II, p. 93.

58. "Proceso criminal contra Simón Váez Sevilla por judaizante, México 1642-1649," AGN, *Inq.*, Vol. 398, exp. 1.

59. 'Denuncia de Gaspar de Villafranca en la audiencia del 2 de abril de 1595,' in the "Proceso criminal contra Manuel Díaz, mercader, por judaizante, México 1595-1596," Pelt Library, University of Pennsylvania, Henry Charles Lea Collection, MS. Lea 25.

60. "Cartas de don Francisco de Valverde Mercado, 1 de julio y 30 de julio de 1606, Puertobelo," Archivo de Indias, Sevilla, *Audiencia de Panamá*, exps. 718 y 725.

61. Eva Alexandra Uchmany, "Simón Váez Sevilla," in *Estudios de Historia Novohispana* IX (1987), pp. 67-93.

62. Boleslao Lewin, *Los Judíos bajo la Inquisición en Hispanoamérica* (Buenos Aires: Dédalo, 1960), pp. 53-69.

63. Tejado Fernández, op. cit., pp. 307-322.

64. José T. Medina, *Historia del Tribunal del Santo Oficio de la Inquisición en México* (Santiago, Chile, 1903), pp. 167–168.

65. "Primer proceso contra Baltzar del Valle, alias Baltazar Díaz, por judaizante, México 1622–1626," in Huntington Library, San Marino California, Vol. 17, HM 35111; and "Segundo Proceso contral Baltazar del Valle. . . por idem, México 1634," in Ibid., Vol. 23, HM 35117; and "Proceso contra Simón López, alias Marcos del Valle, por judaizante, México 1634–1637," in Thomas Gilcrease Institute of American History and Art, Tulsa Oklahoma, *Conway Collection*, Vol. 32.

66. "Testificación de Gaspar de Robles, México 1641," AGN, *Inq.*, Vol. 390, exp. 11, and "Causa criminal contra Francisco Home alias Vicente Enríquez, por judaizante, México 1641," AGN, *Inq.*, Vol. 391, exp. 1.

67. "Autos de Fe de la Inquisición de México, con extractos de sus causas, 1646–1648," in Genaro García, ed., *Documentos inéditos o muy raros para la historia de México* (México: Porrúa, 1974), pp. 132–259.

68. "Proceso y causa criminal contra Jorge de Montoya, fugitivo, por hereje judaizante, México 1642–1649," includes a letter from the Inquisition of Goa announcing the imprisonment and execution of Montoya. Huntington Library, MS 26 HM 35119, exp. 2.

69. Medina, *Historia del Tribunal. . . en México*, pp. 174–213.

70. Lewin, *Los judíos bajo la Inquisición. . .*, pp. 55–60.

71. "Pleitos sobre los bienes de Simón Váez Sevilla, México y Madrid 1660–1668," AHN Madrid, signatura 4806, cajas 1, 2, 3; signatura 4807, cajas 1, 2, 3.

72. "Diligencias contra algunos reconciliados que con pretexto de ir a embarcarse a Veracruz se quedaron en Puebla, México 1649," AGN, *Inq.*, Vol. 432, exp. 3; and "Cartas y órdenes" annexed to the "Proceso contra Simón Váez. . . México 1642–1649," AGN, *Inq.*, Vol. 398, exp. 1.

73. Medina, *Historia del Tribunal. . . Mexico*, pp. 277–280.

74. *Ibid.*, p. 275.

75. *Ibid.*, p. 268.

76. "Proceso del Santo Oficio contra don Diego Muñoz de Alvarado por judaizante, Puebla de Los Angeles 1682," AGN México, *Inq.*, Vol. 644, exp. 3.

77. "Carta a Pedro Muñoz de Alvarado" annexed to the "Proceso. . .contra Diego Muñoz de. . .," in Ibid.

78. Documents related to the property of Diego Muñoz de Alvarado can be found in AGN México, *Inq.*, Vol. 652, exp. 1, 2, 3; Vol. 653, exp. 1, 2, 3; all the documents in volumes 654, 655, 656, and 663.

79. "Proceso y causa criminal contra Fernando de Medina alias Moisés Gómez, francés, por judaizante, México 1691–1699," AGN, *Inq.*, Vol. 704, exp. 3.

80. Medina, *Inquisición de México. . .*, p. 336.

81. Medina, *La Inquisición de Lima. . .*, Vol. I, pp. 196–197.

82. Seymour B. Liebman, *New World Jewry, 1493-1825* (New York: Ktav, 1982), Chapter 8.

83. "Expediente formado con motivo de un abanico...con la historia de la reina Esther, México 1788," AGN, *Inq.*, Vol. 1103, 259-274ff.

84. "El Santo oficio contra Esteban de Zerecedo por hechos suspersiticiosos y judaísmo, México 1776," AGN, *Inq.*, Vol. 1108, exp. 10.

85. *Leviticus* 19:28.

86. "El Santo Oficio contra don Manuel Vázquez, por leer y retener libros de Voltaire y sospechas de judaísmo, México 1783," AGN, *Inq.*, Vol. 1283, exp. 5.

87. "Proceso contra Rafael Gil Rodríguez, fraile de San Francisco en el convento de Santa Ana Grande, Guatemala...por herejía formal y sospechas del judaísmo, México 1788-1795," AGN, *Inq.*, Vol. 1234, exp. 3.

88. "El Santo Oficio contra Pedro Bazán, español, por hereje judaizante, México 1781," AGN, *Inq.*, Vol. 1295, exp. 8.

89. Liebman, op. cit., p. 207.

90. "El Santo Oficio contra José Uruzal o Bruzal, francés, por sospechoso de ser judío, México 1785," AGN, *Inq.*, vol. 1032, exp. 6.

91. "El Santo Oficio contra don José Salomón, médico, por sospechoso de judío, Guatemala 1786," AGN México, *Inq.*, Vol. 1052, exp. 6.

92. Yoseph H. Yerushalmi, "Between Amsterdam and New Amsterdam: The Place of Curaçao and the Caribbean in Early Modern Jewish History," in *American Jewish History* 2 (1982), p. 185; and Jonathan Israel, "The Changing Role of the Dutch Sephardim in International Trade, 1595-1715," in *Dutch Jewish History*, (Jerusalem: Tel-Aviv U, 1984), pp. 44-49.

93. Harold Sharfman, *Jews on the Frontier* (Chicago: Henry Regnery Company, 1977), pp. 139-154.

94. Carta del Santo Oficio al Rey..." apud Medina, *Inquisición de México*, p. 362.

NINE

Cryptojews in Río de la Plata in the Seventeenth Century

Matilde Gini de Barnatán
Translated by Rachel Cassel

The persecutions of the Inquisition created waves of fugitives who, even though forbidden entrance to the New World, filtered through from the beginning, blessed by the sound of their Castilian and Portuguese last names.

The royal attitude forbidding converts from returning to their old faith, stated in the Expulsion Decree of 1492, is emphasized by an author who indicates: "The Inquisition did not come to America to guard the purity of the newly-converted Indians' faith. With the permanent danger of Judaism, the Inquisition was in the New World because of the risk that traditional religion would weaken or become degraded among the Spanish or European settlements separated from Old Christendom."[1]

The Inquisition worked to guard and control the colonies through three tribunals installed in Lima, Mexico, and Cartagena de Indias. The first, established in Lima by Philip II in 1590, was assigned all of South America. To it and the tribunal in Mexico, 1610 saw the addition of the one in Cartagena de Indias comprising New Granada, Tierrafirme, Hispaniola, all of the islands of Barlovento, provinces of Santo Domingo (the archbishopric of this city and of Santa Fe de Bogotá), and the bishoprics of Cartagena, Panamá, Santa Marta, Puerto Rico, Popayán, Venezuela, and Santiago de Cuba.

In all the territories of the provinces of Río de la Plata, only the cities of Mendoza, San Miguel de Tucumán and Asunción had been established. Buenos Aires had not yet been reestablished and was little more than a hamlet, which the arrival of the Holy Office must have affected greatly. The people were isolated, living in remote provinces.

Historical changes happened at the end of the sixteenth and throughout the seventeenth centuries, as the first clandestine Jewish immigration took place. Portuguese Jews fleeing Brazil took shelter in Río de la Plata, in spite of the laws that were in force. At times they came on slave ships protected or furnished with falsified permits by those who were profiting from excellent business.

Their presence is witnessed in vast numbers of documents, sometimes in veiled form as "the Portuguese" or "forbidden persons," or in a clear detailed form. (Keep in mind that at this time the word *Portuguese* was synonymous with *Jew*.[2]) Having achieved entry, the Portuguese took refuge in the inner provinces and formed prolific families. At times, they had the protection of priests who sheltered them in convents and refused to turn them over to the authorities, who came to prison at night and married off many of them to daughters of the city's inhabitants, or who offered a bond for those arrested until it could be proven that they were not 'forbidden' persons. Having thus obtained their freedom, these people fled to Asunción, Corrientes, or Santiago del Estero, where they could rely on the help of their fellow countrymen for absorption into the new environment.[3]

The Portuguese appear in vivid descriptions and accounts of the time, practicing diverse professions and trades—pharmacists, doctors, and craftsmen— with the great majority devoted to commerce so successfully that the Spaniards joined them to achieve greater progress. The difficulties facing business practices in those times—the slow means of communication and all the obstacles of travel— turned business trips into a true challenge to boldness and personal bravery. In spite of the strict watch of the Holy Office, colonial society adopted contradictory measures. Although one of the goals of the Consejo de Indias and the Casa de Contratación de Sevilla was to avoid strangers' coming to Río de la Plata, special licenses of varying duration were issued between 1602 and 1609.

REVEALING DOCUMENTS

In the work, *Comercio Impedido*, by the historian Pellicer d'Ossau, one document states: "These businessmen made full use of licenses, and are established in great number in Seville, Cadiz, Sanlucar, the Low Countries, and German ports." And it adds: "Those same ones have spread from Brazil to the East Indies, to Havana, to Cartagena de Indias, to Portobelo, to Charcas, Buenos Aires, and ports of Peru and New Spain." This happened during the union of Spain and Portugal. Even afterward, in repeatedly seeking the expulsion of the Portuguese, many difficulties arose, given that these people and their families were established both commercially and socially.

Among the diverse relevant sources is a document transcribed by the Argentine historian Vicente Fidel López from the year 1664, in which the governor presents a request "in the name of the neighborhood, asking for exemptions and requesting that the expulsion of their Portuguese neighbors not be carried out, in view of the decline and poverty of the Colony." Another document states: "Not only because they are rich, but because they have married and settled in the city, the measure, although much talked-of in the beginning, resulted in mere display."[4]

INFLUX OF THE PORTUGUESE

The pronounced influx of the Portuguese was especially heavy in the Panamá-Portobelo route[5] and from Brazil to Río de la Plata. Concern over the constant influx of these foreigners is seen especially in the repeated requests of the port officials for the installation of a tribunal of the Inquisition in the port of Río de la Plata. Numerous denunciations taken to the Inquisition in Lima tell of the entrance of Portuguese protected and concealed by coreligionists.[6] In a detailed letter dated 1635, the prosecutor of the court in Charcas, Sebastián de Alarcón, pointed out to his sovereign the problems caused by the presence of "so many innumerable Jews who have entered and continue to enter in greater abundance in these parts. . ."

For his part, the lawyer Francisco de Trejo, in a detailed letter to the Holy Office in Lima also indicates: "We consider as certain that many people will come fleeing, Jews from Spain and from Brazil. . .the ease with which the Jews enter and leave this port cries out for help, for we cannot rectify the situation; as they are all Portuguese, they cover for each other."

In fact, the entry forbidden by the unfortunately famous Statute of Purity of Blood which asserted that "neither Jew, nor Moor, nor heretic, nor son or grandson of a burned one, a reconciled or a dishonored person can enter the Indies. . ." was repeatedly circumvented by way of false documents or false certificates of purity. We see an illustration in the trial records of Francisco de Antonio, from the Archivo Histórico Nacional in Toledo: "And the aforesaid man spoke of many things that had happened in his life in the Indies and in Florence, and how in Florence he had communicated with a Portuguese who was a great Jew and very rich named Enriquillo, who in the time that he was there was the only one with whom he dealt, and who had given false information of being an old Christian to go to the Indies, and that in those parts there were many Jews."[7]

A KEY PIECE

A search of archives reveals real living reports, useful information to clarify the colonial past. In this case, documents from the Sevillian archives throw light on unknown details of one of the earliest groups of people settled in Río de la Plata. It deals with the expedition of Ortiz de Zárate (1570–1572) who obtained "royal permits" after several problems, which required that each passenger not have any debts, be an honest person and, if married, leave his wife and children in favorable circumstances. The intention was to choose "peaceful, upright, and hardworking" people to form a settlement of "up to two hundred men and as many of those as possible married and bringing their wives; and to endeavor to choose honorable people, quiet and peaceful, so that they could handle the affairs of governing the republic and also provide workers for the benefit of those lands." In all, 280 people arrived at their destination, and it is very important to note that these settlers were exempted from having a license of purity of blood, usually required by the Casa de Contratación. This curious document, which awarded the license "without asking any of them or demanding from any of them information,"[8] becomes a very revealing key to the introduction of the phenomenon of Crypto-Judaism in the New World.

If we look at these semi-secret official immigrations from a distance, prominent figures of the colony show up. The first bishop of Tucumán, Friar Francisco de Vitoria, was the object of repeated denunciations due to his Jewish lineage. One of the first trials of the Holy Office in Río de la Plata took place against Diego Pérez de Acosta, brother of this priest, who managed to flee the Inquisition and take refuge in Italy with the help of his brother, as the documents suggest.[9] Relatives of the bishop lived openly as Jews in Europe under the last names of Duarte, Acosta, Nuñez, and Curiel.

THE LEÓN PINELO FAMILY

In this period of contradictory social climate, the noted León Pinelo family, children of the Portuguese convert Diego López de Lisboa, stands out. Although their Jewish origin was well-known, the Inquisition never bothered them, as they had been careful to avoid suspicion on entering the port of Buenos Aires by purchasing references as "Old Christians" from a certain Navarro.

However, a very telling incident unleashed denunciations for suspicion of heretical practices in the very house of Don Diego de Lisboa. It did not go unnoticed by the officials of the Inquisition that Don Diego and other Portuguese people met behind closed doors guarded by a servant one Holy Thursday. It was not a proper night for a game of cards as these people asserted. We find the explanation in the date: they surely were gathered in secret to celebrate the Jewish Passover, coinciding with the Holy Week. (The Jewish celebration of secret rites continually appears in trial records.) Don Diego de Lisboa constantly faced jokes and young people who "called and shouted saying: Come out, you Jew, Diego de Lisboa," or "throw this Jew out of his house," despite his serving as steward for the Archbishop Diego de Ugarte. The priest's protection apparently saved Don Diego de Lisboa and his family from the clutches of the Inquisition. This can be assumed from the professions of his sons: Don Rodríguez de León, his oldest son, was a cleric in Puebla de los Angeles. His second son, the well-known Antonio de León Pinelo, served as court reporter for the Consejo de Indias. And the third, Don Diego de León Pinelo, renowned man of letters in

Lima, held the position of lawyer for the Royal Court. It is extremely interesting to study the destiny of this entire family who continued their lives and professions without opposition in the midst of the social unrest during this period.[10]

A TALENTED SCULPTOR

As we have shown, the integration of the Portuguese into colonial society and their occupations of goldsmith, artesan, silversmith, and businessman speak to strong mercantile activity. Among these people, the famous sculptor Manuel de Coyto stands out, in whose studio other artists were trained and who was the creator of the very beautiful Christ carved at the time for the Cathedral in Buenos Aires.[11] In spite of being sentenced to four years in prison in Validivia, Chile, for certain heretic sentiments, this famous sculptor managed to escape punishment and continued working on a statue of Saint Michael for the fortress of Buenos Aires.

THE ENSIGN RODRÍGUEZ ESTELA

Among the most interesting cases in the Trials of Faith of the seventeenth century is that of the ensign Juan Rodríguez Estela, a Portuguese convict in Lisbon who, fleeing from Brazil, had settled in Buenos Aires with his family many years earlier. Under evidence from Spain, he was imprisoned and his property was seized in 1673. Sent to Tucumán and Potosí, he was placed in secret jails a year later, declaring himself a New Christian on both parents' sides, having been baptized in Lisbon and worked for twenty years as the prefect of the Company of Jesus in that port. Pressured by the officials of the Inquisition and not knowing the prayers of the church, "he ended up confessing that he was of the Jewish faith and raising his hands and in tears he begged for mercy, saying that his father taught him the faith and the ceremonies of the Law of Moses until the age of fifteen when he left Lisbon, and as soon as he entered Río de Janeiro, he forgot it completely."[12]

While Estela remained in prison, the inquires continued, to find more information for the case, but there are no further details to tell us his fate. Nevertheless, the appearance of a valuable document among the early wills in Río de la Plata has allowed me to discover the introduction of the ensign, his wife, and children into Buenos Aires society, useful information that allows us to reconstruct the family's history. The document is a detailed will of Doña Catalina de Aguilar, wife of the ensign Estela. In it appear possessions and the dowry received at the wedding, as well as the couple's children: Juan Francisco, Duarte Rodríguez Estela, and Francisco Pérez de Burgos. We should note that the last son changed his paternal last name for that of his grandfather on his mother's side.[13] Professor Boleslao Lewin points out that Rodríguez Estela is an ancestor of the exalted Juan Martín de Pueyrredón.

TRIAL OF THE HENRÍQUEZ FAMILY

The trial of the Henríquez family sheds light on the proceedings and inquiries carried out by the Holy Office against families who, fleeing Inquisition persecution in Spain, tried to hide in South America. Let us look at some aspects of this case.

On August 30, 1656, a ship arrived at the Peruvian port of Callao. On it were the Spanish doctor Rodrigo Henríquez de Fonseca, his wife Leonor de Andrade, a baby daughter only eight months old, and Leonor's brother, Luis de Rivero—all held prisoner by the Holy Office. After a storm, they arrived and were immediately locked in the secret jails of the Inquisition. They did not know that their possessions, which they had believed lost in the storm—three locked hampers, a trunk, and a slave they possessed—had been seized, as was customary, by the Inquisition.

The Henríquez family were 'forbidden' persons because of their secret clinging to the Jewish faith. The first denunciations came from Málaga, where certain expressions and attitudes of Doctor Henríquez awoke the first suspicions that put the inquisitional machinery into motion, crossing continents and oceans to reach the relatives of those suspected. These people, the majority accused or punished, supplied information for the inquiries.

Several years had passed and the traces of our subjects had been lost when the Inquisition in Lima received new information. In a letter dated 1655, we learn that Doctor Henríquez and his wife had gone from Buenos Aires to Paraguay and Tucumán. On October 30 of the same year, warrants for the arrest of both were issued along with an order for the seizure of their belongings. New information showed that they had moved from Tucumán to Chile, settled in Santiago, and changed their names to Diego and Francisca de Sotelo. Nevertheless, the inquisitors, sure of having found the fugitives, sent the necessary orders in January 1656.

They were soon captured, their possessions seized, and they were sent to Lima on the first boat. Neither the change of name nor the distance was sufficient protection from the danger that lay in wait for them. In a letter to the court of the Holy Office by the Inquisitor Alvaro de Ibarra dated September 1, 1656, he testifies that the Henríquez couple as well as Luis de Rivero, Leonor's brother, were already in jail, although they denied the charge of clinging to the Jewish faith.

However, a little while later, Leonor confessed that her relatives had been imprisoned by the Inquisition of Toledo and Granada. On their part, Andrés de Fonseca, his wife Isabel Henríquez, as well as Luis Henríquez and his wife Guiomar, (parents and brother and sister-in-law of Dr. Henríquez) had not escaped punishment either; they were prisoners in Spain, accused also of Judaizing.

Meanwhile, Luis de Rivero also confessed that all of his family observed the rites and ceremonies of the Law of Moses. The following day he was to denounce his sister. This event meant a certain death sentence for her, but he was found dead in his cell. Faced with that situation, he decided to take his own life, inflicting a deep wound in his arm and bleeding to death.

The trial continued unrelentingly. In another letter from 1660, the inquisitors tell that the accused continued denying the charges, a useless denial in view of the discovery that Doctor Henríquez was circumcised.

In January 1661, they subjected Leonor to torture on the rack, "forcing her with the first turn to confess to whatever they wished." A month later, Don Rodrigo, faced with the same test, resisted four turns without confessing. Placed again under torture a short while later, his strength left him, and he confessed.

Finally, in the *Auto de Fe* held on January 23, 1664, in Acho Plaza, the tormented lives of Rodrigo Henríquez de Fonseca and his wife Leonor de Andrade ended, as they were burned alive.[14] As happened with many children and even entire families in similar circumstances, the fate of the young daughter of the Henríquez couple is unknown.

BUENOS AIRES GENEALOGIES

The groups of relatives who emigrated from certain regions of Spain at the end of the sixteenth century awoke the curiosity of genealogists, who could not explain these emigrations, even when certain keys to the adventure in America appeared in their reports.

> Although not all those listed were relatives, some were, as we have been able to establish. This, in addition to their coming from certain regions on the Spanish map, leads us to believe that it was migrations of tightly knit family units with relatives based in far-off Peru or Chile. The person considered head of the group, once established, assured the possibilities for the success of the new settlers. It can also be assumed that the move was motivated not by a summons from the absent relative in the Indies, but by the invitation implied in news coming from the New World, offering a promising future. Be it one or the other, the migration was not effectuated by chance, but was organized and directed. It is strange, but not accidental, this influx of persons with the same last names, relatives of each other, coming from the same region and at times the same place (city, village, hamlet, or simple settlement), whose inhabitants could not be numerous, judging by the sparsity of the population in those times, when Spain had not yet recuperated from the Reconquest, whose end was contemporaneous with the Discovery.

José Torre Revello, researcher on the colonial period, answers these questions with illuminating information in his book, *La sociedad colonial*:

> Notice that from the beginnings of Spanish dominion the settlers heading for Río de la Plata enjoyed a privilege that perhaps would protect them, which was that there was no investigation into their past, nor their family's past, nor an examination of their nationality. On the other hand,

the sale of licenses to travel, including their falsification, was another door used by many disinherited people to reach our shores.[15]

We find documented examples illustrating these procedures, as well as entry without the aforementioned license, such as in the case taken from the *Revista del Instituto de Ciencias Genealógicas*:

> Don Bernabé González Filiano, born on the island of Tenerife, accused of being a passenger without a royally issued license or profession, must have been Castilian because of the crime he committed before reembarking on the coast. But upon marrying a Castilian woman, neighbor and descendent of the conquistadors (granddaughter of Irala), he was forgiven because the law protected him. Later, he was sentenced to permanent exile. But this was not carried out, given the fact that we find his will.

Numerous denunciations and briefs are brought to the Holy Office, and suspicion abounds in religious matters and heresy; persecution against the Portuguese suspected of secretly practicing Judaism grows greater and greater.

The denunciation of a Dominican priest is remarkable: at his death, another priest of his order, Friar Jerónimo Peña, ordered an Indian to wash the body of the deceased and then to dress it in the Dominican habit. This gave rise to a trial to determine "if he had done so that, knowing the moral position of the criminal, no one could investigate further." Another singular trial in Río de la Plata was that of the Portuguese Juan Acuña de Noroña, who was burned alive in the *Auto de Fe* in 1625, his possessions having been seized. His trial showed that he had descended from Jews, did not attend mass, always spoke about the Old Testament, and his usual saying was: "Praise God, the Lord of heaven be blessed. How great is the God of Israel, Abraham, Isaac, and Jacob. . ."

FRANCISCO MALDONADO DE SILVA: AMERICAN MARTYR

The dramatic trial of Francisco Maldonado de Silva shows in great detail the activity of repressive machination, as an instrument and exercise of terror, intolerance directed toward a minority in society. The tragedy of the Creole Maldonado de Silva who died in the flames for his faith, makes him a symbol of the American martyr.

In the year 1627, Francisco Maldonado de Silva was a doctor in Tucumán, Chile. His father, Diego Nuñez de Silva, was one of the first doctors of the colony and practiced his profession in the province of Córdoba. He had already been tried along with another son of his, and both had completed their sentence. (Both had been accused of Judaism and accepted 'reconciliation,' a term for those who, having been discovered for the first time, formally promised to 'mend their ways.') Diego secretly continued to practice his faith and taught his son,

Francisco, the Jewish tradition from childhood, forcing him to keep it a secret from his mother and sisters. Francisco, married to an Old Christian and father of a daughter, became a fervent Jew through readings of the Old Testament and other texts and carried out the traditions as much a possible, going to the extreme of performing circumcision on himself when his wife was away. When he tried to pass his secret faith on to his sisters, one of them, Felipa, denounced him to the Holy Office. He was then placed in a secret jail, his belongings were confiscated, and he was moved to the prison in Valladolid.

In his first declaration, he refused to swear with his hand on the cross, saying, "I am a Jew, sir, and I practice the Law of Moses, and by it I will live and die; if I have to swear, I will swear by the living God who made heaven and earth and is the God of Israel." This declaration is rare in the history of defendants who generally tried to negate or diminish their charges and show that they were 'repentant.' Maldonado de Silva or "Heli Nazareo," as he decided to call himself, remained true to his faith throughout his trial. With infinite patience, covering every scrap of paper he could find with minute writing, using a pen made from a chicken bone, he tried to reveal his convictions, born from his reflections and his faith, always maintaining that unwavering attitude, in spite of repeated threats and interviews designed to dissuade him.

In this way, he spent twelve years in Inquisition jails. When he finally appears in the *Auto de Fe* to die in the fire, he is "thin, greying, with a beard and long hair, with the books he had written tied around his neck." At three in the afternoon, a wind blew up, something unusual at this time in Lima, whipped around and destroyed the awning of the platform prepared for the evil ceremony. Maldonado de Silva raised his eyes and exclaimed: "The God of Israel has done this so that he can see me face to face from heaven..."[16]

An important fact revealed by the documents on Maldonade de Silva was the connection and communications among American Crypto-Jews. He gave letters to other prisoners to be delivered to the synagogue in Rome. Other documents show the connections of the American Cryto-Jews with others established in Bayonne, La Rochelle, and St. Jean de Luz.

THE UNDERLYING PAST

These brief notes offer only a reflection of a shadowy world. Fugitives in Río de la Plata and other parts of America, many from families decimated by the Holy Office, looking for hope in these lands, practiced silence and furtiveness to save their lives and those of their descendents. A large majority assimilated into that society to the point that they erased their origins and lost their roots in forgetfulness. Other survivors of Crypto-Jewish communities, whose members are descendents of the persecuted ones, keep those traditions to this day, even in times of Jewish-Christian rapproachement. In Río de la Plata, one finds traces of this past in the "Israelita del Nuevo Pacto" group, a Crypto-Jewish community that has survived and keeps Jewish traditions and some religious rites of this symbiosis. The reality of the underlying past can also be glimpsed in the last names of converts and the phenomena which form part of collective memory.[17]

INQUISITORIAL SPIRIT

The most significant fact to emerge from the presence of Jews arriving from Spain and Portugal to form an active part of the society of the time, is the double life and the rise of Crypto-Judaism as a defense against dictatorial power. This phenomenon has left cultural indications which can be traced basically in genealogical studies. Not to be forgotten are the valuable sources of information coming from documents that the Chilean writer José Toribio Medina found in the Archivos de Simancas, as well as in the Archivos de Indias, Archivo Histórico y Biblioteca Nacional de Madrid and others from Spain, the Archivo Histórico Torre y Tombo in Portugal, Archivo General de la Nación in Mexico, Lima, and Chile, and innumerable documents found throughout European and American archives, private family resources, and also the horrifying testimony from the prison of the Holy Office in Lima.

The prolonged development of the inquisitorial legal process has left deep traces in certain structures of modern societies. In fact, recent tragic events in Argentina could not have taken place without the rigid structures modeled after that institution persisting in some social areas. There have been no differences in the introduction of terror, police control, black lists, people's disappearing, trials without the right of defense, driven by power in a society that turns its members into suspects.

To recognize this inquisitorial spirit is to look at the research with new eyes, ridding ourselves of prejudices that mask our knowledge of the historic evolution of America, coming to the phenomenon of the Inquisition and its own basis of ideological and religious content, and the development of 'social control' as a set procedure.

To recognize this inquisitorial spirit is to point out dangerous parallels in contemporary societies and leads to the analysis of areas of interest not only to historians, but also to ethnologists, anthropologists, sociologists, psychologists, students of law and religion, and many others.

To recognize this inquisitorial spirit is, in short, to alert younger generations to study, know, and circulate the historic reality to achieve a more humane society. This same spirit—with its ghosts, infamies, and fires—is not foreign to today's America, so wounded and tattered.

NOTES

1. Marcel Bataillon, Prologue to *Historia de la Inquisición de Lima (1569–1820)*, José Toribio Medina, ed. (Santiago de Chile: Nascimento, 1956).

2. This fact has created confusion in understanding information, presenting the 'Portuguese' settlers as Jews. In those times, that type of information or census was impossible.

3. José Toribio Medina, *La Inquisición en el Río de la Plata* (Buenos Aires; Huarpes, 1945). Carta al Tribunal de Lime, Buenos Aires, Abril de 1619.

4. Vicente Fidel López, *Historia de la República Argentina*, Vol. I, Chap. IX, "Carácter económico de la colonización argentina en sus primeros años" (Argentina: Sopena, 1944).

5. Alberto Osorio O., *Judaísmo e Inquisición en Panamá colonial* (Panama: Instituto Cultural Panamá-Israel, 1980).

6. Toribio Medina, *La Inquisición en el Río de la Plata*, ibid.

7. Archivo Histórico Nacional, Madrid, "Inquisición de Toledo."

8. Archivo General de Indias, Sección y audiencia de Buenos Aires, Lib. IV, fol. 58. Quoted by José Torre Revello, *La sociedad colonial* (Buenos Aires: Ediciones Pennedille, 1970), Chap. I; Guillermo Furlong, *Trasplante cultural y social* (Buenos Aires: Ed. TEA, 1969).

9. Toribio Medina, *La Inquisición en el Río de la Plata*, Chap. VI, "Los portugueses en el Río de la Plata."

10. Ibid., "Sección Documentos, Autos y Diligencias obrados en el Tribunal de Lima, relativo al Licenciado Diego López de Lisboa (Relación de testigos)," in Toribio Medina, ibid.

11. Guillermo Furlong, *Historia social y cultural del Río de la Plata (1536–1810)* (Buenos Aires: Ed. TEA 1969), "Las tallas, escultores y tallistas."

12. Toribio Medina, *La Inquisición en el Río de la Plata*, Chap. X, "Continúan los procesos de fe del siglo XVII".

13. *Genealogía*, Revista del Instituto Argentino de Ciencias Genealógicas, Buenos Aires.

14. José Toribio Medina, *Historia del Tribunal del Santo Oficio de la Inquisición en Chile* (Santiago de Chile: Ed. Universitaria) Chap. IX, "De familia de judíos".

15. José Torres Revello, *La sociedad colonial*, Sección Audiencias de Buenos Aires, Lib. IV, fol. 58.

16. "Proceso Francisco Maldonado de Silva", Inquisición Lima, lib. 1031, Archivo Histórico Nacional Madrid, Sección Inquisición. Toribio Medina, *La Inquisición en el Río de la Plata*, Chap. VII, "Proceso de Maldonado de Silva." José Toribio Medina, *Historia del Tribunal de la Inquisición de Lima*, segunda parte, Chap. XVI.

17. Matilde Gini de Barnatán, "Inquisición y cripto-judaísmo en Hispanoamérica: comunidades actuales," *Maguen* 41 (Publication of the Asociación Israelita de Venezuela y del Centro de Estudios Sefardíes de Caracas).

PART TWO

Language and Literature

Introduction by David M. Gitlitz

The term 'Sephardic Literature' is too broad to have much practical use, even when it is limited to the classic definition of *Sephardic* as pertaining to the Judaic culture of Spain. The scope of the term includes such widely diverse works as eleventh-century philosophical treatises written in Hebrew or Arabic in Al-Andalus; polemical literature of seventeenth-century Castile dealing with the conversion issue; ballads recovered from the oral tradition in Macedonia; the Gongoresque verses and Calderonian plays of seventeenth-century Marrano writers in Amsterdam; Turkish Ladino novels from the 1880s; modern Israeli short stories dealing with Sephardic themes; late medieval responsa and the hymns of the mystics of Safed. The language of composition of these works may be Hebrew, Arabic, Spanish or Judeo-Spanish (Castilian, Catalonian, Galician, or any of their Judeo-dialects), Portuguese, Italian, Ladino, Turkish, English, Serbian, or what have you. The themes may be secular or religious, historical, philo-sophical, contemplative, or fictitious. The span of composition covers a thousand years. The geographic range of Sephardic literatures extends from Spain through the countries of the Spanish *galut*. It includes material by non-Sephardis on Sephardic themes, and by Sephardis on themes which have nothing to do with Judaic culture. The most one can assert, then, is that Sephardic literature is in some way related to Judaism and in some way related to Spain.

The very imprecision of the term, however, gives an indication of the vast wealth of material that exists. Some aspects of this terrain have been well studied. The philosophers and poets of the Spanish Golden Age, people like Maimonides, Halevy, and Ben Ezra have received a lot of attention. In the later Spanish Christian Golden Age, I and some of my colleagues have dealt with Judaic themes in the works of mainstream Christian authors like Cervantes, Lope de Vega, Quevedo, and Alemán. Iacob Hassán and his group in Madrid have cast light on Moroccan Sephardic culture. And there are many superb individual studies dealing with the Sephardic experience in the Americas, Europe, the Maghreb, and the Levant. But even so, the surface has barely been scratched.

The chapters included in Part II are typical of the wide-ranging interests of Sephardic literary and linguistic scholars. Joshua Blau's analysis of the influence of Spanish-Arabic dialects on Maimonides' Hebrew contributes to our knowledge of certain linguistic features of Maimonides' prose and also of the Rambam's attitudes regarding Judeo-Spanish customs. Paul Wexler's brief stemma of the Judeo-Ibero-Romance languages clarifies with remarkable precision the complex linguistic history of the Jews in Spain, making the case for the derivation of dialects such as Judeo-Catalán and Judeo-Galician from Judeo-Latin, and the relative modernity and eventual dominance of Judeo-Castilian. Paloma Díaz Mas' discussion of toponyms and anthroponyms in Moroccan Sephardic *romances* 'ballads' sheds light on the persistence of certain historic and geographic peninsular traditions among the Moroccan Sephardis.

Woven throughout all three of these chapters is a common thread: that during the millennium and a half in which Jews prospered or suffered on the Iberian Peninsula, an indelible Hispanic stamp was put on both their languages and their attitudes about Spain.

These three chapters are similarly indicative of the extraordinary range of topics encompassed by the term *Sephardic*. Carlos Mota's penetrating analysis of Villasandino's fifteenth-century satires against Alfonso Ferrandes provides insights into the complex attitudes toward forced conversion that dominate the literary polemics that survive from the courts of the Trastamara kings. Whether or not Villasandino was himself a convert, it is clear that he had detailed knowledge of the religious and social customs of the New Christians. The bitterly ironic scorn that he heaps on them opens a window for us onto the complex interpersonal relationships of that world. Particularly interesting are Mota's comments on the probable performance characteristics of this courtly satiric poetry.

Helen Shepard's discussion of the intellectual traditions that underlie Camilo Castelo Branco's late nineteenth-century novels ties this Portuguese writer into an important European liberal tradition. Together with people like Disraeli, George Eliot, and Benito Pérez Galdós, Castelo Branco's liberal anti-clericalism condemned the excesses of the Catholic church, as embodied in the Inquisition, and as a corollary praised Hispanic Jews and converts as exponents of liberal ideals.

Sandra Cypess's analysis of two modern Latin American plays involving Jewish characters—Sabina Berman's *Herejía* and Alfredo Dias Gomes' *O Santo Inquérito*—shed light on Brazil's and Mexico's recent interest in their multireligious and multicultural historical past. For these writers, the Inquisition and its persecution of colonial New Christians represent at one and the same time a metaphor for autocratic intolerance and repression, and a criticism of the universal danger of fanatic faith combined with greed.

These chapters are typical of the renaissance of studies dealing with Sephardic themes. Until recently, most mainstream historians, linguists, literary critics, and artists in Spain and in the far-flung homelands of the Sephardic diaspora, have focused their attention on the dominant Christian or Islamic cultures. But as the new generation of scholars has probed the roots of their cultural development, they have come to realize the importance of understanding the Sephardic element in their midst. Sephardim themselves—in the wake of the Holocaust, the establishment of the national homeland in Israel, and the United States—have come to take new pride in the complexities of their history and their power of survival in the face of centuries of pressure to assimilate.

Scholarly momentum is building, but there is still important work to be done. The last generation of Sephardim with personal ties to the ancient homelands is rapidly growing older in retirement communities in Israel and the United States. In a short while, the chance to interview them for firsthand recollections of their experiences in the cultures in which they were raised will be lost to us. One task, then, is to concentrate effort in recording—on tape and on film—as much of this tradition as possible before it is lost.

A second task is to locate and put into the public venue in the world's great libraries manuscripts and other printed material in Ladino (and related languages and dialects) before it, too, crumbles away. Scholars must hunt down the secular and religious books that immigrants brought with them from Turkey and the Maghreb before these materials disappear as households are broken up and the immigrant generation fades away.

Third, the vast storehouse of Sephardic secular and religious literature in the Hebrew University library, the Biblioteca Nacional in Madrid, the Vatican Library, the Library of Congress, Weidner Library, and others must be more accurately catalogued and surveyed so that it can become available to scholars. Some of it, at least the most important works, will have to be transliterated from the *Rashi* script, which is inaccessible to most modern audiences. Some truly seminal works should be translated into English—as *Me'am Lo'ez* has become the *Torah* anthology—or into other modern languages.

Finally, once this wealth of material has been found, catalogued, and made accessible, the exciting work of historical and literary summary and critical analysis can begin in earnest.

TEN

Camilo Castelo Branco and the Portuguese Inquisition

Helen A. Shepard

The problem of the Inquisition and its effect on the intellectual and spiritual values of Spain and Portugal has become an increasingly important theme for Hispanists since the middle of the nineteenth century. The Inquisition was at an end for less than a generation when historians such as Alexandre Herculano[1] and José Amador de los Ríos[2] began researching archives and inquisitional records which spanned three hundred and fifty years of the repressions of the Holy Office in Iberia. In more recent years, Américo Castro,[3] Yitzhak Baer,[4] Cecil Roth,[5] and Julio Caro Baroja,[6] (to mention only a few) have added many volumes and years of research and investigation to help unfold the tale of those who suffered and died for reasons of faith in Iberia. Renewed interest in Hebrew letters and in the contributions of the Jews to the culture of Iberia during the late Middle Ages has given impetus to much new scholarship in this area. In intellectual circles in Madrid in the two decades prior to the demise of the Franco regime, there was a heated polemic as to whether the Jewish Moorish existence in Iberia was or was not a formative factor in Iberian civilization. Américo Castro's theories on the Jewish underpinnings of Spanish culture were used to combat those of the historian, Sánchez-Albornoz, who believed Spain and Portugal since Roman and Visigothic times have been entirely a Christian entity with only slightly lasting influence, if at all, from Semitic sources. These arguments have been carried to Hispanic circles in the United States and there were enclaves of those for and those against Américo Castro's ideas in some university departments. Since the study of Portuguese letters has often been slighted to a great degree in favor of Spanish, the question of Portugal's importance in the Judeo-Iberian problem seldom comes up, although both countries were united for a long period at the height of the Inquisition in Iberia.

In the early nineteenth century in both Portugal and Spain, the dominant intellectual current was the Europeanizing of the Iberian Peninsula. The Napoleonic Wars had brought both French and English ideas to Iberia, and the generation following the end of the Napoleonic Era was one of great intellectual ferment and transition. The anti-clerical feelings of the French intellectuals and the English hostility toward the Church of Rome made themselves felt in every area of intellectual endeavor. Both Spanish and Portuguese writers of the nineteenth century believed that the Europeanization of their countries depended upon a strong stand against clericalism. Even though they were willing to recognize the ideal morality taught by the gospels, they tried not to confuse this idealism with the institutionalized practices of the Church itself. Benito Pérez Galdós, in his novel *Doña Perfecta*, attacked the unconscious bigotry of those who accepted institutionalized Christianity. He, however, never permitted himself an attack against Christian ethics or morality. He avoided the agnostic's view, but he unhesitatingly attacked the abuses of the clergy, intolerance, and prejudice. Like a true liberal of the nineteenth century, he contrasted the advances of science to the medievalism of the state religion.

Camilo Castelo Branco, an older contemporary of Galdós, believed that Portugal could become part of the liberal scientific community only if it freed itself from its adherence to medieval Catholicism. His hatred for the clergy parallels Galdós's written attacks against the ecclesiastical suppressions of the intellectual life of Spain. Camilo believed that by incorporating into his work the most intolerant and fanatical aspects of Portuguese history he could mobilize the sentiments of his readers sufficiently to make them receptive to liberal ideas. In order to emphasize the oppressive system under which the Portuguese had lived for so many centuries, he chose that aspect of Portuguese history that had been repeatedly held up as an example of intolerance by European liberals—the Inquisition. In this he followed Voltaire who satirized the Portuguese Inquisition in *Candide* and *Traité sur la tolerance*. He took up the standard also from his friend, Alexandre Herculano, who had written against the clergy and was to spend the mature years of his life publishing his research on the Portuguese Inquisition. In the course of his research, Herculano discovered that the Inquisition was almost exclusively concerned with the suppression of Judaism. This fact led him to use the Jews as exponents for his liberal tendencies. Camilo follows in Herculano's footsteps and uses inquisitional suppression of Crypto-Jews as the main weapon against the tyranny of the state religion of Portugal. Thus, in Portugal, the Jew hounded by the Inquisition became the representative for liberal thought.

In the nineteenth century, the Jew began to play an increasingly important role in fiction. In the minds of many authors, Christian intolerance of Jews represented the basic impediment to liberalism. A few examples of the Jew in nineteenth-century fiction will reveal the foundation of a Pan-European movement upon which Camilo Castelo Branco built his novel, *O Judeu*.[7]

In 1844, Benjamin D'Israeli wrote his novel *Coningsby*,[8] in which the Jewish character, Sidonia, a philosopher, financier, and diplomat, a native of England, speaks of Christianity's debt to Judaism. D'Israeli attempts to enlighten Englishmen on the position of the descendents of the race whose religion laid the foundations of Christianity, and he goes so far as to regard Christianity as the "Judaism of the multitude." He insists repeatedly that the moral and ethical beauties of Christianity are all Jewish. In his preface to *Coningsby*, D'Israeli asserts his opinions on the Church's place in the politics of England and makes the following shrewd comments on the foundation of Christianity and anti-Semitism, a view antedating Freud's insights by a century. In his essay, *Moses and Monotheism*,[9] Freud sees the origin of anti-Semitism as the reaction of newly converted pagans to the restriction of instinctual freedoms imposed by Christianity. In Freud's view, these restrictions were blamed on the Jews. In D'Israeli's preface to *Coningsby*, he reflects on medieval Christianity:

> The Jews were looked upon in the middle ages as an accursed race, the enemies of God and man, the especial foes of Christianity. No one in those days paused to reflect that Christianity was founded by the Jews; that its Divine Author, in his human capacity, was a descendent of King David; that his doctrines avowedly were the completion, not the change, of Judaism; that the Apostles and the Evangelists, whose names men daily invoked, and whose volumes they embraced with reverence, were all Jews; that the infallible throne of Rome itself was established by a Jew; and that a Jew was the founder of the Christian Churches of Asia.

D'Israeli goes on to say:

> The European nations, relatively speaking, were then only recently converted to a belief in Moses and in Christ; and, as it were, still ashamed of the wild deities whom they had deserted, they thought they atoned for their past idolatry by wreaking their vengeance on a race to whom, and to whom alone, they were indebted for the Gospel they adored.

George Eliot treats Jewish characters with great sympathy in her novel *Daniel Deronda*,[10] one of her more elaborate productions. In preparing for this work, she familiarized herself with Jewish literature and traditions. Her purpose in writing this novel was to correct the intolerant and prejudiced opinions of her countrymen. She expressed this attitude in a letter she wrote to Harriet Beecher Stowe on October 29, 1876:

> Toward the Hebrews we Western people who have been reared in Christianity have a peculiar debt, and whether we acknowledge it or not, a peculiar thoroughness of fellowship in religious and moral sentiment. Can anything be more disgusting than to hear people called 'educated' making small jokes about eating ham, and showing themselves

empty of any real knowledge as to the relation of their own social and religious life to the history of the people they think themselves witty in insulting? And I find men, educated, supposing that Christ spoke Greek. To my feeling, this deadness to the history which has prepared half our world for us, this inability to find interest in any form of life that is not clad in the same coat-tails and flounces as our own, lies very close to the worst kind of irreligion. The best that can be said of it is that it is a sign of the intellectual narrowness—in plain English—the stupidity—which is still the average mark of our culture.

In Spain, Benito Pérez Galdós attacked fanaticism by exposing the anti-Semitism implicit in Spanish life in his novel, *Gloria*, of 1877, written eleven years after the publication of *O Judeu*, Camilo's two-volume novel. So popular was the theme of prejudice against Jews that this novel was immediately translated into English and French and became the foundation of Galdós's European reputation. The plot of the novel is reminiscent of Lessing's one-act drama *Die Juden*. A surviver of a shipwreck is taken into the home of a pious Catholic family in Spain. He is nursed back to health by the daughter of the family, Gloria. The survivor and Gloria fall in love, and all agree to the marriage until it is discovered that the survivor is not merely a German, as they thought, but a German Jew. Both the Jew and Gloria are hounded by an unthinking and illogical prejudice that destroys their lives. Throughout the book, the survivor is the spokesman for a liberal universalism that is almost a transcription of the doctrine of Lessing's play, *Die Juden*, which deals with a traveler who saves the life of a Christian baron who was attacked by a highwayman. This traveler is a man of such outstanding virtue that the baron decides to marry the stranger to his daughter. He learns, of course, that the stranger is a Jew and that the marriage cannot take place. The Lessing play ends with the baron's statement: "Oh how worthy of esteem the Jews would seem if they were all like you." The Jew replies, "And how worthy the Christians if they possessed all your qualities." In *Gloria*, Galdós's interest in Jews is inextricably connected with his anti-clericalism and his hatred of fanaticism. Unlike George Eliot, he did little research on Judaism and used his spokesman only for the liberal tradition. Galdós is an exponent of the Europeanization of Spain and, although he is famous for his historical novels, he is not so bold as to present a specifically Spanish context in his use of Jews as weapons against fanaticism.

In the novel, *Misericordia*, Galdós presents another Jew, Almudena, a beggar in the streets of Madrid. Almudena's religion, although clear to the reader, is hardly recognized by the other characters in the book. The Hebrew phrases he uses are taken as Arabic by his fellow beggars. But the Jew, Almudena, is again a spokesman for universalism. It is he who recognizes that Catholic, Moslem, and Jew are the possessors of a common morality based on the equality of men before God. In *Fortunata y Jacinta* (1886–1887), a long novel about life in Madrid, Galdós is content to suggest the *Marrano* descent of some of the minor characters.

From his novels, one would get the impression that Galdós had little interest in the inquisitional period. He is a contemporary of Amador de los Ríos, whose monumental work, *Historia social, política y religiosa de los judíos de España y Portugal*, was certainly known to one as interested in Spanish history as Galdós. In fact, a bit of biographical data informs us that Galdós had a lifelong interest in the history of the Jews in Spain. This information was given to Pío Baroja, the Spanish novelist, who reported it to his nephew, Caro, whose three-volume work, *Los judíos en la España moderna y contemporánea*, was published in 1961. Even in his historical novel, *Mendizábal*, Galdós is silent on Mendizábal's well-known *Marrano* ancestry and sympathy for the Jews. One must conclude that Galdós wished to avoid the theme of the Inquisition—perhaps from a desire to achieve a certain aesthetic distance. Or perhaps he wished to attack prejudice in a rarified, abstract form that would permit the reader to despise prejudice without despising his own history.

No such delicate feeling affects the work of Camilo Castelo Branco. Camilo, according to the Portuguese archivist, António Baião,[11] had Jewish family origins in the town of Vila Real in Tras-os-Montes in northern Portugal. In his youth, Camilo lived in a small town in this region, which even today is an isolated part of the country where traces of Crypto-Jewish practices were found as late as the 1920s. A sympathy for the Jews became for Camilo a touchstone for his literary theories. Unlike other liberal writers of his epoch, Camilo is not simply denouncing the Inquisition as a brutal excess but rather sees it as a formative element of Portuguese mentality.

In 1866, Camilo published a two-volume semibiographical novel, *O Judeu*, based on research on the family of António José da Silva, a well-known Lisbon playwright who was burned at the stake in 1739 for supposedly having lived a secret Jewish life. Inquisitional documents give the following information on da Silva: He was born in 1705 in Rio de Janeiro to João Mendes da Silva and Lourença de Coutinho. When he was seven, his parents were taken along with other family members by the Inquisition to Lisbon where in 1713 they were tried, penanced, and later released. In 1726, António José, his brothers, and his mother were again taken by the Inquisition and were tortured and sentenced. After release from this incarceration, António José returned to Coimbra and completed his education in law at the university. Between 1734 and 1735, he married his cousin Leonor María de Carvalho who had also been involved more than once with the Inquisition. Between 1733 and 1738, he became well known as a playwright in Lisbon. In October 1737, Antónia José da Silva, his wife, and his mother were again taken prisoner, and in 1739, at thirty-four years of age, "O Judeu" was burned at the stake. His wife and mother were released.[12]

In Camilo's novel, *O Judeu*, the characters fall into three categories. The first are Old Christians with high-ranking lineage who are depicted as heartless, superstitious, hypocritical, or morally depraved. The second are Portuguese Crypto-Jews who are secretly loyal to the tenets of Judaism. These latter Camilo treats in great detail as to the customs of marriage, religious upbringing, and learning. Camilo's romanticized version of underground Jewish life in the town of Covilha is replete with all the secret apparatus one could imagine belonging to a family hiding their customs and ways of life from the Inquisition in subterranean passages under the house. The library of Hebrew books hidden behind a secret panel in the house of Simão de Sá is protected by a large painting of the Sermon on the Mount. The Crypto-Jewish customs depicted in O *Judeu* are described by Camilo in detail, and he treats this segment of society as learned, compassionate, and loyal to their families. The third category of characters in the novel are those who neither believe in Catholic dogma nor in the Law of Moses. They believe in freedom of choice in religion and are the mouthpieces for Camilo's own liberal views, his deism, and his skepticism. The character of António José da Silva fits this latter category, as does the character of Francisco Oliveira, who is portrayed as a close friend of António José. Xavier de Oliveira is a skeptic, a liberal, and a true son of the Reformation. The historical Cavalheiro de Oliveira was exiled from Portugal, renounced Catholicism, and became a Protestant in London. He is chiefly remembered in European letters for publishing a periodical and pamphlets condemning the evil practices of the Portuguese church-state and for claiming that the Lisbon Earthquake of 1755 was a divine and just retribution for the Inquisition. For this and other printed heresies, he was made one of the last martyrs of the Inquisition in an *Auto-de-fe* on September 20, 1761. Padre Gabriel de Malagrida also claimed the earthquake was a punishment from God for the evil doers. The latter was committed to the flames in the flesh while the Cavalheiro de Oliveira was only burned in effigy. Malagrida and Oliveira were the last two victims of the Portuguese Inquisition, although the latter was fortunate enough to live to the ripe old age of eighty-two. He died in Hackney, England, in 1783.

In dealing with Crypto-Jewish practice, Camilo's descriptions are quite accurate if compared with details published by Cecil Roth in his chapter entitled "The Religion of the Marranos," published in *Gleanings* in 1967. In matters of the Inquisition's obsession with fasting on a large scale, diet, and changing of clothing on the Jewish Sabbath, Camilo depends on documentation from the inquisitional records. He shows a clear understanding of the psychosis that caused people to live double lives of a schizophrenic nature. The family of António José da Silva in public are Christians but live as Jews in private. Camilo refers to da Silva as "o hebreu" in spite of his depiction of him as a skeptic in religious matters. In this novel, only those who live double lives seem morally acceptable. Sincere Catholics in the novel are inevitably represented on a low moral level. They are depicted as hypocrites of the lowest order if their behavior contradicts Christian practice, whereas those who are forced to live a double life are never accused of hypocrisy in spite of the contradiction in their public and private statements and beliefs.

The nervousness displayed by the *conversos* in *O Judeu*, their restlessness, and their flight from place to place, even without real cause, is another example of Camilo's grasp of the mentality of potential victims of the Inquisition. In the space of two years, the characters Sara and Jorge live in five different places, from Brazil to Rome. Although Camilo has them blame their wanderings on the adverse climate and Jorge's health, their being constantly on the move insinuates a nervousness that was so common to potential victims of the Inquisition.

Unlike other liberal writers of his epoch, Camilo is not able to simply denounce the Inquisition as a brutal excess. He sees it as a formative element of Portuguese mentality. The fact that he dwells obsessively on the specifically anti-Semitic aspect of the Inquisition shows that he was preoccupied, not only with the abstract objections to persecution but with the specific direction it followed using historical victims as his protagonists. Other authors such as Galdós attempt to avoid specifics and cast the anti-Semitic policies of the Inquisition into a more universal framework. Perhaps Camilo's knowledge of his own *converso* ancestry gave him a special empathy for the persecution and torture that António José da Silva underwent.

In his preface to *Os ratos da Inquisição*,[13] published in 1883, seventeen years after *O Judeu*, Camilo shows compassion for the plight of the poet Serrão de Castro that even surpasses his sympathy for António José da Silva. Serrão de Castro, a pharmacist and poet of extraordinary constitution, had the misfortune of landing in the inquisitional dungeons for ten of his most productive years. Serrão de Castro lived through his tortures and was released from prison in an *Auto-de-fe* on May 10, 1682. His son, Pedro, was less fortunate and was condemned in the same *Auto* to be "relaxed in the flesh" along with three others.

In his latter years, Camilo spares us no detail of those horrible descriptions that he hesitated to give in *O Judeu* of the torture and the *queimadeiro*. *Os ratos da inquisição* is perhaps the only piece of literature written in an inquisitional dungeon that managed to survive. Serrão de Castro turned his suffering into a bitterly satiric yet burlesque long poem in clever and complicated verse that describes living conditions in his cell. The inquisitional rats rob food, clothing, and peace of mind from their long-suffering victim. In a mocking tone, Serrão compares the rats to his incarcerators. Camilo believes in his preface that Serrão de Castro found an antidote for despair and terror in his comical rats.

For Camilo, it is perhaps a ray of hope that another man more desperate than he could laugh at his misery and evoke a charitable smile from the inquisitors themselves. Camilo, like Serrão de Castro, was going blind when he wrote the preface to *Os ratos da inquisição*, and several years later he was in total darkness when he put a bullet through his head. He left Iberian letters with a unique contribution to the literature of the Inquisition, one of empathy for victims of the Holy Office and a hatred for the fanaticism, corruption, brutality, and superstition practiced by those in power.

NOTES

1. Alexandre Herculano, *History of the Origin and Establishment of the Inquisition in Portugal*, trans. John C. Branner (Stanford: Stanford Univ. Press, 1926).

2. José Amador de los Ríos, *Historia social, política y religiosa de los judíos de España y Portugal* (Madrid: Aguilar, 1960).

3. Américo Castro, *España en su historia: cristianos, moros y judíos* (Buenos Aires: Editorial Losada, 1948).

4. Yitzhak Baer, *A History of the Jews in Christian Spain*, 2 vols., trans. Louis Schoffman (Philadelphia: The Jewish Publication Society of America, 1961).

5. Cecil Roth, *Gleanings* (New York: Block, 1967).

6. Julio Caro Baroja, *Los judíos en la España moderna y contemporánea*, 3 vols. (Madrid: Arión, 1961).

7. Camillo Castello Branco, *O Judeu*, 2 vols. (Oporto: Moré, 1866).

8. Benjamin D'Israeli, Earl of Beaconsfield, *Coningsby* (London: Longmans, 1923).

9. Sigmund Freud, *Moses and Monotheism*, trans. Katherine Jones (New York: Vintage, 1967).

10. George Eliot, *Daniel Deronda* (New York: The Jefferson Press, n.d.).

11. António Baião, *Homenagem a Camilo no seu centenário, 1825–1925* (Coimbra, 1925).

12. António Baião, *Episódios dramáticos da Inquisição portuguesa*, 3 vols. (Lisbon, 1955).

13. António Serrão de Castro, *Os Ratos da Inquisição*, preface by Camillo Castello Branco (Oporto: Ernesto Chardron, 1883).

ELEVEN

The Inquisition and the Jew
in Latin American Drama

Sandra Messinger Cypess

Although the term 'Latin America' stands for a heterogeneous region varied in history, culture, and social experiences, the area is often treated as a uniform whole. The evolution from its discovery to its contemporary configuration results from the historical clash between Amerindians and Christian Europeans, with some variation added by the emigration of Africans because of the slave trade. It is significant that little can be found in standard reference material relating to the Jewish presence in Latin America, whether in the post-Independence period or during the Colonial era.[1] The work of Judith Elkin and the Latin American Jewish Studies Association has done much to advance the dissemination and promotion of knowledge about Latin American Jewry, but the traditional historical record is almost silent regarding Latin American Jewish inhabitants because of the political and cultural power of the Inquisition. That institution most affected the ability of Jews in Latin America to live according to their religious customs and traditions and to express their spiritual and intellectual presence. Until recently, the literary texts of Latin America have also largely ignored the Jewish experience as a theme and bypassed the Jew both as literary character and as writer.[2] Because of a current departure from this trend, one can now document the emergence of both historians and Jewish artists exploring Jewish themes. Two Latin American plays which offer a literary interpretation of the relationship between the Inquisition and the Jews are the focus of this essay—Sabina Berman's *Herejía (Heresy)* from Mexico, and *O Santo Inquérito (The Holy Inquiry)* by the contemporary Brazilian playwright, Alfredo Dias Gomes.[3] Each play explores the possible ways in which the topic of the Inquisition and the Jew can be treated, either as a specific element in the sociopolitical world or as a symbol of a general phenomenon.

161

I first began to investigate the topic of Jewish themes in Latin America when the noted Mexican dramatist Emilio Carballido strongly recommended that I read the work of a new young playwright, Sabina Berman. Her play, *Heresy*, was awarded the Premio Nacional de Teatro in 1983. Set in colonial Mexico, the play deals with the subject of those Spaniards who had Jewish blood and their status as *conversos*—Crypto-Jews or New Catholics—vis-à-vis the Inquisition. As a result of my interest in her play, I began to investigate the theme of the Inquisition and the figure of the Jew, a topic which had received little attention from Latin American historians and sociologists, in part because of its emotional and highly charged nature.[4] Another reason to explain the lack of attention to the topic derives from the conception that there was no Jewish presence, since practicing Jews had been expelled from Spain in 1492, and in 1523 an edict prohibited New Christians from emigrating to the New World. Nevertheless, as the *Encyclopedia Judaica* notes, although Jews were prohibited officially from settling in the New World, one could detect the presence of Spanish Crypto-Jews in almost every town in New Spain.[5]

The view that Jews were absent from Latin America during the Colonial period has been supported by historians such as E. Bradford Burns, who in the fourth edition of *Latin America: A Concise Interpretive History* (Englewood Cliffs, NJ: Prentice Hall, 1986) makes no reference to the fact that Jews arrived with Columbus, or that their presence posed any problematics that differed from the pattern of European-Indian-Black relationships. In *Latin American Culture: An Anthropological Synthesis* (New York: Harper and Row, 1975), Emilio Willems, who has written on aspects of religious pluralism in regard to Protestantism and Catholicism, includes no consideration of the Jews as a possible topic in his index, nor are they referred to in his book in any meaningful way. Michael D. Olien, in *Latin Americans: Contemporary Peoples & Their Cultural Traditions* (New York: Holt, Rinehart, & Winston, 1973), notes in a few brief lines that because the presence of Jews was illegal in New Spain, no continuous identifiable community existed during the Colonial period—that is, from 1521 to 1821. I would suggest that these Latin Americanists ignore the implications of the sociocultural realities of the Inquisition and its relation to Jewish identity and therefore dismiss the presence of covert Jews and their contributions to the cultural and economic development of the New World. Perhaps the key to the misunderstanding of this historical record can be found in the different ways the definition of the 'Jew' has been interpreted. If one defines a Jew in terms of adherence to the full practices of orthodoxy or according to Spanish legal qualifications, then Jews were not a presence in the New World. Gerson D. Cohen has suggested that "the historian is not at liberty to restrict his definition of Jewishness to one laid down by rabbis or their adherents. . . . no matter how christianized the Marrano way of life may become, they need not—and apparently did not—cease to be a Jewish group historically, sociologically, or even religiously."[6] Cohen's broader interpretation is echoed in the *Encyclopedia Judaica* (see Note 5) and refers to the presence of

Jews either as *conversos*—that is, those who officially converted to Christianity—or as Crypto-Jews, those who practiced the Jewish religion in secret. The Mexican historian of the colonial period, Alfonso Toro, confirms the presence of Jews in the broader sense: "There were many Israelites who went to the New World and who took part in its conquest and discovery as well as in the formation of colonial society; moreover, they could be found in all the social classes, performing all kinds of professions and occupations."[7] According to Cecil Roth in *A History of the Marranos*, the Jews grew so rapidly in influence and number that, before the sixteenth century was over, it was considered necessary to make special provisions against them.[8] The Inquisition worked zealously to that end. It is a great irony that the well-kept records of the Inquisition itself enable us today to reconstruct the lives and the fates of those very people whom the Inquisition wished to blot out from history.

The topic of the Inquisition and the Jew in Mexican literature appears to have become a theme in a number of narratives written in the period of strong nationalist tendencies which began in the mid-1880s and continued after the French invasion and the defeat of the Habsburg empire.[9] These texts are romantic novellas which stress the themes of liberty and independence from Spain, hence their critique of any institution of Spanish origin.

According to my investigations, Berman's play is the first dramatic work in Mexican literature to take up the specific theme of the Inquisition's treatment of Crypto-Jews. Hers is not, however, the first Latin American play to deal with the topic of the Inquisition and the Jew in the New World. In nineteenth-century Brazil, one of the founders of Brazilian national theater, Domingos José Gonçalves de Magalhães (1811–1882), chose as the topic of his first play the tragic treatment of the colonial playwright and Crypto-Jew, António José da Silva (1705–1739). In 1838, he staged *António José ou O poeta e a Inquisição* (*Antonio Jose or the Poet and the Inquisition*), a five-act verse tragedy in the Romantic style. Despite the success of Magalhães's work, only one other Romantic piece, the novel *O Judeu* (1866) by Camilo Castelo Branco of Portugal, reproduces the story of the most famous Brazilian Inquisitional martyr. (A discussion of the work of Castelo Branco can be found in the Chapter 10 of this volume.) This topic was not repeated in a literary work until one hundred years after the publication of Castelo Branco's work, when Bernardo Santarena presented in Portugal a play with the same title as the novel, *O Judeu*. In the same year, 1966, the Brazilian dramatist, Alfredo Dias Gomes, produced "*O Santo Inquérito*, the second Latin American play I will discuss here.

The Dias Gomes play represents the works which refer to the Inquisition as a general symbol of repression. Rather than focusing on the particulars of the relationship between the Inquisition and the Jews, the play uses the theme "as a dramatic metaphor for the intolerance and repressive climate of contemporary times," according to George Woodyard, the Latin American drama specialist.[10] Woodyard points out that the reference to the Inquisition functions in the Dias Gomes play as another example of the universal repressive systems which afflict humanity, like Fascism or McCarthyism.

As in Berman's work, *The Holy Inquiry* ostensibly recreates a colonial event.[11] The Brazilian play, however, uses the historical record of the Inquisition's persecution of Branca Dias and her family in order to encode a message about the contemporary period. Because the political situation in Brazil at the time of the play's production prohibited any criticism of the political or social structure, Dias Gomes was able to present his critique of the repressive regime by using the Inquisition as an allegory for the situation in Brazil of the 1960s, a technique used with frequency by contemporary Hispanic writers, whether in Spain or Argentina, to avoid censorship.[12]

Until this day, Branca survives in the folklore of northeastern Brazil as a kind of Joan of Arc figure. She was persecuted by the Inquisition because she refused to agree to their accusations that she was a Crypto-Jew—that is, a heretic who secretly practiced Judaism. According to Dias Gomes's version of her story, Branca saves a priest from drowning by applying mouth-to-mouth resuscitation procedures. The physical contact of the innocent and beautiful young woman arouses the priest and, in order to cover up his sexual interest in Branca and the contradictions she stimulates within him, he interrogates her and questions her innocent motives. Finally, to avoid coming to terms with his own sinful feelings, he accuses her of having practiced Judaism as a child and denounces her to the Inquisition. Branca insists she is a Christian like her fiancé, Augusto. She bravely asks the Inquisitors: "But what do you want? Should I consider myself a heretic although I am not?. . .I was not a convert, I was born a Christian and as a Christian I have lived until today" (pp. 100, 102).[13] It soon becomes evident that her grandfather had left Lisbon as a New Christian but in secret had clung to his Jewish faith, a fact her father knew and hid from her. In terms of the dramatic action seen by the audience, however, Branca and her family reveal no particular behavior which could be considered identifiably Jewish practices. Branca's father admits he is a Crypto-Jew, yet he readily recants his faith under the pressure of torture. Unlike her father, Branca did not know about her family's Jewish origins, but at one point she is also willing to confess to being a Crypto-Jew in order to save the life of her fiancé. Augusto, also falsely accused of heresy, persuades Branca to stand firm and refuse to submit to the pressure of torture. Her strength of character is contrasted to the weakness of her father with the result that the play offers a negative view of both the Crypto-Jew and the Inquisition. Ironically, Branca is persecuted as an enemy by the very Christian faith she wanted to preserve. Her refusal to give up her principles and acquiesce to the demands of the Holy Office is interpreted as a rebellious act, as the Inquisitors express it: "Thousands of people, like yourself, consciously or unconsciously, propagate revolutionary doctrines and subversive practices" (p. 100).[14] As represented here by the Holy Office, the Church symbolizes a totalitarian system that allows no opposing theological, social, or political practices. Most readers of the play would agree with Woodyard that it is "based upon the concept of religious freedom, and whether or not the church has the right to legislate beliefs, restrict liberty, or demand conformity to a particular set of religious principles" (pp. 70–71). Despite the polarity set up between the Inquisition and the Jew by the nature of the topic, in the actual enactment of the play the lack of specific Jewish religious references enables the reader or viewer to bypass the Jewishness of the characters or the theme in order to concentrate on the universality of their plight. The protagonists of Dias Gomes's plays die not for a particular faith, but for the right to believe freely and to identify with whatever they choose.[15] The Brazilian play, therefore, by using the Inquisition and its persecution of Jews as metaphors for universal situations, in effect makes transparent the real suffering and injustice inherent in the historical situation because it encourages the spectator to bypass the particular reality for a metaphorical reading.

In contrast to Dias Gomes's generalized political treatment and metaphorical use of the Inquisition, Berman's presentation contains specific linguistic and kinesic codes which relate her characters to an identifiable and concrete Jewish world. In addition, Berman includes the complicating element of the internal conflict within the protagonist regarding his identity as a Jew, a theme which does not concern the Brazilian text. Berman's play foregrounds the particular Jewish experience while the Dias Gomes work quickly erases the particular to project the universal. I do not mean to imply that Berman's play is so culturally specific as not to be universal; rather I would stress that her text explores the diversity and complexity of Mexican identity vis-à-vis the Jew in particular. The existence of the Inquisition as a concrete reality is addressed in order to shed light on the circumstances involved in the country's complex beginnings, which have led to its present diversities.

As indicated by its title, *Heresy* focuses on the religious aspects of dissent, or denial of dogma, the crime of which the Crypto-Jews were judged to be guilty by the Inquisition. Concerned with the purity of the faith, the Holy Office was ostensibly not so much interested in the persecution of Jews, since they were legally not present in New Spain, but in those individuals who professed to be Catholics but practiced Judaism in secret. Berman illustrates the tactics of the Inquisition through the experiences of one of the most prominent families of New Spain to have been persecuted by the Inquisition.

The Carbajal family represents a prototypical case of Crypto-Jews in that each member exhibited in the privacy of the home varying degrees of adherence to Catholicism or Jewish law. The Governor, for example, prays with his rosary and recites the Hail Mary, while his niece entones Hebrew prayers, lights the Sabbath candles, and recites her credo of faith, the Shema. Unlike Dias Gomes, Berman emphasizes the Jewish nature of her characters by including not only the Hebrew language, but also the enactment of important events of Jewish life:

a circumcision, a wedding with its attendant ceremonial configurations (the witnesses, the *chupah*, the wine glass), and Sabbath observances.

The events surrounding the Carbajal family are well-documented in the Archives of the Inquisition in Mexico. From time to time since the sixteenth century, a number of monographs have been generated about the family, most of which focus on the figure of Luis de Carbajal el mozo (the Younger).[16] He was a poet who left a diary of his experiences and, unlike his uncle, appears to have been a practicing Jew. Berman uses his diary, Toro's *La familia Carvajal*, and the Mexican archival documents as texts for her play. In that way, she follows the techniques of documentary theater as a means to validate the somewhat controversial material, substantiate the objectivity of her perspective, and avoid the emotionally explosive nature inherent in the topic of the Carbajals' persecution and torture.[17]

One of the more polemical premises suggested by several historical sources and reproduced by Berman in the play is the belief that Governor Luis de Carbajal need not have been apprehended by the Holy Office. Rather, he and his family were chosen for punishment because of an underlying motive: the viceroy of New Spain at that time wished to transfer the large Carbajal property and possessions to his own holdings. In this interpretation, Berman follows historians such as Richard Greenleaf who suggest that the persecution and torture of the victims of the Inquisition were not always based on religious grounds, but were motivated by economic factors, personal jealousy, and ignorance.[18] Don Luis, as an example, was not only a conquistador, but the designated governor of the lands he discovered, called the New Kingdom of Leon in northeast Mexico, which included many rich silver mines. For these reasons, he was counted among the most wealthy and powerful people of New Spain. Because his title and possessions were to be handed down in perpetuity to his heirs, the economic status of don Luis is not unimportant nor unrelated to his persecution by the Inquisition, nor to the Inquisition's persecution of his designated heir, Luis el Mozo. The viceroy's envy of the governor was supported by the weaknesses and jealousies of other members of the Carbajal entourage, with the result that the betrayal of the family to the Inquisition was not difficult. Richard E. Greenleaf states that:

> There were many more Protestants and Jews in sixteenth-century Mexico than is commonly supposed, and the documents hint that only a small number of these ever came before the Holy Office. . . . Except when they challenged the Church or Spanish authority in an open manner or when they particularly rankled the peninsular Spaniard as a business competitor or political rival, these heretics did not appear in the halls of the Inquisition (p. 3).

In *Heresy*, the dialogue supports this observation through the interaction of Felipe Nuñez, the governor's aide, and two Inquisitors. Felipe had informed on the Crypto-Jews of the Carbajal family after the niece of the governor, Doña

Isabel, had spurned his frequent offers of marriage. Felipe, to be sure, claims that he believes in the innocence of his master, Don Luis. Nevertheless, being ingenuous, as he describes himself, and not denying his own jealousies of the Carbajals as motivations for his act, he denounces the members of the family, thinking that the governor will remain untouched by the Inquisition. Too late, as one of the key dialogues reveals, he discovers the realities of the *modus operandi* of the Inquisition and the viceroy:

FN: Those cries. . . Ave Maria Purisima; those are the cries of my master Don Luis.

Inquisitor 1:   You're imagining things. Calm yourself.

Inquisitor 2:   And if they were, what of it?

FN: What do you mean? The viceroy swore that Don Luis himself would be respected. His nieces and nephews are the Jews. He was always the faithful Christian.

Inquisitor 2:   We shall see.

FN: Then you are torturing him! But he has nothing to confess. How long will you make him suffer?

Inquisitor 2:   Until he confesses.

FN: But he has nothing to confess!

Inquisitor 2:   We'll see about that (pause)

FN: Vile viceroy, evil, ambitious man. So all this has happened in order to appropriate the New Kingdom of Leon. How naive I was: He said that I ought to help him free Don Luis from his corrupt family members. He said that they were placing the honor of Don Luis in jeopardy. He said. . .

Inquisitor 1:   He didn't lie to you, he simply connot fulfill his word. Within the domain of the Inquisition, the word of the viceroy has no effect.

Inquisitor 2:   Enough of your groanings, hypocrite. Your left hand knew very well what your right hand was doing and was waiting with open palms for recompense. Who, once his relatives were imprisoned, would be the heir of Don Luis? Whom did you expect it to be? Answer. You? (p. 196)[19]

This dialogue reiterates what the researchers have discovered after studying the trials and the records—that local politics and economic rivalries often were the motivating reasons for the denunciation of the Crypto-Jews.

Berman's play reproduces the documentation of the Carbajal family in a dramatic yet impersonal way so that the events may be evaluated, judged, and remembered by today's audiences. One particular conclusion to be reached in regard to *Heresy* is that the work reflects not only a Mexican nationalist political interpretation of the Inquisition, for Mexico is an anti-clerical state, but also a growing consciousness of the Jewish theme and its relation to nationalist expressions in Latin America.

A broader reading of *Heresy* shows that Berman belongs to the tradition of Latin American writers who have started on the road to a profound re-examination of the foundations of Latin American society, its complexities, and its diversities. I would like to suggest that Dias Gomes's play can be said to vitalize the Inquisition when he stresses its role as a symbol of eternal repression that continues to this day. Berman's play, in contrast, subverts the very goals of the Inquisition to blot out from existence the people who dared to dissent. By means of *Herejía*, she rescues from the hidden documents of the archives a forgotten people and brings to them the victory of survival that the Inquisition tried to prevent.

NOTES

1. The same silence that I have documented in Latin American historical texts regarding the presence of the Jew was noted by the historian Gerd Korman in reference to the treatment of the Holocaust in American textbooks. See Korman, "Silence in the American Textbooks," *Yad Vashem Studies on the European Jewish Catastrophe and Resistance*, ed. Livia Rothkirchen (Jerusalem: Yad Vashem, 1970), pp. 183–202.

2. Exceptions to the rule always exist, and in regard to work on the topic of Jews in the New World, Seymour Liebman is a historian who has devoted much research and skill toward filling the void. His general book on the culture of Latin America, *Exploring the Latin American Mind* (Chicago: Nelson Hall, 1976), refers to the presence of Jews, unlike the investigators referred to in my discussion. In his article, "Los judíos en la historia de México," *Cuadernos Americanos* 26, 150 (1967), Liebman categorically states, *"De 1521 hasta la fecha no ha habido un sólo período durante el cual los judíos no hayan sido residentes de Nueva España y México"* (From 1521 until the present, there has been not one period in which Jews have not been residents of New Spain and Mexico) (p. 145). The Latin American Jewish Studies Association also works toward documenting the presence of Jews in the area, and can be reached by contacting Judith Elkin at the University of Michigan, Ann Arbor. See her *Resources for Latin American Jewish Studies* (Ann Arbor: LAJSA, 1984). The literary journal *Hispamerica*, edited by Saul Sosnowski, dedicated part of an issue to several papers presented at a symposium on "Jewish Literature in the Americas." See xiv, No. 42 (December 1985).

3. Sabina Berman, "Herejía," *Teatro* (Mexico: Editores Mexicanos Unidos, 1985). Alfredo Dias Gomes, "*O Santo Inquérito* (Rio de Janeiro, Editôra Civilização Brasileira, 1966). Subsequent references to and quotations from these plays will be identified in the study by page number in parentheses and translated by me.

For a study of the Jew in English and American drama, consult Ellen Schiff, *From Stereotype to Metaphor: The Jew in Contemporary Drama* (Albany: State University of New York Press, 1982).

4. David M. Gitlitz, "The New-Christian Dilemma in Two Plays by Lope de Vega," *Bulletin of the Comediantes* 34, 1 (1982), pp. 63–81 analyzes examples of the treatment of the Jews in plays of the Golden Age theatre of Spain. His comments parallel my findings in relation to the emotional and cultural sensitivities surrounding the theme: "But critics seem to agree that it was impossible to bring to the stage the emotional traumas of Spanish New-Christians who were persecuted by the old-Christian majority" (p. 63). For further work on Jewish images in the Spanish *comedia*, see Gitlitz, "The Jew in the Comedia of the Golden Age," (diss. Harvard University, 1968); E. Glaser, "Referencias antisemitas en la literatura peninsular de la Edad de Oro," *Nueva Revista de Filología Hispánica* 8 (1954), 46ff.

5. *Encyclopedia Judaica*, 3rd printing, Jerusalem 1974, Vol. 11, p. 1454.

6. Cohen is quoted by Seymour Liebman, *The Inquisitors and the Jews in the New World* (Coral Gables: U. of Miami, 1974), p. 30.

7. Alfonso Toro, *Los judíos en la Nueva España.* (Mexico: Publicaciones del AGN, 1932), quoted by Rafael Heliodoro Valle, "Judíos en México," *Revista Chilena de Historia y Geografía* 81, No. 89 (1936), p. 222; my translation: "fueron muchos los israelitas que pasaron al Nuevo Mundo, y que tuvieron parte en su conquista y descubrimiento, así como en la formación de la sociedad colonial, pues se les encontraron en todas las clases sociales, ejerciendo toda clase de profesiones y oficios."

8. Cecil Roth, *The History of the Marranos* (Philadelphia: Jewish Publication Society, 1947), p. 275.

9. For a discussion of the themes of the historical novel in nineteenth-century Mexico, see John Brushwood, *Mexico in Its Novel* (Austin and London: Univ. of Texas Press, 1966), especially Chapters 3 and 4.

10. George W. Woodyard, "A Metaphor for Repression: Two Portuguese Inquisition Plays," *Luso-Brazilian Review* 10, 1 (1973), p. 68. Further references to this article will appear in the text.

11. For a discussion of *O Santo Inquérito* and the other plays of Dias Gomes, see Leon F. Lyday, "The Theater of Alfredo Dias Gomes," *Dramatists in Revolt*, eds. Lyday and George W. Woodyard (Austin: Univ. of Texas Press, 1976) pp. 221–242. Consult Arnold Wiznitzer, *Jews in Colonial Brazil* (New York: Columbia Univ. Press, 1960), for historical information on the period.

12. Herbert Lindenberger, in *Historical Drama* (Chicago: Univ. of Chicago Press, 1975), comments that "historical plays are at least as much a comment on the playwright's own ties as on the periods about which they are ostensibly written" (p. 5). See the plays of Antonio Buero Vallejo in Spain (*Un soñador para un pueblo, Las meninas, El concierto de San Ovidio*), and Griselda Gambaro

of Argentina (_La malasangre_) as contemporary examples of the use of historical allegories to comment on current events in a repressive regime.

13. "Mas que querem? Que eu me considero uma herege, sem ser?...Não fui convertida, nasci cristã e como cristã tenho vivido até hoje" (pp. 100, 102).

14. "milhares que, como você, consciente ou inconscientemente, ropagam doutrinas revolucionárias e práticas subversivas" (p. 100).

15. Fred M. Clark and Ana Lucia Gazolla de García, _Twentieth-Century Brazilian Theatre: Essays_, Estudios de Hispanófila, #50 (Chapel Hill: Estudios Hispanófila, 1978), p. 102.

16. The historian Alfonso Toro published a two-volume opus on the whole family (_La familia Carbajal_ [Mexico: Editorial Patria, 1944]), which Berman refers to as part of her documentation; most works have tended to focus on the nephew, Luis el Mozo, who took on the name "el Alumbrado" (the Enlightened One) when he openly professed his Judaism. See Alberto María Carreno, "Luis de Carvajal el mozo," _Memorias de la Academia de Historia de México_ 15 (1956), pp. 87–101; Martin A. Cohen, _The Martyr_ (Philadelphia: Jewish Publication Society of America, 1973); Seymour B. Leibman, _The Enlightened: The Writings of Luis de Carvajal, el Mozo_ (Coral Gables: Univ. of Miami Press, 1967); Pablo Martinez del Río, _Alumbrado_ (México: Porrúa, 1937). It should be noted that the surname Carbajal is spelled with the _b_ by Berman, although other sources use a _v_: Carvajal; in either case, the pronunciation is identical in Mexican Spanish.

17. For a helpful discussion of documentary theater, see Franz Haberl, "Peter Weiss: Documentary Theatre," _Books Abroad_ (now _World Literature Today_) 43 (1969), 359; Pedro Bravo-Elizonda, "La realidad latinoamericana y el teatro documental," _Texto crítico_ (1979), pp. 200–210.

18. Richard E. Greenleaf states that "local politics and economic rivalries" were often "reasons for denunciations of heretics," _The Mexican Inquisition of the Sixteenth Century_ (Albuquerque: Univ. of New Mexico Press, 1969), p. 5. Further references to this work will be noted in parentheses in the text. For similar views that, in addition to its religious duty, the Inquisition used its power for political and economic ends, see also Felipe Antín, _Vida y muerte de la Inquisición en México_ (México: Editorial Posada, 1973), who stresses the function of the Inquisition as an "instrumento político-policíaco," p. 8; Patricia Aufderheide, "True Confessions: The Inquisition and Social Attitudes in Brazil at the Turn of the XVII Century," _Luso-Brazilian Review_ 10, 2 (1973), 208–240. Stanley M. Hordes, "Historiographical Problems in Study of the Inquisition and the Mexican Crypto-Jews in the Seventeenth Century," _American Jewish Archives_, 34, 2 (1982), 138–152.

19. FN: Esos gritos...Ave María Purisima; son gritos de mi amo don
    Luis.

    Inquisidor 1: Te imaginas cosas. Sosiégate.

    Inquisidor 2: Y si lo fueran, ¿qué?

FN: ¿Cómo qué? El virrey juró que la persona de don Luis sería respetada. Son sus sobrinos los judíos. El me consta, fue siempre, un fiel cristiano.

Inguisidor 2: Ya se verá.

FN: Entonces sí lo torturan. Pero no tiene qué confesar. Hasta cuándo lo harán sufrir?

Inquisidor 2: Hasta que confiese.

FN: iPero no tiene qué confesar!

Inquisidor 2: Ya se verá. (pausa)

FN: Villano virrey, malditos ambiciosos. Así que todo ha sido para que se apropie del Nuevo Reino de León. iQué ingenuo fui!: dijo que debía ayudarlo a librar a don Luis de sus familiares corruptos. Dijo que ellos ponían en peligro la honra de don Luis. Dijo. . .

Inquisidor 1: No te mintió, sencillamente no te puede cumplir. En los ámbitos inquisitoriales la palabra de virrey es nula.

Inquisidor 2: Basta de gimoteos, hipócrita. Tu mano izquierda sabía muy bien lo que hacía tu diestra y esperaba ahuecada la recompensa. ¿Quién, encerrados los parientes, heredaría a don Luis? ¿Quién te imaginabas? Responde. ¿Tú? (196)

TWELVE

Anthroponyms in the Collection of Moroccan Sephardic Ballads

Paloma Díaz-Mas
Translated by Judith A. Long

More than a presentation of conclusions or the exposition of a subject, this chapter is the description of current research. I had already done various studies of the Sephardic and Spanish ballad when, in 1984, I became interested in a little-studied aspect: the use of proper names in the ballad. I worked on the assumption that the modern oral ballad—traditional poetry—possesses its own language and some specific literary conventions of the genre (facilitated by its form of transmission through the centuries) divergent from the language and the conventions of other literary genres. I sensed, too, that proper names (of both places and people) play a very special role in that ballad language, a role not limited to indicating where the action takes place or what the people are named, and that the presence of a given name in one version of a ballad could not be justified by mere 'archeological' survival of old forms.

In order to test the truth of these hypotheses, the first step was to choose a corpus of ballads with which to work, because to tackle the study of the uses and functions of proper names in all the known versions of all the ballads of all the geographic traditions seemed to be an overwhelming task which I could not complete.

If the chosen body consisted of published collections of traditional Moroccan ballads, it was due not only to the fact that I knew the Moroccan tradition well, thanks to previous studies, but also because it presented some ideal characteristics. Morocco was sufficiently isolated from peninsular reality so that the toponyms or anthroponyms of Hispanic origin that might appear in the texts would not refer to too close a reality. On the other hand, there was sufficient contact—in the recent past—with the peninsula so that relatively current influences of the peninsular collection would be reflected in the Moroccan tradition. In other words, the collection of Moroccan ballads presented the advantage of having developed in an environment independent of the one from which its primitive toponyms and anthroponyms evolved but without the difficulty of being so isolated that conclusions would have been difficult to extrapolate to other ballad collections.

I preferred to limit the study to published collections, because not all of the unpublished recent compilations (quite numerous and rich, I must say)[1] were accessible to me or to my expected readers. I concentrated on the more than six hundred and fifty texts contained in the sixteen published collections that include Moroccan ballads.[2]

I decided to begin by studying toponyms or place names. Various publications and papers presented,[3] concentrating above all on the function of those place names in the ballad tradition, have been a product of the study. I was able to verify how, besides the obvious function of indicating where the action takes place, the toponyms at times perform functions that until now have not been noticed, from serving as a trait defining a character to emphasizing the superiority or lineage of a person or the value of a possession or gift. It is likewise clear that some toponyms have become specialized in indicating ideas such as distance, splendor, or the magic character of an environment or situation. Other functions of the toponyms—as well as their important role in key sequences of the narration, especially beginnings and endings—need a more detailed study.

I recently began the second phase of the study, dealing with *anthroponyms* or names of people that appear in ballads from the same Moroccan collections. Although the study is still in a very initial stage (only part of the largest collection—Larrea Palacín's ballads—has been critically analyzed) it is possible to point out some interesting aspects which (although we cannot yet offer conclusions) seem to deserve special attention.

1) In the first place, it is a good idea to specify which proper names we are including in our study:

1.1.a) Personal names that identify characters in the ballads (actors in the fable, in semiotic terms), including those which are the combination of a toponym and a title or position, of which we will see examples later.

1.1.b) Proper names that may appear in introductions—so frequent in popular ballads—as, for example, in one about captives (Larrea 226):

En el nombre de *Jesús*
y la *Virgen Soberana*
te escribo, esposa querida,
esta lastimosa carta.

and those in which—as they almost always have to do with references to Christianity—we sometimes find interesting variations tending toward dechristianization, such as in this version of *La esposa cautiva* (Larrea 225), in which the name of Jesus is avoided, substituting another proper name for it:

Noche de San Juan Bautista
muy resplandeciente y clara
en la que *Juana* nació
de aquellas puras entrañas
de *María*, Concebida
de aquel Cordero sin mancha.

1.1.c) Those included in the speeches of the characters, even when they do not refer to other characters, as, for example, in invocations like the monologue in *Bucar sobre Valencia* (Larrea 8):

Ay, Valencia; ay, Valencia;
Valencia la bien cercada;
primero fuistes del moro
que de cristianos ganada.
Y ahora si *Alá* me ayuda
a moros seréis tornada.

Or in the lamentation of the unfortunate daughter-in-law of *La mala suegra* (Larrea 94) who is about to give birth:

—Oy, mi Dios, y quien me diera
una sala en aquel valle,
y por compañia buena
Jesucristo y a su madre.

Or in the plans that the faithful wife makes in *La vuelta del marido (e)* (Larrea 32), having decided to become

Monja yo de *Santa Clara*,
Monja yo de *Santa Inés*

and which in another text (Larrea 36) converts the founding nun of each order into authentic, real-life people:

Tres hijitas que yo tengo
Cómo las repartiré?
La una con *Doña Clara*,
La otra con *Doña Inés*.

1.2) We do not include the proper names used to specify time, such as the "Noche de *San Juan Bautista*" previously mentioned, or the "Mañanita de *San Juan*" which is the beginning of several ballads.

2) In the second place, let us note what aspects are to be considered in the study, and the points on which the research focuses.

2.1) Aspects that we could call 'statistical':

2.1.a) Presence and absence of people's names, as much in ballad themes as in specific versions of a ballad.

Although the majority of ballads include anthroponyms, characters are also frequently identified only by common nouns, such as "el caballero" (the gentleman), "la linda dama" (the pretty woman), "la niña" (the girl), "el buen rey" (the good king), "la princesa" (the princess), "la infanta" (the king's daughter), "el conde" (the count), and so on.

A single ballad, on the other hand, often presents, in its different versions, the same characters with different names, or a character in one version has a proper name, while in another he is identified by a common noun. For example, in *El nacimiento de Bernardo del Carpio*, characters appear who have taken their names from ballads about El Cid:

Hermana tiene el buen *Sidi*
que *Ximena* se llamaba
        (Larrea la)

but in another version (Larrea lb), *Sidi* loses his name and is referred to by a common noun:

Hermana tenía el *buen reye*
que *Ximena* se llamaba.

2.1.b) Possible link between the contents of the ballad and the presence or absence of anthroponyms.

Although it is still early, and conclusions will have to wait until the whole body of works is catalogued and analyzed, we can ask if the presence or absence of anthroponyms has some relation to the type of ballad (epic, Carolingian, biblical, historical, novelistic, etc.). A first impression is that anthroponyms are common in epic, historical, or religious ballads, something to be expected if we bear in mind that, in those ballads, reference to specific characters whose deeds or events were narrated—at least originally, when they were composed—was fundamental. Existing versions have preserved, more or les faithfully, specific characters and their names. On the other hand, novelistic ballads more often have nameless characters or those identified by a common noun which converts them into a type (maiden, king, father, etc.).

2.2) The anthroponyms in current versions compared to those in older versions (when these are known).

It is a question of analyzing the relation of anthroponyms which appear in modern oral versions to those in the original versions—or those most similar to the original: the old versions found in sixteenth-century collections. Regarding toponyms, present-day versions are not identical to old versions, and not even the presence or absence of a toponym in a modern version always coincides with the old ballad. Not only have toponyms that were in sixteenth-century texts disappeared, but others that were not present have appeared in modern versions—aside from the multiple recreations, substitutions, and reinterpretations of old toponyms which are seen in modern traditional versions. We can assume that a similar process has taken place with anthroponyms. It would, therefore, be a good idea for us to consider the following points:

2.2.a) Survival of original anthroponyms:

Occasionally, Moroccan Sephardic versions have preserved accurately character names which must have been in the original ballad. It is not strange, for example, to find biblical characters' names in ballads of this type, especially in some that seem to be of Jewish creation, such as *La consagración de Moisés* (Larrea 44), where the names of the characters are in Hebrew form:

> Mosé salió de Misrain
> huyendo del rey Parhó
> y se fue derecho a Midián
> y se encontró con Yitró
> le dio a Cipora su hija
> porque era temiente de Dios.

Others, Spanish in origin, preserve the names of Jewish characters in their Hispanic form.

But it is not only the biblical ballads in which original anthroponyms are accurately preserved. In a historical ballad such as *La muerte del maestre de Santiago* (Larrea 9), the memory of the fourteenth-century killer king remains, although the brother who died by his order has gone from the historical *Fadrique* to a mythological *Alfonso*:

> Estábase don *Alfonso*
> en silla de oro sentado;
> cartas le habían venido
> del rey don *Pedro* su hermano.

Similarly, the name of the deceived husband in the historical ballad *Juan Lorenzo* is retained. Or those of *Zaide, Zaida,* and *Tarfe* in the Moorish ballads in which Lope sings of his love of Elena Osorio—ballads which had a long and fruitful life on the lips of the Moroccan Sephardim.

2.2.b) Sometimes an anthroponym is retained, but the original name is replaced by another. For example, in some peninsular versions of *La muerte del príncipe don Juan*, we find the mention of "Doctor *Parra*," the real name of the Catholic monarchs' famous doctor who attended the prince. In Sephardic versions, the reference to the doctor remains, but with a change in name:

> Ya mandan por los dutores,
> dutores de toda España;
> los unos le miran el pulso,

los otros le miran la cara;
todos dizen a una voz:
—Mi señor no tiene nada.
Si no n'era el más chiquito
que *Asebastián* se llamaba
(Larrea 17)

2.2.c) Even more frequent is modification, distortion, or reinterpretation of the original anthroponym. Sometimes, curiously, the distortion is closer to the original etymon than the original name, as in *Fátima y Jarifa* (Larrea 20), where the name of the second protagonist, undoubtedly influenced by Morrocan Arabic, becomes distanced from sixteenth-century Moorish ballads, only to acquire a still more Moorish form:

Cuáles son las dos hermanas
las que son de amor trocadas?
La una se llama *Cherifa*,
la otra *Fátima* se llama.

2.2.d) Quite often the so-called distortion is actually a reinterpretation of the name, generally under the influence of popular etymology or of a search for names with meaning. So, in *Tamar y Amnón*, very well-known both in Morocco and southern Spain, the name of King David is kept, but his children receive 'names with meaning.' The girl's refers to the sea (*Altamar, Altamares*: not in Larrea), while her brother's seems derived from the verb *hablar* (to speak):

Un hijo tiene el rey *David*
que por nombre *Ablón* se llama
(Larrea 45)

Likewise, the name of the protagonist's father in *Moriana y Galván* adopts diverse forms depending on the version. In some, (such as Larrea 78) it is a more of less neutral *Xuane*, or a sonorous *Grismane* (Larrea 79). In another (Larrea 81), his proper name conveys the justice-giving character which corresponds to a king:

Siete años hacían, siete,
que estoy por este lugare
comiendo hierbas del campo,
bebiendo agua de un xarale
en busqueda de *Juliana*,
hija del rey don *Juzgante*

2.2.e) We must also consider the points made in 2.2.a–d in relation to the different types of ballad. Again we must ask ourselves—without attempting, for the moment, to reach a conclusion—if the 'better' or 'worse' preservation of a person's name through oral transmission across centuries has any relationship to the type of ballad in which it appears. To put it another way, we must ask if ballads of a certain type are prone to the preservation of anthroponyms and in those of another type names are more likely to be suppressed, substituted, or reinterpreted.

2.2.f) Perhaps more helpful than the above would be to study the link that may exist between the presence of certain anthroponyms and the time when that ballad came into the Judeo-Moroccan repertoire, or recent influence of the modern peninsular tradition.

A good example is the previously cited *Tamar y Amnón*, where it is strange that two names so familiar to a Jewish singer, such as the example of King David's children, have been distorted and/or reinterpreted. The mystery is cleared up if we consider that the ballad is also very popular in Andalusia, where those names were changed. *Altamar* and *Ablón* are, then, the result of recent influence of the peninsular tradition.

Another clear example is the ballad of *Don Bueso y su hermana*, also called *La hermana cautiva*, in which the name of the brother, in the oldest Moroccan versions (hexasyllabic), is *Güezo* or *Bueso*:

—De dónde tu conoces
los campos de olanda?
—Mi hermano don *Güezo*
en ellos paziaba.

(Larrea 58)

However, in octosyllabic versions, recently brought to Morroco from Spain, the brother's name is different:

—Lloro porque en estos campos
mi padre a cazar venía,
con mi hermano *Moralejo*
y toda su cortesía.

(Larrea 59)

Lloro porque en estos montes
mi padre a cazar venía
con mi hermanito *Alejandro*
que era toda su compañía.

(Larrea 60)

2.3) Another interesting point of study is that of anthroponyms which are, however, not people's names.

2.3.a) The apparent contradiction clears up when we realize that common nouns are frequently used as character names. The previously cited *Moriana y Galván* provides a good example. Its usual beginning is:

Juliana en el castillo
con ese moro *Galane*
              (Larrea 81)

in which the editors are confronted with a serious problem in capitalization. Is
Galane a proper name or an adjective? One of Larrea's informants seems to have
been inclined toward the former (text 80):

Xuliana en el castillo
con ese moro *Galanes*

where *Galanes* as an adjective would not agree with *moro*. Here the final *s*, rather
than a plural form, is a proper name of Carolingian influence.

2.3.b) It is also customary to give characters proper names that are actually
the result of joining a title or position with a toponym. In the previously cited
Muerte del príncipe don Juan, the prince is only mentioned as the "King of
Salamanca." In one version of *Conde Alarcos* (Larrea 85), the noble protagonist
is the "Count of Almería." The victim in *La muerte del duque de Gandía* is the
"Count of Seville."

2.4) The last points to consider in this study are the name-character
relationship and the possible functions of anthroponyms within the ballad
narration. As in the case of the toponyms, they can be expected to go beyond
the merely indicative.

2.4.a) To begin with, we must raise the problem of the correspondence of
one and only one proper name to each character in each version. I do not refer
only to the fact that, in a single version, a character can have two different but
equivalent names, as for example, in *Diego León* (Larrea 83):

En la ciudad de Madrid,
en la ciudad de Granada,
ahí se ha criado un manzebo
que *Griego León* le llaman....
Un día se vieron juntos,
dize *León* a su dama....

I refer to a more complex and surprising phenomenon. In a considerable
number of texts, the names of certain characters are altered arbitrarily or even
contradictorily, giving the impression that it is not as important to identify each
character by name as to assign names, perhaps arbitrarily, to all the characters
who take part. Thus, in a version of the same *Diego León* (Larrea 82), the name
Pedro is given to the bride's father and also to her suitor, who had just previously
been called *León*:

ni le aprovecha el dinero
con que *León* negociaba...
Un día por la mañana

a don *Pedro* se encontrara;...
—Don *Pedro*, dame a tu hija,
a tu hija doña *Juana.*
—Mi hija no es de casar
porque aún es chica y muchacha.
Por hacer burla del caso
a su hija lo contara:
—Don *Pedro* te ha pedido;
váyase en hora mala.

Likewise, in one version of *Búcar sobre Valencia* (Larrea 8), the protagonist
and the rival receive the same name—*Sidi*—with the additional complication that
it is the same *Sidi*—a Christian—who tells his daughter to delay the Morrish
enemy, with these words:

—Cuando pasare ese *Sidi*
entretenle con palabras

where it is likely that *Sidi* is not a proper name but has the etymological sense
of 'gentleman.'

More spectacular is the tangle of names in one version of the popular ballad
of *Melchor y Laurencia* (Larrea 61), where the protagonist sometimes is *Laurencia*,
sometimes *Laudencia*, and sometimes *Lucrecia*, and her suitor is both *Menchol
Veleza* and *Menchol Vileza.*

There are numerous examples of this phenomenon. It clearly can be argued
that these changes are due to occasional errors committed by singers or reciters.
That is true, but these cases indicate the mobility, flexibility, and instability of
anthroponyms in ballads.

A result of that mobility, that instability, is a series of phenomena that need
to be studied with properly analyzed texts:

2.4.b) For example, the frequency—or infrequency—with which a character
appears with the same name in all versions of the ballad. There is the impression
that the protagonist has the same name in but a few very specific ballads. (*Virgilios*,
for example, with merely phonetic variations; or *Juan Lorenzo*; or *Diego León*.
It is quite significant that, in all three cases, the character's name is the title of
the ballad.) In the majority of cases, the characters—protagonist or not—receive
different names depending on the informants.

2.4.c) Or also the apparent existence of names which can be applied to various
characters, although they come from a specific type of ballad. Such seems to
be the case of *Sidi* and *Jimena* which, originating in ballads on El Cid, can appear
in historical, novelistic, and even Moorish ballads. The Carolingian *Alda* is utilized
at times as a woman's name in ballads that have no Carolingian elements. There
are others, such as *Alonso* or *Albar.*

2.4.d) This takes us to a last question. Does some degree of specialization
exist, as in the case of toponyms, of specific anthroponyms in specific uses? Are

there characters whose name defines their traits? Does the fact that a character is called *Bueso*, *Blanca Niña*, or *Alda* provide some implicit information to a Sephardic listener? Do certain names have a connotative value that lets them transmit additional information?

We cannot conclude anything for the moment—nor do we want to—until the systematic analysis of the whole body of works is finished. Let the possibility stand for the moment.

NOTES

1. As an example of recent compilations totally or partially unpublished, two realized in Israel can be cited. One is by Moshe Shaul, resulting from his program in Judeo-Spanish on Kol Israel, some samples of which have been broadcast on that program or published by the journal, *Aki Yerushalayim*. There is also the compilation by musicologist Susana Weich-Shahak, in the record library of the Jewish National University Library of Jerusalem, from the Moroccan texts, of which I am preparing an edition in collaboration with Krinka Vidakovic. Besides these, several libraries have manuscript collections in which the Sephardic families of Morocco were wont to gather the songs that they knew, a good part of which were ballads. A description of one of them (that of Luna Bennaim) done by the owner of the manuscript, Iacob M. Hassán, and me, will soon appear in *Estudios Sefardíes* of *Sefarad*; I am also preparing an edition of the more than two hundred texts contained in it.

2. The ballads are included in the following publications: Africano Fernández, *España en Africa y el peligro judío: Apuntes de un testigo desde 1915 a 1918* (Santiago: 1918); M. Alvar, *Cantos de boda judeo-españoles*, (Madrid: CSIC, 1971); M. Alvar, *Poesía tradicional de los judíos españoles* (Mexico: Porrúa, 1966—only the primary texts); M. Alvar, *Textos hispánicos dialectales: Antología histórica*, 2 vols. (Madrid: CSIC, 1960): II, pp. 729–792; O. Anahory Librowicz, *Florilegio de romances sefardíes de la diáspora (Una colección malagueña)* (Madrid: Cátedra-Seminario Menéndez Pidal, 1980); S. G. Armistead et al., "Antología" in Vol. III of *El Romancero judeo-español en el Archivo Menendez Pidal (Catálogo-índice de romances y canciones)*, 3 vols. (Madrid: Cátedra-Seminario Menéndez Pidal, 1978); S. G. Armistead and J. H. Silverman, *En torno al Romancero sefardí (Hispanismo y balcanismo de la tradición judeoespañola)* (Madrid: Cátedra-Seminario Menéndez Pidal, 1982); M. J. Benardete (col.), *Judeo-Spanish Ballads from New York*, ed. S. G. Armistead and J. H. Silverman (Berkeley: Univ. of California Press, 1981); P. Bénichou, *Romancero judeo-española de Marruecos* (Madrid: Castalia, 1968); J. Benoliel, "Dialecto judeo-hispano-marroquí o Hakitía", *Boletín de la Real Academia Española* XIV (1927): pp. 137–168, 196–234, 357–373, and 566–580; P. Díaz-Mas, *Temas y tópicos en la poesia luctuosa sefardí* (Madrid: Univ. Complutense, 1982); A. de Larrea Palacín, *Cancionero judío del Norte de Marruecos: Canciones rituales hispano-judías* (Madrid: CSIC, 1954); A. de Larrea

Palacín, *Cancionero judío del Norte de Marruecos: Romances de Tetuán*, 2 vols. (Madrid: CSIC, 1952); J. Martínez Ruiz, "Poesía sefardí de carácter tradicional (Alcazarquivir)," *Archivum* XIII (1963): pp. 79–215; Z. Nahón (col.), *Romances judeoespañoles de Tánger*, ed. S. G. Armistead and J. H. Silverman (Madrid: Cátedra-Seminario Menéndez Pidal, 1977); and M. L. Ortega, *Los hebreos en Marruecos*, reprint of the 2nd edition (Madrid, 1934).

3. "Topónimos en el Romancero sefardí de Marruecos," paper presented at the Second International Congress for the Study of Sephardic and Oriental Jewry (Jerusalem, Misgav Yerushalayim, December 1984), in press for the proceedings: "Madrid en el romancero sefardí de Marruecos", paper for the I Jornadas de la Comunidad Autónoma de Madrid sobre Madrid Tradicional (San Sebastián de los Reyes, Universidad Popular, December 1984), published in the proceedings of that meeting (San Sebastián de los Reyes: Univ. Popular, 1985): pp. 11–15; and "La mención de Granada en los romances sefardíes de Marruecos," paper for the Congreso Internacional sobre lengua y Literatura en época de los Reyes Católicos (Madrid-Hita-Pastrana: CSIC, July 1986), in press for the proceedings.

THIRTEEN

"Plázeme de tus Enojos": Alfonso Alvarez de Villasandino against Alfonso Ferrandes Semuel

Carlos Mota
Translated by George K. Zucker

L et us read Alfonso Alvarez de Villasandino's verses in the *Cancionero de Baena* condemning the convert Alfonso Ferrandes Semuel:

1280
Ms.: PN1 140 (45 r) Este dezir fizo e ordenó el dicho Alfonso Alvarez de Villasandino contra Alfonso Ferrandes Semuel, el más donoso loco que ovo en el mundo.
Alfonso Alvarez de Villasandino composed and arranged this poem for Alfonso Ferrandes Semuel, the most amusing crazy man the world has ever seen.

I Pues non tengo qué fazer
   ora con los contadores,
   contar quiero tus dolores,
   Alfonso, a quien bel ver;
   todos deven bien creer,   5
   que, quanto en aquesta hedat,
   non nació tal *mesumad*
   nin creo que ha de nasçer.

I Since I have nothing to do
   now with accountants,
   let me count your troubles,

185

Alfonso, the good-looking;
everyone should believe   5
that, although in this age,
such a *meshumad* was not born
nor do I think he will be.

   II Ya passan de los sesenta
     años malos que nasçiste,   10
     que cada día corriste
     grant fortuna con tormenta,
     resçibiendo çiertamente   (f. 45 v.)
     de palos e bofetadas:
     si padesçen tus quixadas   15
     tu nariz lo repressenta.

II It is now more than sixty
    evil years since you were born,   10
    when every day you experienced
    great fortune with torture
    certainly receiving   (f. 45 v.)
    your buffets and blows:
    if your jawbones suffer   15
    your nose shows it.

   III En quanto fuestes judío
      —bien quarenta años o más,
      Simuel *fide*, salta atrás—
      noble fue tu atavío: 20
      en invierno passa frido,
      en verano roça poco;
      estonçes, mançebo loco;
      agora, viejo atrevido.

III As for when you were a Jew
    —a good forty years or more,
    Shimuel son of Salta Atrás (= Jump Backwards)—
    your dress was noble: 20
    in winter you feel the cold,
    in the summer little goes through;
    then, a crazy young man;
    now an insolent old man.

   IV E pues eres behetría   25
      de Ayala entre parientes
      —donde perdiste los dientes—,

ruégote por cortesía
que dexes la garçonía,
oso viejo e sin sabor,   30
pues nunca serviste amor
nin fuste en su compañ[í]a.

IV And since you were a confusion   25
    among relatives from Ayala
    —where you lost your teeth—,
    I beg you for courtesy's sake
    to leave youthful mannerisms,
    old bear with no flavor,   30
    since you never served love
    nor were in its company.

V   Plázeme de tus enojos,
    Dios me perdone si peco,
    pues soliés nadar en seco   35
    do te cosieron los ojos;
    [a] vezes me toman antojos
    de te ver de aquesta guissa:
    tú descalço e sin camisa
    sin jubón trillando abrojos.   40

V   I am pleased about your troubles,
    God forgive me if I sin,
    since you used to swim high and dry   35
    where they sewed up your eyes;
    sometimes I feel
    like seeing you that way:
    barefoot and with no shirt
    or doublet, raking thistles.   40

1281
Ms.: PN1 141 (45 v.)
Total vv.: 6 (2, 4); *Estribote*
    Estribot de Alfonso Alvarez para Alfonso Ferrandes Semuel
    Refrain by Alfonso Alvarez for Alfonso Ferrandes Semuel

I   Alfonso, capón corrido,
    tajar te quiero un vestido.

I   Alfonso, abashed capon,
    I want to cut some clothing for you.

Balandrán de quatro quartos
bien senbrado de lagartos:
desque fueren en ti fartos,   5
quedarás loco atordido.

Cassock with four holes
well sown with lizards:
since there were enough on you,   5
you will remain a hopeless crazy man.

1282
Ms. PN1 142 (45 v.-46 r.)
Total vv.: 56 (7 x 8); *Dezir*
    Este dezir fizo el dicho Alfonso Alvarez por manera de testamento contra
el dicho Alfonso Ferrandes quando finó.
    This rhyme was composed by Alfonso Alvarez as a will for Alfonso Ferrandes
when he died.

    I   Amigos quantos ovistes
        plazer con Alfonso en vida,
        de su muerte tan plañida
        sed agora un poco tristes,
        o reíd como reístes   5
        sienpre de su dessatento
        oyendo su testamento:
        quiçá tal nunca lo oístes.

    I   Friends who took
        pleasure with Alfonso during his life,
        of his so-lamented death
        be now a little sad,
        or laugh as you laughed   5
        always at his impoliteness
        listening to his will:
        perhaps you have never heard such.

    II Testamento e codeçillo
        ordenó como christiano,   10
        e mandó luego de mano
        mandas de muy grand cabdillo:
        que le fagan un luzillo
        en que sea debuxada
        toda su vida lazdrada,   15
        su[s] corrençias e omezillo.

II Testament and codicil
　he ordered as a Christian, 10
　and he then sent it by hand
　as if he were a great leader:
　that they make him a little light
　in which would be portrayed
　his whole miserable life, 15
　his verbosity and insults.

　III Manda a la Trenidat
　　un cornado de los nuevos;
　　a la Cruzada, dos huevos
　　en señal de christiandat; 20
　　e por mayor caridat,
　　manda çient maravedís
　　para judíos, avís
　　que non labren en Sabad.

III He leaves to the Trinity
　a new coin;
　to the Crusades, two eggs
　(as a sign of Christianity); 20
　and, as greater charity,
　he leaves a hundred maravedis
　to Jews, you know,
　so that they not work on Saturday.

　IV Manda que'l ponga la cruz 25
　　a los pies: ved qué locura;
　　el Alcorán, nesçia escriptura,
　　en los pechos al marfuz;
　　el Atorá, su vida e luz,
　　en la cabeça, la quiera 30
　　destas leis, quien más podiere,
　　esse have este abestruz.

IV He orders the cross put 25
　at his feet: what craziness;
　the Koran, stupid scripture,
　on the chest of the renegade;
　the Torah, his life and light,
　at his head, let him love it 30
　for its laws, whoever best can,
　that bird, this ostrich.

 V Si moriere oy o cras,
  manda su opa la blanca
  que la den en Salamanca   35
  o aquí [a] algunt *samaz*,
  porque'l reze en el *homaz*
  e le canten con buen son
  una *huina*, un *pizmón*,
  bien plañidos por compás.   40

V Should he die today or tomorrow,
 he directs that his white cassock
 be given in Salamanca   35
 or here to some *shamass*,
 so that he will pray for him in the *humash*
 and will sing for him in good voice
 a *huina*, a *pizmon*,
 well mourned in rhythm.   40

(f. 46v.)

 VI De su asno e sus fardeles
  e de su opa de seda,
  manda fazer almoneda
  para dar a los donzeles,
  porque l'non sean crueles   45
  —aunque otri los conseje—;
  nin lo traigan a ereje
  arrastrando con cordeles.

VI His ass and his packs
 and his silk tunic,
 he orders to be auctioned
 to give [funds] to the young men,
 so that they not be cruel to him   45
 —even if someone else advises them to—
 nor bring him up as a heretic
 dragging him with ropes.

 VII Faze su testamentario
  para complir todo aquesto   50
  un judío de buen gesto
  que llaman Jacob Çidario,
  al qual manda su sudario
  en señal de *çedaquá*
  porque reze *tefilá*   55
  desque fuere en su fonsario.

VII He makes his executor
to carry all this out
a good-tempered Jew
named Jacob Cidiario
to whom he bequeaths his shroud
as a sign of *tsedaka*
so that he will pray *tefillah*
once he is in his grave.[1]

To begin with, it is not easy to assign exact dates to these poems. Nevertheless, it seems logical that they were composed *in vita* and *in morte* of Ferrandes Semuel, in at least two different time periods—to which the poems refer directly—thus forming a small humorous burlesque *cancionero* which Baena's compilation has preserved as a series of scenes. But we cannot even affirm that much definitively, especially if we look at the genre which, in my opinion, the third poem imitates, a burlesque versified will. It could well be entitled *The Convert's Will* (similar to a *testamentum porcelli*, cat's will, drunkard's will, and so many other last will and testaments in both verse and prose, which are humorous or didactic, ultimately representative of certain professions or conditions). Clearly, the basic condition, which may be no more than fiction—that is, an *ad hominem* mockery, albeit somewhat macabre—is the death of the supposed testator whose wishes are being made public.[2]

The best possible reading of these poems requires knowing their dates. Villasandino's work comprises about a third of the *Cancionero de Baena*, one of the oldest of the great fifteenth-century collections of Castilian poetry meant specifically for the entertainment of King Juan II and his close family members.[3] It is generally agreed that a poetic work as extensive as Villasandino's—with few parallels in terms of quantity—would have seen the light between the early 1370s and 1424.[4] That is to say, it was published during the first half-century of the reign of the dynasty which, between 1369 and 1492, would finally control all of the Spanish kingdoms, impel the discovery of the New World, eliminate the last Islamic kingdom in Western Europe, and expel the Jews from Spain. These deeds are more than just the fruits of governmental action on the part of the Trastamara monarchs—in their various branches—and, doubtless, more than the doings of just the Catholic monarchs. In such a context, even if only for its demonstrable testimonial value, Villasandino's work, the work of a courtier, seems worthy of a more detailed study than it has enjoyed up to now.

Yet it is difficult to tell for sure if the large quantity of Villasandino's work in the *Cancionero de Baena* reflects the poetic tastes of the courts of the first Castilian Trastamaras (from Enrique II to the early reign of Juan II)[5] or is a result of the preferences of someone closely connected to the *Cancionero*'s compiler, Juan Alfonso de Baena[6]—perhaps even the compiler himself. It may be his homage to a notorious (or a petty) personage[7] in the court, a former colleague, unworthy and mercenary except for his poetic talent and loyalty to the crown, for whose library the volume was being compiled—loyalty *pro pane lucrando,* but not necessarily toward the whole royal family. The poet's longevity could as well account for the quantity of work. Or it might be the peculiar wish of Villasandino—or of one of his friends—to always have on hand, in more or less orderly fashion, the majority of his poetry, which (we must not forget) was not merely the product of his spare time, but rather one of his means of livelihood.

We can be reasonably certain, at least, that the poems under consideration were first heard between 1390 and 1424—and that they were, in more than one sense, representative of a common literary reaction to a phenomenon which could be considered new if only by its unusual extent at that time: the forced conversions to Christianity. That thirty-year period was among the most bitter experienced by the Jews in medieval Spain, times which, despite their ominous character, had their ups and downs, and which no one has documented better than Yitzhak Baer.[8]

Regarding the *terminus a quo* of 1390, bear in mind that it is the decade when Villasandino and other poets of his generation abandon in practical terms the use of Galician as a vehicle for expression, with few exceptions. There is more than one cause for this change of language, thus breaking with the Castilian troubadour tradition but, as Ramón Menéndez Pidal notes,[9] it would be unlikely for Villasandino and his colleagues to have suffered an attack of Lusophobia, so to speak, given the situation in the court after the reversal of Juan I's policies— and his spirit as well[10]—as a result of the defeat of Castile's troops by the Portuguese in Aljubarrota in August 1385. One result of that disaster might have been the historical abandonment of Galician as a poetic language in Castile, although, as Rafael Lapesa notes, that phenomenon began before the battle and its immediate antecedents, with roots that were historical, literary, and esthetic, as well as political and social.[11] With this fact in mind, I have chosen as an obvious, and perhaps overcautious, *terminus ante quem* the year in which we lose sight of our poet—1424.[12] Dating from around that year, we have a good number of texts which show Villasandino's ultimate loyalty to the cause of his young sovereign, badgered by the intrigues of the Infantes of Aragon, and the importunate and derelict image of the poet, already quite aged. It is precisely this image—because it is the one which most characterizes him—that has caused his devaluation in the eyes of Spanish literary historians, especially Marcelino Menénedez y Pelayo.[13]

This rapid review, despite its sketchiness, shows that many historical lines and literary and life experiences intersect in these poems. In view of all this, a search for two dates with the mentioned characteristics is not arbitrary; not if we bear in mind, on one hand, the language in which they are written, and, on the other, the realization that almost nothing of Villasandino's later work differs from that begging character to which I referred earlier.[14]

Both literarily and historically, it would be well to recall (again briefly) what happened to the Spanish Jews during the years we have accepted as possible dates (1370 and 1424). First, the crucial year of 1391 marks the culmination (not the beginning, despite its notorious and multiple effects) of a convulsive anti-Jewish attitude. This climate was due overwhelmingly to four factors. Religiously and culturally, the establishment and growth of universities during the thirteenth century was of capital importance for western Christian culture, and the effects of the Fourth Lateran Council's decrees on the Church led to the growth and renewal of *coram populo* preaching due, among other factors, to the appearance of new religious orders. In the social and economic arena, the crisis which struck Europe during the first half of the fourteenth century and the Bubonic plague epidemic, attributed in many places to presumed plots and criminal actions of the Jews, are certainly factors. The year 1391 also marks the appearance of the first *pogroms* in Castile (begun in the Andalusian Jewish communities by Ferrán Martinez's agitation of the masses), and they quickly spread to the neighboring kingdom of Aragon. It becomes clear that only the presence of the king or a militarily powerful delegate in an area could save the Jewish community from looting and its population from being forced to choose between baptism and death. Such is the case of Zaragoza, where King Juan I of Aragon was when, within a few weeks' time, attacks took place in Valencia, Barcelona, Gerona, and other towns and cities of the realm. Above all, 1391 is a year of bloodshed and massive conversion to Christianity, due to sheer physical terror unseen until that time, at least in so great a degree.

Over the course of the thirteenth and fourteenth centuries, many left Judaism for the most diverse reasons—especially after the war between Pedro I and Enrique II of the House of Trastamara and the rather negative results of that conflict for the Jews. Even if many of them did not abandon their beliefs of their own accord during that period, it is certain that the process was due less to the effects of fear than to the development of an attractive advanced culture nearly incompatible with the strict discipline of Jewish life and to the efficacy of persistent Christian apologia on the powerful as well as on the weak. Add to all this the long-term effects of an economic and political crisis which pardoned neither Christian nor Jew, closing off, especially for the latter, many possibilities of advancement and—in the majority of cases—survival, with increasingly restrictive juridical and moral standards. The die is cast for Iberian Jews from 1391, despite the fact that the fifteenth century will see an economic and demographic renaissance of some Jewish communities and a major remission of violence (which will, nevertheless, reoccur here and there with some frequency). Anti-Semitism has yet to meet figures such as San Vicente Ferrer—whose preachings range throughout Europe (and who was a major factor in the ascension of a Trastamara to the throne of Aragon in 1412)—and Benedict XIII, the Aragonese Pedro de Luna, who put Judaism on the gallows at the Dispute of Tortosa.[15]

What most interests us around 1391 is the world of the *conversos*, a world to which Alfonso Ferrandes Semuel belongs, if not exactly chronologically (and there is no way to know that), then certainly spiritually. Although there is no way to know it, we can gather from Villasandino's words in lines 17–18 of poem 1280—*En quanto fuestes judio, / bien quarenta años o más*. . .(As for when you were a Jew—a good forty years or more. . .)—that Ferrandes Semuel was baptized as an adult, having been a practicing Jew for many years, and the baptism was some twenty years earlier: *Ya passan de los sessenta/años malos que naçiste*, vv. 9–10 (It is now more than sixty/evil years since you were born). Given that, a conversion at that time of life, and in those times, was likely due to societal pressure. Furthermore, if it is not very probable that such poems were written before 1385 or 1390 for historical, linguistic, and literary reasons, nor is it likely that they were written after 1424 or 1425, since that was the time when Villasandino disappeared, the most plausible hypothesis would have Ferrandes Semuel converted in 1391 or shortly thereafter (because of what went on during that year), at the time when such societal pressure was at its most acute. If all this is correct, we simply need to add to 1391 the twenty years that Villasandino says have passed since Ferrandes Semuel's conversion to find the date of the poems' composition, in or near the year 1411.

Let us not, however, yield to the temptation of taking converts or—worse yet—the descendents of converts as necessarily Jews or Judaizers, regardless of the sincerity of conversion or the amount of free will that led to that conversion. This matter may also be a posthumous 'triumph' of the xenophobic attitude toward the 'other person'—be that Jew, Moor, *converso*, or whoever—heretofore hidden under many layers of Old Christianity. That is the mentality that Villasandino exhibits in these poems, albeit for different motives. Whether it was done consciously, unconsciously, or subconsciously matters little now: literarily, and for the sake of the comic effect sought, the poet could not have chosen a more effective approach.

The convert, simply by virtue of being who he is, is a false convert, an opportunist, probably a Crypto-Jew. It is not useful, sensible, possible—or prone to literary satire—for him to believe in the authenticity of his new faith. Furthermore, someone capable of renouncing his ancestors' faith, even if obliged by the sword to do so, is, like his beliefs, inconstant and, consequently, a target for ridicule. One step further makes him as verbally executable as a Jew; he is as much the 'other person' (and therefore suspect, false, tainted) as is the Jew, only more so because of his deceit, first presumed and then taken for granted. Baptism of a convert, for the mentality here sketched, is, or should be, a mark of exclusion (just like the *sambenito*), and not a safe-conduct which, in any case, attests to the precarious situation of one who exhibits it on demand—often simply because he is known to be a convert. It therefore is not correct to consider the convert as integrated into society, as socially rehabilitated, or as redeemed by and for Christianity, but rather, on the contrary, as someone deservedly punished, insalvageable because of his own nature and condition. At the time these poems were written, especially if that time is, indeed, around 1411, it would be neither recent nor unheard of to find the reappearance of the traditional hatred, envy, and ridicule of the Jew applied now equally to the convert who is well-situated socially or who holds a good position because of baptism. For the active antagonist in this relationship, the convert is not a new Christian, but the same Jew as always, disguised—a renegade, but a Jew (allowing the establishment of the equation *renegade = Jew*); an especially Jewish Jew because he has gone back on his original faith. For the anti-Semite, Judaism is a nefarious essence, not an accidental circumstance. In any case, that is what is in his best interest to believe and, in certain cases, he interiorizes it sincerely as the only correct interpretation of reality. A good illustration is the fact that, according to the portrait Villasandino offers us in poem 1280, Ferrandes Semuel could certainly not be a motive for hatred or social or economic envy to even the most impoverished (except, perhaps, if he were better at begging).[16]

One need only look at the first of the texts (in the order in which they appear in the *Cancionero de Baena*), to realize that only the presence of a mentality like the one described, or one very close to it, can reasonably account for the mockery these verses try to achieve and, consequently, they give us a reasonable idea of the conditions under which these poems were originally published. Nevertheless, the cruelly ingenious characteristics of that attitude show up most clearly in the burlesque will which is poem 1282, laced with Hebrew terms used to indicate malicious knowledge—which converts this poem into a sort of *qab*, as well as a perversely intentional dwelling on one's weaknesses—precisely because these characteristics are present in the voice that speaks in the poem, even supposing, as the contents indicate, that these words come after Ferrandes Semuel's death. This all allows us to affirm that the phenomenon is not simply a rhetorical recourse with demeaning purpose, but rather a form of expression which comes from a mentality disposed to reacting with black humor in situations such as poor Ferrandes Semuel's.

Consequently, a series of complex linguistic acts are generated. It would be a question of attitude, like the one in Quevedo's famous anti-Gongora sonnet. And, of course, it is in the same tradition, in both rhetoric and thought. If Quevedo threatened to anoint his verses with bacon so that Gongora would not dare consume them—as corresponded topically to the descendent of converts who are therefore, willy-nilly, suspect of Cryptojudaism—Villasandino, tongue in cheek, uses the greatest possible amount of Jewish liturgical terminology, the clearest cultural indication (and even part of the Castilian social scene) to emphasize his quips. Products of a thorough knowledge of the Jews, their religion and way of life, they accuse Ferrandes Semuel of being an apostate of his old faith and, at the same time, they remind him inequivocally that he belongs to a group marked for exclusion. An especially cutting example is the reference to Ferrandes Semuel with the Hebrew *mesumad* (apostate) in line 7 of the first stanza of the first poem, which is constructed entirely on the basis of malicious witticisms, of words and phrases with double meanings, direct ancestors of the polemic repartee of the Baroque poets. Some examples:

A. *contadores-contar*—(after the ambiguous *fazer con*—equivalent to 'be busy with' or 'criticize'. Its likely context is the habitual tardiness of the bookkeepers in paying his salary, a situation of which Villasandino complains on one occasion to the king). It may mean both things at once (which seems most probable), and it behooves us to remember that bookkeeping had been, and still was, especially the work of Jews and former Jews, a fact which places the joke in a broader and more tensely significant framework. Or is it—tremendous suspicion that would contradict much more than all of the interpretations to date of these lines—that the author of this poem was the Contador Mayor, Alfonso Alvarez de Toledo, who evidently had very good reasons for having business with the bookkeepers (*tener qué fazer con los contadores*)?

B. *ver/creer*—add to this the fact that, according to what Villasandino guilefully says later in lines 35–36, Ferrandes Semuel had been blinded. And do not overlook the possibility that this may well be a malicious evangelical echo (especially in such a text, since the Resurrection is the most obvious manifestation of Jesus' divinity and a basic article of faith for Christianity) of "Happy are those who have believed without seeing," ("Beati qui non viderunt et crediderunt" with which the resurrected Christ admonishes Thomas, once the latter recognizes him by the sight and feel of the stigmata.

C. *todos deven bien creer*—a phrase which, opportunely taken out of context, can be read perfectly well as an admonition against the Jews who would consider Ferrandes Semuel to be a *mesumad*, etc. In this stanza we see the greatest concentration of these double entendres, completely deliberate as I see them.

In the remaining poems—except the last one—everything is much more uncouth. For example, the classic mention of the peculiar size and shape of his nose here becomes particularly sinister if we speculate that perhaps what is meant by *fortuna* ('fortune,' and also 'storm') and *tormenta* ('storms'), the blows and punches that collapsed this unfortunate convert's jawbones so that his nose was forced to grow, thus acquiring its characteristic appearance (lines 11–16)—may be experiences like the *pogroms*. Or consider the probably sarcastic allusion to the clothing and physical appearance (*noble atavío*) in the era in which Ferrandes Semuel had been Jewish—because Jews were required to look different from Christians in their clothing and the way they wore their hair and beards—beyond the ridiculous clothing that was habitual among the court jesters (where monks' cassocks certainly occupied a prominent place).

This *manner* is not an adornment of the first and last stanzas of the text, a 'brilliant' beginning and end, but rather the backbone of this poem, from its sounds to the most recondite of its senses. And think, too, of the second of the two dimensions needed for the complete understanding of this medieval poetry. (First is obviously the music. It would be no surprise if these texts were accompanied by an imitation as malevolently burlesque as the double and triple meanings previously mentioned.) I refer here to mimicry and histrionic inflections of voice—a complete *poétique de la voix*—which require, in an era of exaggeration like few others, an effective public interpretation of poetry so full of verbal winks. This procedure finds its best and most complete representation in the formulation of the title of these lines: *Plázeme de tus enojos,/Dios me perdone si peco* ('I am pleased about your troubles,/God forgive me if I sin' [lines 33–34]), where I cannot help but hear the abominable wordplay *Plázeme de tú sen ojos* ('I'm pleased about you without eyes') as the background of its already horrifying meaning (in which—and in all similar references throughout the poem—aside from the actual blindness of Ferrandes Semuel, it has to do with the topic common in apologetics and iconography, of *caecitas judaeorum*).

Of course, there could be more than an easy rhyme in the *antojos* ('whims') of line 37. We know from another of his poems in the *Cancionero de Baena* that when Villasandino was older—probably at about the time of the poems in question—he used eyeglasses [*anteojos*] for reading and writing (See *Cancionero de Baena*, 216, v. 3 [Dutton, *CIPC*, 1356]). The same is true of *abrojos* ('thistles' = 'with eyes open' [*con los ojos abiertos*]) a word first documented in Castilian in the *Castigos e documentos para bien vivir ordenados por el Rey don Sancho*. Its etymology seems to be as follows: "contraction of the Latin phrase *aperi oculos* 'open your eyes', originally a warning to those mowing a field full of thistles so they would be careful, and subsequently the name of the plant."[17]

Francisco Cantera Burgos, in his review article of the latest edition of the *Cancionero de Baena*, recalled the double-edged possibility of Villasandino's being a convert himself.[18] And he, in turn, echoed the cruelty shown to former coreligionists by many influential New Christians. Not only the eminent behaved this way, nor was it always because of the somewhat less than permanent worth which the rest of Spanish society attributed to them over the course of centuries. But there is no indication which would allow us to go beyond the suspicion stated, not without reservations, by the master of Hebraists and which, by itself, would add little more than pathos to a fuller understanding of these poems. It is sufficient to record that we probably find ourselves in the presence of a typical wretch who enjoys—and makes other enjoy—publicly ridiculing the wretchedness of those worse off than he. However much he might take delight in these texts before an audience which knows him as both jokester and target, the pot's calling the kettle black, so to speak, could turn out to be especially humorous.

The beginning of the burlesque will (and the title of the first poem, but that is another story) calls to mind the image of the unfortunate Ferrandes Semuel and presents the atmosphere of a courtly feast—although really quite sordid and dissolute at heart—where there was no place for distinctions of race or religion, and barely for social status, when it come time to call each other names wittily (and not so wittily) as pure diversion. It is the ideal atmosphere for the initial recitation, live and perhaps with appropriate musical accompaniment, of verses such as these.

Maxime Chevalier has indicated the probable importance of courtly name-calling (especially during the time of Carlos V, and in previous eras) to explain certain characteristics of Hispanic literary conceptism beyond purely burlesque and courtly themes and situations.[19] We may have here an early example of the same exercise, closely related to the *cantiga d'escarnho*. It is circumstantial poetry, yes, but not merely that: it is a major component of the poetry of the 1400s, a fountain and source of wealth of some of the best-known literary and linguistic creations of the Golden Age. And also a vignette of an era which, for many reasons, may well be considered darker and more transcendent than has been believed to date.[20]

NOTES

1. The numbers of the poems and the sigla of the manuscripts are those given in the *Catálogo índice de la poesía cancioneril del siglo XV*, by Brian Dutton et al (Madison, WI: Hispanic Seminary of Medieval Studies, 1982) (from here on, *CIPC*). The edition of the texts and the punctuation are mine. I have kept in mind in these matters several interesting interpretive suggestions in the article by Francisco Márquez Villanueva, "Jewish Fools of the Spanish Fifteenth Century," *Hispanic Review*, L (1982), pp. 385–409. For other readings and interpretations, see the editions of the *Cancionero de Baena* by P. J. Pidal and E. de Ochoa (Madrid, 1851), Francisque Michel (Leipzig, 1860), and José María Azáceta (Madrid, 1966), those by Raymond Foulché-Delbosc in his *Cancionero castellano del siglo XV* (Madrid, 1912–1915), Vol. II, or Francisco Cantera Burgos in his summary review of the edition of José María Azáceta, "El *Cancionero de Baena*: judíos y conversos en él" in *Sefarad*, XXVII (1967), pp. 71–111 (specifically pp. 89–93). Translations are relatively literal; the baroque word-plays in Spanish could not be meaningfully transferred into English.

2. In fact, the genre so freely imitated here is identified with this fictitious character. In addition, in this case, given the fact that the supposed *author* of the will, Ferrandes Semuel, is a real person, Villasandino would take advantage of that characteristic of the genre to seek an even more emphatically humorous effect by attributing to the convert (still alive?) presumed wishes designed to make the situation absolutely clear to the public so that readers could laugh at the ideas. I have said that the genre of the burlesque will is freely imitated by Spanish poets: that explains why Villasandino seeks the opportunity to include his own voice, a voice which appears as the notary who, rather than simply reading the text, refers summarily to the content of Ferrandes Semuel's document (which he does not quote directly, nor put in the dead man's mouth). On burlesque wills in Spain, see José Vidal, "Testamentos de bestias," *Revista de Dialectología y Tradiciones Populares* (hereafter *RDTP*) III (1947), pp. 524–550; José Luis Pérez

de Castro, "El testamento del gato y una canción de corro en Figueras (Asturias),"
RDTP IX (1953), pp. 350–357; and Pilar García de Diego, "El testamento en la
tradición popular,"*RDTP* III, (1947) pp. 551–557; "El testamento del gato." *RDTP*
IV (1948), pp. 306–307 and "El testamento en la tradición," *RDTP* IX (1953), pp.
601–666, and X (1954), pp. 400–471.

3. Remember the well-known dedication of the *Cancionero de Baena* in
the Bibliothèque Nationale de Paris (PN1, according to Dutton's index, *CIPC*)
to King Juan II, Queen Maria, and the prince Don Enrique, and to the royal
family above all; also the observations on the value and the characteristics of
the text transmitted in that manuscript (which was not the one given to the
king, since it is copied on paper made in Pistoia ca. 1460), by Barclay Tittmann,
"A Contribution to the Study of the *Cancionero de Baena* manuscript," *Aquila*
I (1968), pp. 190–203, and by Alberto Bleuca, " 'Perdióse un quaderno. . .': sobre
los Cancioneros de Baena," *Anuario de Estudios Medievales* IX (1974–79), pp.
229–266. See also Brian Dutton, "Spanish Fifteenth-Century Cancioneros: A
General Survey to 1465," *Kentucky Romance Quarterly* XXVI (1979), pp. 445–460.

4. This conclusion has been almost generally accepted since Erasmo
Buceta's article, "Fecha probable de una poesía de Villasandino y de la muerte
del poeta," *Revista de Filología Española*, XVI (1929), pp. 51–58.

5. In his famous *Carta prohemio al Condestable Don Pedro de Portugal*, the
Marqués de Santillana reserves an outstanding place for our poet, inspired by
reading the dedication of the *Cancionero de Baena* (*Unicuique gracia est data
secundum Paulum relata*) or, more probably, from Villasandino's works in general.
I use 'the reign of Juan II' to mean from the time he achieved majority and was
no longer under the regency of his mother, Queen Catalina of Lancaster, and
his uncle, Fernando.

6. Regarding whether of not Juan Alfonso de Baena was a convert, much
has been written since the beginning of the reconsideration of said collection
in the middle of the last century, depending largely—and perhaps excessively—
on how critics read the word *indino/iudino* in the dedication. The question has
been resolved by Azáceta's observations in the prologue to his edition of the
Cancionero (1966), I, pp. 4–5n., where he summarizes the main points of the
argument, supported by Cantera Burgos in his earlier-cited review article. Baena's
opponents recall his diet and other customs typical of Jews, as well as his baptism,
and leave little doubt as to the likelihood of his being a convert. To those factors
there has recently been added conclusive documentary evidence by Manuel Nieto
Cumplido, "Aportación histórica al *Cancionero de Baena*," *Historia, Instituciones,
Documentos* VI (1979), pp. 197–218. But, on the other hand, what we read in
the manuscript now in Paris is the word *indino.*

7. "Personilla," as he is called by Pedro M. Cátedra in his *Exégesis, ciencia,
literatura: la exposición del salmo "Quoniam videbo" por Enrique de Villena* (Madrid,
1985), p. 25, where he raises the interesting question—which would necessitate
reevaluating matters that today are considered commonplaces regarding

Villasandino and the *Cancionero de Baena*—that, at least in the case of the *pregunta que fizo fray Pedro Imperial a Alfonso Alvarez* (0171 in Dutton, *CIPC*) "señor Alfonso Alvarez gran sabio perfecto," mentioned in the first line of the poem, would be Alfonso Alvarez de Toledo, finance minister (*contador mayor*) for Juan II, not Villasandino. In fact, as Cátedra remarks, the *Respuesta* (Dutton, *CIPC*, 0172 R 0171) to the aforesaid *pregunta* is attributed to Villasandino in the *Cancionero de Baena*, in contrast to three other *cancioneros*: the *Cancionero de Juan Fernández de Ixar* (MN6: ed. José María Azaceta [Madrid, 1956]), the *Cancionero de Roma* (*RC1*: ed. M. Canal Gómez [Florence, 1935]), and Bibliothèque Nationale de Paris MS. Esp. 233 [*PN10*]. Giovanni Caravaggi's "Villasandino et les derniers troubadours de Castille," *Mélanges offerts à Rita Lejeune* (Genbloux, 1969) I, pp. 395–421, is a very accurate general survey of Villasandino's social status and activities.

8.   In his classic *Historia de los judíos en la España cristiana*, 2 vols. (José Luis Lacave's translation into Spanish of *Toledot ha yedudim bi-Sefarad ha-nosrit*, 1945, 1959) (Madrid, 1981). See also Charles F. Fraker, Jr., "Judaism in the *Cancionero de Baena*," *Studies on the "Cancionero de Baena"* (Chapel Hill, 1966), pp. 9–62.

9.   *Poesía juglaresca y orígenes de las literaturas románicas* (Madrid, 1957) p. 217ff.

10.   In fact, for two years, the king would not wear any royal insignia, nor did he want any celebrations in the palace because of the grief that the military disaster had caused him. The *cortes* in Briviesca in December 1387 asked him to return. On this matter, see *Cortes de León y Castilla*, published by the Real Academia de la Historia, II (1863), p. 398 (quoted by Menéndez Pidel, *op. cit.*, 218 n.)

11.   See Rafael Lapesa, "La lengua de la poesía lírica desde Macías hasta Villasandino," *Romance Philology* VII (1953–54), pp. 51–59. From a more historical-literary perspective, Alan Deyermond, "Baena, Santillana, Resende and the Silent Century of Portuguese Court Poetry," *Bulletin of Hispanic Studies* LIX (1982), pp. 198–210. Also, Guiseppe Tavani, "A arquivación dunha experiencia poética," and "Os epígonos en Castela e en Portugal," in his book *A poesia lirica galego-portuguesa* (Vigo, 1986), pp. 37–49, and pp. 268–273 respectively.

12.   See Erasmo Buceta, "Fecha probable de una poesía de Villasandino y de la muerte del poeta," *Revista de Filología Española*, XVI (1929), pp. 51–58.

13.   Although this is based on Marcelino Menéndez y Pelayo's judgment on the *cancionero* poetry with a love theme and on the continuation of that judgment, Keith Whinnom's analysis of this matter is very important; see *La poesía amatoria de la época de los Reyes Católicos* (Durham, 1981), especially pp. 9–20.

14.   I hope to demonstrate this fact convincingly in the critical edition of Villasandino's complete poetic works which I am currently preparing. Beyond what Caravaggi (see Note 7) states regarding Villasandino's professional decline, F. Márquez Villanueva's statement (see Note 1, p. 386) that "in Spain the moment

of transition from *jongleur* to jester is clearly documented by the *Cancionero de Baena. . ."* seems to the point. He illustrates the observation as follows: "A perfect hybrid of the *jongleur* and the court jester was found in Alfonso Alvarez de Villasandino. . ."

15.   The best and most detailed explanation of this time period may be seen in Baer, op. cit., Vol. I, Chap. VII and VIII (pp. 239–378), and Vol. II, Chap. IX, X, and XI (pp. 383–546), *passim*. For material relative to the famous dispute, see Antonio Pacios López, M. S. C., *La disputa de Tortosa* (Madrid-Barcelona, 1957), 2 vols.

16.   I agree with Márquez Villanueva that "Villasandino was performing. . . on a crowded stage" (cited article, 388), and his reading of the relations between Villasandino and Ferrandes Semuel seems very suggestive in terms of competition among jesters; but evidently there is much more behind it.

17.   J. Corominas and J. A. Pascual, *Diccionario crítico etimológico Castellano e hispánico.*

18.   Op. cit., pp. 89–93. Aside from a detailed discussion of the major obscure, and probably corrupt, passages of these texts, there is also a good explanation of the Hebrew terms found in them, indicative of the complete precision with which Villasandino uses them. See also Josep M. Solà-Solé and Stanley E. Rose, "Judíos y conversos en la poesía cortesana del siglo XV: el estilo políglott de Fray Diego de Valencia," *Hispanic Review*, XLIV (1976), pp. 371–385.

19.   Maxime Chevalier, "Fama pósthuma de Garcilaso," in Víctor García de la Concha, ed., *Actas de la IV Academia Literaria Renacentista: Garcilaso* (Salamanca, 1986), pp. 165–185.

20.   In such a sense, I agree only to a certain point with the statement of Kenneth Scholberg, *Sátira e invectiva en la España medieval* (Madrid, 1971), p. 340, when he says of poem 1282 that it is "an invitation to laughter, and not to hatred"—especially when in these poems, and all those in which Villasandino satirizes Jews or converts, he points out that "it is in these compositions that the troubadours tried to demonstrate their talent for insult; they should not be taken too seriously" (Ibid., 349).

FOURTEEN

Maimonides, Al-Andalus and the Influence of the Spanish-Arabic Dialect on His Language

Joshua Blau

A few years ago, in 1985, Jews, Muslims, and Christians alike, in Spain and all over the world, celebrated the 850th anniversary of Maimonides's birth, and thus taught us the lesson that the ancient Talmudic saying, שבשתא כיון דעל על ('a mistake once accepted remains'), does not apply to everyday life only, but to scholarship as well. It was once an accepted truth that Maimonides was born in 1135, and it was on this basis that his 850th anniversary was celebrated. Yet for a long time it has been known that, according to the colophon of his *Commentary of the Mishna*, as preserved in all the reliable manuscripts, he was only thirty years old when finishing this work in Egypt in 1168, and accordingly, his correct birth date is 1138.

The fact that Maimonides was born three years later than thought is not entirely without importance for his standing as a Spaniard. Forced to leave Spain as a young man, the fact that he was cut off from his native country when three years younger than generally assumed is of some consequence. It shows that Maimonides was only a child of about ten when the *Muwaḥḥidûn* conquered Spain and his family had to flee from Cordova, and in his early twenties when they had to leave Spain for good.

Nevertheless, although less than one-third of his life was spent in Spain, that span included the formative years, and he always considered himself a Spaniard, attached to Judeo-Spanish ways of life and extolling Judeo-Spanish customs. He continued to refer to whatever was in vogue in Spain as being used ʿ*indanâ* ('chez nous'), and it was only Spain that he referred to with this expression. Thus, in his famous responsum about a *qaṭlânît*, a woman who had been widowed twice and was therefore superstitiously suspected of causing her husbands' death (see my collection of Maimonides' responsa no. 218), he urges to emulate the model of Spanish rabbis (mentioning them later expressly) with the words: וגאיה אהל אלורע ענדנא ('and the utmost pious people do *chez nous*'). And one may not claim that he wrote these words when still in Spain, since in the immediate sequel he continues: והכדא אפתינא נחן ופעלנא פי דאר מצר מנך חלולנא בהא ('and thus we decided as our legal opinion, and have so actied in Egypt since we have arrived here').

Scholars, to be sure, had difficulties in digesting this adherence to Spain and tried to explain it away. As a matter of fact, in addition to plain 'indanâ, Maimonides used two somewhat expanded versions of this expression. Sometimes he expressly stated, 'indanâ fi-l-andalus ('chez nous, in Spain'), and even more often he used, 'indanâ fi-l-maghrib, etc. ('chez nous in the Maghrib'). The latter expression was misinterpreted as always referring to northwest Africa, to the exclusion of Spain. According to Abraham Geiger (at the beginning of the nineteenth century, the first to discuss this expression), Maimonides always uses 'indanâ to refer to the country in which he happened to write that particular passage—'indanâ fi-l-maghrib indicating that it was composed in northwest Africa and 'indanâ fi-l-andalus referring to its Spanish origin. This view was accepted and used for determining the country where various parts of Maimonides' works had allegedly been composed. It is, however, contradicted by the occurence of 'indanâ fi-l-andalus in passages written in Egypt, as in Maimonides' *Book of Precepts*, and still further by the use of 'indanâ in reference to Spain in the responsum previously cited, although it was written in Egypt. I. Friedlaender, therefore, in the introduction of his *Arabisch-Deutsches Lexikon zum Sprachgebrauch des Maimonides* Frankfurt a.M: V. J. Kauffmann, 1902), proposed Maimonides' use of 'indanâ in two different senses. When he wrote 'indanâ fi-l-andalus, he used it even after he had fled from Spain, in an exclusive sense, "we" referring to Maimonides only, with the exclusion of his audience (as if I were to say "at our place in Israel," to the exclusion of an American audience). On the other hand, he used the same 'indanâ in the phrase 'indanâ fi-l-maghrib only when he was already living in northwest Africa, using 'indanâ in an inclusive sense—"we" referring not only to Maimonides, but including his Maghrebine audience as well. Thus, Friedlaender assumed that *maghrib* and so on always referred to northwest Africa to the exclusion of Spain. Yet Maimonides did refer to *maghrib* and so on even in passages in which he enumerated Spanish rabbis as witnesses (as in responsum no. 269) and did speak of the visibility of the sun in various countries, in Ethiopia, Yemen, Babylon, Palestine, Egypt, and Maghrib (responsum no. 134). Is it conceivable that he omitted just Spain? The only possible explanation, therefore, is that Maimonides used *maghrib* both in a limited, exclusive sense, referring to northwest Africa, and also in a broader, inclusive sense, including Spain. And, indeed, even geographers used *Maghrib* in this broader sense (e.g., Maimonides' contemporary,

Ibn Jubayr; see his *Travels* (2nd ed.), [Leiden: Brill, 1907, p. 50, 16]). Therefore, one will refrain from accepting Friedlaender's proposition as to the double (inclusive and exclusive) usage of *'indanâ*, and rather postulate that *maghrib* and so on may include Spain, and that *'indanâ* is in both expressions—*'indanâ fi-l-andalus* and *'indanâ fi-l-maghrib*—used to the exclusion of the audience, always referring to Spain and thus demonstrating that he had never ceased from proudly considering himself a Spaniard, a representative of the Spanish branch of Judeo-Arabic culture.

Although Maimonides' attitude toward Judeo-Spanish customs can be reconstructed with reasonable certainty, it is much more intricate to fathom the extent of the influence of Spanish-Arabic on his language. In the following, we shall refrain from collecting as many Spanish-Arabic features in Maimonides' writings as possible. This would only fit an article devoted to Arabic studies. In a framework dealing with Sephardic studies, even in the broad sense of the word, it seems more appropriate to content ourselves with describing the typology of characteristic Spanish-Arabic features used by Maimonides and the processes generating them.

It goes without saying that we cannot make any direct statement about the *spoken* language of Maimonides in the second half of his life, during his stay in Egypt, for want of any document written in plain dialect emerging from Maimonides (or, as a whole, of any Judeo-Arabic document of this kind). All we can do is to cull from the writings of Maimonides linguistic features which deviate from Classical Arabic, and which, according to outside evidence, seem to reflect dialectal forms. We are limited, of course, by the very complicated linguistic structure of Judeo-Arabic works written in what we dub 'Middle Arabic.' These Middle Arabic texts were intended to be written in Classical Arabic, but as a rule they imitated the post-classical style in which science, philosophy, and so on were composed. Accordingly, features deviating from Classical Arabic need not reflect genuine vernacular (in the case of Spanish authors, genuine Spanish-Arabic), but may exhibit post-classical constructions or, even more often, pseudo-corrections (including hyper-corrections), stemming from the author's unsuccessful desire to utilize Classical Arabic. Even if we do succeed in isolating genuine Spanish-Arabic features from Maimonides' writings, mostly written or at least completed in Egypt, in order to appreciate their proper standing, we must evaluate them against the background of the general linguistic situation in Fustat-Cairo in general and its Jewish population in particular. A political, economic, and cultural center, Fustat-Cairo attracted people from the whole Arabic-speaking world, including Jews. We do know now, in light of the studies of Behnstedt and Woidich, how complicated the linguistic dialectal setup of Egypt is, and it stands to reason that it was, to say the least, no less so in the twelfth century. Besides, most Judeo-Arabic documents stemming from medieval Egypt contain Maghrebine features (to which dialectal group Spanish-Arabic belongs; see my *The Emergence and Linguistic Background of Judaeo-Arabic*, (2nd ed.) [Jerusalem:

Ben-Zvi Institute, 1981], p. 57). Against this background of great dialectal diversity
and the preponderance of Egyptian Jewish dialects of the Maghrebine type, it
seems unlikely that Maimonides made any conscious efforts to change his native
Spanish dialect when speaking, the more so since, as we have seen, he was proud
of his Spanish origin. On the other hand, it is also quite improbable that he
made special efforts to employ it. It stands to reason that he wanted to be properly
understood, and so preserved his native dialect—the most natural thing to do—
when he could hope to be correctly comprehended, yet was ready to resort to
dialectal forms to help proper understanding. This quite reasonable *a priori*
assumption as to the use of Spanish dialect features in his speech can be buttressed
by the intentional use or avoidance of words stemming from Spanish-Arabic in
his *Commentary of the Mishna*. In this work, Maimonides often had to explain
implements, and since his book addressed the whole world's Arabic-speaking
Jewish audience, and not only the audience in Egypt (where he finished his
commentary), he sometimes adduced their Arabic equivalents in more than one
dialect, including Spain, Maghrib (in both its broad and narrow sense), and Egypt,
as (ed. Qafih vi 151, 6) ‏קמטרה" אלתי נסמיהא באלאנדלם אלעתידה ופי מצר‎
‏אלקמטרה‎ *'qamtra* is called in Spain *'atida* and in Egypt *qamṭra*, using on *purpose*[1]
Spanish and Egyptian dialect words, thus indicating that he was guided only
by the desire of making himself properly understood.[2]

On the other hand, we have express indication that Maimonides did abandon
Spanish dialect words when they were apt to impair proper understanding. In
Spanish-Arabic, *thamara* denotes 'fruit *tree*,' and it occurs in this sense often in
the *Commentary of the Mishna*. Then, presumably after he had discovered in Egypt
that this meaning was unknown outside Spain[3] and thus *thamara* was apt to
be mistaken for 'fruit,' Maimonides started substituting *shajara* for it in his personal
copy. Yet, as always in cases like this, he was not able to be consistent enough
to rewrite all the passages in which *thamara* ('fruit tree') occurred, and from one
of these passages (or perhaps from an earlier version of his commentary), this
Spanish dialectal word penetrated Tanhum Yerushalmi's dictionary[4] (sub voce
‏סגניות‎; it was influenced by vi 150, 5).

While it is easy to recognize the reason for Maimonides' attempt to expurgate
the use of *thamara* in the sense of 'fruit tree,' it is more difficult to understand
what caused him to systematically substitute classical forms of verbs *iii y*,
terminating in the third person singular feminine of the perfect in *-at* (as *zanat*
'she fornicated'), for Spanish (and general Maghrebine) forms ending in *-ât* (as
zanât) in his personal copy of the *Commentary of the Mishna*. Here no misunderstanding was involved in the use of the Spanish forms. I regard the following
explanation as the most likely: in Egypt, Maimonides encountered dialectal forms
terminating in *-at* (identical with the classical forms), and this made him realize
more clearly that his usage of the Spanish vernacular forms terminating in *-ât*
contravened classical usage. Wanting, basically, to use Classical Arabic, as did
Judeo-Arabic authors in general, he attempted to expurgate this native dialectal

feature.[5] However, he was not always successful. Thus he changed בקאת to בקת, although the classical form is *baqiyat*.

At any rate, Maimonides was basically correct when substituting *iii y* forms terminating in ה- for those ending in את-. In other cases, however, he was less lucky in his quest for classical forms, substituting post-Classical features for Classical ones. Thus, in his personal copy of the *Commentary of the Mishna*, he systematically tried to substitute אבאע, a pseudo-correct feature (in all likelihood, arising by backformation from the pseudo-correct passive אביע), which had become quite frequent in post-Classical texts, for classical באע 'to sell.' The linguistic setup of Judeo-Arabic texts was so intricate, with the interchange of Classical, post-Classical, vernacular, and pseudo-correct features, that one could hardly avoid such pitfalls.

As we have seen, Judeo-Arabic authors in general and Maimonides in particular wanted to write in Classical Arabic, deliberately using dialectal forms only when the context demanded it (as in the case of the explanation of implements). Therefore, they were quite successful in avoiding distinct vernacular features, but were less able to refrain from the usage of vernacular forms which in other syntactic environments were identical with classical features. This is the reason that of *naf'al: naf'alû* ('I shall do: we shall do'), the hallmark of Spanish-Arabic (including Maghrebine), it is only *naf'al* that is well attested in his writings, whereas I have noted *naf'alû* only in the *draft* of his *Mishna Commentary Shabbat* xii 3 נדאעו ('we pay attention') (the final version ii 63, 4; 5 being נדאעי).

In spite of the decisive influence exerted by Classical orthography on Judeo-Arabic spelling, thus blurring possible phonetic dialectal features, Maimonides' writings contain some forms reflecting phonetic characteristics of Spanish-Arabic. Thus, קד[6] for *qad* apparently reflects the influence of the allophonic distribution of *d* and *dh* in the local Romance languages, and גבד ('to pull, draw') = metathesis. The rather frequent use of infinitive forms with long vowel in the second syllable, as תלאף ('ruining, wasting'), especially of the pattern *fa'îl* denoting material operations, as טחין ('grinding'), כביז ('baking'), is perhaps connected with the decay of the short vowel system characterizing Maghrebine dialects in general. Even more frequent is the plural *fa'âlil* instead of *fa'âlîl*, as *mabâṭil* ('crippled ones') from the singular *mabṭûl*, presumably reflecting a stress system in which the first of two syllables containing long vowels was stressed.

Sometimes Maimonides' writings even contain Spanish-Arabic dialectal forms attested elsewhere only marginally (as the use of הו, and so on as demonstrative pronoun) or not attested at all, as the use of the demonstrative pronouns as mere actualizators, reflecting the tendency to describe realistically and *in concreto* (see for example, *Guide for the Perplexed*, ed. S. Munk, Paris: Frenck, 1856–66, iii 36a, 6ff.

לא אעתקד בונה אן הדה אלורקה סקטת בענאיה כהא ולא אן הדא אלענכבות
אפתרס הדה אלדבאבה בקצא אללה...ולא אן אלבזוקה...נזלת עלי הדה
אלבעוצה פי מוצע מכצוץ פקתלה בקצא וקדר ולא אן הדה אלסמכה למא
אכתטפת הדה אלדודה...

I do not by any means believe that *this particular* leaf has fallen because of the providence watching over it, nor that *this particular* spider has devoured *this particular* fly because God has decreed...nor that the spittle...came down in a *particular* place [note that here 'particular' is expressed by מכצוץ, rather than by the demonstrative pronoun, thus conveying that their meanings are identical!] upon *this particular* gnat and killed it by a divine decree and judgement, nor that, when *this particular* fish snatched *this particular* worm....

Often it is difficult to discern whether a syntactic feature deviating from Classical Arabic reflects genuine dialect (in our case, Spanish-Arabic) or rather post-Classical Arabic, possibly with Spanish-Arabic tinge. Cases in point are the use of אנמא in the sense of אמא, a clear Spanish-Arabic usage[7]; further *idh wa-* ('because'), in the main a Spanish-Arabic feature[8] (though it is not restricted to Spain), which, especially frequent in Maimonides' works, was imitated by his son Abraham, as well as by Tanhum Yerushalmi and Yemenite authors.

I would like to conclude with a negative feature: the use of *an* marking a following indefinite attribute is so frequent in Spanish-Arabic texts that it was even surmised that its origins stem from Spain. Yet, curiously enough, its use is rather restricted in Maimonides' writings.

In summary, although Maimonides had spent only a comparatively small part of his life in Spain, he always considered himself a Spaniard, referring to Spain as '*indanâ 'chez nous'*. He did not use (Spanish-Arabic) dialect words on purpose, except when he had to explain certain implements. Otherwise, as Judeo-Arabic authors in general, he attempted to write Classical Arabic. When confronted with certain Egyptian forms, he became aware that the Spanish-Arabic forms he used were not Classical, and he would go to great lengths to eradicate them. However, he was not always successful and sometimes substituted post-Classical forms for Classical ones. Conspicuous dialect features (as *naf'alû* ['we do']), therefore, are very rare (as is, curiously enough, *an* marking a following indefinite attribute). Even reflections of phonetic features occur, along with dialectal forms not yet attested elsewhere or attested only marginally. Sometimes it is difficult to discern whether a syntactic feature deviating from Classical Arabic reflects genuine (Spanish-Arabic) dialect or rather post-Classical Arabic, possibly with a Spanish-Arabic tinge, as is *idh wa-* ('because'), so frequent in Maimonides' writings that it penetrated the writings of his son Abraham, Tanhum Yerushalmi, and several Yemenite authors.

NOTES

1.   Maimonides sometimes expressly states that a word is used by the common people, as *ibid.*, vi 62, 6 אלקמע והו אלדֹי תסמי אלעאמה ענדנא באלקמא 'the funnel, called by the common people *chez nous* (i.e., in Spain) *qimâ*.

2. *Obiter dictum*, Maimonides was not always consistent in adducing dialectal features. Thus (*ibid.*, vi p. 168, 1), he opposes these dialect words, as if they differed: אלעתאיד ואלקמטראת and in the second volume of this commentary (which he completed, it seems, before arriving in Egypt) p. 71, -5 he simply states "שדה" אלעתידה "*shidda*' means ʿ*atida*, citing the Spanish dialect word only, without mentioning the Egyptian one, whereas the Eastern author Tanhum Yerushalmi, in his dictionary to Maimonides' היד החזקה entitled אלמרשד אלכאפי, *s.v. shiddâ*, simply states that it is תאבות צגיר יסמי עתידה ויסמי קמטרה a small chest, called ʿ*atida* and called *qamtra*' without mentioning their dialectal affiliation. At any rate, through Maimonides' influence, this Spanish dialectal word has penetrated into the writing of an Eastern author, indicating how complex the linguistic evaluation of a Judeo-Arabic text may be.

3. In R. Blachère, M. Chouémi, C. Denizeau, *Dictionnaire arabe-français-anglais* (Paris: Maisonneuve, 1967). This meaning is cited in a passage from the *Egyptian* Maqrizi (fifteenth century). I could not locate this passage, not having the cited edition at my disposal. In the Qoranic passage quoted there, at any rate (it is xvi, 11, and it is adduced while skipping some words), *thamarât* can be interpreted as 'fruit' as well. Yet, even if the passage from Maqrizi turns out to be authentic, it may not only reflect marginal use, but linguistic usage might also have changed between the twelfth and fifteenth centuries.

4. See Note 2.

5. Against this background, it is quite interesting that in a Yemenite(!) dictionary from the fourteenth or fifteenth century, which frequently quotes Maimonides's *Commentary of the Mishna* and which was published by H. Shay, *taʿudâ* 3.181–213 (1983), צסמאת 'she was named' is attested (188, -3; 189, -2; 191, -2). It stands to reason that the Yemenite author had as his *Vorlage* an earlier version of the *Commentary of the Mishna*, in which the original תסמאת had not yet been corrected to תסמת, and he copied it to the letter, causing the Yemenite version to become "more Spanish" than Maimonides' final version.

6. V. here and in the following the appropriate *lemmata* of my forthcoming *Dictionary of Medieval Judaeo-Arabic*. Through Maimonides' influence, קֿ was used also by his grandson David, as I learn from P. Fenton.

7. This use of אנמא, as well as that of פאיד instead of פאידה 'advantage,' also occurring in Maimonides's writings, was subject to severe criticism by a so-far-unknown Spanish rabbi (v. D. Z. Baneth, אוצר יהודי ספרד 4.14–15 [1961]). In the main, he reprimanded his unknown antagonist in matters of Jewish law, scolding him, *inter alia*, for his stupidity, arrogance, and aggression, and dubbing him "a donkey turning the scoop-wheel." Yet, surprisingly enough, he digressed from his main subject and reproached his opponent also for his faulty Arabic, adding that he does so because of his antagonist's boasting about his eloquence, although "he is more stupid (and wilder) than a billy goat in a storeroom of jugs." Thus he scolded his opponent for the aforementioned usage of אנמא and פאיד (although he himself, while reprimanding him, did not refrain from using an

even more vernacular expression [תאעמי 'to boast']). When doing so, he was in theory—but in theory only—correct, because these two expression are, indeed, post-Classical. In practice, however, the aforementioned two expressions reflected customary Spanish usage, because it was in theory only that Jews wrote Classical Arabic; in practice, they preferred to use post-Classical style.

8. I am obliged to S. Hopkins, who called my attention to F. Corriente, *A Grammatical Sketch of the Spanish Arabic Dialect Bundle* (Madrid: Instituto Hispano-Arabe de Cultura, 1977), p. 140, Note 231, who adduces *idh wa-*.

FIFTEEN

Uncovering the Origins of the Judeo-Ibero-Romance Languages

Paul Wexler

There are two goals to a detailed analysis of all Judeo-Ibero-Romance languages (fragments of Judeo-Catalan, Judeo-Aragonese, Judeo-Castilian, Judeo-Portuguese, and Ladino from the thirteenth through the fifteenth centuries; post-Expulsion Ladino texts; and contemporary Judezmo and Ḥakitía dialects), Christian terminology relating to Jews, transcripts of Jewish and Marrano speech recorded in Inquisition proceedings, Christian stereotypes of Judeo-Ibero-Romance speech (twelfth through seventeenth centuries), as well as Iberian Judeo-Greek and Judeo-Latin inscriptions (approximately sixth through eighth century): they (1) allow us to reconstruct the linguistic behavior of the Iberian Jews through time and space, and (2) elucidate the paths of diffusion and relative chronology of Jewish settlement and the interplay of Arabic and Romance culture among the Iberian Jews.

In reconstructing the linguistic history of the Iberian Jews, I attribute paramount importance to the comparative study of non-native components in the Ibero-Romance speech of the Jews from Catalonia, Aragon, and Castile. For example, a Judeo-Greek and Judeo-Latin impact (both in the form of loans and models for loan translations) appears better preserved in the Catalonia-Aragon areas than in Castile. Conversely, the Castilian speech of the Jews (including the colonial descendants, Judezmo and Ḥakitía) shows a marked Judeo-Arabic substratum, while in its native Romance component it deviates little from coterritorial Christian dialects. Judeo-Catalan vestiges also appear to preserve a slightly larger percentage of Judeo-Latin expressions than Castilian (Ladino) texts. I believe the small corpus of Judeo-Latin and Judeo-Greek elements in Judeo-Castilian and modern Judezmo and Ḥakitía can be ascribed to a Judeo-Catalan impact not older than the fourteenth century.

On the basis of the linguistic facts, I hypothesize that the Catalan and Aragonese Jews could be descended directly from the Judeo-Latin and Judeo-Greek speakers who first settled in the Peninsula in the Roman period. The Castilian Jews, however, were originally Arabic-speaking Jews for the most part who became (re-)romanized relatively late—in large numbers perhaps only two or three centuries prior to the expulsions of 1492–98. In the fourteenth century, the newly judaized Castilian speech spread to non-Castilian areas, supplanting Judeo-Catalan and Judeo-Aragonese. Only Judeo-Castilian (Judezmo and Ḥakitía) survived the expulsions. Further confirmation for the theory that the Catalan and Castilian Jews have radically different origins comes from the pronunciation norms and the corpus of Hebraisms in Judeo-Ibero-Romance speech which can be recovered from both Jewish and Christian documents.

In the following figure, I offer two models for representing the relationship of Judeo-Ibero-Romance to Judeo-Latin; both models entail a correction to Blondheim's and Max Weinreich's scheme in which Judeo-Romance languages were all seen as direct descendants of Judeo-Latin. Judaized French, Provençal, and Italian are assumed to be direct outgrowths of Judeo-Latin, though this remains to be proven.

Examples of Judeo-Greek and Judeo-Arabic elements in the Judeo-Ibero-Romance languages are given.[1]

I. Judeo-Greek influence: primarily in Northeast Judeo-Ibero-Romance languages.

1. Colloquial JAram *rībbī* 'rabbi' > JGk, JLat *rebbi* (Mérida, c. 6th-8th cc?) > JCat *reebi* (Girona 1380), Nav *rebi* (Tudela 1407) (and in JItal, JFrench, Yiddish, JArabic) vs. arabized *arrab(i)*, *rabi* in Cast, Nav, Arag, Port.

2. JGk *sxolē* 'synagogue' (New Testament) > Cat, Prov, Fr, Ital (and Yiddish *šul*) vs. Cast, Pt *esnoga*, etc. (‹ *sinagoga*), Judezmo *eznoga* 'women's section in a synagogue'.

3. JGk *aladma, alalma,* etc. 'rabbinical excommunication' < JGk *'anaΘēma* appears in Arag, Nav, Cat, Val 1205ff. Extremely rare in Cast documents.

4. Jud *meldar* 'read (Jewish religious books)' < GK *meletáō* 'be occupied with'. Surface cognates in JPort, JFr, JIt, etc.; among Christians, in Southern Ital and Catalan. Earliest Ibero-Rom attestation is in the Catalan area.

5. Occasionally get JGk expressions exclusively in Cast and Port. For example, JAram *jōmā' rabbā'* 'Kippur' > JGk *hē megalē hēmera* > JLat *dies magnus* > Jud *el dia grande*, Marrano Port *dia grande.*

6. Jud *talamo* 'bridal canopy; seats of honor for the bride and her consorts; talit held over head of bride(groom) during the wedding ceremony' < Gk *Θalamos* 'bridal chamber', etc. Also, in JFr, JIt,

Figure 15.1

Two models for representing the relationship of Judeo-Ibero-Romance to Judeo-Latin:

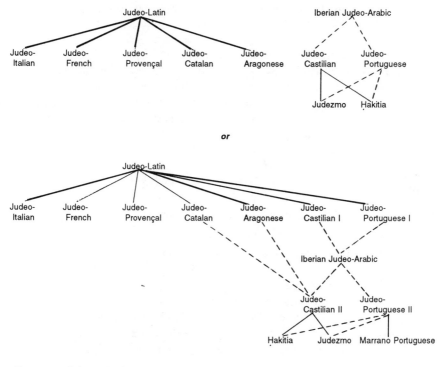

Key: ____evolutionary development
      ------language shift

Marrano Port and Western Yiddish. Semantic features "chair" + "religious ceremony" shared by Jud and Catalan: see Cat tàlem 'nuptial bed; thalamus; receptacle for carrying a holy image in a procession'.

7. He *nidduj* 'excommunication' > Arag *nenduy* (Zaragoza 1331), Port *nelduy* (1496). Dissimilation of geminated consonants is typical of Judeo-Greek (e.g. *sambata* < He *šabbāt.*

II. *(Judeo-)Arabic components in Judeo-Ibero-Romance languages: greater in number in JCast and JPort than in the Northeast JIbRom languages.*

1. Terms shared by Cast Jews and Muslims: *fadas* 'naming ceremony for a child', *alxad* 'Sunday'.

2. Terms in Christian Cast and Port from Arabic with exclusive Jewish or Jewish + Muslin connotations: Pt *almocávar*, etc. 'Jewish or Moorish cemetery', Val *azuna* 'law code of Jews or Muslims', Cast, Cat *alfaquim*' honorific title for Jewish translator, physician', etc., Pt *genesim* 'room, school where rabbis expound on Bible; tax paid for such a room' (1433ff) (< JArab *knīs* 'synagogue'?).

3. Jud has fewer Arabic loans than Castilian.

4. Few unique Arabisms in Judezmo, e.g. *adefina* 'Sabbath food prepared on Friday' < Arabic 'bury'. JRomance languages use or translate JAram *ḥammīn* while JArab translates He *ṭāman* 'conceal'.

5. Jud preserves Arabic features more faithfully than Cast, e.g. Arabic /x / and order of consonants, as in Jud *alxavaka* vs. Cast *albahaca* < Arabic *al-ḥabaq(a)* 'sweet basil'.

6. Arabic influence also on JCast Hebraisms—e.g., *albedin*, etc. 'rabbinical judge' < He *bēt dīn*.

7. Jewish terminology in JCast (and Judezmo) largely of Arabic origin.

III. *Tendency to de-Arabization in Judeo-Castilian prior to the Expulsions of 1492–98.*

1. Replacement of Arabized romanisms by non-Arabized cognates: *el djo* (~ Arab ʿ*allāh*, ʿ*arrab*) > *dios* (15th c).

2. Jewish anthroponyms, e.g. *Axibil* (1321), *Axivil* (1352) > *de Sibilia* (1372), *Sevillano* (late 15th c).

3. Replacement of Arabized hebraisms by non-Arabized cognates: *atora* 'Torah' > *tora*; *albedin* 'rabbinical judge' > *bedin*, etc.

4. Replacement of an Arabism by a native Romance synonym: *domingo* 'Sunday' (Calahorra, c. 1259–1340) (~ contemporary *alxad*).

NOTES

1. Further details may be found in my *Three Heirs to a Judeo-Latin Legacy: Judeo-Ibero-Romance, Yiddish and Rotwelsch* (Wiesbaden: Otto Harrassowitz Verlag, 1988).

SIXTEEN

Problems of Transcribing Sephardic Texts into the Roman Alphabet

George K. Zucker

Judeo-Spanish documents are generally written in *aljamiado*—that is, in the Judeo-Spanish language, but using Hebrew characters. Transcription into the Roman alphabet makes these documents accessible to a much larger corpus of scholars and, indeed, that has been done in many cases. Just a few years ago, for example, Yolanda Moreno Koch, of the Universidad Complutense in Madrid, published an annotated transcription of the *Taqqanot* 'Laws' written in Valladolid in 1432 to govern the Jewish communities in Castile. Transcription would thus seem to solve the problem of having texts available for any and all who are interested in reading or studying them. However, the transcription process itself raises additional problems.

The Hebrew alphabet consists of consonants only; vowels appear as dots or dashes above, below or beside the letters. Yet the vowels are semantically significant in both Spanish and Judeo-Spanish: e.g., *mes* ('month') vs. *más* ('more'); *lo* (masculine direct object pronoun) vs. *la* (feminine direct object pronoun) vs. *le* (indirect object pronoun). The *aljamiado* writing system, which developed in Spain in the Middle Ages but was not formalized until the advent of printing houses in the Ottoman Empire after the Jews' expulsion from Spain, solved this problem, but only partially, by co-opting a limited number of consonants which would generally serve as vowels. Here is a list of the Judeo-Spanish vowels and the letters used to represent them in *aljamiado*:

a: *aleph* in any position but word-final; *hay* in word-final position.[1]

e: *yod* in all positions; prefaced by an *aleph* (with no phonetic value) in word-initial position.

i: *yod* in all positions; prefaced by an *aleph* (with no phonetic value) in word-initial position. Sometimes double *yod* is used when it is a semivowel.

o: *vav* in all positions; prefaced by an *aleph* (with no phonetic value) in word-initial position.

u: *vav* in all positions; prefaced by an *aleph* (with no phonetic value) in word-initial position. This is true for both the vowel and the semivowel.

The system used has its problems; the front vowels *e* and *i* are not differentiated from each other, since both are represented by the *yod*,[2] nor are the back vowels, *o* and *u*, distinguished from each other. The *aleph*, in addition to representing the vowel *a*, serves to introduce words which begin with other vowel sounds, and to break what would otherwise be diphthongs. For example, the word *vio* ('he saw'), a single syllable, would be written with *yod vav* for the vowels. *Navío* ('ship'), however, which breaks the diphthong, would appear with *yod aleph vav* for the final vowels. Thus, in terms of vowels, *aljamiado* text is a reliable indicator of the pronunciation only of *a*.

Consonants, too, can be problematic, in two aspects. First, there are consonantal sounds in Judeo-Spanish which did not exist at the time of the expulsion from Spain (when phonetic development of Judeo-Spanish stopped following the same course as in Spain). There is also the fact that Judeo-Spanish has consonantal sounds which do not exist in Hebrew. The problem arose of how to represent the sounds of *ch* and the Old Spanish sibilant *j*, or *g* before a front vowel. That question was solved by incorporating a *rafé*, a tick above the Hebrew letter, with *gimel* and *zayin*. But now the reader must rely on the scribe to include the *rafé* where it belongs and not to write it in other cases. Remember, through, that we are dealing with a language written by native speakers for native speakers, so that the words would be recognized whether or not they were 'spelled' correctly. If we see, for example, *mem vav gimel vav*, the word is obviously not *mugo* (which does not exist), but rather *mucho*, with a missing *rafé* above the *gimel*.

The other difficulty comes from a single sound's being represented by more than one Hebrew consonant. The most troublesome of those cases deals with the *s*, which can be written with either the *samekh* or the *sin*. *Sin* is the one most commonly used, both within words and in word-final position as the sign of plurality in nouns and adjectives, and of second-person-singular in verbs. But does that mean that the *samekh* represents a different *s* sound? Rather, it may simply be an alternation of phonetic equals.

An additional problem posed by the *sin* is that the same letter, with a dot on the opposite upper corner or, in *aljamiado*, with a *rafé*, is the *shin*, pronounced

/sh/. That sound, which does not exist in modern Spanish, was part of the late fifteenth-century Spanish phonetic inventory, and is still present in Judeo-Spanish. Represented in Old Spanish by the letter *x*, it could appear in either word-initial or medial position. However, Judeo-Spanish has made the difference between /s/ and /sh/ semantically significant in second-person forms of the verb: -*s* marks the second-person singular forms, while the Judeo-Spanish marker for second-person plural is -*sh*.

If the *rafé* is regularly and consistently used—which is often not the case—there is no problem, for the *rafé* converts *sin* to *shin*. Certainly, the writer of a document—and, most likely, the document's recipient—knew whether the 'you' addressed was singular or plural, but the contemporary reader often has no idea. So, while the *rafé* may have been optional for understanding when a document was written, it may, in fact, change the thrust of the contents for a reader of that same document today.

These are just the problems involved in reading a document written in *aljamiado*, and they will certainly be reflected in attempts to transcribe such documents into the Roman alphabet. Unfortunately, the problems of transcription do not end there. Transcription will often reflect dialectal differences in Judeo-Spanish as well. Do we, upon finding *aleph yod zayin* with *rafé vav*, write *ijo* or *iju*? Both are legitimate, contemporary pronunciations of the Judeo-Spanish word for 'son' or 'child'; the difference is regional. Since *vav* represents both of those final vowels, both are legitimate renderings of the word in *aljamiado*.

Then there is the problem of differentiating between transcription and transliteration. In a panel discussion on transcription problems held at the international and interdisciplinary Sephardic Studies conference at SUNY-Binghamton in April 1987 (whose participants were Joshua Blau [Hebrew University] as chair, with Alan Corré [University of Wisconsin-Milwaukee], Moshé Lazar [University of Southern California], and Isaac Jack Lévy [University of South Carolina] as speakers), Professor Blau pointed out the distinction between the two processes—a distinction which is too often overlooked. Transcription, he said, is used "in the sense of transcribing a whole word," using the example of *lamed yod* and transcribing it as the third-person indirect object pronoun *le*. Transliteration, on the other hand, is the regular and consistent substitution of a given Roman letter for a given Hebrew letter, and the transliteration of *lamed yod* would be *ly*. Is it our aim, then, to transcribe or to transliterate? The former results in a readable document; the latter is intelligible only to a linguist: *beth vav yod nun vav* becomes *bueno* if transcribed, but *bwynw* if transliterated.

The system used by the Instituto Arias Montano in Madrid for transcribing *aljamiado* texts attempts to be all things to all people, and thus fails by creating barriers to understanding for all save those trained in linguistics: it attempts to transcribe and, at the same time, transliterate. There are three symbols each for the voiced bilabial occlusive /b/, the voiced dental alveolar /z/, the voiced prepalatal affricate /j/ and voiced prepalatal fricative /zh/. Unvoiced prepalatal fricative /sh / is represented by two symbols. Dots below *b, d, v,* and above *g* indicate that those sounds are occlusive in Judeo-Spanish, although not in Spanish in those positions, and an apostrophe is used to indicate the voiced pharyngeal fricative *ayin,* which has no equivalent in Western languages. If this sounds complicated, imagine trying to read a text written this way, especially if the reader has no training in linguistics!

The basic problem, however, is that there is no universally accepted system for the transcription of *aljamiado* text into the Roman alphabet. The sound /sh /, for example, will appear as *sh* if the transcriber's native language is English, as *ch* if that language is French, and as *s* plus cedilla if the language in question is Turkish. And what about the sound /ch /, which, for a speaker of Italian is *c* before a front vowel?

At the Binghamton conference, Professor Isaac Jack Lévy noted, among problems caused by the lack of standardized transcription, the near impossibility of using dictionaries. Regarding Joseph Nehama's *Dictionnaire judeo-espagnol français,* his comment was, "I've just finished translating many, many poems on the Holocaust, and when I didn't know a word, half the time I couldn't find it in Nehama, because I didn't know how he spelled it. It was a labyrinth."

Speaking about the transcription of relatively modern texts, such as novels and poetry, Professor Lévy summed up his point of view by stating: "Our need is not for a sophisticated linguistic system, but for a practical, standard alphabet." His system would include a strictly phonetic representation of sounds with, for example, the letter *k* to represent the hard *c,* and *y* for the front semivowel in a diphthong to contrast with *i* when that vowel has its own syllabic value. Thus, the word *beth* with *rafé yod vav* would appear as *vyo* ('he saw'), a single syllable, while *nun aleph beth* with *rafé yod aleph vav* would be written *navio* to indicate that the last two vowels were separate syllables. Accent marks, which are not used in *aljamiado* (although they are a feature of Spanish orthography) would have their acceptance in Professor Lévy's system in those cases where stress was semantically significant—e.g., *avlo* ('I am speaking') vs. *avló* ('he spoke')—and for words, generally of non-Spanish origin, whose stress falls on a normally unaccented syllable: *berahá* ('blessing').

An interesting counterview was presented by Professor Moshé Lazar, who was then working on the transcription of the sixteenth-century Ladino Bible.[3] First, he pointed out the not-infrequent problem of "misprints, miswritings by scribes, mispronunciation by a reader." We need, he added, "to figure out, the same way as in the Middle Ages we are trying to live in, how the scribe transcribed a manuscript in a scriptorium, or how the printer worked at the printing press. We have to remember that we are reading texts which have their limitations in the fonts, in the pieces of wood which the printer has.

Indeed, we cannot always take for granted that texts in *aljamiado,* either printed or handwritten, were correct. The presence or absence of the *rafé* should not cause us to read *abe* in a fifteenth- or sixteenth-century text when all Ladino speakers say *ave*. That kind of mistake, according to Professor Lazar, is not even worth recording, "because there is no meaning to it. It doesn't represent a phonetic reality."

Transcription serves the purpose of making Sephardic texts available to a large group of readers who do not know the Hebrew alphabet, the vast majority of whom are "not interested in. . . sanctifications or sacrelizations of mistakes by printers and misspellings by scribes. They have nothing to do with the phonetic reality," asserts Professor Lazar. He uses a transcription system which is closest to the Spanish of the time in which the document in question was written. The text with which he works date from the fifteenth through seventeenth centuries, and consequently, he says, "I am going to transcribe them in the closest possible way to the phonetic reality of the Spanish language [at that time]."

Transliteration, according to Professor Lazar, defeats the purpose of rewriting *aljamiado* texts in the Roman alphabet. For example, to write *lyybandwlw* for *llevandolo* results in a situation in which "the reader has to do more work to read. . .than I have to do to read it in the original." In summation, he stated, "I am for the language of man whenever it is possible."

Professor Corré brought up an entirely different matter, based on current technology—computers and desktop publishing. Any system agreed upon at this time should "be amenable to the computer." He asked that we "bear in mind that great changes in technology are taking place and, if we seize the occasion, they can be very useful." His appeal was for "some kind of consistent transcription, and one that is compatible with the computer."

Here, then, appears another consideration—one which had not been dealt with previously, and which certainly has the potential to create further difficulties in the attempt to arrive at a standardized transcription system.

We are, unfortunately, still a distance away from any proposal for transcription which would be found acceptable on a more-or-less universal basis. That system would need to take into account the various native languages of transcribers and readers, the purpose for which the transcription is being made, and the amount of transliteration which should be included. There remain several questions to be answered before such a system can even be proposed, if it is to have any chance of being successfully adopted by Sephardists:

1. Should a single system be used, whether the text in question is relatively recent, or for a non-technical audience, or if we are dealing with a historical text?
2. Is it necessary to indicate what Hebrew characters were used to represent specific sounds?
3. Should misprints/misspellings be recorded in the transcription?
4. Should the transcription represent any specific current dialect of Judeo-Spanish, or should it attempt to approximate, as much as possible, current Spanish pronunciation?

5. What 'computer-friendly' symbols should be used in cases where they prove necessary?

Perhaps we need not one, but various systems—systems, however, which are universally used and accepted. It seems clear that transcriptions done for linguists would better serve their targeted audience if they did indicate the Hebrew characters used, and perhaps even misprints or misspellings. And it would seem to make sense to transcribe documents according to Spanish spelling of the time in which those documents were written. But none of these matters can be decided unilaterally, for the intrinsic interdisciplinary nature of the field of Sephardic studies requires that any transcription proposal have the blessings of practitioners of anthropology, history, linguistics, and so on.

The imediate barrier, then, to the proposal of any unification of transcription of Sephardic texts into the Roman alphabet is the difficulty of getting experts in various academic disciplines together to find what is acceptable (or, perhaps even more important, not acceptable) in transcriptions used for each of those disciplines. What is needed is an interdisciplinary Sephardic studies conference whose specific topic is the problem of transcription of texts into the Roman alphabet. That can provide the starting point for the resolution of the problem.

NOTES

1. Final *-a* is generally the sign of feminine gender in nouns in Spanish and Judeo-Spanish; *hay* serves that same function in Hebrew.

2. This factor may well be the cause of one notable difference between Spanish and Judeo-Spanish. The first-person singular preterite ending of first-conjugation Spanish verbs is *-é*, the same form in second- and third-conjugation verbs ends in *-í*, and the corresponding form of the strong preterites is *-e*. In Judeo-Spanish, all first-person singular preterites end in *-í* or *-i*. The morphological change may have been caused by reading pronunciation in generations after the expulsion, when all of those words were seen ending in *yod*. For a discussion of the phenomenon of reading pronunciation, see Jesse Levitt, "The Influence of Orthography on Phonology: A Comparative Study (English, French, Spanish, Italian, German)," *Linguistics*, 208 (June 1978): 43–67.

3. *Ladino Pentateuch (Constantinople, 1547)*, ed. Moshe Lazar (Culver City, CA: Labyrinthos, 1988).

PART THREE

Ethnography and Folklore

Introduction by Walter P. Zenner

In examining fields of inquiry, we often find that narrative and intellectual history are the preferred modes when the history of a group is dramatic and marked by 'great men,' while folklore, sociology, and ethnography are the preferred modes where the cultural field appears mundane and ordinary. The history of Jews in and from the Iberian Peninsula, from Hasdai Ibn Shaprut (tenth century) through Shabbtai Zevi (seventeenth century) is marked by the former, while more recent considerations of Mediterranean and West Asian Jewry are marked by the latter.

The division of the study of Sephardim into studies stressing elites and great men on the one hand and the folklore of the masses on the other is really a false one. In Steve Siporin's study of that community, we find folklorists relying on deliberate literary efforts by authors who are part of a well-educated elite. At the same time, some medieval historians, such as the late and lamented S. D. Goitein, are increasingly ethnographic in their orientations.

There are several characteristics which mark the anthropological approach, besides its focus on materials derived from all segments of society and which differentiate it in part or whole from other approaches.

1) Anthropology, like area studies, is interdisciplinary by nature. Within anthropology departments in the United States, one finds linguists, biological anthropologists, and archaeologists as well as ecologically oriented and symbolically oriented cultural anthropologists. Integration of all these subdisciplines is impossible, yet cross-fertilization takes place.

2) Since the subject matter of anthropology is human diversity, anthropologists find themselves studying human beings who are apparently different from themselves. This entails several problems.

a) The first is, How does the study of the Other relate to the person who is undertaking this research? Since most anthropological and folkloristic research is in the form of participation-observation fieldwork, the self is immediately engaged in a way in which laboratory experimentation, survey research in which the analyst does not interview personally, and documentary historiography does not involve one's being. For instance, studying one's own family or ethnic group is not the same as studying another group. Thus Dina Dahbany-Miraglia, a Yemeni Jew born in the United States, has a different standpoint from S. D. Goitein, Laurence Loeb, Herb Lewis, or Lisa Gilad in studying Yemeni Jews. Walter Zenner and Yael Zerubabel have different views of Syrian Jews than Syrian Jewish researchers such as Joseph Sutton or Dianne Esses. Yet the very act of writing about one's group involves self-consciousness and even marginality. The problem is a real one though the advantages and disadvantages of studies by insiders and outsiders vary.

b) Making human diversity the focus of attention implies cross-cultural comparison. While all historical and social scientific research implies comparison, the anthropological enterprise ultimately is concerned with using comparison of human groups to obtain models of human nature. While this is a goal rarely reached, it is still a central concern.

c) This concern with comparison leads anthropologists and folklorists to a Janus-faced approach to the common Western assumptions about the inevitability of progress, Westernization, and modernization. The view of progress as a bandwagon which we must jump on or perish is held by Westerners and many other peoples throughout the world. It underlay the often force-fed acculturation of West Asian and Mediterranean Jews by the Alliance Israelite Universelle and the Jewish Agency. While many anthropologists accept the idea of cultural evolution which moves from societies which are technologically primitive and socially simple to those which are more complex on both counts, they also question whether such movement is for the better. Most would question whether the particular ideologies or customs which have accompanied such development are necessary for technological development, whether it is eating with a fork or ideas of economic rationality. Thus, anthropologists do not privilege the latest fad or technological innovation as superior to traditional forms.

d) The fieldwork experience, however, also prevents anthropologists from rejecting all change out of hand. Musicians, singers, storytellers, and craftsmen constantly revise and improvise. They adopt new techniques and adapt their forms to them, and new content is constantly poured into old molds.

This raises the problem of authenticity. At the 1987 Conference on Sephardic Studies at SUNY-Binghamton, a concert was presented by Flory Jagoda and her family. The Balkan Sephardic songs were played on Spanish guitars. At a panel discussion the next day, the musicologist Israel Katz pointed out that this performance, like many others, such as the new klezmer bands which have sprung up in the 1980s, are not authentic in the historical sense. They do not use the same instruments. Klezmer music, which was improvisational, now may be played from written scores. Instruments are used today which were not used traditionally, Katz acknowledged that Flory Jagoda brought with her a folk ambience from Bosnia but, even so, this performance should not be mistaken for a genuine Balkan Sephardic performance which would use Turkish rather than Spanish instruments.

Later in the same panel, Dov Noy, the dean of Israeli folklore studies, replied that we should not consider folklore as static, and we should acknowledge change. Therefore, the use of non-traditional instruments or arrangements does not invalidate the ensemble as standing in a Sephardic tradition. Traditions are constantly being discarded, reinterpreted, and invented. This is part of the process with which we are concerned.

Both Katz and Noy represent legitimate concerns, but Noy is closer to the view of anthropologists who are less concerned with deciding what is legitimate and more with process. Of course, anthropologists will comment sardonically about the recent inventions of tradition, but the field tends to be more permissive than other fields in the humanities and social sciences in this regard.

In the present volume, some of the aspects which mark anthropology appear in the section on History and Philosophy. The chapters by Schroeter, Genot-Bismuth, and Trigano exhibit the interplay between history, sociology, anthropology, and other social sciences.

The present section consists primarily of chapters by folklorists who are concerned with custom and folk literature. In the study of Judeo-Spanish speakers, the study of folk literature is, in fact, much stronger than other branches of ethnographic research. That we have three chapters dealing with folktales, proverbs, and wedding songs from this speech community is not surprising. Ben-Ami's article is comparative. Even though the title specifies "Sephardic and Oriental Jews," he gives us enough examples from the Ashkenazic sphere to make us see it as an article about Jews in general. The article by Siporin is about an earlier ethnographer of Italian Jewry, but is related to his own work on Italian Jewish folklore.

All of the articles in this section are based on fieldwork, either by the author or others. The article by Isaac Jack Lévy and Rosemary Lévy Zumwalt is of particular interest because it illustrates the ultimate in fieldwork by interviewing a family member, their mother (and mother-in-law respectively). Augusto Segre, whose work is analyzed by Siproin, also used observations in his own community and family. The papers by Haboucha, Ben-Ami, and Anahory-Librowicz are based on fieldwork carried out previously.

The various articles show us the particular ways in which universal themes are expressed. Both Ben-Ami and Anahory-Librowicz utilize the concept of 'rites of passage' with regard to marriage, pregnancy, and birth. Anahory-Librowicz, for example, explores the alternation of moralistic, erotic-lyrical, and bawdy themes in Judeo-Spanish wedding songs as they express moods present at marriage ceremonies. Ben-Ami proceeds from the universal desire for children and anxiety over the process of childbirth to the specific longings of the Jewish people for continuity. In both these chapters, the dialectic between nature and culture, order and chaos, which Levi-Strauss and other anthropologists see as pervading myth, folklore, and ritual are played out.

Reginetta Haboucha similarly mediates between the universal and the local in her analysis of attitudes toward women's power in a Balkan Ladino folktale. She, like Ben-Ami, Siporin, and an increasing number of folklorists and anthropologists, sees the influence of the written tradition on the oral, as well as vice-versa. She points to the alternating images of faithful wives/maidens and evil women in the Old World patriarchal societies, which include Judaism. Her paper illustrates a feminist perspective of such texts.

The chapters in this section illustrate the concern of anthropologists and folklorists with the expressive side of culture. The interest which many anthropologists have in the economic and political system is similar to what we find in papers by such historians as Schroeter, Trigano, and Genot-Bismuth. The analysis of expression found in the folkloristic view help us to deepen our view of Mediterranean and West Asian Jewry, while social and economic studies broaden our vision of the Sephardic role in their region and in the world as a whole.

SEVENTEEN

Memories of Jewish Life

Steve Siporin

SEASON

Here is how it begins:

Late September, the first faint autumn mists, the time for *selichot* (penitential prayers). The pleasant and savory cool of the night, together with the sharp smell of the grape harvest—which already is spreading from the wine cellar—fills your lungs and stings your nose. It is still dark. The old stones which pave the narrow lanes on the way to the Holy Temple reflect the faint light of the few lampposts. The city sleeps, but in the small Jewish quarter, where the ghetto once was and where many Jewish families still live, someone is already getting up. Meanwhile, the coffee in the coffee pot, prepared the evening before, is being heated, and it mumbles. Old Giacubin is ending his morning rounds to warn the faithful that the hour of prayer is close at hand. For years he has been carrying out this job. He gets up early, slips on his hobnailed military boots and an old military jacket—bought many years ago for little money from his friend *sur* Elia—and he goes slowly from house to house, knocking on the doors with his cane and shouting in a stentorian voice, '*Selichoth! Selichoth!*' In the silence of the night, the banging of the cane and the sound of the voice resound and fade out in the distance. Meanwhile, Giacubin stops to catch his breath, sometimes taking a pinch of tobacco; then he resumes his route, his slight and swaying figure stretching out upon the shining stones of the alleys. For how long has he been fulfilling this charge of the Community which lasts from the week before Rosh ha-Shana (New Year) until the Eve of Kippur

225

(Atonement)? From time immemorial. It almost seems as if the ancient *selichoth* were born with him, as he is old they are old, like the faults and sins of man or the yearning desire to ask of the Lord, at least once a year, that greatly desired forgiveness. His seems to be the eternal, timeless voice, an anonymous voice which comes from a distant world and is regularly reawakened in us towards autumn, when the red and yellow leaves of the rows of Monferrato vines seem to remind us that everything ends and that the moment for prayer and meditation has arrived.[1]

This opening scene in Augusto Segre's reminiscence of Jewish life in Italy, *Memorie di vita ebraica: Casale Monferrato, Roma, Gerusalemme: 1918–1960*, evokes a Jewish world which exists today as memory alone. Due to the sparseness of ethnographic fieldwork among Italy's disappearing Jewish communities, we must turn to native writers like Segre for the folklife of Italian Jewry.[2]

Segre did not write, as the passage above clearly shows, as a folklore fieldworker or an ethnographer, trying objectively to describe a reality as he observed it. He wrote as a nostalgic native, remembering and recreating scenes more than a half-century old, set in a world which had been virtually destroyed. At the same time, Segre was a rabbinical scholar and historian, a leader of Italian Jewry, and he served for many years as editor of the major journal of Italian Jewish culture, *Rassegna Mensile di Israel*. Thus, his perspective might be described as that of the educated insider. As editor of *Rassegna Mensile di Israel*, Segre was a strong proponent of research on Italian-Jewish history, and he published many articles on the Italian communities. We must read his book with both caution and respect—caution for the subjective nature of reminiscence with all its inherent flaws, but respect for one who would be an ideal oral informant.[3] By utilizing information about other Jewish communities and their folk practices, it may be possible to learn something about Italian-Jewish folklife from the *Memorie*.

The passage cited above, for instance, describes a practice—the *shamash* going from door to door to awaken the community—which is associated with the saying of selichoth during the period preceding Rosh ha-shanah. In Eastern Europe, the practice was similar:

> From the beginning of the month until Rosh Hashanah the shammes makes nightly rounds, pounding on the shutters of each house and calling, 'Jews, get up, it's time to go to "pardons!"'[4]

This practice is a familiar one in other Jewish communities as well. With Segre, we see a widespread Jewish practice. But for Monferrese Jews, the season also has local associations which are related to the climate, the grape harvest, wine-making, and the architecture of the town. These associations become part of the subtle yet substantial *local*, Italian-Jewish sense of the fall holidays.

In other passages, Segre tells us more about the local meaning of the season:

> The month of September and the weeks of the *selichoth* were, though only generically, festival days; though it might seem like a contradiction, it really was so. September was something lively that broke the drowsy vacation period which for us lacked the sea, the mountains, and very often the countryside....Thus with September—with its coolness, with its grapes and peaches of the harvest—the time of the *selichoth* returned. The small Community revived practically at once, reawakening from its summer lethargy; hence our expectations and festive joy.[5]

There is a certain appropriateness in the shamash waking the community from its summer drowsiness—its symbolic forgetfulness of God—which may be more than literary. The reciting of selichoth had a meaningful niche in the folklife of this community. In most places, selichoth have the connotation of seriousness and sobriety. But in Casale Monferrato, at least for the children, local conditions made the days of selichoth almost festive.

CHARACTER

The characters who peopled this post-Ghetto world, especially in light of their characteristic occupations, are one of Segre's major descriptive concerns. One character, Mandulìn, is a consummate *schnorrer*, a sponger:

> The door opened and was slammed shut again immediately afterward because the person who entered did not bother to close it gently. This was also a way to attract attention. Tall, bony, with long shoes, shuffling along more than necessary in order to announce his presence, Mandulìn appeared. He took his place in one of the last rows, an optimum observation post for seeing who came in. He leaned on the reading stand, which in the meantime he had raised, sighing and shaking his head. Turning to Babandu, he exclaimed in a low voice, 'Oh, poor me! What times, *ulam hafukh* (the world turned upside down).' As if to console himself, he took a snuff-box from his pocket, put a pinch of tobacco in his long nose—which was eternally red and runny—meanwhile never ceasing to shake his head. While accomplishing all this—which for him was almost a ritual—he was also checking, out of the corner of his eye, to see if there might be some 'foreigner' among those present. For him this word had something magical about it and referred to coreligionists who had moved to other cities but who returned to their native Community for the annual ceremonies, or to others who, also coming from afar, were travelling. In both cases it always meant good oppor-

tunities for renewing acquaintances or making new ones, and above all, obtaining a certain immediate advantage in cash. If he were dealing with an ex-fellow countryman, Mandulin went up to him without any hesitation, reminding him of the ancient maxim that 'the poor of your own city take precedence over others,' assuming the tone of a creditor who flaunts one of his rights. If instead he ran across a new person, he studied the new subject deeply and astutely, before making his own move—ably as always. He took a big yellow handkerchief out of his pocket—which he shook before opening—and, covering his nose, blew it loudly. Babandu peered at him maliciously, but he didn't say a word; he knew better than to hazard a conversation with Mandulin. He was, perhaps, the most characteristic figure representing the 'old ghetto.' He had inherited all its misery, worries, sighs, laments, and also the hopes—nurtured by the practiced (sometimes ingenious) imagination of the poor, who were compelled each day to invent ruses in order to get themselves at least a bowl of soup and to go forward toward the less miserable. It was said that he was truly first-rate—a *schnorrer* (sponger) at a professional level—because he was unsurpassed at contriving new systems for obtaining what he needed and at making his requests like a true schnorrer: that is, as one who asks only to have his legitimate rights fulfilled, not as one who waits upon dubious generosity or an act of beneficence.[6]

This last phrase—"as one who asks only to have his legitimate rights fulfilled, not as one who waits upon dubious generosity or an act of beneficence"—for all its humor, is deeply rooted in widespread Jewish notions of charity. Later, when recounting stories about Mandulin's exploits, Segre writes:

On day, rejoicing, Mandulin appeared before the Community to announce the birth of his twelfth son, exclaiming, 'Here is *Yaakov* [Jacob] and the twelve tribes. There was also, in this proud communication, the certainty of immediate and spontaneous assistance which would take account not only of his precarious economic conditions, but which would also be a sign of recognition for one who had so seriously committed himself to increasing the population of his Community. In Casale every birth was by now becoming an important event, because births were not so frequent as in the past. Mandulin, therefore, was glad to offer up joy and evidently, responsibility, before all his fellow Jews. This time, however, the Secretary had heard him with less enthusiasm than usual and shaking his head, had said to him, '*Mazal tov* (congratulations), Mandulin, but still, listen, listen to me: I think that now you should be a bit more careful considering your situation.' But Mandulin, almost shouting, interrupted him saying, 'How can the Community interfere in my strictly personal affairs and give me such orders? Is this how you receive someone who contributes as he can to the life of the Community? It's a shame, a real shame.' Having said this, he went toward the door, but suddenly he stopped. Turning to face the secretary, trembling with rage and shaking his finger menacingly, he exclaimed, 'Well then, I'll tell you what. Next year I will come here again to announce to you— with the help of the Holy One, blessed be He—the birth of another child.' It is told that that was one of the few times in his life that he kept his word precisely.[7]

The very use of the term 'schnorrer' may lead us to wonder if the character of Mandulin is a fictional borrowing from London or Eastern Europe. Has Segre romanticized the Italian post-Ghetto era through the influence of someone like Israel Zangwill, Sholom Aleichem, or other Yiddish writers?

A citation from a dictionary of the Jewish-Venetian dialect, *giudeo-veneziana*, indicates that both the character-type and the term (in the form *znora*—begging) were well-known in Venice:

> The old Ghetto certainly did not lack figures such as these [schnorrers], and *znora* [begging] became an art which had its major and minor practitioners.[8]

Thus, whatever modifying effects Yiddish literature may have had upon Segre, there seems to be a basis in Italian-Jewish folklife for this character-type.[9]

PLACE

We also find examples in Segre's *Memorie* of the legends and other folklore connected to the physical Ghetto of Casale Monferrato itself:

> These stones also concealed their own secret, a long and not always happy history—if one thinks of the families that ascended and descended them, often running in fear, anxiety, and dismay during the long period of the ghetto. Sur Elia remembered well that when he was still a boy, one of his old relatives (noted for his oddities) had shown him some steps and a corner projecting from the wall where there were certain signs which, according to the relative, were sword strokes. Lower down were very dark stains, which almost everyone said were simply the work of humidity, but which were, for that old relative, blood stains: 'There was so much,' or so he said, 'that the wall had drunk it up, so to speak, in a gulp and preserved it; then with the passing of time it took on that very dark color.'[10]

In similar fashion, Jewish suffering in the Ghetto of Venice has been recorded in folk memory through a legend attaching itself to a particular physical feature of the Ghetto environment.[11] Such topographic folklore was probably attached to all the Ghettos in Italy. I found in Venice, for example, that an indigenous Jewish 'mental map' of the Ghetto could still be assembled from oral interviews in 1978—almost two hundred years after the abolishment of the Ghetto.[12] To the extent that the physical Ghetto and the memory of its social dynamics remains, there also remains a certain knowledge of the world view of the Jews of the Italian Ghetto, as Segre demonstrates for Casale Monferrato:

> These shops represented one of the historic boundaries of the ghetto, which was situated right behind them. Before the 29th of March 1848—the glorious and unforgettable (to the Jews) date of the Albertine emancipation—whoever had a shop was thus able to enjoy the not insignificant advantage of having access to it (by entering from the back) without having to exit from the *chazer* (courtyard, ghetto). They opened their stores, and thus they could appear facing the free world, which was granted to them during certain hours. In compensation, the *goim* [non-Jews] who came to them to make their purchases were always numerous, since—everything notwithstanding—it was known, especially among the country people, that with the Jews one could make good deals.[13]

MARGINALITY

Segre's description of the periphery of the Ghetto's architecture objectifies the social, psychological, and spiritual condition of the late Ghetto and post-Ghetto era Italian Jew. The shop on the boundary of the Ghetto—with access from the inside—is a remarkable instance of physical marginality and transition which parallels a mental and historical condition. Not only does the shop stand midway between inside and outside (the Ghetto); it is literally and symbolically midway between Jewish and Christian, sacred and profane, domestic and public, oppressed and free, safe and dangerous, dark and light, community and nation. The marginal status of the shopkeeper, placed in clear relief in Segre's description, carried over into much of Italian-Jewish folklore of the post-ghetto era, as Segre demonstrates:

> He [the President of the Community] was interested in everything that happened, and he was extremely well informed about every private or community dispute. This attitude was explained by the usual mischief-makers by the fact that he had made a 'mixed marriage.' It was told that once, when he met Rabbi Castelbolognesi, he introduced his wife saying, 'Here is my wife. She is not Jewish, but she knows how to make Kosher goose salami.' (Kosher goose salami was a specialty of Casale, known and appreciated throughout Italy.) To this remark, however—which could have been interpreted as a tentative, though naive, partial justification

for his marriage—the Rabbi, not at all convinced, had replied, 'And here is my wife, who does not know how to make kosher goose salami, but who is Jewish...'[14]

This stinging narrative, a story utilizing an Italian-Jewish ethnic food specialty, addresses the confusion about Jewish identity in the post-Ghetto era. The tension Italian Jews experienced in this era is one of the main themes of Segre's book and, undoubtedly, of the folklore of the era he describes. In several places, he describes what must have been a constantly recurring, but always varying, scene:

> From one side came a fusilade of questions, formed with a slightly ironic smile by one of them, a brilliant graduate, who put them to Papa to see if he would be unnerved. On the other side was the *murenu*[15] who responded calmly, serenely, not allowing himself to be confused by "science." Even in those sitting-room discussions, the usual themes of the old and "superceded" traditional Jewish quasi-world and the new, more broadly attractive horizons of assimilation, re-emerged in their essence. My father—I would say to his good fortune—did not have a university education, but rather a solid, Jewish culture and a faith which no philosophical and scientific theory could scratch. The hosts paraded their learning with an almost ostentatious pride and affected language, and they strained to make the *murenu* understand that many Jewish religious values were being recast.... Assimilation and tradition clashed even among the grapevines of Monferrato.[16]

CONCLUSION

Thus far I have presented some examples of Italian-Jewish folklife from one locality, Casale Monferrato, as protrayed in the reminiscence by Augusto Segre, *Memorie de vita ebraica*. In closing, I would like to describe the scholarly context and status of the study of Italian-Jewish folk culture.

JEWS IN ITALY

A Jewish people and a Jewish culture do exist in Italy today. Both the people and their culture have deep roots in the past. But Italian Jewry has often been overlooked or else wrongly subsumed under either Ashkenazic or Sephardic Jewry. Sergio della Pergola notes that:

> Because of the ancient origins of the Italian Jewish communities, part of the Italian Jews cannot be considered either as Sephardim or Ashkenazim, since they are direct descendants of the original inhabitants of Palestine.[17]

Italian Jewry may be distinguished on the basis of language, liturgy, and custom as well as descent. Nevertheless, the waves of Ashkenazic and Sephardic immigrants who have arrived in Italy over the centuries have affected local Jewish cultures enormously. Such immigrants continue to arrive today. The last twenty-five years have witnessed the arrival of both Russian and Libyan Jews, the continuation of a long tradition.

Although, historically, immigrants were assimilated to the local culture, they also brought additions and in other ways changed the 'native' Italian-Jewish culture. Segre himself came from a family which recognized its Sephardic origin although it had been in northwest Italy for centuries. The situation one finds in Italy today is complex, each community varying in its configuration of Ashkenazic, Italian, and Sephardic cultural attributes.

Nevertheless, in order to recognize and identify this current of world Jewry, Italian Jews have been referred to as *Italkians*[18], from Hebrew *Italki* (Italian), and it has recently been suggested that their local Italian-Jewish languages be collectively called *Italkian*.[19]

SCHOLARSHIP

Historical scholarship dealing with Italian-Jewish communities is extensive.[20] But folk culture—which is at the heart of any ethnic group's continuity—has been dealt with mainly in terms of Italian-Jewish languages.[21] Outside of folk language, the subject of Jewish folk culture in Italy is rarely approached, and little exists in the way of collected Italian-Jewish folk material.[22]

The reasons for the absence of folklore fieldwork lie more in the biases of scholarship than in the objective reality of Italian Jewry. Fieldwork and other kinds of research have perhaps been blocked by hasty assumptions about folklore and assimilation. Cecil Roth wrote, for instance, that in the late nineteenth and early twentieth centuries

> Italy became a byword in the Jewish world for the completeness of emancipation on the one hand, for its deadly corrosive potentialities on the other.[23]

This observation echoes the broader description of Lucy S. Dawidowicz:

> Western Jews could not resist the lures of enlightenment, emancipation, and the opportunity to enter the larger society. They rushed to embrace it....In a brief span, Western European Jewish communities were decimated, having paid heavily for emancipation with conversion.[24]

These statements may be largely true, but perhaps they have discouraged the closer examination of traditional culture in Western Europe. This widespread opinion partially accounts for the lack of objective research into the *actual* state and evolution of Jewish culture, especially at the folk level, in Italy over the last one hundred and fifty to two hundred years.

Cecil Roth also wrote that "the folklore of the Italian Ghetto has never been collected and now [i.e., 1940s] it is unhappily too late."[25] As I have shown elsewhere,[26] Italian-Jewish folk customs that may even predate the Ghetto could still be observed and collected in 1978. Early twentieth-century Italian-Jewish scholars themselves—who were clearly the best equipped to engage in folklore research in Italian-Jewish communities—regarded their own folk culture as basically defunct, as only the memory culture of the oldest people:

> Born too late, we have never, to tell the truth, heard this dialect
> from the lips of anyone who spoke it regularly, since it has already been
> dead for a while. But we have had the help of someone who is proficient,
> even though he, too, though born a bit earlier than us, was also born
> too late.[27]

A final bias may lie with the Jewish folklorists of the early twentieth century who were concerned on the one hand with Ashkenazic folklore and on the other hand, as Dan Ben-Amos argues,[28] with the most exotic of the Jewish communities. Italian Jewry falls between these categories—neither part of Eastern Europe nor far enough from the mainstream to be considered exotic.

STUDYING ITALIAN-JEWISH FOLK CULTURE TODAY

Given the loss of time and people, what sources are available for the study of Italian-Jewish folk culture today?

The people themselves—contemporary Italian Jews should still be considered the most valuable source. It is remarkable that Paola Diena, a linguist, found a large vocabulary of Jewish-Piedmontese dialect terms among more speakers in the 1970s than had been recorded by scholars—complaining that it was already too late—in the early twentieth century.[29] During my fieldwork in Venice in 1978, I recorded language, proverbs, songs, customs, foodways, and topographical lore that was still important to contemporary Venetian Jews. Jewish life in Italy, through the 1930s, clearly shared even greater continuity with the past. To those living in the pre-war era, what was left of traditional culture did not seem significant because, like Segre, they knew that much more had existed in the nineteenth century. But from a post-Holocaust perspective, Jewish Italy of the 1920s and 1930s seems worthy indeed of ethnographic description. Italian Jews who are now (1992) in their seventies should be interviewed about this era.

The situation today is as pressing as ever, and perhaps more so. According to Sergio della Pergola, the leading authority on Jewish demography, the small and medium-sized Italian-Jewish communities, in places such as Florence, Venice, Padova, and Genova, will not survive the twentieth century.[30] Only Milan and Rome will contain orgainzed Jewish communities in Italy in the twenty-first century.[31] Thus, fieldwork, ironically at this late stage, still remains the most important strategy for documenting Italian-Jewish folk culture.

THE REMINISCENCE: SEGRE'S WORK

Another source is what you have sampled here, the personal reminiscence, a literary form. I do not know how widespread this kind of document may be among Italian Jews, but there are several published examples.[32] Augusto Segre's *Memorie di vita ebraica: Casale Monferrato, Roma, Gerusalemme: 1918–1960* is certainly a masterpiece of this genre, and the examples cited here illustrate the book's importance to a description of Italian-Jewish folklife in a small post-Ghetto city during the early part of this century. Segre's work gives us a chance to re-evaluate Italian-Jewish folklore and to realize that the subject has been overlooked more because of scholarly biases than because of objective reality. Reminiscences such as Segre's clearly must be read with reference to whatever ethnographic or historical records exist, since they are prone to the flaws of memory and nostalgia. Nonetheless, when so little is available on the folklife of a community—as is the case with Jewish Italy—reminiscences such as Segre's *Memorie* become invaluable documents, one of our few windows into communities just beyond our grasp.

NOTES

1. Augusto Segre, *Memorie di vita ebraica: Casale Monferrato, Roma, Gerusalemme: 1918–1960* (Rome, Bonacci, 1979), 19–20.

2. For fieldwork in the 1970s, see Paola Diena, "*Il Giudeo-piemontese: Tracce Attuali e Testimonianze Sociolinguistiche*," [Jewish-Piedmontese: Actual Traces and Sociolinguistic Testimony] (*Tesi di Laurea* in Italian Dialectology, *Universitá degli studi di Torino*, 1979/80); and Steve Siporin, "Tradition and Innovation in the Jewish Festivals in Venice, Italy," Ph.D. dissertation, Indiana University, 1982.

3. As, in fact, he was for me during a field trip to Israel in 1985.

4. Mark Zborowski and Elizabeth Herzog, *Life is With People: The Culture of the Shtetl* (New York, Schocken, 1974), 392.

5. Augusto Segre, *Memorie*, 46, 51.

6. Augusto Segre, *Memorie*, 35–36.

7. Augusto Segre, *Memorie*, 38–39.

8. Umberto Fortis and Paolo Zolli, *La Parlata giudeo-veneziana* (Assisi and Rome, Carucci, 1979), 346.

9. In the case of Venice, Yiddish forms one of the contributing languages to the local dialect since Jews immigrating from Germany were an early part of the Jewish population. The first ghetto, created in 1516, was expressly for German Jews. There are a few terms of Yiddish origin listed in the dictionary of Jewish-Venetian by Fortis and Zolli. The term *orsai*, for example, meaning the anniversary

of someone's death, derives from Yiddish *yorzait* and is found in other North Italian Jewish dialects (Fortis and Zolli, 325).

10.   Augusto Segre, *Memorie*, 21.

11.   See Adolpho Ottolenghi, *"Per il IV Centario della Scuola Canton: Notizie Storiche sui Templi veneziani di rito tedesco e su alcuni Templi privati con Cenni della vita ebraica nei secoli XVI–XIX: Commemorazione tenuta nella Scuola Canton la sera del 6 Dicembre 1931 - 26 Chislev 5692*, [For the Fourth Centenary of the Canton Synagogue: Historical Notes on the Venetian Temples with Allusions to Jewish Life from the Sixteenth to Nineteenth Centuries: A Commeration held in the Canton Synagogue the evening of the Sixth of December, 1931 - 26 Kislev 5692], (Venice, *Gazzettino illustrato*, 1932), 18–20.

12.   Steve Siporin, "Tradition and Innovation in the Jewish Festivals in Venice, Italy," Ph.D. dissertation (Indiana University, 1982), 267–303.

13.   Augusto Segre, *Memorie*, 22–23.

14.   Augusto Segre, *Memorie*, 41–42.

15.   Jewish Piedmontese dialect term meaning 'rabbi,' literally 'our teacher,' from Hebrew *morenu* 'our teacher.'

16.   Augusto Segre, *Memorie*, 49–50.

17.   Sergio Della Pergola, *Anatomia dell'Ebraismo Italiano: Caratteristiche demografiche, economiche, sociali, religiose, e politiche di una minoranza* (Anatomy of Italian Judaism: Demographic, Economic, Social, Religious, and Political Characteristics of a Minority), (Assisi and Rome, Carucci, 1976), 65.

18.   Solomon A. Birnbaum, "The Jewries of Eastern Europe," *Slavonic and East European Review* 29 (1950): 420–443, as cited in David L. Gold, "The glottonym *Italkian*," *Italia, Studi e ricerche sulla cultura e sulla letteratura degli ebrei d'Italia* 2 (1980): 102.

19.   David L. Gold, "The glottonym *Italkian*, *Italia: Studi e ricerche sulla cultura e sulla letteratura degli ebrei d'Italia* 2 (1980): 98–102.

20.   Jews have lived in Rome continuously at least since 63 B.C., according to Cecil Roth, *The History of the Jews in Italy* (Philadelphia, Jewish Publication Society, 1946). Other south Italian Jewish communities may date from even earlier times. The recent archaeological discovery of a synagogue at Ostia Antica, Rome's ancient seaport, confirms the presence of a Jewish community there at least by the third century A.D. (Umberto Fortis, *Jews and Synagogues*, Venice, Storti, 1974). At a later date, southern Italy seems to have been the link in communicating Jewish mystical tradition from the Middle East to Germany, via the Kalonymus family. (See Gershom G. Scholem, *Major Trends in Jewish Mysticism*, Jerusalem and New York, Schocken, 1974 edition, pp. 101–102.) Southern Italian communities such as Bari and Otranto enjoyed serious reputations for Hebrew learning from the ninth through the twelfth centuries (see Roth, pp. 58–66). Venice was a major center for scholarship and printing in the sixteenth and first half of the seventeenth centuries. (See Roth, *History of the Jews of Venice*, Philadelphia, Jewish Publication Society, 1975 edition.) The major bibliographies are Aldo

Luzzato and Moshe Moldavi, *Biblioteca Italo-Ebraica, Bibliografia per la storia degli Ebrei in Italia, 1964–1973* (Rome, Carucci, 1982); Attilio Milano, *Biblioteca historica italo-judaica* (Florence, Sansoni, 1954), and *Supplemento, 1953–1964* (Florence, Sansoni, 1965); G. Romano, *Bibliografia italo-ebraica !1848–1977)* (Florence, Olschki, 1979).

21. *La Parlata Guideo-Veneziana* (The Jewish-Venetian Dialect), by Umberto Fortis and Paolo Zolli (Assisi and Rome, Carucci, 1979), is a dictionary of one Jewish-Italian language. This dictionary is well-annotated and includes scholarly citations of equivalent or related terms which appear in other Jewish dialects. It contains the best bibliography available on Jewish-Italian languages. *Giudeo-Italiano: Dialetti Italiani Parlati dagli Ebrei d'Italia* (Jewish-Italian Dialects Spoken by the Jews of Italy) by Giovanna Massariello Merzagora (Pisa, Pacini, 1977), is an attempt to synthesize earlier works on individual Jewish-Italian languages. *Il Giudeo-Piemontese: Tracce Attuali e Testimonianze Sociolinguistiche* (Jewish-Piedmontese: Actual Traces and Sociolinguistic Testimony) by Paolo Diena (*Tesi di Laurea* in Italian Dialectology, *Universitá degli studi di Torino,* 1979/80) utilizes historical material but also is based on fieldwork and questionnaires from the late 1970s, indicating that there is still a living population that has some knowledge of this language. *La Rassengna mensile di Israel* is an Italian-Jewish journal which over the years has printed the bulk of the published scholarship on Jewish-Italian languages. Recent work has begun to appear in Israel in the journal, *Italia: Studi a ricerche sulla cultura e sulla letteratura degli ebrei d'Italia.*

22. A practically unheeded call for the collection of Italian-Jewish folklore appeared as "*Ricerche folkloristiche e linguistiche degli Ebrei d'Italia*" (Folkloristic and Linguistic Research on the Jews of Italy) by Riccardo Bacchi in *La Rassegna Mensile di Israel* 2 (1926): 24–30. Fortis and Zolli, above, contains proverbs. Also see Steve Siporin, "Passover, Shavout and Simhat Torah in Venice: Elite Innovations and Their Acceptance by the Folk," *La Rassegna Mensile di Israel* 50 (1984): 23–41; " 'The Table of the Angel' and Two Other Jewish-Venetian Food Customs," *Lares* 50 (1984): 357–365; " 'To Hold High Their Glorious Origins': The Jewish Festivals in Venice," *Shofar* 8 (1989): 30–46; and "Continuity and Innovation in the Jewish Festivals in Venice, Italy," Ph.D. dissertation (Indiana University, 1982).

23. Italy, 506.

24. *The Golden Tradition* (New York, Chicago, and San Francisco, Holt, Rinehart, and Winston, 1967), 5.

25. Italy, 389.

26. 'The Table of the Angel' (already cited fully in note 22).

27. Bene Kedem, "*La Gnora Luna: scene di vita Ebraica Fiorentina*" (Miss Luna: Scenes of Jewish Florentine Life), *Rassegna mensile di Israel* 6 (1932): 547.

28. "Folklore in Israel," *Schweizersches Archiv für Volksunde* 59 (1963): 14–24.

29. Diena, "*Tracce Attuali.*"

30. Della Pergola, *Anatomia Dell'Ebraismo italiano.*

31. Ibid.

32. These examples include Letizia Morpurgo Fano, *Diario: Ricordi Di Prigionia* (Venice, n.p. 1966); Marco Herman, *Diario di un ragazzo ebreo* (Cuneo, L'Arciere 1984); Emilio, Pardo, *Luci ed Ombre: Il Ghetto di Venezia alla fine del 1800 ed al principio del 1900* (Venice, n.p. 1965); Enzo Levi, *Memorie di una vita (1889–1947)* (Modena: S.T.E.U. Muchi, 1972); Marco Momigliano, *Autobiografia di un Rabbino Italiano* (Palermo: Sellerio, 1986 [1897]); Dan Vittorio Segre, *Memoirs of a Fortunate Jew: An Italian Story* (Bethesda, Maryland: Adler and Adler, 1987).

EIGHTEEN

Misogyny or Philogyny:
The Case of a Judeo-Spanish Folktale

Reginetta Haboucha

Sephardic Jews do not escape the wavering views about women which are found throughout the ages in Jewish writings as well as in Jewish oral tradition.[1] In this chapter, I examine a Judeo-Spanish folktale which represents a powerful illustration of this ambivalent attitude toward women. This narrative, collected from Bitolj (Monastir) in the early 1930s, deals with examples of marital behavior and female responses to adverse circumstances. It had appeared, untitled, in Cynthia Crews's early collection of Sephardic tales[2] but was given the name *Tale of the Talking Birds* at a later date.[3]

The *Tale of the Talking Birds* uses the framework of a supernatural narrative to provide the structure which introduces and links two distinct realistic stories within it. In the end, the frame tale returns to wrap up the entire narrative into one entity.[4] Thus, we have three different tales incorporated into one text. In this beautiful narrative, King Solomon is assigned a premarital task by an unidentified beloved:[5] to win her hand, he must secure a feather from every species of birds. All the birds obey the king's command except two—the owl and the nightingale. When repremanded, each of the culprits justifies its negligence by recalling the event which had distracted it from its duty to the king. After the birds have told their respcetive tales (Tales 1A and 1B), the narrative reverts to the frame story of King Solomon and his bride. At that time, the owl and the nightingale deliver their respective feathers to Solomon, thus helping him complete the assigned task to the satisfaction of the bride. The couple marries (Tale 1).[6]

During the internal digressions, the owl speaks first and narrates the tale of the *Matron of Ephesus* (Tale 1A),[7] in which a woman mournfully weeps day and night by the side of her beloved husband's grave. Out of deference for her tears, the execution by hanging of a condemned man is postponed. When the convict subsequently escapes, the widow suggests that he be replaced at the gallows with the corpse of her dead spouse. She then runs off with the executioner.

In turn, the nigtingale gives a version of the tale type entitled *The Faithful Wife* (Tale 1B).[8] It is a more complex story of a virtuous but destitute woman who is made to marry a rich but depraved man. Under the influence of his good wife, the husband appears to reform. Later, however, he leaves home to seek adventures and finds himself in a land of cheaters, where royal succession is determined by whether a cat holds up a mace or drops it. The cat is trained to hold it up so that no one can win the throne. Like other dupes before him who gamble against the cat's concentration, our man loses and ends up in prison. Later, the wife suspects the wiles of a treacherous impostor who tries to lure her away from home and uncovers from him the predicament and the whereabouts of her missing spouse. Dressed up as a man, she goes to his rescue and is subjected to the identical cat trick. She, however, distracts the cat with mice so that it drops the mace. The disguised wife thus wins the throne, becomes 'king,' and frees her husband. She takes him home, humbled.

Because folklore is, in part, a traditionally communicative process,[9] due attention should be given to the symbolic significance of some of the elements present in these texts. A symbol proper "is a dynamic and polysymbolic reality imbued with emotive and conceptual values...."[10] A symbolic expression, therefore, must be functional within the social pattern of a determined community and must be imagined within a total social situation. The purpose of this chapter is to examine the symbolism of the tales and to interpret the ambivalent messages about women they seem to convey.

TALE 1

The framework of the suitor task, with speaking birds as helpers, belongs to the realm of the extraordinary. The motifs are folktale commonplaces, except that the suitor is identified as King Solomon, perhaps to give authenticity to the tale but simultaneously giving it a Jewish stamp. It befits Solomon to frame the tales of an unworthy widow and a reliable wife. In Jewish popular belief, Solomon is considered the father of wisdom but symbolizes human weakness as well. The son of David had little good to say about women in his writings: he considered them more bitter than death and was unable to find one virtuous woman among a thousand. Thus, he thought that any man who escaped from their clutches was beloved by God.[11] If a good woman were to exist, however, he prized her as a jewel above rubies.[12] And yet Solomon is fabled to have loved a thousand women and married a multitude of them.[13] It is thus logical that our narrative, which well illustrates this ambivalence, should belong to the cycle of Solomon's legends.[14] It addresses both his proverbial wisdom and his legendary weakness for women.

As a symbol of Man, Solomon submits willingly to the remarkable demand imposed by the woman he loves.[15] In variants of our tale, Solomon agrees to build a palace with the bones of birds. A rebel bird upbraids him for submitting to the whimsy of his lover and condemns those men who obey their women meekly, thus betraying the superiority of their sex.[16] Our own version is less misogynic but no less cynical and cautionary. Since popular tradition has it that Solomon understood the languages of birds and beasts, and that all animals submitted to his judgment and command,[17] he is able thus to fulfill the suitor task without extraordinary difficulty. In return, however, he must listen to exempla illustrating the two faces of Eve.[18] The practical lesson of these illustrations is meant to expose the dichotomous nature of women and to alert men about to select a mate to the necessity of being wary of women and of choosing a bride wisely. Once the task is accomplished and the couple is married, Solomon's tale concludes in typical escapist fairy-tale manner: "i bibyerun alegris para tode su bide."[19]

Solomon's bride represents Woman and is depicted as an active, decisive character. While appearing to play a secondary role in the tale, she, in fact, provides the springboard for the rest of the narrative. She does not shy away from dealing directly with her suitor, eliminating the need for conventional intermediaries. The difficult suitor task she imposes is not whimsical. It is not set as a contest of cleverness or skill against rival suitors or as a barrier to discourage or get rid of the royal lover but, rather, as a way to test his love and resolve before consenting to marry him. The assignment and performance of the suitor task are the pivotal events of the frame tale. They establish the supernatural or symbolic background against which the bird anecdotes unfold and they permit the transformation of the bride from a demanding female to one who fades into a benign uxorial role. No moral judgment is passed.

In the *Tale of the Talking Birds*, it is not difficult to recognize the cultural value and the symbolic meaning of the owl and the nightingale which introduce the internal tales.[20] Throughout the centuries, birds of prey often incarnated evildoers, while birds that sang melodiously symbolized the faithful and virtuous.[21] Here, they effectively represent the two dramatically conflicting views of women prevalent in Jewish society, as well as universally. Tales 1A and 1B are examples of extreme female conduct which are offered to Solomon as life truths and to the listener/reader for condemnation or praise.

TALE 1A

The classical literary tale of the widow of Ephesus appears in Aarne-Thompson in the division *Stories about a Woman*, under the subdivision *Other Anecdotes of Women*. Although he lists oral versions from northern, western, and eastern Europe, as well as literary treatments of AT 1510,[22] Thompson writes that the tale "has itself never become popular among the folk, but it has given rise to a number of similar anecdotes of faithless widows.[23] In all of these the central point is that the wife plans her new marriage on the day of the husband's funeral."[24] This tale, however, appears to be popular in Jewish folklore in general[25] and particularly among Sephardim.[26]

In our version, *The Matron of Ephesus (Vidua)*[27] is told by the owl as a tale of bitterness. The owl is a nocturnal bird of prey which has always been regarded as an evil omen.[28] It has been associated with evil and misfortune almost everywhere, but it has also often been used as a symbol of wisdom.[29] Both these characteristics are present here. In the Bible, the owl symbolizes destruction, misery, and desolation.[30] One of the biblical species of owls is the lilith or 'night monster' (screech owl).[31] Interestingly, in the Aggadah, Lilith is the name of a night demon,[32] described in the Talmud as having long black hair.[33] In Semitic folklore, Lilith is a dominant female demon, perhaps the 'first Eve' or first wife of Adam who successfully fought against his domination.[34] Considered a harmful spirit, it has various roles, one of which is to prey on males, trying to seduce them and destroy them. In the *Zohar*, it is known as Lilith the harlot, the wicked, the false, or the black.[35] Widespread, also, is the identification of Lilith with the Queen of Sheba,[36] a noteworthy connection for us in view of the identification in another version of our tale of the unnamed bride of Solomon as the Queen of Sheba.[37] With all of this in mind, it is logical that the owl be symbolically associated with behavior considered by society as unsuitable, morally offensive, and censurable, and that it be assigned to voice a tale of gloom, disloyalty, and betrayal.[38]

Further along, the figure of the man about to be hanged may have a profound and complex symbolism. It may suggest a silent (dead) married man subject to a domineering/castrating wife who permits indignities to be committed against his body. The Hanged Man is Enigma # 12 of the Tarot pack of cards, which "in the positive sense stands for mysticism, sacrifice, self-denial, continence."[39] The convenient disappearance of the condemned man may symbolize the actual renunciation of these self-sacrificing characteristics by the pragmatic widow. She seems to forget her dead spouse the moment a possible new suitor appears on the scene. On the day of her husband's funeral, and despite her apparent grief, she does not hesitate to suggest the perfidious substitution of corpses, as well as propose marriage to another man.

On the surface, Tale 1A is an illustration of female treachery. Although the widow is depicted as decisive and pratical, these characteristics are not presented as favorable traits. Rather, they are interpreted as proof of her being unfathomably heartless and indecently disloyal to the memory of the deceased. This antipathetical description of the heroine's behavior, with the stress on the speed of her betrayal and the ignominy of her actions, is flagrantly overstated so that moral condemnation is inevitable. The tale aims to rally the sentiment of the listeners against the heroine because she does not conform to the social and moral behavior expected of a widow. Once her conduct is implicitly censured, the tale has no further aim; it ends abruptly. The moral to be derived from this narrative is that women are fickle, hypocritical, and untrustworthy by nature.[40]

Looked at from a less biased perspective, however, the tale may transmit a less misogynic message. It presents a woman who demonstrates independence and courage, and who displays complete disregard for conventions by defying societal rules of decorum. While mourning the death of her loved one, she considers the reality of life and acknowledges the necessity of looking out for herself. Her decisive rejection of the accepted rules of propriety may be prompted by her immediate need for comfort, companionship, and economic support. She wastes no time on the conventional mourning period[41] because her decision to take a new husband is a practical one and has to be made without hesitation, as soon as a potential suitor appears. There is no room or time for love, wooing, preliminaries, or even decency in the urgency to resolve her predicament.

TALE 1B

To offset the alleged perfidy of women as illustrated in Tale 1A, the nightingale narrates a conglomerate version of a *Romantic Tale* found in the AT subdivision of *Fidelity and Innocence*. It combines AT 888,[42] AT 888A,[43] and AT 217.[44] The sweet song of the nightingale having always been admired, it is easy to accept that this bird, which appears in the Bible only once, as 'zamir', in a joyous description of spring in Israel,[45] symbolizes a pleasing and harmonious situation. Its use here to introduce praiseworthy behavior in a happy tale is consistent with that image.[46] The tale also supports the well-known proverb which states that behind every good man stands a good woman.

Unlike Tales 1 and 1A, this narrative follows the conventional Jewish matchmaking procedure. With the respective fathers acting as brokers, romantic notions are eliminated as superfluous. Economic and practical considerations tip the balance. A willing wife for the worthless son of a rich man is difficult to find, however. No man wants to grant his daughter's hand to him except the heroine's father, who is destitute. He gives her away in marriage to the unworthy but wealthy groom without asking for her consent. She is thus depicted as a passive character, totally subjected to male authority. The background as described is not unrealistic within the social and economic context of the tale and of the Sephardic milieu in which it was transmitted.

Not surprisingly, the focus of this tale is not on the irresponsibility and bad habits of the husband but on the utter commitment and extraordinary capability of his wife. It is, however, the husband's inadequacy which creates the stage for the display of his wife's abilities. Her initiative and intelligence surface only as a result of and in contrast to his foolishness and immaturity. Reforming him requires difficult tests of her constancy, astuteness, courage, guile, and determination. It takes a remarkable woman to succeed. Such a woman symbolizes the perfect mate for any man: she is wise, faithful, steady, and unafraid. In fact, this model wife is so 'devoted' to her husband that, even when he abandons her to seek adventures, she takes enormous risks to rescue him from the darkness of prison where he ends up. After astonishing adventures, husband and wife are finally reunited.[47]

This tale's apparent intent is to stress the wife's outstanding personal superiority,[48] and to show how influential she can be in a marriage.[49] To reach the final denouement, however, this particular woman is forced to break with convention. She cannot succeed in the tale as a traditional woman. To free her husband from confinement, she goes out into the world incognito, disguised as a man, and cheats the cheaters by carefully planning her strategy. The skills and talents she displays to attain her goals are characteristic male traits and not traditionally acceptable in a woman. Thus, she can only succeed when she misrepresents herself as a man. Only aided by her transvestism can she achieve her goal and reform her husband. The unintended message derived shows that women need to prove themselves as men before they can be accepted as the equals of men.

In contrast with Solomon's bride in Tale 1, the heroine here is transformed from a nonentity to a decisive and aggressive woman after she marries. Her success in reforming her husband is demonstrated twice. The first time is when she forcefully ends his association with his wayward confederates: she confines him to their home and becomes his sole moral support and friend.[50] The second time is when the man tries to reassert himself by leaving home but is easily tricked and imprisoned by strangers: she rushes to his aid and rescues him, but she brings him home only after she humbles him and he becomes a broken man. In both instances, she acts as an emasculating woman. She does so, however, with the full approval of society as represented by her father-in-law himself who, after the betrothal, promises to give her jewels as an incentive to reform his son. The wife is thus given license to act as she does and is actually offered a prize to do so.

There is no doubt that Sephardic oral tradition is ambivalent about women. It wavers uncertainly between misogyny and philogyny. As we have seen, these Judeo-Spanish examples are full of female initiative. Heroines are challengers and unafraid of confronting the world to reach their objectives. As such, however, they are threatening to their male counterparts. Thus, the tales themselves become symbols which are uniformly consistent in tacitly reinforcing traditional female traits and communicating their message: women's role is to conform to an established image, fashioned after a male ideal. They are expected to adapt themselves to the prevailing standards, except perhaps in unrealistic or super- natural surroundings (Tale 1). Although women play major roles in the tales, the shadow of men always looms large over them. Their world may be defined by achievement, aggressiveness, self-confidence, and self-reliance, but these characteristics continue to be seen in traditional masculine terms and remain unacceptable as female traits. The successful female protagonists in the tales are those who can and do assume these masculine qualities in order to succeed in a traditional man's world. If they do so openly, however, it has to be in the service of men or else they are censured and condemned.

The strikingly conflicting attitudes toward women found in Biblical, rabbinic, and Jewish oral literature[51] are not altogether surprising in the context of the prevailing patriarchal view of women. This ambivalence does not mean that women have not been respected throughout the centuries[52] or that they have not occupied an important place in Jewish society.[53] Rather, it symbolizes universal male fears and fantasies about women and adds to them a distinctive Jewish coloration. Whether women in Judaism are admired or hated is not always clear. It is obvious, however, that they are often misunderstood and mistrusted.

NOTES

1. See R. Haboucha, "Women in the Judeo-Spanish Folktales," in "The Sephardic Scholar, Series 4, 1979–1982, 32–47, especially 32–33 and notes 1–13, 43–44. Moses Gaster, in *The Exempla of the Rabbis* (New York: Ktav Pub. House, 1968), xxii, writes: "In Jewish lore on the whole are neither despised nor held in contempt. Still a few misogynous tales . . . are validated by such verses . . ." as Eccles. 7:28. See also H. Schwarzbaum's article, "Female Fickleness in Jewish Folklore," in *The Sephardi and Oriental Jewish Heritage*, edited by I. Ben-Ami (Jerusalem: Magnes Press, 1982), 589–612.

2. Cynthia M. Crews, *Recherches sur le judéo-espagnol dans les pays balkaniques* (Paris: E. Droz, 1935), Tale No. 5 (Bitolj), 91–97.

3. See R. Haboucha, *Classification of Judeo-Spanish Folktales* (Ph.D. dissertation, Johns Hopkins University, 1973), Tale Type **538, 147–151.

4. *The Thousand and One Nights* is a classic example of a frame tale. The cohesive plot device concerns the efforts of Sheherazade to keep her husband, Shariar, legendary king of Samarkand, from killing her by entertaining him with a tale a night for one thousand and one nights.

5. Another version, a Jewish tale from Egypt housed at the Israel Folklore Archives (IFA 5378), identifies Solomon's bride as the Queen of Sheba. In the tenth century B.C., the biblical queen of Sheba made her famous visit to Solomon (I Kings 10). Louis Ginzberg writes (in note 21, p. 389, VI, of *The Legends of the Jews* [Philadelphia: Jewish Publication Society, 1959], 7 vols.): "The legend about Solomon's marriage with the Queen of Sheba is perhaps of Arabic origin, as it is not found in old Jewish sources antedating the Mohammedan period. The name Bilkis, however, given in Arabic sources to the queen of Sheba, seems to be the Hebrew 'concubine', and this would point to the Jewish origin of the legend." Solomon's marriage to the Queen of Sheba is stated in 2 Alphabet of Ben Sira, 21b, a Midrash of the geonic period.

6. For the sake of clarity and expediency, the frame tale of Solomon will be identified as Tale 1, the tale told by the owl (*The Matron of Ephesus*) as Tale 1A,

and the one told by the nightingale (*The Faithful Wife*) as Tale 1B. The structure of the Crews version, therefore, is thus: Tales 1 + 1A + 1B + 1. This structure is not universal. The frame story and the complete version of the tale are not extant in the Aarne-Thompson index. To identify the type as it appears in Crews, we have to refer to N. P. Andreyev's index of Russian folktale plots, *Ukazatel' Shazocnich Sjuzhetov po Sisteme Aarne* (Leningrad, 1929), Type *981 I, also adopted by Heda Jason in "Types of Jewish-Oriental Oral Tales," *Fabula* VII (1965), p. 175, and in her *Types of Oral Tales in Israel*, Israel Ethnographic Society Studies 2 (Jerusalem: Israel Ethnographic Society, 1975), p. 65.

7. AT 1510 in Antti Aarne and Stith Thompson, *The Types of the Folktale: A Classification and Bibliography*, FF Communication No. 184, Second Revision (Helsinki, 1973), hereafter referred to as AT. The type is described as follows: "A woman mourns day and night by her husband's grave. A knight guarding a hanged man is about to lose his life because the corpse has been stolen from the gallows. The matron offers him her love and substitutes her husband's corpse on the gallows so that the knight can escape."

8. This tale combines several AT types. See notes 42, 43, and 44 below for a breakdown.

9. Dan Ben Amos, "Toward a Definition of Folklore in Context," *Journal of American Folklore* 84 (1971): 9.

10. J. E. Cirlot, *A Dictionary of Symbols*, 2nd edition, translated from the Spanish by Jack Sage (New York: Philosophical Library, 1976), xi.

11. Eccles. 7:26–28. See Ginzberg, *Legends*, Vol. IV, 135–136, for a tale about Solomon's demonstration of the truth of this saying. See also Vol. VI, pp. 286–287, note 32. See Gregory Bar Hebraeus, *The Laughable Stories*, trans. by E. A. W. Budge (London: Luzac, 1987), p. 67, sardonically states in the thirteenth century: "A good woman is like a raven with white legs, that is to say, she cannot be found."

12. Prov. 31:10–31. This final chapter of the Proverbs is ambiguous, as it depicts a situation in which the virtue of the woman appears to be defined mostly by her selfless labor to benefit her family, thus making her subordinate. Traditionally, Bat-Sheba, Solomon's mother, is counted as one of the twenty-two virtuous women whose praise is sung by him, while Sarah represents the ideal "woman of valor". See Ginzberg, *Legends*, Vol. V, p. 258, note 271, for a listing of the other twenty women.

13. I Kings 11. See Ginzberg, *Legends*, Vol. VI, p. 298, note 76. Solomon married more than the eighteen wives permitted to a monarch (Deut. 17:16–17; Sanhedrin 21a; I Kings 11:1–4), including many foreign wives. Among them were Necha, Pharaoh's daughter, and the Queen of Sheba.

14. See Schwarzbaum, "Female Fickleness," 590, note 4.

15. The assignment of a task to a suitor by a prospective bride is less usual than its imposition by the father of the maiden. See S. Thompson, *The Folktale* (Berkeley: Univ. of California Press, 1977), 106.

16. Jason's *981 I (Andrejev) describes several tales from the Israel Folktale Archives: "According to his wife's wish, the king wants to build a palace of bird bones; a single bird does not come, and afterwards, when it arrives, it announces that it counted whether there are more men or women. It found out that there are more women, because those who obey women are the worst of them; the king abolishes his order" (p. 65 of *Types* and p. 195 of "Types").

17. This is based on I Kings 5:13 and is often referred to in Midrashic literature but hardly appears in the older literature. See Song R. 1:1, no. 9; Tanhuma B., Introd., 157. Bereshit R. 34.12 reads: "The power over the animal world, lost by Adam through his sin, was regained by Solomon."

18. In rabbinic literature, women are seen as having a positive side (passive, loyal, nurturing, and supportive) and a negative side (assertive, enticing, seductive, and destructive). See Howard Schwartz, "Jewish Tales of the Supernatural," in *Judaism*, Summer 1987, 36:3(143), 343.

19. The Judeo-Spanish equivalent of "And they lived happily forever after". Thompson (*Folktale*, 103), writes: "Most of the favorite folktales involving lovers and married couples are laid in a world of unreality and are filled with the supernatural."

20. These birds are often used together. The Middle English poem, *The Owl and the Nightingale*, is a good example. Probably written about the beginning of the thirteenth century by Nicholas de Guildford of Dorsetshire, it describes a debate between the sober owl and the merry nightingale as to their respective merits. See *The Owl and the Nightingale*, edited by J. W. Atkins (New York: Russell and Russell, 1971), and *The Owl and the Nightingale: The Poem and its Critics*, by Kathryn Hume (Toronto and Buffalo: Univ. of Toronto Press, 1975). See note 26 below for birds that appear in other versions of our tale.

21. *Dictionary of Symbols*, 28.

22. See AT, p. 430, for a listing of parallels. D. L. Ashliman, in *A Guide to Folktales in the English Language* (New York: Greenwood Press, 1987), lists other variants of the type on p. 256.

23. Motifs T231ff. and K2213.1 in Stith Thompson's *Motif-Index of Folk Literature* (Bloomington, Indiana: Indiana Univ. Press, 1955–58). In his *Motif-index of Talmudic Midrashic Literature* (Indiana University, Ph.D. dissertation [Ann Arbor, 1954]), Don Neuman (Noy) lists under K2213.1 the following bibliographical entries: Tosafot to Kod 80b (R. Hananel Gaon, 11th century); *Jewish Quarterly Review*, Vol. VI, p. 516; *Zeitschrift der deutschen morgenlandischen Gesellschaft* (Leipzig, 1847ff.), Vol. XXVII, p. 563.

24. In *Folktale*, p. 209. See A. S. Rappoport, *The Folklore of the Jews* (London: Soncino Press, 1937), 157ff.

25. The Ephesus story is alluded to in a Talmudic source, Tosafot to Kiddushin 80b. For parallels, see M. Grünbaum, *Judisch-Deutsche Chrestomathie, zugleich ein Beitrag zur Kunde der Hebräischen Literatur* (Leipzig: F.A. Brockhaus, 1882), and *Jüdische-Spanische Chrestomathie* (Frankfurt am Main: J. Kauffmann,

1896), 119. See also M. Gaster's *Ma'aseh Book* (Philadelphia: Jewish Publication Society, 1934), Vol. I, pp. 193–195, #107 ("Women are fickle—But not all"); Gaster's *Exempla*, p. 176, #442, ("Widow Comforted"); and M. J. Bin Gorion, *Der Born Judas: Legenden, Märchen und Erzählungen* (Leipzig: Insel-Verlag, 1916–1922), Vol. III, pp. 240ff., 315; also Bin Gorion's *Mimekor Yisrael, Classical Jewish Folktales* (Bloomington and London: Indiana Univ. Press, 1976), Vol. III, pp. 1141–1143, #24–26. For additional parallels, see Gaster's *Exempla*, notes to #442, pp. 268–269; Bin Gorion's *Mimekor Yisrael*, p. 1523, notes to #24–26; and note 18, p. 599, in Schwarzbaum's "Female Fickleness." For a comprehensive study of AT 1510, see Schwarzbaum, *Mishlé Shu'alim (Fox Fables) of R. Berekhih Ha-Nakdan, a Study in Comparative Folklore and Fable Lore* (Kiron: Institute for Jewish and Arab Folklore Research, 1979), pp. 394–417.

26. Another Sephardic version, apparently earlier than our 1930 tale, can be found in Max Grunwald's "Spanioloc Jewish Folktales and their Motifs," in *Edoth* II (Jerusalem, 1947), p. 237, #46, and also in his *Tales, Songs and Folkways of Sephardic Jews, Texts and Studies*, ed. by Dov Noy, Folklore Research Center Studies VI (Jerusalem: Magnes Press, 1982), with the English summary of the tale in p. xxxiii, #56, the Hebrew text on pp. 80–81, and its classification and relevant bibliography on p. 105, in which it is mentioned that eight versions from Morocco, Lybia, and Afghanistan can be found in the Israel Folktale Archives. A humorous version is given by J. E. Hanauer, *Folklore of the Holy Land* (London: The Sheldon Press, 1935), 186–187. For additional versions, see Schwarzbaum's article "Female Fickleness," 603–612. He examines several Jewish Oriental and Sephardic versions of this folktale on pp. 605–612. Two versions, the Grunwald tale and the Egyptian one mentioned in note 5 here, are almost identical to Crews's, with the frame story and the two internal tales perfectly analogous except that in the Egyptian version the bride is identified as the queen of Sheba and the two birds as an eagle (one of the species of owls mentioned in Isa. 13:21 is the Palestinian eagle owl) and a parrot. The disobedient birds in Grunwald's tale are the same as in Crews—the owl and the nightingale.

27. See listing of parallels in Thompson, *Motif Index*, Vol. IV, p. 483, under Motif K2213.1.

28. See Motif B147.2.2.4. As they often inhabit ruins and utter a hooting cry like a groan, owls sound as though mourning over the devastation; thus they are considered birds of darkness and death. In Rome, their hooting presaged death (of Augustus, Emporor Commodus Aurelius, and Caesar).

29. In ancient Greece, as the bird of Athena, who personified wisdom, the owl was auspicious.

30. See Lev. 11:16, 17; Deut. 14:15, 16; Ps. 102:6; Isa. 34:11; Isa 13:21. The Talmud mentions it being bad luck to dream of owls. See Berahot 57b.

31. Isa. 34:13, 14, 15. It is referred to there as a beast of prey or spirit that will lay waste to the land on the day of vengeance.

32. Niddah 24b.

33. B. Erubin 100b.

34. For the legend of Lilith, see the *Alphabet of Ben Sira*, edited by M. Steinschneider (Berlin, 1868), reprinted in *Otzar Midrashim*, edited by J. D. Einstein (New York, 1915). See also Schwartz's article, pp. 339–351.

35. Zohar I, 14b, 54b; II, 96a, 111a; 19a, 76b. She is seen as the negative side of Eve.

36. See Schwartz, 343–34. He writes that *The Testament of Solomon*, an early apocryphal text, connects Solomon with Lilith, the leading female demon in Jewish demonology.

37. IFA 5378; see note 5 in this section.

38. As an attribute of Satan, prince of darkness, the owl typifies deception.

39. In the negative sense, it denotes a Utopian dream world. See *Dictionary of Symbols*, p. 138–139, and Oswold Wirth, *Le Tarot des imagiers de moyen Age* (Paris: E. Nourry, 1927).

40. According to Jewish writings, women are often depicted as grasping, lazy, jealous, querulous, prying, unreliable, and talkative. See Gen. R. 45:5; also *Jewish Values* (Jerusalem: Keter Books, 1974), pp. 150–155, by Rabbi Dr. L. Jacobs, especially pp. 152–153. Eve is considered the first sinner, putting out her hand to take the forbidden fruit and thus bringing sin into the world. Other biblical women are described as niggardly, mendacious, and eavesdropping (Sarah); jealous and talkative (Rachel); deceitful (Delilah); haughty (daughter of Zion); talebearers (Miriam); gadabouts (Dinah); and vain (Dinah and Leah, who liked to be looked upon). They are also seen as curious and unreliable or "light-minded" (Shabbat 33b). The faults of the matriarchs and other biblical women are far more numerous than their virtues. These same negative traits are not similarly criticized in men.

41. The custom of a widow remaining unmarried for a year may have developed from the belief that it was indecent for her to marry until her husband's body rotted and his soul found another home.

42. The broad description of our tale is found in this type: "*The Faithful Wife*: The enslaved husband is rescued by his wife disguised as a pilgrim. The white handkerchief." In our tale, instead of a white kerchief as a token between husband and wife, there is a glossy photograph which arouses the lust of the treacherous imposter. In his *Guide to Folktales* (p. 180, Type 888), Ashliman lists variants of this tale and summarizes them as follows: "*A Wife Rescues her Husband from Slavery*: A count fell into slavery in Turkey. His shirts, which his wife has made for him, never soiled, a sign of her continuous fidelity. She disguised herself as a pilgrim and, through her great skill as a harpist, accomplished his release." For the variants, see J. and W. Grimm, *Grimm's Other Tales*, selected by Wilhelm Hansen, translated by Ruth Michaelis-Jena and Arthur Radcliff (Edinburg: Canongate, 1984), 128, "The Faithful Wife"; A. Lang, ed., *The Violet Fairy Book* (New York: Dover Publications, 1966), p. 70, "The Lute Player"; and W. A. Clouston, *Popular Tales and Fictions: Their Migrations and Transformations* (Detroit: Singing Tree Press, 1968), Vol. 1, p. 168, "Tests of Chastity." In Grunwald, *Tales*,

p. 105, it is mentioned that eight versions of this type, from Morocco, Tunisia, Libya, and Turkey exist in the Israel Folktale Archives. See also p. 105 for bibliography.

43. This type gives a more detailed description: "II. *The prince enslaved*: (a) The prince sets out to win his fortune but is enslaved. (b) The chess game and the trained cat. (c) The youth in the land of cheaters. III. *The rescue*: (a) The wife disguised as a man frees her husband. (She overcomes the courtesan in a chess game by loosing mice which the trained cat chases.)"

44. This type is based on the motif of the trained cat. "*The Cat and the Candle*: A man has a cat trained to hold up lighted candles on its head. The king has a mouse let loose. The cat drops the candle and chases the mouse. (Often used as a method of cheating in a game.)"

45. The Hebrew word is mentioned in Song 2:12. It refers to a singing bird, not specifically the nightingale but all singing birds that fill the air with melodious song in spring. See also Is. 25:5. The word is often translated as 'psalmist' or 'song.' *New American Standard Exhaustive Concordance of the Bible*, edited by Robert L. Thomas (Nashville: A. J. Holman, 1981), 1514.

46. The nightingale also symbolizes anticipated happiness and sweetness.

47. Thompson, (*Folktale*, 103) writes: "In a considerable number of these romantic tales we find a faithful wife who goes on a long search for her husband—a thoroughly realistic search filled with high adventure instead of magic and mystery." See also 108–110.

48. Niddah 45b declares explicitly that "God endowed women with more intelligence than man." Gen. R. 17:1, on the other hand, expresses the opposite view: "It is the way of woman to remain at home and for man to go to the market-place and learn intelligence from other men." See A. Cohen, *Everyman's Talmud* (New York: Schocken Books, 1978), 161.

49. How decisively a woman can affect her husband's behavior can be seen in Gen. R. 17:7: "It is related of a pious man who was married to a pious woman that, being childless, they divorced one another. He went and married a wicked woman and she made him wicked. She went and married a wicked man and made him righteous. It follows that all depends upon the women." See Cohen, 160. Gaster includes a tale about a virtuous woman in his *Exempla* (p. 114, #310), which is very similar to ours: "A pious and poor man's wife was not tempted by a rich man; she also saved her husband from prison and misery by her courage and virtue."

50. I am grateful to Dr. Samuel Morell and the University Center of SUNY-Binghamton for calling my attention to a Responsum by R. Moses Trani regarding a similar situation: A man in the habit of carousing with friends was prevailed upon by his wife to swear, under penalty of becoming a Samson Nazirite, never to eat in the company of three people except in his own house. The question posed to R. Trani sought to clarify the true meaning of the vow. The issue was whether, as the husband thought, he was bound to the literal words of the vow.

The comments of the respondent identified the binding principle as a commitment to avoid drunkenness and wayward friends rather than to avoid social gatherings altogether. *She'elot ve Tshuvot* (Lemberg, 1861), Part II, Question 168.

51.   See Nehama Aschkenasy, *Eve's Journey: Feminine Images in Hebraic Literary Tradition* (Philadelphia: Jewish Publication Society, 1968).

52.   The prophets compare the love of God for Israel to the love of a husband for his wife.

53.   There were seven prophetesses in the Bible: Sarah, Miriam, Deborah, Hannah, Abigail, Huldah, and Esther. Sotah 11b shows that Israel was redeemed from Egypt on account of the virtue of its righteous women. Miriam, alongside her brothers, is considered one of the three emancipators from Egypt. See Micah 6:4.

NINETEEN

Customs of Pregnancy and Childbirth among Sephardic and Oriental Jews

Issachar Ben-Ami

P regnancy and childbirth among Sephardi and Oriental Jewish groups are subjects which have been paid very little attention. Scholars are of the opinion that all we have available to us today are descriptions which, for the most part, are incomplete.[1] We need not mention that this material has not been subject to serious scientific analysis other than on the level of isolated and specific studies.[2] This situation also applies to other groups and to many cultural phenomena associated with them.

The purpose of this chapter is not to take inventory of customs related to pregnancy and childbirth among the Sephardi and Oriental Jews (however desirable such inventory might be), but on the basis of selected examples, to try, on the one hand, to expose rules, principles, and concepts which feed this complex of customs, and to illustrate, on the other hand, the milieu and the atmosphere in which these customs existed and developed.

Precise observation of the system of customs related to such an important point in life, in all cultures and throughout all time, raises a number of fascinating distinctions. First, consider the general background: the love of children, the desire to carry on the family heritage through offspring, the fulfillment of religious duties through male descendants, the expectation of help and support of children in old age, the strong survival instinct characteristic of ethnic religious minorities frequently living within a hostile environment, and perhaps, above all, and weighed against all the aforementioned factors, the terribly high mortality rate of infants, which characterized earlier generations.[3] All these elements influenced the customs associated with pregnancy and childbirth in the sociocultural framework within which these traditions were practiced.

Pregnancy and childbirth are an integral part of the life cycle of human beings. The examination of different beliefs which certify the existence of life in any form before birth[4] and after death enables us to draw an infinite line comprising three points which represent three main stations in the life of humans—birth, marriage, and death—or a closed circle comprising these same three points.

The customs associated with pregnancy and childbirth may be divided into five separate groups:

1. The newly married woman and barren woman, until the moment that she becomes pregnant
2. The pregnant woman until time of childbirth
3. The period from birth until 'pidyon ha-ben'[5], or the first month of the infant's life
4. The period from the end of the first month of life until the age of five[6]
5. The period from the age of five until the age of 'mitzvot'[7]

A widespread belief among the Muslims is that a barren woman is not affiliated with any religion.[8] In fact, she is considered to be outside of social and religious bounds. In contrast, the Muslim woman who has given birth to ten children or who has died in childbirth is considered to be deserving of a place in heaven.[9] A Jewish proverb, cited however in a different context, says that "seven sons secure for their parents a place in heaven; seven daughters, a place in hell."[10]

The Jewish woman, like the Muslim woman, does everything in her power to reject or even cancel her state of barrenness. She believes that the fetus is asleep in her womb or that it has fainted, and thus a variety of methods of treatment are employed in order to awaken the fetus or encourage it to emerge. Another explanation of barrenness is that the woman's belly is cold,[11] and thus she drinks alcoholic beverages or eats foods that warm the belly.

Like most cultures, the Jewish culture is rich in various magic formulas aimed at canceling out the condition of sterility, and at dealing with all situations related to conception, preservation of pregnancy, childbirth, protection of the infant, and so on.

The many folk medicine books in existence are clear witness to the existence of such formulas. They are derived, for the most part, from the animal and vegetable worlds, not excluding materials that ordinarily would not be touched by man. More animal than plant materials are used. This phenomenon is clear: the parallel process of pregnancy and birth in animals is far more closely related to reality.

Systematic investigation of the formulas which appear in the folk medicine books[12] under the rubric "For the woman who has difficulty in giving birth," raises a number of interesting distinctions. This expression refers, on the one hand, to the barren woman who is unable to become pregnant and thus has difficulty giving birth, and on the other hand, to the pregnant woman who suffers difficulty at the time of childbirth. The formulas prescribed for the first condition are suitable also as preventive measures—that is, they may be used during the course of pregnancy to ensure easy birth. Other formulas are used at the time of birth with the intent of drawing the child out of his mother's womb, dead or alive. More than eighty percent of these formulas are intended for the treatment of both husband and wife together. Very few of the formulas deal solely with sterility in the male, but they nevertheless should not be ignored.

It is interesting to note that, in close to ninety-five percent of the cases, the man is responsible for bringing the materials necessary to treat the woman. Only in very few cases does the woman treat herself directly. This may be seen not only as shared responsibility and a shared desire to succeed in the production of the offspring and, in fact, recognition of a shared problem, but perhaps also as a compensation for the negative image that the woman, alone, is responsible for her infertility.

The animal materials used against sterility have clear symbolic meaning and include the skin of a fox or a rabbit which is burnt to ashes, the gall bladder of a wolf or black chicken, camel urine, sheep excrement, the claws of a hoopoe, the stomach of a rabbit, the milk of a bitch or mare or she-ass, a rabbit, a she-bear, a cow or a nanny-goat, the genitals of a pig, brain of a dove, a fish that is found inside another fish, a snake, the gall bladder and tongue of a black raven, the womb of a rabbit, and so on.[13] The use of some human materials is not unknown, such as menstrual blood, hair, nails, bone marrow, and so on. The ingestion of foreskin by a barren woman was very common, and occurs even in our day.

The use of plants was also quite widespread. One focus of special activity in this context was the holiday of Tu-Bishvat. At this time, the women of Kurdistan used to go in the evening to a fruit tree and recite as follows:

Pregnant tree,[14] you shall not conceive.
I shall conceive with this intent.
This year my body will be filled.

Or another version:

Oh tree, your pregnancy to me and mine to you
This year I shall conceive.
Just as you give fruit
So shall I give fruit.

A similar tradition existed during the Middle Ages among other Jewish communities of Europe, where barren Jewish women would dip a piece of paper into menstrual blood, tie it to a fruit-laden tree, and say: "I am giving you my illness and my weakness; you will give me your power to bear fruit."

Similar as well as dissimiliar formulas are found in many cultures. In Salonica, the Jews believed that on Tu-Bishvat the trees embrace and copulate. They used to hang a pitcher full of fresh water, well water, or rosewater between the trees, and in the morning the barren woman would be given some of the water to drink. It was believed that these waters that had witnessed the copulation of the trees were charged with the reproductive power of the trees and the power to cancel infertility.[15]

One important measure taken by a barren woman was the pilgrimage to a holy place.[16] Once again, this custom is apparent in other cultures: the woman would sleep in a holy place for a few days or sometimes longer, until the saint gave her some sort of sign, in a dream or some other manner, of the remedy of which she was in need. Sometimes the woman would be referred by the saint to another saint whose speciality was to cure sterility. It is interesting to note that if a baby was born as a result of such a visit to the saint, the baby would usually bear the holy one's name and a kind of 'covenant' would be made between the child and the saint, which the child would honor his whole life by making pilgrimages to the holy place.

In summary of this issue, we would note that the great number, the nature, and the variety of formulas for the treatment of sterility are an indication of the strong desire of the barren woman not to make light of any opportunity to cancel this situation.[17]

An additional group of less well-known customs aimed at helping a barren woman to become pregnant is associated with the marriage celebrations. The purpose of these many customs is to ensure that the woman will be fruitful and will bear male children. The presence of small children at various stages of the celebrations symbolizes the hope that the bride will have many children to take care of later on. For example, children may be placed on the nuptial bed immediately before the couple goes on it, or a small child may be held in the lap of the bride when she is brought to the groom's house on horseback. Here we see the transference of one situation to another by means of sympathetic magic.

A woman who becomes pregnant within a reasonable period of time will do everything to safeguard the fruit of her womb (and all the more so a previously barren woman whose problem has been solved). Safeguarding pregnancy, in popular conciousness, is parallel to actual struggle for existence.

The pregnant woman greatly fears the 'evil eye' from women who are unable to become pregnant. She is also afraid of ghosts and spirits, especially the spirits that inhabit the house in which she lives. When an Iranian-Jewish woman suspects that a woman has cast the evil eye on her, she will attempt to obtain a piece of the woman's garment, burn it, and scatter the ashes on the threshold of her house. In this way, she has burnt the woman and her evil eye. When a woman throws water in her house, she precedes her action with the word *beware* so that the spirits will not be harmed by the water.

All must be done to ensure that the birth tract will be open and the birth will follow smoothly. The Jewess of Salonica used to leave everything open in her house—doors, cupboards, drawers, and so one. Many families did not lock their houses during the entire nine-month period of pregnancy, even at night.

The time of birth is, in itself, a special situation which is both looked forward to and feared. This is a dual situation wherein the woman gives life, while she, herself, is in mortal danger and the newborn infant, too, is in danger. According to popular belief, this is the moment when all the forces of evil come together and try to overcome the two weak creatures. The great number of formulas related to the act of giving birth are an indication of the difficulties and fears surrounding it. For example, the room of the woman in confinement is succoured with holiness: earth from the grave of a righteous man is brought and spread around the room, prayers are offered and psalms recited. Thread is tied to a Torah scroll and its other end is tied to the woman's bed, the shofar is blown, the key to the synagogue is placed under the woman's bed, and so on. If a woman was having difficulty giving birth, the German Jews would whisper a passage from Exodus 11:8 in her ear: "Get thee out and all the people that follow thee." In Iran, the children would climb up onto the roof of the house in which the woman is in difficult labor, and shout: "Lord, save her!"

When a son was born, the Moroccan midwife would shout in Hebrew, "*Baruch Habah*" (welcome), and if a daughter was born, she would shout in Arabic, "*Mas uda mimuna*" (You shall be blessed and happy). When the midwife finishes cutting the unbilical cord and wrapping the baby, she holds the baby, approaches the mezuzah and recites the following prayer:[18] "May your name be blessed. May you grow up to be wise and may your mouth be filled up with the Torah. May you be happy and blessed by Israel and by your family. May you reach the chupah and do good deeds during your parents' lifetime." Then she puts sugar in the infant's mouth and says: "May the Torah be as this sugar in your mouth."

Every night until the circumcision (*Brith Milah*), the father holds the baby in his arms, touching him, whispering the *aleph-beth* (alphabet) in his ears, blessing him, and kissing him. These traditions are loaded with symbolism and bear witness to the ideals and aspirations of the society.

From the hour of birth until the day of circumcision, the threats and dangers are centered around the fantastic image of Lilith,[19] a female spirit that occupies a central position in Jewish demonology and who is mentioned by this and similar names as far back as the third century B.C.E. Lilith was, according to the Midrash, the first wife of Adam before the creation of Eve. The strife that broke out between them transformed her into a spirit and into the greatest enemy of the descendants of Adam. May one see in the parting of this couple and the terrible evil that resulted from their separation a projection of the popular teaching that rejects the separation of a couple and hints at the extent of responsibility that man bears for his own destiny?

Many measures were taken in order to neutralize the evil of Lilith. The similarity of these measures among different ethnic groups is surprising. The use of metal (charms, knives, etc.) against Lilith and other spirits stems from the principle of using a strong substance against a weaker substance. The metal may crush spirits born during the stone ages. The use of other strong and hard materials, not only because of their physical properties, but also because of their smell and taste (for example, garlic, salt, and the like) stems from the same principle.

Another very common measure is the 'guardian page.'[20] On the guardian page were written Psalm no. 126, the names of the angels involved in the punishment of Lilith (Sini, Sinsini, and Samangloch), the names of Adam and Eve, the names of the patriarchs and the matriarchs, and the passage, "Thou shall not suffer a sorceress to live" (Exodus 22:17). These charms were usually written out by a scribe, a rabbi, or a learned man. Most of the time, *cheder* pupils (pupils of religious elementary school), accompanied by their teachers, would personally deliver the charms and hang them in the room of the new mother, while singing and reading various passages from the Torah. In earlier times, the content of the charm was written directly onto the walls of the woman's room.

Many rituals escorted the infant from the hour of his birth to the time of his *Brith* (circumcision) and, of course, thereafter. Some of them were repeated daily, but it should be noted that this activity increased, especially during the night preceeding the Brith. In popular consciousness, there was a strong belief that the night before the Brith was the last opportunity for Lilith and her friends to conspire against the infant. The lack of name and of personal identity placed the infant on the margins of society and thus, from this point of view, made him vulnerable to danger.

The night before the Brith is known by different names in the Jewish diaspora[21] and is the focus of special and intensive activity. A ritual which is interesting and rich in content exists among the Jews of Morocco. It is called 'Tachdid': friends, relatives, and neighbors come every night to the house of the new mother and read portions of the *Zohar*[22] and sing. Two poetesses compete with each other in riddles and rhymes, making sharp comments to each other.[23] At midnight, the doors of the house are locked, one of the men present (the father of the child, a 'Cohen,' or one of the honorable visitors) takes a sword and strikes the walls of the house and makes circles in the air in order to banish the spirits. The sword is then placed under the mother's pillow. All remain awake throughout the night. The mother of the woman who has given birth or an old woman who practices this ritual professionally, sings special songs until the light of dawn.[24] This ritual, in one form or another, is also found among the Jews of the Diaspora and among Muslims living in Mediterranean countries. It was also widespread in Ashkenazic countries (Central and Eastern Europe, especially Germany). Evidence of this exists as far back as the thirteenth century. In Ashkenaz, a sword inscribed with the phrase "Thou shalt not suffer a sorceress to live" was used. According to the congregation of Worms, the new mother was forbidden to leave the house for a period of forty days, and every night circles were made around the mother and child. In Alsace, the ritual of the circles began at the time of birth.[25]

The tradition of the 'week of the son' (the week before circumcision) is an ancient one. The Talmud places special emphasis on the night before the Brith. For example, the Sanhedrin (32:17) states: "There shall be celebration on the eve of the Brith."

A common belief, and one that still exists today, is that there are other spirits besides Lilith that would harm the newborn child. Of these, the most important is the spirit-double of the mother, who has also just given birth to a spirit infant and wishes to exchange it for the human infant.[26] This spirit will exchange the infants at a time when the human infant is left unguarded.

According to a number of traditions, the spirits often take a human midwife to aid a spirit who is about to give birth. The human midwife is in great demand by the spirits, and so when she is called out at night to aid in childbirth, she must carry a lighted candle, sprinkle salt, and other substances which ward off spirits along the way, and murmur all sorts of prayers and formulas against the spirits. Her proximity to the spirits sometimes caused a fear of the midwife herself.[27]

How could one know whether a human infant had been exchanged? Some of the signs of the exchange are if the baby stops developing, loses its appetite, or becomes ill for no apparent reason. In order to ascertain whether an exchange has indeed been made, in Morocco the infant is taken and placed on the grave of a righteous man or an unmarked grave in the graveyard. If, after an hour or two, the infant cries, this is a sign that the spirits have returned the human infant. If the infant does not cry, this is taken as a sign that the baby will die.

In Yemen, in order to exchange a spirit infant for a human infant, the baby is passed under the wheel of a water well (since spirits tend to dwell in wells). One person passes the baby, and another person receives it, and they say to each other, "Take yours and give us ours." If this does not help, the baby is taken to a special place where spirits are believed to dwell, and the ritual of passing the baby is repeated seven times.

Another well-known custom among many groups is concerned with the death of infants. A woman whose sons die at an early age traditionally betroths her baby son to a baby girl that has just been born. Another possibility is to sell the infant to another person. Such a sold infant is called 'Mercado' if male, or 'Mercada' if female. The child will, in fact, live on account of the person who bought him or her and is helped by the neighbors. It is believed that something in the parents causes the death of their children, and thus the sale, like the betrothal, removes the infant from the domain of the family. This situation can continue until the child reaches the age of *bar mitzvah*, when he becomes responsible for himself. The tradition of selling the child has painful significance from many points of view and continues over a long period of time, without any proportion to other customs of the same genre. As said, in this war of destruction between the forces of darkness and the forces of light, when the existence of the young and delicate must be safeguarded, all must be done in order to secure the continuing chain of life.

An interesting group of customs has to do with the manner in which the birth of a child is announced. Such announcements take many and varied forms. In Yemen, at the moment that the child comes into the world, the members of the family pass the good news to one another by saying *"!fak Allah!"* (G-d saves). Immediately following, all the members of the family are gathered together, big and small, and are sent out to the neighbors, relatives, and friends. In order to spread the news as follows: the news-bearer knocks on the door and waits for the answer, *"Mann?"* (Who's there?). If the bearer of the news is the son of the woman who has given birth, he calls out, *"Qad wuladat Ummi"* (My mother has given birth.) If he is not, he says, *"Qad waladat fulane"* (Someone has given birth). The woman who receives the news then asks; *"Ma waladat?"* (What did she have?), and the reply *"Wald"* is given if the infant is male, or *"Bint"* if the infant is female. The woman then gives blessing,[28] *"Ghanne be'afiyate"* (I am happy for her health).

In Libya, the room of the woman who has given birth is traditionally decorated with colored scarves (especially red), which are hung on either side of the entrance to the room.[29] In Yemen, immediately after the birth, myrrh is burned in a clay or copper stove filled with burning coals and sometimes gum-benjamin is added. Everyone passing in the vicinity of the house smells the special, familiar scent and knows a child has been born. The day after the birth is referred to as *"Yom Al-harish"* (the day of harish). On this day, great quantities of harish are cooked. Harish is a dish made with wheat grain and which is eaten with butter and honey. The children of the neighbors, relatives, and friends are the first to eat this food. Next, the daughters of the house and the neighbors' daughters gather, and each takes a few portions of the harish to the houses of the relatives, neighbors, and the learned. The heavy movement of guests, *cheder* pupils, and visitors of all kinds during the eight days before the Brith helps to spread the good news.

In Libya, the remains of the spices that are prepared especially for the Brith ceremony are taken by a member of the family to the Jewish shops in the market, and everyone is given the opportunity to smell the spices and make a blessing. The blesser asks the child's name and blesses him with good fortune. If more than one Brith occurs on the same day, the man offering the spices calls out all the names of the infants to be circumcised.

The moving of the chair of Elijah the Prophet from the synagogue to the house, the performance of the Brith in the synagogue, and the special prayer that is recited on the Sabbath before and after the Brith are all measures that help to spread and affirm the proclamation of the birth.

The central function of this group of customs is, without doubt, to strengthen the feeling of security of the Jewish minority. The birth and its celebration do not belong to the individual or the family, but to the entire community. Hence, the great involvement and participation between the family and community. The entrance of the child into the covenant of Abraham, the patriarch (by way of the Brith) is a symbol of the strenghthening of the Jewish community and an additional link in the chain of eternal Jewish existence. The beliefs, the customs, and the religious ritual all strengthen this feeling.[30]

A world unto itself is the world of different myths that describe the earth as a living being, a virgin, as married to G-d, or the heavens, coming together with the heavens in order to be impregnated, the creation of man from the earth, of the earth as the mother of all living creatures, that is, of people, animals, and of course, the plant world. These myths, found in all cultures, shed a light on not a few customs and beliefs. The idea of a Mother Earth arises from the parallel between the human life cycle and the cosmic course (the annual cycle). The concepts of mating, birth, growth, aging, and death, characterize the world of humans as well as the rest of the natural world and find clear expression in these myths.[31]

The idea that the earth is the mother of all living things and the mother of all the children of the universe creates and strengthens the idea of the unity of nature. As has been said, the earth and all its features of nature (rocks, trees, rivers, caves) possess the power of fertility which man can utilize through physical contact according to certain rules. Here, too, the superiority of man is recognized. Man takes from the world of nature the characteristics he desires and transfers to nature his negative burden.

The sage's view of the state of the fetus, that the son faces downward because he is looking at his mother, the earth (opinion of the Rabbi Chanina), and the daughter faces upward because she is looking at a rib, is an expression of this belief. Rabbi Yehoshua adds to this by saying: Why must the woman put on scent and not the man? Because the man comes from earth and the woman from bone, and the earth, as is known, is odorless.

The burial of the placenta in the earth immediately after birth (even on the Sabbath) and, similarily, the laying of the dead on the earth immediately after death are both symbols bearing similar meanings which stress the attachment of man to the earth in life and death.

The examination of the many customs and beliefs related to pregnancy and childbirth shows us that, although they are so numerous and varied, they are connected in a surprising unity and form the parts of an astonishingly perfect and harmonious structure. There is no doubt that some of these customs are in accordance with Van-Gennep's theory of transfer,[32] however they express special cultural reality of the nation of Israel, a reality loaded with values, ideology, and outlook. The child that comes into the world is the continuance of the chain, a lifeline that begins before birth and continues after death. The struggle for the child's survival against the forces of evil is aided by traditional assets (Elijah the Prophet, the angel of the covenant, and the promise made to him by Lilith), by magic, and by the utilization of resources that have been made available to man by nature. Here, not only does the idea of nature as a world in which every event has an influence over another part of being find expression, but also the certainty that nature was created for mankind. Not only must nature nourish mankind, but also protect him and even be used as a substitute, to receive human diseases, including death.

Animals as well as plants may serve as atonement for the imperfection of man. The news of the child's birth, as happy as it is, is an event that reaches beyond the family framework and becomes the property of the society and the nation as a whole. The infant joins not only the family group, but also a wider framework. His birth, his existence, and his life are the fruit of communal effort and not just that of his parents.

The struggle against sterility and the protection of the life of a child is common to both the parents and their immediate environment. This is to say, the arrival of a baby promises existence and a name, not only for the family, but also for the Jewish nation, and symbolizes continuity and the possibility of realizing the longings of the Jewish nation. It is not surprising that the Mitzvah (good duty) of being a godparent is raised to a very high level from the religious point of view, and that this duty secures, to an extent, the physical existence of the child or of other parts of society. Thus it is natural that the status of birth is often accompanied by national, religious, and messianic tension.[33]

NOTES

1. See Yom-Tov Lewinsky, *Encyclopedia of Folklore: Customs and Tradition in Judaism* (Hebrew), Vol. I (Tel Aviv, 1970), 84–86, 305, and other entries; Y. Bergmann, *The Jewish Folklore* (Hebrew) (Jerusalem, 1953), 24–32; A Ben-Yaacov, ed., *Yalkut Minhagim* [Hebrew] (Jerusalem, 1967), 40–41 [Babylonia], 67–68 [Kurdistan], 93–96 [Libya] 115–116 [Morocco], 129 [Iran], 149–150 [Tunisia], 163–164 [Djerba], 178 [Yemen]; A. Vasertil, ed., *Yalkut Minhagim*, Part 2: "Ashkenazi Communities (Jerusalem, 1975), 45–47, 106–107, 137, and 167; A. Stahl, *Sources for the Study of the Culture of Oriental Jews* (Hebrew), Part 2, Book 3, "Family, Sons (Jerusalem, 1987); David Knaani, *Studies in History of the Jewish Family* (Hebrew) (Tel Aviv, 1986); A. Sperling, *Taamei ha-Minhagim m-Mekorei ha-Dinim* (Hebrew) (Jerusalem, 1961), 567–568; Yehoshua Bar-Yosef, *The Enchanted City* (Hebrew) (Tel Aviv, 1969); E. Toledano, *Brit Milah n-Minhageiha* (Hebrew) (Haifa, 1977); E. Brauer, *The Jews of Kurdistan* (Hebrew) (Jerusalem, 1948), 128–146; J. Kafih, *Halichot Teman* (Hebrew) (Jerusalem, 1963), 156–182; H. Mizrahi, *The Jews of Iran* (Hebrew) (Tel Aviv, 1959), 69–76; Y. Mazuz, *The Judaism of the Djerba Island* (Hebrew) (Safed, 1978), 124–127; Y. Gur-Arieh, *"The Life of a Jew"* (Hebrew) in *Reshumot*, ed. Y. T. Lewinsky, Y. Twersky (Tel Aviv, 1953), 350–367; Joseph

Yuspa Hahn, *Yossef Ometz* (Hebrew) (Frankfurt, 1928); *Mahzor Vitry*, ed. S. Hurwitz (Berlin, 1889–1983); Joseph G. Moses (1420–1488), *Leket Yosher* (Hebrew), ed. J. Freiman (Berlin, 1903–1904); Eleazar ben Ydhuda of Worms, *Sefer Hochmat Hanefesh* (Hebrew), (Lemberg, 1876); A. M. Luntz, "Within Jerusalem," *Yeda 'Am*, Vol. XIV, No. 33–34 (1968), 3–23; T. H. Gaster, *The Holy and the Profane* (New York: C. W. Sloane Associates, 1955), 3–77; M. Molho, *Usos y costumbres de los sefardíes: de Salónica* (Madrid: CSIC, 1950), 49–90; Elie Malka, *Essai de Folklore des Israëlites du Maroc* (Paris: CIPAC, 1976), 13–45; H. C. Dobrinsky, *A Treasury of Sephardic Laws and Customs* (New York: Yeshiva Univ. Press, 1986), 3–29; H. Pollack, *Jewish Folkways in Germanic Lands 1648–1806: Studies in Aspects of Daily Life* (Cambridge: M.I.T. Press, 1971); T. Schrire, *Hebrew Amulets* (London: Routledge and K. Paul, 1966); G. Sternberg-Stefanesti, *Portrait of a Romanian Shtetl* (Oxford: Pergamon Press, 1984); M. Zborowski and E. Herzog, *Life is with People: The Culture of the Shtetl* (New York: Schocken, 1964); E. Shorter, *A History of Women's Bodies* (Harmondworth: Penguin, 1984); N. Zerdoumi, *Enfant d'hier: l'education de l'enfant en milieu traditional algérien* (Paris: Maspero, 1970); J. Mathieu and R. Manneville, *Les Accoucheuses musulmanes traditionnelles de Casablanca*, Publications de l'Institut des Hautes Etudes Marocaines, Tome LIII (Paris: Impr. Administrative Centrale, 1952); J. Mathieu, *"Notes sur l'enfance juive du mellah de Casablanca,"* in *Bulletin de l'Institut d'Hygiène du Maroc* (1939); J. Trachtenberg, *Jewish Magic and Superstition* (Cleveland: Meridian, 1961); R. Patai, *On Jewish Folklore* (Detroit: Wayne State Univ. Press, 1983); H. Zafrani, *Mille ans de vie juive au Maroc* (Paris: G.-P. Maisonneuve & Larose, 1983), 49–67; M. Gaster, "Birth (Jewish)," in J. Hastings, *Encyclopedia of Religion and Ethics* (Edinburgh: T. and T. Clark, 1909), Vol. II, 655–658; J. Gutwirth, *Vie juive traditionelle* (Paris: Editions de Minuit, 1970), 315–319.

2.   An example is from Patai on the treatment of barrenness: R. Patai, "Jewish Folk Cures for Barrenness," in *Folklore*, Vol. LV (1944), and Vol. LVI (1945). Another example is to be found in J. Z. Lauterbach, "The Naming of Children in Jewish Folklore, Ritual and Practice," *Yearbook of the Central Conference of American Rabbis*, Vol. XLII (1932), 1–45.

3.   S. Kottek, "Pratiques magiques liées à la protection du nouveau-né," in *La Mèdicine infantile*, 88 année (Sept.–Oct. 1981) 675–700.

4.   See *Tan huma-pikudei* and also *Nidda 30*; H. N. Bialik and Y. H. Rawnitzki, *Sefer ha-Aggadah* (Hebrew), (Tel Aviv, 1973), 451–452. Among the Ashkenazi Jews: "When a male child is born, the congregation is invited the Sabbath Eve before the Brith Milah to the house of the baby's family. Refreshments are served to the guests in order to console the child for the Torah that he knew before he was born and lost at the time of his birth." See Rabbi A. Una, "From the Traditions of the Jews of Ashkenaz" (Hebrew), in *Yalkut Minhagim* by A. Vesertil (ed.), op. cit. p. 45. See also B. Landoi, "From the Traditions of the Jews of Ashkenaz (Prushim), in *Eretz Israel* (Hebrew), p. 106: "On the Sabbath Eve that falls between the birth and the Brith Milah, Shalom

Zachar celebrations are held in the house of the woman who has given birth. Friends and family come to wish Mazel Tov (good luck) and are honored usually with certain legumes (Arbes) in remembrance of the loss to the son who forgot his Talmud when he left his mother's womb."

5. Ceremony of redemption of the first-born son. It takes place on the evening of the thirty-first day after birth.

6. "*Quand l'enfant atteint l'âge de cinq ans, on célèbre une fête familiale au cours de laquelle sont servis des gâteaux et du thé. C'est encore un rite de passage. L'enfant cesse d'être un bébé. Il entre maintenant dans la catégorie nouvelle des petits garçons ou des petites filles. Il est par conséquent louable ou blâmable . . . A l'occasion de cette fête l'enfant met au cou un talisman ou des bijoux en or portant l'inscription* "Chadday" *(le Tout Puissant) car, il entre le premier jour de sa cinquième année dans une nouvelle période et ainsi il est sensible au mauvais oeil.*" Elie Malka, *Essai de folklore des Israélites de Maroc,* op. cit., p. 41; "*Hacia la edad de cinco o seis años, el hijo varón era enviado a una escuela de Garrio. . .*" M. Molho, *Usos y costumbres,* op. cit., p. 92; M. Bamberger, "Aus meiner Minhagimsammelmappe," *Jahrbuche fur Jüdische Volkskunde,* ed. M. Grunwald, 1923, 331–332.

7. For boys the ceremony of the Bar-Mitzvah takes place at the age of thirteen years or earlier. Girls reach the age of majority (Bat-Mitzvah) at twelve years.

8. "*La femme stérile est méprisée. On dit qu'elle est entre toutes les religions. Elle n'est ni musulmane, ni juive, ni chrétienne. On croit que Dieu pardonne toutes leurs fautes aux femmes qui ont enfanté. C'est une injure de traiter une femme de stérile, en même temps qu'un mauvais sort.*" Legey, *Essai de folklore marocain,* Paris: P. Geuthner, 1926, p. 69. The Jews of Yemen use the following proverb in relation to an infertile woman: "A tree that doesn't give fruit should be cut down." A. Stahl, *Proverbs of Jewish Communities* (Hebrew), Tel Aviv, 1975, 238.

9. Legey, op. cit., 79–80.

10. Y. Bergmann, op. cit., 25; H. Zafrani, op. cit., 49.

11. Cold here is a symbol of non-existence of life, of death, according to the known biological situation, and therefore it is necessary to create conditions of heat in order that the womb will absorb life.

12. See I. Bacher Eliezer, *Rifuah ve-Haim mi-Yerushalaim* (Hebrew), (Jerusalem, Bakal Publication; R. Ochana, *Mareh ha-Jladim* (Hebrew), (Jerusalem, Bakal Publication); Y. N. Katz, *Mif'alot Elokim* (Hebrew), (Jerusalem, Bakal Publication); Y. Rosenberg, *Sefer Raphael Hamalach* (Hebrew), (Jerusalem, Bakal Publication); Rabbi A. Avidani, *Tishah Sifrei Sgulot, Rifuot ve-Goralot* (Hebrew) Jerusalem, 1976; Ha-Rav Zacharuah, *Sefer Zechirah ve-Ynianei Sgulah,* 1848; Ytshak Ytshaky, ed., *Lachash ve-Kamea* (Hebrew), Tel Aviv, 1976.

13. The following are some examples of the materials that are found in one book: ram (a ram's organ, ashes of ram's horn, a ram's horn), kite, lion (skin of a lion), goose (excrement of a goose), rabbit (stomach, brain, heart, fat, leg), she-ass, spleen of cattle, an animal's heart, rump, sinew, ostrich, camel, fish (fish bile),

bear (bear's milk), hoopoe (hoopoe's egg, tongue), wolf (eye, a wolf), donkey (bile), rat (heel), pig (fat), cat, dove (blood, excrement, doves, a white dove), dog (heart, hair, a mad dog, a she-dog's urine or milk), sheep (a living sheep, bile, spinal cord, bladder), louse, lion, lizard, buffalo, snake (snake skin, powder of snake skin), tiger, ants (ant legs), vulture, horse (foot), scorpion (eggs), leeches (sucking leeches), crow (leg, a black crow, a small crow), bat (blood), mouse (tail), spider (a living spider), goat (bile, milk, bladder, toenails, hooves of a goat), chicken (bile), elephant, flea, cow (nails, milk of a red cow), placenta of a calf, frog (blood), deer (skin, organ), bird (excrement of a sparrow, a sparrow), a night bird, womb, fox (eggs, skin, blood), bull (bile), worms (red, worm oil, worms from garbage), turtle dove (tongue), barn owl, silent he-goat (liver, lungs, kidneys, hand, "innards"), cock (comb, excrement, a black cock, liver, right eye, skin from the face of a cock), chicken (slaughtered, tongue, a small chicken, bladder). Ytshak Ytshaky, op. cit., 264–268.

14. E. Brauer, op. cit., 275.

15. *Salonique, Ville mère en Israel* (Jerusalem and Tel Aviv, 1967), 188.

16. I. Ben-Ami, *Saint Veneration among the Jews in Morocco* (Jerusalem: Magnes Press, 1985), 57, 58, 71, 75, 78, 80, 83, 91, 169, 170, 171, 172, 194, 210, 236, 242, 243, 244, 246, 247, 262, 267, 299, 303, 304, 307, 315, 325, 328, 348, 378, 379, 390, 404, 405, 446, 448, 459, 460, 467, 469, 472, 498, 522, 538, 539, 550, 584.

17. The Muslim woman of Morocco who wants to give birth: "*Cherchera une souris qui vient de mettre bas et lui prendra sept petits. Elle les roulera dans la farine et les avalera, tout vivants, avec de l'eau.*" A. R. de Lens, *Pratiques des Harems Marocains*, Paris: P. Geuthner, 1925, 37; E. Westermarck, *Ritual and belief in Morocco*, Vol. II, 1926, 370–433; E. Mauchamp, *La Sorcellerie au Maroc* (Paris: Dorbon Aine, n.d.), 113–126.

18. "Praise and thanks to your Great and Holy Name on the redemption of the birthing woman and the fruit of her womb. Let it be thy will that this son grow up with the Torah and good deeds. May he be wise and God-fearing during the lifetime of his father and mother and may he bring blessing and redemption to the nation of Israel." E. Toledano, op. cit., 61.

19. On Lilith and the struggle connected to the guarding of the child, see: G. Scholem, *Kabbalah* (Jerusalem: Keter Publishing House, 1974), 356–361; L. Blau, *Das altjüdische Zauberwesen*, Budapest: n.p., 1898; M. Caster, "Lilith und die drei Engel," *Monatschrift fur Geschichte und Wissenschaft des Judentums*, XXXIX (1880), 553–565; H. H. Winkler, *Salomo und die Karina* (Stuttgart: W. Kohlhammer, 1931); M. Gaster *Studies and Texts in Folklore, Magic, Mediaevel Romance, Hebrew Apocrypha and Samaritan Archaeology* Vol. II (London: Maggs Bros., 1925), 1005–1038, 1252–1265; idem., "Two thousand years of a charm against the child-stealing witch," *Folklore* II (1900); 129–162; I. Levy, "Lilite and Lilin", *Revue des Etudes Juives* 68 (1914); 15–20; R. Patai, *The Hebrew Goddess* (New York: Ktav Publishing House, 1967), 207–245; J. A. Montgomery, *Aramaic Incantation Texts from Nippur*, (Philadelphia: University Museum, 1913); I. Zoller, *Lilit* (Rome, 1924);

S. Hurwitz, *Lilith die erste Eva* (Zurich: Daimon Verlag, 1980); E. Doutté, *Magie et religion dans l'Afrique du Nord* (Alger: A. Jourdan, 1908); J. Naveh, S. Shaked, *Amulets and Magic Bowls* (Jerusalem: Magnes Press, 1985) also: (Leiden: E. J. Brill, 1985); G. G. Scholem, "Samuel and Lilith" (Hebrew), *The Hebrew Encyclopedia*, Vol. 26 (1974), 105–107; G. G. Scholem, "New chapters relating to Ashmadai and Lilith" (Hebrew), *Tarbitz*, Vol. 19 (1948): 160, 175; S. Shaked, "On Literature of Witchcraft of the Jews of Muslim Lands; Comments and Examples" (Hebrew), *Peamim* (1979), 15–28; R. Marcaliot, *Malachei 'Elion* (Hebrew) (Jerusalem, 1964).

20.   Y. Shachar, *Feuchtwanger Collection, Jewish Art and Tradition* (Jerusalem, 1971); H. Golnytsky, *Be machzor ha-Yamim* (Hebrew) (Haifa, 1963); P. Sebag, R. Attal, *La Hara de Tunis* (Paris: Presses Universitaires de France, 1959), 83; P. Flammand, *Un mellah en pays Berbère* (Paris: Demnate, 1952), 103–108; Leon de Modena *Historia de Riti Hebraici* (Venezia, 1683), Chap. 8, p. 3; G. Morosini, *Via della Fede* (Venezia, 1638), 113, 114; E. Coypel, *Le Judaisme* (Mulhouse, 1876), 94; D. Stauben, *Scènes de la vie juive en Alsace* (Paris: Michel Levy, 1860); J. M. Babo, *Vollstandige Darstellung der Gebrauchen un Ceremonien der Israeliten* (Strasburg, 1824), 95; F. Raphaël, "La Médecine populaire juive en Alsace," in *Médecine et Assistance en Alsace, XVI–XXe siècle;* A. Goldman, "The Wachnact among Vienna Jews," *Filogische Schriften*, I (1926), 91–94; F. Raphaël, "Rites de naissance et médecine populaire dans le judaisme rural d'Alsace," *Ethnologie Française*, I (1971), 36; E. Davis, "Amulettes Hebraiques," *Ariel*, Num. 45–46 (1978), 111; A. Milano, *Ghetto di Roma*, II (1963), 107–108, 166–180; J. C. G. Bodenschatzens, *Kirchliche Verfassung der heutigen Juden* (Frankfurt, 1748), 57.

21.   It is called la Vegghia or la Viola (Italy), lilt al-ziba (Yemen), al-ras (Iraq), leil Eliahu Hanavi, leil Hazohar, Lilade (among the Jews of Tunis), see P. Sebbag, R. Attal, op. cit., 74.

22.   The Book of Kabbalah, presumed to have been written in the third century by Rabbi Moshe de Leon.

23.   Chapters of Tachid and examples of these songs appear in different folk books. See *Kol Sasson* (Luggassi Publication), (the "Tachdid" chapter); *Yismach Tzaddik* (Hebrew), (H. S. Suissa: Lugassi Publication), 33–46.

24.   See *Salonique, Ville-mère en Israel*, op. cit., p. 190; M. Attias, *Romancero Sefaradi* (Jerusalem: Instituto Ben-Zewi, 1961) 46.

25.   So is it also in Morocco: "Les Juifs tracent dans l'air un cercle magique autour de la femme en doulers avec un grand sabre interdisant ainsi aux génies mauvais de le franchir..." Legey, op. cit., 81; F. Raphaël, "Rites de Naissance," op. cit., 85; I. Goldziher, "Eisen als Schutz gegen Dämonen," *Archiv fur Religionwissenschaft* 10 (1907): 41–46; J. J. Schudt, *Jüdische Merkwürdigkeiten* (Frankfurt, 1715); P. C. Kirchner, *Jüdisches Ceremoniel* (Nuremberg, 1724).

26.   According to the tradition, the baby will become 'avoltado' or 'mgelleb' (Morocco), as it is said, he changes, he becomes something else. See M. Attias, op. cit., 55. In Yemen it is called 'mibbadal,' J. Kafih, op. cit., 163.

27. I once interviewed a midwife from the Spanish region of Morocco. She told me that once she was summoned to assist a woman in childbirth. The midwife was brought to a specific place and assisted the woman as requested. The next day the midwife found a bag filled with gold coins in her case. It was then that she understood that she had assisted a woman-spirit.

28. See Kaf, op. cit., 159.

29. "I heard once from Ami-Shadai Gueta that he heard from old people that the reason for the choice of the color red has its source from the days of the Marranos. They were afraid to circumcise their sons according to the laws of Israel, with a certified *mohel* and a *minyan* of ten Jews. Since they could not advertise the Brith Milah for fear of the enemy, they traditionally hung red women's scarves that represented the blood of the brith. In that way the Marranos would know that there was a Brith Milah taking place in the house and they would come," P. Zuaretz, *Yahadut Luv* (Hebrew) (Tel Aviv, 1960), 368.

30. It is interesting to point out, from this viewpoint, the complex and rich chain of festivities related to the birth that go on for about six weeks after the birth in Yemen and in other places. See J. Kafih, op. cit., 178–182.

31. R. Patai, *Man and Earth in Hebrew Custom, Belief and Legend* (Hebrew) (Jerusalem, 1943).

32. A. Van Gennep, *Les Rites de Passage* (Paris: E. Nourry, 1909).

33. "On the day before the Brith Milah, women come at dusk to the house of the woman in confinement, in order to prepare perfumes. During the preparation, the women, who are specialists in singing and come to every house where there is a Brith Milah, sing holy songs, while sitting under Elijah's chair, about the Messiah Elijah the Prophet, the patriarchs, Moses and Aaron, Joseph the Righteous One and Eretz Israel, praise for the Torah and more. These songs are sung in spoken Arabic, in a folk melody that captures the heart. The content is full of strong longing for all holy things. It expresses the longings of the generations for the *Geulah*, the Redemption and the return to Eretz Israel and to its Torah. The songs express the strong belief that only in Israel will they be able to live and return to the glory of the past. See P. Zuaretz, op. cit., 386–387.

TWENTY

A Conversation in Proverbs:
Judeo-Spanish Refranes in Context

Isaac Jack Lévy and Rosemary Lévy Zumwalt

In our work on Judeo-Spanish proverbs, we might recall the words of Ali A. Mazrui about his account of his native Africa: "I think it was agreed that I would tell my story the way I wanted to tell it. I told them I would be using numerous proverbs because to me, proverbs are the main ingredient in a dish of conversation."[1] So also for the Sephardim, Judeo-Spanish *refranes* provide the spice for conversation. Just as in Sephardic cooking, in Sephardic verbal expression one does not consciously measure out the ingredients. The proverbs are called forth spontaneously from the deep inner knowledge of the culture and used in generous portions. J. Cary Davis emphasized in *"El lenguaje de los refranes,"* that "(Proverbs) are so much a part of our existence that we use them unconsciously to flavor our every day speech."[2]

The metaphor of proverb as the food of speech expresses a key to the importance of *los refranes* for the Sephardim. It brings us to the essence of the proverb in context as a means not only to convey wisdom and authority by calling forth past knowledge, but also to create meaning out of the present circumstance. The past and the present are blended in the contextual use of the proverb. And the richness of the stock of proverbs among the Sephardim of the eastern Mediterranean basin and the Balkans reflects the inheritance from many cultures—Spain, Portugal, Turkey, Greece, Bulgaria, and Rumania—as well as from the religious writings of their forefathers. Important also, though to a lesser extent, were the French and Italian schools as sources for proverbial lore.

In cooking, one ingredient could be used to replace another; so in proverb use, a Turkish, Greek, or Spanish proverb might be drawn forth. In the words of Isaac's mother, Caden Mussafir Israel, originally from Milas, Turkey and the

Island of Rhodes, just as *"la kaza siempre estava yena"* ("the house was always full") for the selection of cooking ingredients, so also was the repertoire of proverbs always full; if one was forgotten, there were others to be used.[3] While the larder was filled with the heritage of many cultures for the Sephardim this was *theirs*. Perhaps when asked the source of a proverb, one might say *"Era de los gregos"* ("It belonged to the Greeks") or *"Era de los turkos"* ("It belonged to the Turks"). In most cases, they were not even aware of the origin, but claimed it as their own: *"Era la mamá ke lo dezia"* ("It was mother who used it"), or *"Era del papá"* ("It was father's"). To give still more authority, the origin was attributed to the patriarchs, to biblical characters, even to famous rabbis: *"Era de muestros padres"* ("It was from our forefathers"), they would proudly emphasize.

The proverbs provided a sense-making mechanism for the Sephardim. Certainly this might be seen in terms of the emigration experience of our parents' generation. From Turkey, to Rhodes, to Morocco, to the United States, from the old world to the new, the changes span continents and widely varying ways of life. But their world is still ordered by the wisdom of the past which is called forth to inform the present.

Our work is based on research we have carried out in Turkey, Israel, Greece, France, and the United States, and by correspondence with people in other parts of the world. We have also drawn from the years of proverb research conducted by Isaac Jack Lévy, from his book, *Prolegomena to the Study of the Refranero Sefardí*, from two of his articles on the subject, and from his collection of over twelve thousand proverbs. These sources, as well as his notes and letters, have been culled for the contextual use of proverbs.

The largest portion of the research for this paper was conducted with Isaac's mother, Caden Israel, now living in Atlanta, Georgia. By necessity, since we were interested in context, we collected the proverbs as spoken, noting the situation and what prompted their use. The harvest was plentiful: we reaped not only proverbs, but also traditional sayings, folk beliefs, *konsejas* (folktales), riddles, and even ballads. Driving to Columbia, South Carolina, from Atlanta, watching the game show "Wheel of Fortune" on television, shopping at Kroger's supermarket, washing dishes, talking of the family—these were the typical situations in which we, ever vigilant, caught the proverbs in speech. Mother, in playful exasperation, would remark, "I can't say anything without you writing it down! I'm going to quit talking!" And we, in turn, would threaten to wire her for sound. One of us would turn to the other in the midst of a conversation in Judeo-Spanish with Issac's mother, and say, "She just came out with another one." "Write it down! Write it down!" we would say to each other frantically. What resulted were scribbled notes on bank deposit slips, paper napkins, manila envelopes, paper bags, and, once, toilet paper—anything at hand which might be used at that moment to record the proverb and the context.

The title for this chapter was inspired by an evening spent with friends in Tel Aviv, Israel, an evening which was a virtual conversation in proverbs. First, sitting outside at a café on Dizendorf Street, and later in our friends' living room eating watermelon, we talked and laughed and exchanged stories. Threaded throughout were a series of proverbs which strung together the themes of discourse. We quote in detail from that evening (August 11, 1985) with Salamon and Renée Bivas, who originally came from Salonika, Greece, and are survivors of the Nazi death camps.

Our evening began over ice cream sundaes and talk of our families, of children and parents. We recounted how Isaac's mother did not want to live with us, because she worried she would cause problems. Renée, in turn, told of her choosing an apartment a distance away from her children, and summed it all up with a proverb:

"*La flor di lonje da mejor guezmo.*"[4]
("The flower from the distance gives better smell.")
"A flower has a better fragrance from a distance."

We moved then from Dizendorf Street to their home. Isaac spoke of the sea wall at the beach in Tel Aviv and how it had deterred erosion, and Renée added that it was really for defense. Isaac commented that one was also needed at Ashdod but that there was no money. And Renée said:

"*La bolsa del riko se vazia i la del prove no se inche nunka.*"
("The purse of the rich itself empties and that of the poor not itself fills never.")
"The purse of the rich empties and that of the poor never fills."

Immediately, Isaac asked how the people in Israel lived without much money. Renée responded:

"*Ojos ke no ven korason ke no yora.*"
("Eyes which no see heart that no cries.")
"What the eyes do not see, the heart does not yearn for."

Our conversation now was consciously fixed on proverbs, since we were writing down what was said and speaking about the research. Salamon had shown us a book on Greek proverbs. And Isaac recounted the reaction of the Sephardim to his article, "The Proverbs and Popular Sayings of the Spanish Jews,"[5] which included several selections that were scatalogical in nature. One in particular, "*Aharva kulo ke no pido,*" ("Strike the ass that did not fart") outraged several individuals, even to the point of prompting one, a medical doctor, to tear out the page. Repeatedly, a few elderly women, close friends of the family, scolded Isaac gently, "*Izak, kerido, esto no se uza!* ("Isaac, darling, this is not used!") Isaac waited his chance. Several months later, he visited his mother in Atlanta. Four ladies gathered for a card game. One of the women who had scolded him, again asked Isaac, "Why did you write that?" And Isaac defended himself, "I picked it up from you people." She denied that it was ever used. Seconds later, in the midst of the game, when she was wrongfully accused of discarding a card, she unconsciously exclaimed, "*Na, mira! Aharva kulo ke no pido!*" And Isaac said, "You see!" Her only response was to blush. Renée's reaction to the story was:

> "*Din para ti i non para mi.*"
> "Judgment/The Law for you and not for me."

Isaac, pursuing Salamon's book on Greek proverbs, read one, "*Bolsa vazia no son*" ("An empty pocketbook does not ring"), and remembered his mother's using it in reference to a person with no education. "Nothing in the head. . . nothing comes out." Renée's immediate response was:

> "*Kuando ay aki* [slapped her rear] *no ay aki* [slapped her head]."
> ("When there is here, there is not here.")
> "When there is here, there is not there."

This proverb, in turn, reminded Renée of her mother's saying,

> "*Kuando se asenta sovre el kulo se inche el pulso.*"
> ("When one sits on the rear it fills the pulse.")
> "When you sit on your rear your pulse [wrist] fills up [moves]."

While most proverbs are readily understood, a number of them are enigmatic and cannot be comprehended out of context or without some explanation. So is the case with Renée's last proverb, which was befuddling to us until she clarified it. Her mother, who could not sew, insisted that her eldest daughter take lessons. The mother realized that young girls would resent sitting down for long periods, rather than playing. She cited the proverb, "When you sit on your rear your pulse fills up," which means that by sitting down and sewing for long periods, one produces more, thus earning or saving money, either by sewing for one's family or for employment.

Still another example of enigmatic meaning came up in a conversation with Isaac's mother on September 26, 1985. The talk, concerning a friend and a violation of confidence, elicited the following proverb from her:

> "*Mi ija a la eskondidas, mi boz ala meshkita.*"
> ("My daughter to the hiding, my voice to the mosque.")
> "To my daughter secretly, my voice to the mosque."

His mother asked Isaac, "What does it mean?" Not comprehending the meaning, even knowing the context, Isaac guessed, "Do you mean, my daughter is doing things wrong. That is, my daughter is bashful or she's having an affair or something. And then the mother or the father goes to the mosque to pray for her?" Mother shot back, "And you're a professor? What it means is: "*Yo avlo avagar, i tu lo dizes a todos*" ("I speak softly, and you spread it all over,"), like the Muezzin, the crier, who calls the faithful to prayer from the minaret. In this instance, the meaning was clarified only through explicit explanation.

In some instances, the proverbs themselves actually reflect the dynamics of the situation. We recall a conversation in 1967 between Isaac and Rabbi Isaac Alcalay, then Chief Rabbi of the Sephardic community of the United States. Isaac asked, "Where are we all going? What is the future of the Sephardic community?" And the rabbi replied,

> "*Esta eskrito en la palma, lo ke deve yevar el alma.*"
> ("It is written in the palm, that which must carry the soul.")
> "What is written in the palm, is that which must come to the soul."

In this situation, the community is equated to the palm, and what is written there, or what is happening now in the community, is a reflection of the future. The proverb moves from the specific, that which can be seen, to the more abstract, the soul or the future of the community. Rabbi Alcalay also meant it as a compliment to Isaac for his work in Sephardic studies—that his present work (that which was written in the palm) will insure the future of the community (that which must come to the soul). This movement in the proverb from the material which was of substance, "*la palma*" (the palm), to the immaterial, "*el alma*" (the spirit), was reflected in the other proverbs which Rabbi Alcalay used to support his statements. The Chief Rabbi made the point that the Sephardic scholars could not attack their own people by saying:

> "*Mas valen mis dientes ke mis parientes.*"
> ("More are worth my teeth than my relatives.")
> "My teeth are worth more than my relatives."

Here, "*mis dientes*" (my teeth) are equated with my people, and "*parientes*" (relatives) with outsiders. In other words, the teeth, or the Sephardim, are part of one's own body, which one is reluctant to attack. Again, the movement in the proverb is from the more specific, the teeth, to the more general, the relatives, or outsiders. And, finally, Rabbi Alcalay spoke about having tried to get help from apathetic but wealthy Sephardim. With sad resignation, he remarked:

> "*Mas da el duro ke el desnudo.*"
> ("More gives the hard than the naked.")
> "The tight-fisted give more than the destitute."

A person without means, even if he wants to give, cannot; so one must go not to the destitute, *"el desnudo,"* but rather approach with persistence the tightfisted, *el duro,"* who eventually contributes out of shame or fatigue. In this case, the proverb moved from the material substance, the *duro,* or the hard, to the lack of substance, the *desnudo,* or the destitute. In all three instances, there was a movement from a specific or concrete to the more general or less substantial. In a sense, this reflects a function of the proverb, to inform a specific situation with a general wisdom. And it also allowed the rabbi to make critical comments about specific situations in the community, but to veil these in the traditional medium of the proverb.

Just as Rabbi Alcalay could express negative sentiments in the metaphorical language of the proverb, so do others criticize obliquely through proverbs. Listening to a colleague complain about the excessive number of literature courses he had chosen to teach, Isaac, true to his Sephardic tradition, responded,

> *"El ke se aharva kon la mano ke no yore."*
> ("He who himself beats with the hand that no cry.")
> "He who beats himself with his own hand should not cry."

In response to the suggestion that something could be put off for another day, Mrs. Israel said,

> *"Asperad azno a la yerva mueva."*
> ("Wait jackass to the grass new.")
> "Wait, jackass, for the new grass to grow."

When Isaac tried to tell his mother how to hold her great-granddaughter, she retorted,

> *"Venid, sinyor, vos ambezare a azer ijos."*
> ("Come, sir, to you I will teach to make children.")
> "Come, sir, I shall teach you how to have children."

And, finally, we offer an example of correction through the use of proverbs which came up in the midst of writing this paper. Isaac was trying to articulate an idea and Rosemary kept interrupting. In exasperation, he said:

> *"La kavesa avierta si ambeza mas."*
> ("The head open itself learns more.")
> "An open head/mind learns more."

Thus, the proverbs as a means of criticism allow one to hit the mark without necessarily piercing the flesh.

The contextual use of Judeo-Spanish proverbs, in some instances, is closely tied to the Judeo-Spanish language and to humor as an expression of ethnicity. The accounts which we give illustrate another important aspect of proverb use, that it can be embedded in narrative. Isaac tells the story about a young, uneducated man from Rhodes, who had journeyed to Paris in search of work. Unsuccessful in his quest for employment, he returned to his native island after a two-month absence and pretended that he had forgotten all his Judeo-Spanish. His mother met him at the dock. As he disembarked from the ship, they embraced and then she asked him what he would like to eat for the Sabbath breakfast. The following conversation ensued:

Young man: *Je veux...je veux...un...un...*
            (I want...I want...a...a...)
Mother: *Burekitas?*
            (Burekas?)
Young man: *Non, non, non, non.*
Mother: *Buyikos?*
            (Boyos?)
Young man: *Non, non, non, non.*
Mother: *Guevos hamenados?*
            (Hard boiled eggs?)
Young man: *Non, non, non.*
Mother: *Pastilikos, kerido?*
            (Pasteles, sweetheart?)
Young man: *Oui, oui! Je veux des pastilé que les mujeré font en viernizé.*
            (Yes, yes, I want some pasteles that women prepare on Friday.)[6]

His whole family was very proud of his returning so cultivated. An educated man, who also went to the pier to meet one of his relatives, overheard this exchange and said,

"*Hamor se fue, azno mus vino.*"[7]
("Jackass himself went, ass to us he returned.")
"Jackass [Hebrew] he left, an ass he returned to us."

In this instance, the humor derives from the incongruous situation of the young man pretending to have forgotten all of his native language and mannerisms in two months and claiming that he could speak only French, which was regarded as more sophisticated. Thus, his final comment was a bastardized mixture of two languages: five words in French—*Oui, oui. Je veux des*—and then the Judeo-Spanish word "*pasteliko*" pronounced as it would be in French, *pastilé.* He continued with two words of French—*que les*—and, again, with the Judeo-Spanish *mujeres* with French pronunciation, *mujeré. He concluded with two words in French, font en,* and the Judeo-Spanish *viernes* rendered in his French by *viernizé*. The proverb summed up the situation—that one cannot change one's inner substance: "Jackass he left, an ass he returned to us."

In another narrative which plays on linguistic knowledge, the situation involved learning a new language in a new land. When Isaac first came to this country, he was taking a course on Shakespeare and having difficulty with the language. As a friendly joke, someone suggested that he go see Mr. Almeleh, a shoemaker. The latter took the book on Shakespeare, put it in a machine that shines shoes, and said, "That's what I can do." Then he added:

"*El ke las save, las tanye.*"
("He who them knows, them plays.")
"He who knows it, plays it."

There was a bit of Djuha in Mr. Almeleh's humor. He pretended to be dumb, and in so doing, showed his wisdom. His message was, one does what one can do. No artifice here—Mr. Almeleh was an expert at making shoes and knowledgeable in the culture of his people, but for teaching English he could be of no help.

In the preceding two examples, the proverb was used to sum up the situation. Frequently, the proverb is interspersed throughout the conversation as an integral part of the discourse. Such an instance was recorded by Isaac in 1964, in Atlanta, Georgia. Several elderly women, who were from Turkey and Rhodes, but had been living in the United States for over thirty years, had come to Mrs. Israel's house for a short afternoon visit. Isaac recorded the following conversation:

1—C. Israel: *Ke haber maná Rahel? En bon ora venga.*
(How are you Mrs. Reina? May you come in a propitious time.)

2—R. Franco: *En bunora mi tengas kirida.*
(May you also have a good fortune, darling.)

3—B. Beton: *Stavamus pasandu kuandu vimos il karu i entrimus para una kavé.*
(We were walking by when we noticed the car and came in to have a cup of coffee.)

4—C. Israel: *Il uidu mi istava kumiendo; kumpania divía di ser, li dishi a la mamá.*
(My ear was itching; we must be having company, I told mother.)

5—R. Franco: *Andi stá Isaac?*
(Where is Isaac?)
(Isaac enters)

6—C. Israel: 'Nombra al guerku i aparesi'.
               ("Speak of the devil and he appears.")
7—I. Lévy: Hi, Mrs. Reina. Good afternoon, Mrs. Bohora.
8—R. Franco: Ke haber kiridu? Ya sta la mamá alegri di tinerti in kaza.
               (How are you darling? Your mother is happy to have
               you home.)
9—I. Lévy: Yes, Ma'am.
10—C. Israel: Ah! Penas para verlus venir, penas kuandu si van.
               [Ah! Agony to see them come, agony when they leave.]
11—R. Franco: Mi alma, estu es la vida. 'Lu bueno prestu si va.'
               (Dear, this is life. "The good is quickly lost.")
12—C. Israel: Ma, mucha pena kriar estus karvonis.
               (But, it is a great agony to raise these rascals [coals])
13—B. Beton: Kayada. 'Nombra lu buenu para ki salga buenu.' La vida
               es estu; otros muz krian i mosotros tambien.
               (Hush. "Speak of the good so that it may come." This
               is life; other people raise us, and we raise others too.)
14—R. Franco: Kuanta sufriensa entri medius!
               (How much suffering in between.)
15—C. Israel: Antanyus era difirenti. Luz padris i lus ijus eran mas
               kirinsiozus.
               (In the past it was different. The parents and the
               children were closer.)
16—B. Beton: Lu ki si dizi es vidrad, 'Una madri para sien ijos, i no sien
               ijos para una madri.'
               (What they say is true, "A mother for a hundred
               children, and not a hundred children for a mother.")
17—R. Franco: La mamá, no esta in kaza?
               (Isn't Mama home?)
18—C. Israel: Si, salyo dil banyu. Si esta trukando. Aora va vinir.
               (Yes, she just got out of the bath. She is changing. She'll
               be here in a minute.)
19—R. Franco: Avagar ki sea. Para salud i aligria ki si banyi. A lus banyus
               di Isaac ki lu viyamus.
               (She should not rush. Let her bathe in health and in
               happiness. May we see the ritual bath of Isaac's [bride].[8]
20—C. Israel: Ishala! Il Dyo ki sienta una boka santa.
               (God willing! May the Lord listen to a saintly voice.)
21—R. Franco: Mi alma, 'kuando la ora dil Dyo vieni, ningun binadán
               lo dizaze.'

(Darling, "When the hour of God arrives, no human being undoes it"/"If it is God's will, no human can undo it.")

22—B. Beton: *'Kon il tiempo todu si ayega.' Entri irmana Sarota.*
("Everything will come in time." Come in Mrs. Sarota.)

23—S. Musafir: *Buirum! Azi muchu tiempo ki no moz vemos.*
(Welcome! It has been a long time since we have seen each other.)

24—B. Beton: *Agora ez duro. Kuandu los ijos mos dravean ya ez buenu.*
(Nowadays it is difficult. When the children drive us it is OK.)

25—C. Israel: *Asenta mamá, vo a miter il kafé.*
(Sit down, Mother, I am bringing the coffee.)
Vengan a la meza. Mamá trae unos biskuchikus.
(Please come to the table. Mother bring some cookies.)

(The table is set. Mrs. Beton spilled some of her coffee.)

26—B. Beton: *Ay! Estas manus negras. 'La vijes es mas negru ki la miel.'*
(Ah! These bad hands. "Old age is worse than honey.")[9]

27—R. Franco: *No importa. Ya si lava il mantel.*
(It does not matter. The tablecloth can be washed.)

28—S. Musafir: *La vida ki nu mus manki. Aora in il washer todu ez fasíl. 'Kuandu ay salud todu ez fasíl.'*
(That is O.K. as long as we are alive. Now, in the washing machine all is easy. "When there is health everything is easy.")

29—R. Franco: *Bindicha seas. Estu ez: 'Oy una koza, manyana otra.'*
(God bless you! You are right. "Today it is one thing, tomorrow another.")

30—S. Musafir: *'Los males van krisiendo komo la yerva mala.'*
("The misfortunes grow as the weeds.")

31—I. Lévy: *Buirum mujeres, ki si va yilar la kavé.*
(Welcome/Please come Ladies! The coffee will get cold.)[10]

In this short excerpt of an afternoon gathering, there are thirty-one exchanges containing ten proverbs interspersed throughout. Approximately thirty-three percent of the responses included proverbs. A study of them in their context and a knowledge of the performance—including voice tone, facial expression, and gestures—will show the following components:

a. Folk belief: #6, #13
b. Humor: #6
c. Religion: #21
d. World view: #11, #16, #22, #26, #28, #29, #30.

As can be seen in the text and in the above list, the women used the proverbs to reflect both what was happening and to sum up their views about health, life, customs, and happiness. Thus, the mundane conversation encompassed notions about religion, superstitions, and a total way of life.

The proverb is part of a deep cultural reservoir which is often tapped spontaneously. Once uttered, it is forgotten. This we have found in our work with Isaac's mother. If we were not able to record a proverb immediately, then it was gone until it came around again, as a natural part of discourse. There are exceptions, of course, such as Isaac's aunt, Mrs. Rachel Musafir, of Izmir, Turkey. Not aware of her special interest in proverbs, Isaac noticed a continuous use of this traditional form in her speech. When asked where she had gained her knowledge, she replied that it came first from the family, and second from her own curiosity. She showed him a little black booklet in which she had recorded proverbs as she encountered them in either speech or literature. At the beach resort of Cheshme, Turkey, they sat together after dinner and by two o'clock in the morning, they had recorded over four hundred proverbs, in many cases with their origin and context.[11] This is an exception, however, since Mrs. Musafir was an amateur collector, and thus consciously attuned to proverb use.

As an integral part of the culture, proverbs can be used in elliptical fashion. "*Una madre para sien ijos...*" ("One mother for a hundred children...") is enough for the audience. They know the rest: "*pero no sien ijos para una madre,*" ("but not one hundred children for a mother"). In still another example of elliptical reference, the first line of a ballad is cited, "*Ningun ombre si dezespere...*" ("No man should despair..."). The hearers mentally complete the last three lines of the stanza, which make up the proverb:

Ningun ombre si dezespere	:	Let no man despair
Ni piedra la esperansa	:	Nor lose his hope
Despues di mucha fortuna	:	After a big storm
Viene la buena bonansa	:	Comes a good catch.

Mrs. Israel said exactly this when she saw Isaac upset about the potential loss of the University of South Carolina basketball team to the State University of Florida. She meant to give him encouragement, after all—"No man should despair"—but her words were prophetic since the University of South Carolina won the game. And in another instance, while watching "Wheel of Fortune," she referred to the same proverb when a contestant, who on one spin of the wheel had gone bankrupt, went on to win the game.

As a part of cultural knowledge, proverbs are subject to rules for proper use, and their selection is influenced by the social situation. Thus, in addition to the spontaneous utterance of a proverb, there is also the element of an informed selection. The members of the culture can vary the proverb to fit the situation. For example, the rather neutral, "*Muevos tiempos, muevos vientos*" ("New times, new winds,") and "*Muevos arvoles, muevas frutas*" ("New trees, new fruits"), might be rendered more emotional by the following: "*Tokan piernezikas se olvidan tetikas*" ("They touch the thighs and forget the breast"). The latter was Caden Israel's response to her son when he joked with Rosemary, who was seated by his side, that his mother should buy a black and white polka dot dress advertised in *The New York Times*. Her remark referred to Isaac's acquiring a wife, represented by the thighs (*piernezikas*), and forgetting the breasts (*tetikas*) that had nourished him.

Ruth Finnegan has remarked on this aspect of selection in "Proverbs in Africa":

> A knowledge of the situations in which proverbs are cited may also be an essential part of understanding their implications, and this is complicated further by the fact that the same proverb may often be used according to the context, to suggest a variety of different truths, or different facets of the same truth, or even its opposite.[12]

The emphasis on the appropriate use of proverbs in context is part of what Alan Dundes and E. Ojo Arewa have called "the ethnography of speaking folklore."[13] In "Proverb Usage in a 'Natural' Context and Oral Literary Criticism," Arewa further emphasized the necessity for collecting proverbs in context and eliciting the people's own interpretations of them.[14] In our work, we have found a study of context to be crucial for an understanding of meaning. Without the proverb *in situ*,[15] one will only be able to give the generally accepted meaning, which in no way can encompass the subtleties and complexities of proverb use. For example, "*Yerva mala nunka muere*" ("Weeds never die") can be used in a literal sense, as Isaac did, in frustration, when looking out our back window at the lushness of the weeds. The same proverb has also been used in a metaphorical sense to refer to an evil person who will never change. The proverb used in a metaphorical sense has its parallel: "*Azno nasyo, hamor muryo*," (Born an ass, died an ass"), or the previously mentioned "*Hamor se fue, azno mus vino*" ("Jackass he left, an ass he returned to us"), while the literal use of "*Yerva mala nunka muere*" would not permit such a variation.

At the moment of utterance, each proverb carries with it an implicit meaning which at times is influenced by the person to whom it is directed. For instance, we have noted a difference between how Isaac's mother uses the proverb:

> "*No ay mejor amiga ke la madre i la ija.*"
> ("Not there is better friend than the mother and the daughter.")
> "There is no better friend than mother and daughter."

This depends upon whether she is speaking to her sons, Isaac and Julian, or to her daughter-in-law, Rosemary. With her sons, she uses it when she is depressed, as a way of saying that she is lacking the daughter she needs for companionship. To her daughter-in-law, she uses it in a literal sense, as reference to the closeness between Rosemary and her daughter, and to that which existed between herself and her mother, from whom she was never separated for more than a few days. She also recalls that her mother alway said this to her. Clearly, this proverb conjures up the past.[16]

Our research on the Judeo-Spanish *refranes* has further reinforced our position that compiling lists alone will not get at the meaning. While there is value in recording them, still one must ask to what purpose does one compile a corpus of proverbs? In a sense, the list of Sephardic proverbs might show very little difference with lists from other cultures. There is also, of course, the difficulty of a too-facile classification of the Sephardim. These people are not all the same, either in terms of culture or linguistics. In this light, to work toward a total Judeo-Spanish corpus of proverbs might overlay the complexity of the pan-Sephardic world with a façade of uniformity. Therefore, the context, with emphasis on the specific region, is crucial for the understanding of the cultural meaning of the proverb. This task must be undertaken without delay, since the people who speak the proverbs no longer reside in their original communities, and their numbers are decreasing.

In her work, "Proverbs in Africa," Ruth Finnegan remarks on the importance of context for the crucial aspect of meaning. She quotes a Fante elder who says, "There is no proverb without the situation."[17] Thus, the proverb alone, stripped of its life, loses its vital element. It cannot speak to us in fullness. It is merely a text. An Ibo youth echoed this sentiment from his own perspective. Educated in the European tradition, he had been removed from the tradition of his parents. As he said, "I know the proverbs, but I don't know how to apply them."[18]

NOTES

1. Ray Benson, "After Four Years in the Making, 'The Africans' Premieres Tonight," *The Columbia Record*, Oct. 7, 1986, Section B, p. 6, col. 3–4. Ali A. Mazrui, a native of Kenya, is a professor at the University of Michigan and the creator of *The Africans*, a nine-hour series produced by WETA/Washington, D.C., an Annenberg/CPB project.

2. J. Cary Davis, "El Lenguaje de los refranes," *Language Quarterly* X, No. 3–4 (1972), p. 6.

3. The orthography does not follow that of Castilian, but the Judeo-Spanish alphabet. For the translation of the proverbs from Judeo-Spanish to English, we have, in most instances, provided first a literal translation in parentheses followed by a free translation.

4. On another occasion, when asked to move with us, Mrs. Israel used the following version: *"La flor guele mejor di leshos,"* ("The flower smells better from far away"). In another instance, she has also used: *"La kompania i el pishkado fiede despues de tres dias"* ("Company and fish smell after three days")

5. *Sephardim & a History of Congregation Or VeShalom,* edited by Sol Beton (Monroe, Georgia: Walton Press Inc., 1981), pp. 64–74.

6. *Burekas* are crescent-shaped dough filled with mashed potatoes and cheese. *Boyos* are square-shaped dough filled with mashed potatoes, spinach, or pumpkin. *Pasteles* are cup-shaped dough filled with meat. The *pasteles* are miniature meat pies with sesame seeds sprinkled on top.

7. A variation of this proverb appears in Louis Combet, *Recherches sur le 'Refranero' Castillan* (Paris: Société d'édition "Les Belles Lettres," 1971), p. 344: "Fuime a Palazio bestia, i vine asno" ("I went to the palace a beast/ignorant and I returned an ass"). We also recorded a different version of the proverb on October 2, 1985. Isaac had taken his mother shopping for a sweater. She failed to find one and, on her return home, she said: "Vazio fui, lonsu vine." ("Empty I went, and a bear [= stupid/empty-headed] I returned.")

8. It was customary among the Sephardim for the bride and her female relatives and friends to go to the Turkish bath for a ritual cleansing prior to the wedding. The ceremony was held in a joyous spirit.

9. Whenever possible, the Sephardim avoid direct reference to negative terms. For instance, in this proverb, *miel* ("honey") is used for *fiel* ("bile"), which is bitter. In the same manner, they refer to the cemetary as the *Bet Ahaim* ("The house of the living") instead of "the house of the dead."

10. This conversation is taken from Isaac Jack Lévy, *Prolegomena to the Study of the Refranero Sefardi* (New York: Las Americas Publishing Company, 1969), pp. 96–97. We are taking the liberty of changing some of the spelling, including an English translation, and giving the names of the participants.

11. From the conversation of this evening, Isaac Jack Lévy published an article in Judeo-Spanish entitled "El refran sano i bivo entre los sefaradis," in *Aki Yerushalayim,* anyo 5, No. 19–20, Oktobre 1983–Enero 1984, pp. 55–56. There are other Sephardim, who, like Mrs. Musafir, have been collecting proverbs, with the intent of preserving their heritage. For the most part, they simply recorded the proverb and not the context, since to them this was obvious. Unfortunately, these lists are unpublished, and thus, unavailable to the scholar. In one instance, the son of one such collector refused to allow access to the list, even though he could neither speak nor understand Judeo-Spanish; he viewed the collection as part of his family's treasure.

12. In Alan Dundes and Wolfgang Mieder, editors, *The Wisdom of Many: Essays on the Proverb* (New York: Garland Publishing Inc., 1981), p. 19.

13. Ojo E. Arewa and Alan Dundes, "Proverbs and the Ethnography of Speaking Folklore," *American Anthropologist* 66, Part 2, No. 6 (1964), pp. 70–85.

14.   Ojo E. Arewa, "Proverb Usage in a 'Natural' Context and Oral Literary Criticism," *Journal of American Folklore* 83 (1970), pp. 430–437.

15.   For a discussion of the proverb *in situ*, see Barre Toelken, *The Dynamics of Folklore* (Boston: Houghton Mifflin Company, 1979), pp. 93–121.

16.   The variations of this proverb convey the idea of closeness—in the first instance, between the mother and her children, and in the subsequent versions, between the mother and her daughter:

1.   "*No ay mas amigos ke la madre kon los ijos.*" ("There are no better friends than the mother with her children").
2.   "*La ija yena la kaza*" ("The daughter fills the house").
3.   "*Ija, la palavra ya basta*" ("Daughter, the word is enough").
4.   "*La ija para los dias negros*" ("The daughter is for the black/bad days").
5.   "*La ija ez para la vejes*" ("The daughter is for the old age").

The first, more general in reference, identifies the strong relationship between the mother and her children. The remainder, numbers 2–5, focus on the daughter—(#2) she fills the house with her presence, (#3) she understands the mother implicitly, without further explanation, and (#4) she is there for the bad days, or times of depression, and (#5) for old age. In the last two mentioned, one can see the equivalence made between bad days and old age. A proverb which contrasts the mother's relationship with her daughter to that with her daughter-in-law follows: "*A ti te lo digo mi ija para ke lo entienda m'ilmuera*" ("I tell it to you my daughter so that my daughter-in-law will understand it"). And in one other example which compares the daughter to the daughter-in-law, Mrs. Israel said when both she and Rosemary yawned at the same time: "*Busteja mi ija di la tripa vazia. Busteja m'iluera di la tripa yena*" ("My daughter yawned from an empty stomach. My daughter-in-law yawned from a full stomach").

17.   In *The Wisdom of Many, Essays on the Proverb*, p. 27.

18.   Arewa and Dundes, p. 70.

TWENTY-ONE

Expressive Modes in the Judeo-Spanish Wedding Song

Oro Anahory-Librowicz

Although there have been many studies of the Judeo-Spanish oral tradition, very few have explored the wedding song.

The extensive collection of A. Larrea Palacin[1] and the fundamental study of M. Alvar[2] stand out as the only representatives of this neglected aspect of Sephardic lyrical poetry[3]. The present study does not claim to bring to light texts not contained in these two collections, which were made during the 1940s, nor to add a new critical methodology to Alvar's exhaustive and perceptive study. Instead, the main thrust of my study is to discuss an aspect of Judeo-Spanish wedding songs which does not seem to have been explored to date, an aspect which I shall refer to as *expressive modes*.

Unlike *romances*, most wedding songs do not relate a story. They reflect a state of mind, with specific references to the festivities which accompany the lengthy and complex Sephardic traditional wedding—for example, the *tufera*[4] the display of the trousseau (*ajuar*), the farewell to maidenhood, the reading of the marriage contract (*ketubba*), and the ritual bath. The repertoire of Moroccan Judeo-Spanish wedding songs, to which this study is limited, has a wide range of expressive modes, which I will attempt to define here.

The wedding, as a rite of passage par excellence, is a classic occasion for the preservation of customs and traditions. Of all traditional Judeo-Spanish songs, the ritual songs (wedding and para-liturgical) are perhaps those which will take

This article was originally prepared in Spanish for publication in the *Revista de dialectología y tradiciones populares* (Madrid). It was translated into English for this volume by Judith R. Cohen, who also prepared the musical commentary.

the longest to disappear[5], while the *romances*, separated from their traditional family context, constitute a much more vulnerable repertoire which may be doomed to oblivion. As well, the structure of the wedding songs is more flexible and open than that of the *romance*, so that verses can be added or omitted without altering the basic nature of the song. This flexibility means that, for wedding songs, surviving fragments may be meaningful texts. On the other hand, a partially remembered *romance*, retaining only certain elements of the narrative, loses its vitality and much of its interest. A wedding crystalizes the hopes, yearnings, and fears of an entire lifetime; these emotions are reflected in the wedding song repertoire, whose expressive modes range from the most intimate lyricism to the crudest vulgarity, passing through various intermediary modes along the way.

EROTIC LYRICISM

The wedding songs reflect women's amorous feelings in their most refined aspect. In text #1 of this study, the groom's sluggishness is countermanded by the bride's intense love and desire, exalting the wedding night as a sublime moment which she would not exchange "for a hundred ships."

Other songs refer to the dream world of women. The young girl's dream reflects a subtle desire and eroticism:

Y anoche, mi madre,
cuando me eché a acordar (= dormir)
soñaba un sueño
tan dulce era de contar:
que me adormía
y a orias del mar.
            (Alvar VI, Version A., 2nd verse)[6]

(Last night, mother,
when I lay down to sleep,
I dreamed a sweet dream:
that I fell asleep
on the seashore.)

The symbolic presence of water enhances the erotic quality of both poems.

The bride's deepest feelings about different stages of her life are also expressed—the flirtatiousness of the young girl, the wistfulness of leaving maidenhood, and, on a more elevated level, faith in creation and the Creator:

¡Ay, qué bueno que es lo bueno,
lo mejor el Dio del cielo!
Y ay qué buena es la esperanza,
quien espera bien alcanza,
se le cumple la demanda.
            (Alvar XXXII, refrain)

(Oh, the good is good indeed,
but the Lord of the heavens is the best.
How good is hope,
and to wish for good is to achieve it
and have desires fulfilled.)

THE POETIC TONE

Alongside these lyric songs in which the bride speaks in the first person, revealing her private world with its longings and apprehensions, other equally poetic tests may be found, whose central common theme is praise of the bride's beauty.[7] In these poems, the woman is admired and her aesthetic qualities praised in the third person. An outstanding example of this category is *Dize la muestra novia* (Our Bride asks...), a cumulative wedding song known to virtually everyone in the Judeo-Spanish community, which describes the bride in a series of attractive metaphors: head = spacious field;[8] hair = strands of silk; forehead = shining sword; eyebrows = weaving ribbons; eyes = beautiful look-out points; nose = date of the date tree; face = rose of the rosebush; lips = threads of coral; teeth = slender pearls; tongue = sweet bearer of bread; chin = crystal goblet; arms = oars of the sea; breasts = lemons of the lemon tree; insides = river for swimming.

Arrelumbre, #2 in this study, is another poetic hymn to the beauty of a woman: the bride shines like gold and enamel, like the dawning sun. The cult of feminine beauty is the central or secondary theme of a large number of wedding songs. Frequent expressions used to describe the bride include: "gallant," "elegant," "face like a moon," "svelte/lovely body."

THE EXEMPLARY TONE

Included in the didactic vein of Sephardic literature are certain *romances* which are sung at weddings, such as (1) *Rahel lastimosa* (M7), (2) *¿Porqué no cantáis, la bella?* (J4), (3) *El marido disfrazado* (T3), and (4) *Repulsa y compasión* (S5) + *Bernal francés* (M9).

1. Rahel is the adulteress whose example is not to be followed: her conduct leads irrevocably to death.[9]
2. The king's daughter represents faithfulness, as exemplified by the patience and heroism of the young girl who vows to become a captain and rescue her lover, who is away at war.
3. The exemplary wife refuses to let herself be seduced by her husband, disguised as a page.
4. *Bernal francés*, with the deadly punishment of the adulteress, transforms the diversionary *romance*, *Repulsa y compasión* into an exemplary narrative.[10]

The wedding, which is chiefly a religious ceremony, evokes the patriarchs (Abraham, Isaac, Jacob) and Moses as models of virtue, and refers to Jewish law as the light which must guide the married couple's new life (see *El Zejut de los abot, #3*).

Still, exemplary or didactic songs are not the predominant genre of the Sephardic wedding song. One of the favorite themes is the relationship between the bride and the groom before the wedding ceremony.

THE PLAYFUL OR DIVERSIONARY TONE

This relationship is alluded to in a playful or diversionary tone. The traditional encounter at the foot of a fountain or by the shores of a river creates delicate situations in which the bride, at once seductive and modest, sidesteps her suitor's amorous advances:

> Tate, tate, caballero,
> deja el amor para mañana.
> Lavaré mi lindo cuerpo,
> me pondré nagüita blanca
>   (Alvar XVII, version C)

> ("Hold on, young man,
> leave love for tomorrow.
> I'll wash my pretty body
> and put on my white shirt".)

Songs which refer to bathing reflect the double symbolic dimension of water: it is at once purifying and erotic.[11]

A more daring bride is described in #4 of this study, in which the woman goes to market to buy herself a husband. She chooses a carpenter, and has him build her a chest "with golden keys and silver locks," an undeniably erotic metaphor (see below for the commentary on the author's collected version of this song).

THE BAWDY OR OBSCENE TONE

There are some songs which are even more polarized, combining very lyrical verses with others which are extremely bawdy. For example, both *¡Qué hermoso pelo tienes tú, Rahel!* and *La novia destrenza el pelo* start in a poetic mode and end with bawdy verses. Verses 3 and 4 of the first song, and verse 1 and the last verse of the second song are good examples of this:

> (3) ¡Qué hermosos ojos tienes tú, Rahel! (bis)
>   Los ojos tuyos, las miradas mías.
>   No me espartiré de ti. (bis).

(4) ¡Qué hermoso coche tienes tú Rahel! (bis)
El coche tuyo el motor mío
No me espartiré de ti. (bis).
(As sung by Solly Levy, of Tangiers; Montreal, Oct. 1982)

(3: What beautiful eyes you have, Rahel! Your eyes and my gaze; I'll never leave you.

4: What a beautiful car you have, Rahel! Your car and my engine; I'll never leave you.)

(Verse 1) La novia destrenza el pelo, se desmaya el caballero. (Last verse) Shawil se pone las botas, se le miran las pelotas.

(The bride lets down her hair and the groom faints. Shawil puts on his boots and everyone sees his balls.)

The bawdy verses, which are not really part of the original song, are a relatively recent regional addition from a Moroccan town. It is not for nothing that Alvar points out the Council of Agde's edict (506) against erotic songs and dances during weddings. The latter have always been ripe occasions for all manner of licentiousness, during the Middle Ages and in traditional societies such as the Sephardic community.

Recent songs in *haketía* (Moroccan Judeo-Spanish) include a large number of short compositions of a bawdy and playful nature. For example, *Jacob y Mazaltov* (#5 of this study) is a bawdy wedding song in which culinary metaphors are used to allude to the sexual activities of the two protagonists.

The well-known *romancillo, Fray Pedro* or *Paipero*, a peninsular song introduced fairly recently to Marocco, belongs to an indisputably goliardic tradition and is a perennial favorite among Sephardic Jews. It features a self-indulgent monk with few inhibitions, a hundred and twenty ladies who seduce him, and a detailed description of an orgiastic scene worthy of Rabelais. All this takes us to the opposite end of the refined and subtle songs which were discussed near the beginning of this overview.

The Judeo-Moroccan wedding song is a very old form which, like the *romancero*, has been enriched by recent imports from the Peninsula. The wedding songs, largely because of their ritualistic nature and context, have maintained more vitality than the *romances*, and have inspired recent compositions in *haketía*; these often bawdy verses have their own interest for folklore researchers. Although their themes are less varied than those of the *romance*, they reflect a greater variety of expressive modes. Love and related themes are given a wide range of treatments, from highly refined to actually obscene.[12] The open structure of the wedding songs, which permits additions and interpolations, makes it possible for a song of this genre to not only have an almost unlimited number of verses, but also to contain several different states of mind and expressive modes in the same poem.

Without the wedding songs, no panorama of traditional Sephardic poetry would be complete. The narrative dimension of the *romance* is complemented by the wedding songs' lyrical and intimate character, which deserves serious study on the part of researchers.

THE TEXTS OF THE SONGS

In this section five texts will be presented, representing the five expressive modes discussed above. The main criterion for selection was the degree of originality of the versions collected, except for #2. In this category, my collected versions were not unusual in any way. I recorded these songs in different countries and from different informants, some recently, others several years ago.

To transcribe this dialect of Judeo-Spanish, the following signs are used:

c̲, s̲ or z̲ = voiced alveolar fricative or voiced s̲ (e.g., hiz̲o, las̲).

Z = voiced palatal fricative (e.g. muZer).

x = unvoiced palatal fricative (e.g. dixo).

H = unvoiced laryngeal fricative, corresponding to Hebrew *het* or Arabic *ha* (e.g. IsHaq).

h̲ = unvoiced glottal fricative, corresponding to Hebrew *he* or Arabic *ha* (e.g. cah̲al).

Text 1: Ni por cien navíos

Casóme mi madre   con un mercader.
La noche de novia   se me echó dormir.
Amor y recordís,*1   recordís, mi amor,
y non dormáis, no.
-Cien navíos   tengo a orillas del ri,
Tomis̲los vos, la novia,   y dexaime dormir.
Amor y recordís,   recordís, mi amor,
y non dormáis, no.
-Ni por cien navíos,   ni por otros ciento,
en la noche como esta   me echaré a dormir.
Amor y recordís,   recordís, mi amor,
y non dormáis, no.

*1 *recordís*: wake up! (See Alvar p. 220).

As sung by Mary Levy de Peres, approximately forty-five years old, native of Tangiers, resident in Toronto, Canada. Recorded in Montreal, June 1982. Bibliography: Alvar XLIII.

This poem appears for the first time in Alvar, in a less complete version which lacks the first verse and the refrain. The poem is fully comprehensible only with the first verse of the text presented above; otherwise, it is not clear that the song is really a dialogue between two newlyweds, and that its theme is the sexual tension between them. This tension between the amorous bride and the sleepy groom[13] is resolved in a final verse sung by my informant's brother, Solly Levy, in 1973, some years before I recorded Mary L. de Peres' version:

Le di un pellizquito, le hi̱ze arrebuir.

una noche como esta no me iré a dormir.

Amor y recordís. Recordís, mi amor,

y no digáis no.

(1-3: My mother married me to a merchant, and on the wedding night he fell asleep. Wake up, love, and don't sleep. I have 100 boats on the shore; take them, my bride, and let me sleep. Wake up. . .Not for 100 boats, nor for 100 more, would I sleep on a night like this. Wake up. . .4: I gave him a good pinch to rouse him. I will not sleep on a night like this. Wake up, love, and don't say no.)

Text #2: *Arrelumbre + Ansí se me arrimó*

Arrelumbre y arrelumbre y arrelumbre tu mazale. *1.

como arrelumbra esta novia delante de todo el cahale *2.

La novia de cara pintada *3 donde el novio se resmiraba.

(bis) Y asi se me arrimó i hacia la cama

i a ver las almohadas si eran de lana

(bis) i a ver la nuestra novia si era galana.

(bis) Por Dios, la nuestra novia, cuello garrido.

¿Qué vos ponís en escondido,

vos ponís arrayarte*4 y oro molido?

¡Qué bien le parecís a vuestro marido!

(bis) No me puso mi madre cosa ninguna.

La cara de esta novia como la luna.

(bis) La cara de esta novia como la luna.

*1 Hebrew: *mazal*: luck, fortune
*2 Hebrew: *kahal*: community, congregation.
*3 cara pintada: idiomatic Judeo-Spanish for "beautiful face"
*4 arrayarte: read *albayalde*.

As sung by Mercedes Tamesti, approximately thirty-nine years old, native of Tangiers, resident in Caracas, Venezuela. Recorded in Caracas by Soly Anahory de Cohen, 16-4-72 and sent to 0. Anahory-Librowicz. Bibliography: *Arrelumbre*: Alvar XXIV (A & B); Larrea 40. *Ansí se me arrimó*: Alvar XXXVII; Larrea 45, 46, 47.

This text does not differ significantly from the published versions; in fact, it is representative of common variants. The twinning of two or more wedding songs with similar or even different melodies is a common phenomenon in oral tradition.

(May your fortune shine, like the bride before her congregation. The bride with her beautiful face which the groom gazes at. And so I went to inspect the bed, to see if the cushions were of wool, to see if the bride was truly a virgin. In God's name, o bride of the graceful neck, what have you put on in secret: ceruse, ground gold? You will be so pleasing to your groom! My mother has not put anything on my face. The face of this bride, like the moon.)

Text #3: La fragua de la Casa Santa + El zejut*1 de los abot*2

(Hagad) is la tebá*3   de oro fino
para que suba este novio   a dar el anillo.
¡Rejmidor*4 rejmidor   de toda' las alma'!
A ti llamo, señor,   tarde y mañana,
que me cumpláis mis deseos   y mis demandas.
¡Rejmidor, rejmidor   de toda' las alma'!
A ti llamo i'señor   ta(rde y mañana.
Que el Dio es uno,   su nombre es uno,
crió cielo y tierra   y afirmó el mundo.
¡Rejmidor, rejmidor   de toda' las alma'!
Y hagadeis la teba   de oro y plata
donde suba este novio   y a dar las anda.
¡Y a mí, rejmidor   de toda' las alma'!
A ti llamo, señor,   tarde y mañana,
que me cumpla mis deseos   y mis demandas.
Hagadeis con Isha   güestro querido
que después de cincuenta años   fue cercucido*5.
¡Rejmidor, rejmidor   de toda' las alma'!
A ti llamo i'señor   tarde y mañana,
que me cumpla mis deseos   y mis demandas.

*1 Hebrew: honor, integrity
*2 Hebrew: patriarchs, fathers
*3 Hebrew: the bridal throne
*4 Judeo-Spanish: redeemer
*5 read: circuncidado.

Sung and recorded by friends and family of Nina Almozni, native of Tangiers, in Tetuán, 5-5-57. Tape given to O. Anahory–Librowicz in Caracas, Venezuela, June 1972.

(Summary: Refrain: Redeemer of all souls, I call on you night and day to grant my wishes.

Build the bridal throne of gold, that the groom may go up to it with the ring; the Lord is One, his name is One, He created heaven and earth and the world; build the bridal throne of gold and silver, where the groom will go up to give them.

Be like our beloved Isaac, who was circumcised when he was over fifty years old.)

To my knowledge, this text is otherwise unpublished, at least in the collections of Alvar and Larrea. Still, the theme of divine omnipotence and of man's dependence on God's will is not unknown in Moroccan Sephardic wedding songs. It is found, for example, in three texts in Alvar:

"Y el deseo que deseaba
cumplióme el Dio" (XXXI, 5–6);
"Y agradezco a Dio del cielo. . . .
que tal marido me ha dado" (XXXVI, A., 1,3);
"Qué lo bueno qué es lo bueno,
lo mejor: el Dio del cielo" (XXXII, refrain).

("And God fulfilled my desires"; "and I thank the Lord of heaven. . .who has given me such a husband"; "the good is good, but the best is the Lord of heaven".)

The last verse of my version, which belongs to the text *El zejut de los abot*, constitutes a serious historical error: Isaac, son of Abraham, was not circumcised at fifty years old. According to the Bible, his *father* was circumcised, at the age of ninety. The song exhorts us to follow the examples of Isaac, who "offered his throat to the executioner" and of Jacob, "for from his seed were born the twelve tribes."

Text #4: Levantíme madre

Hecha está la cama   como de novia honrada
con cinco almadraques   y sábanas de holanda.
Con el guelindón.*1
Levantíme, madre,   un lunes de mañana.
Fuérame al mercado,   y como alboreaba,
Con el guelindón.
Mercara un marido   de honra y de fama.
Carpintero era,   y maestro le llaman.
Con el guelindón.
Maestro, maestro,   adobaisme*2 este arca.
Las llaves de oro   y la chapa de plata.

Con el guelindón.
Y a la medianoche   prima la llamaba:
-Más blanca sos, prima,   que la rosa fina.
Con el guelindón.
Vos me parecías   una rosa encendida,
vos me parecitis   una luz del día.
Con el guelindón.

*1 guelindón: penis
*2 from *adobar*: repair (see Alvar, p. 193).

As sung by Solly Levy (thirty two years old), native of Tangiers, resident of Montreal, Canada. Recorded in New York City, July 1976. Bibliography: Alvar XL; Larrea 5, 6.

The unusual element of this version is the refrain, which is a unique variation of this song and suggests a vein of realism. The texts in Alvar and Larrea have refrains which are more lyrical in nature: "*Y ay pastor a mí / para mí pastor / y ay pastor a mí*" (See pp. 293 and 27–28 respectively) ("And, oh, my shepherd. . ."). Its adjacent elements of refinement (verses 5 and 6), eroticism (3 and 4), and realism (refrain) place this version of the song on the border between the playful and bawdy modes.

(The bed is made up, as befits an honorable bride, with five mattresses and Holland sheets. I arose, mother, one Monday morning, and went to the marketplace at dawn. I bought a husband, well-known and honorable; they call him a master carpenter. Master, fix up this chest for me, with golden keys and a silver lock. At midnight he says she is fairer than the rose, she appears to him as a flaming rose, the light of day.)

Text #5: Jacob y Maẓaltov

Pescado frito   vende Ya'acó,
¿ande*1 lo frió?   En la sartén Maẓaltó;
ajay*2 qué sartén   que tiene Maẓaltó,
¿quién se la caientó?   El señor Ya'acó.
Pan caiente   vende Ya'acó,
¿ande lo coció?   En el forno de Maẓaltó;
ajay qué forno   que tiene Maẓaltó;
¿quién se lo hameó*3   El señor Ya'acó.
Perejil y culantro,   vende Ya'acó,
¿ande lo jarpeó*4?   En el fedán*5 de Maẓaltó;
ajay qué fedán   que tiene Maẓaltó,
¿quién se lo hafteó*6   El señor Ya'acó.

The asterisked terms are common ones in *haketía*,
Moroccan Judeo-Spanish.

*1 *ande*: where (Spanish *donde*)
*2 *ajay*: ah, oh! (Sp. ay!)
*3 *hamear*: to heat up
*4 *jarpear*: to plant
*5 *fedan*: marketplace, plaza
*6 *haftear*: to steal

As sung, with tambourine (*sonaza* accompaniment, by Raquel Garzón de Israel (approximately forty–eight years old), native of Tetuán, resident of Madrid. Recorded in Madrid by O. Anahory Librowicz and Jacob M. Hassán, 9-7-84. Bibliography: Larrea 54.

This bawdy song, published in Larrea, contains two metaphors not found in his version—bread and parsley. Larrea's erroneous transcription obscures the meaning of the song: the Hebrew woman's name *Mazaltov* (good fortune), is transcribed *más alto* (higher, the Most High), probably because of the Judeo-Spanish pronunciation, *Mazaltó*.

(Jacob is selling fried fish: where did he fry it? In Mazaltov's frying pan. Oh, what a frying pan Mazaltov has! Who heated it up? Mister Jacob. Jacob sells hot bread. . .baked in Mazaltov's oven. . .who heated the oven—Mister Jacob. Jacob sells parsley and cilantro. . .planted in Mazaltov's plaza. . .who stole it? Mister Jacob.)

NOTES

1. *Canciones rituales hispano-judías* (Madrid: CSIC, 1954).
2. *Cantos de boda judeo-españoles* (Madrid: CSIC, 1971).
3. Other researchers have published wedding songs, but without according them their own analysis separate from the *romancero*. See bibliography in Alvar, pp. 3–7.
4. *Tufera* means 'braid' and refers to the ceremony which is celebrated at the bride's home the same day as the display of the trousseau, six days before the wedding ceremony. The bride unbraids her hair, binds it with a circlet sent by the groom, and covers it with a silk handkerchief or *meherma*, which she will wear the rest of her married life. In fact, Jewish tradition requires a married woman to keep her hair covered for reasons of modesty. She may only uncover it in front of her husband or in the presence of one or more women with no other men present. This custom is still practiced today by very observant women. For a description of the various stages of the traditional Sephardic wedding, see Larrea, 13–19.
5. In fact, from the 1970s until the present, ever since I have been recording traditional Sephardic songs, I have observed that the *romance* repertoire has been diminishing, while the wedding songs still maintain considerable vitality. I have even met informants who have sung nothing but wedding songs for me.

6. All the texts quoted in this study are part of the author's unpublished field collection, which includes some forty-five Moroccan Judeo-Spanish wedding songs collected in Spain, Israel, Venezuela, the United States and Canada. Nevertheless, because wedding songs vary very little from one informant to another, the already published texts of Alvar and/or Larrea Palacin will be cited with their numbers for the reader's convenience. When a particularly interesting variant is to be quoted, the author's text will be cited. The translator of this article, Judith R. Cohen, prepared the English language summaries of the texts cited in this study.

7. Note that certain elements of these songs (speaking in the voice of the woman, and calling on the mother) can be related to Galaico-Portuguese lyric poetry, especially the *cantigas de amigo*. For a detailed study of the metrical and thematic relationships between Sephardic wedding songs and the early Hispanic lyric, see Alvar, pp. 46–63 and 97–118 respectively.

8. Mrs. Clara Benchimol (a Montreal, Canada informant originally from Tetuán), gave me an interesting variant as a metaphoric term for 'head': billiard ball. To my knowledge, this is a unique variant which does not figure in Larrea, Alvar, or the numerous versions of this song I have recorded. The modern connotation of this metaphor shows that the song has been able to maintain its vitality and continues to generate original variants in our own epoch.

9. For a more detailed interpretation of the didactic aspects of *Rahel lastimosa* see O. Anahory-Librowicz, *Florilegio de romances sefardíes de la diáspora* (Madrid: Cátedra-Seminario Menéndez Pidal, 1980), 58–60.

10. For a fuller study of the interrelationship of these twinned *romances*, see *Florilegio* 77–79.

11. For a detailed study of the significance of water immersion in antiquity and the Middle Ages, see Alvar, 30–32.

12. The wedding songs could perhaps be classified according to expressive mode, because their thematic material is too sparse for the system used to classify the *romancero*.

13. Note the irony of the first line. The groom, who can consider sleeping through his wedding night, is none other than a merchant; a frequent butt of satire in medieval and Golden Age literature. This beginning is reminiscent of another wedding song (Alvar XXXIX), in which the satirical portrait of the merchant is taken to an absurd extreme: he is described as a "flamingo, with huge feet like a camel's" (Alvar, 291).

TWENTY-TWO

The Music of the Songs: Musical Transcriptions and Commentary of the Songs Discussed by Oro Anahory-Librowicz in "Expressive Modes in the Judeo-Spanish Wedding Song"

Judith R. Cohen

The music of Judeo-Spanish songs has not been widely studied, and most of the studies published have dealt with the *romances* or ballads. Alvar[1] and Larrea[2] contain generous numbers of wedding song transcriptions. The transcriptions in Alvar are fewer, but are at least briefly discussed by their transcriber, Maria Teresa Rubiato; those in Larrea are far more numerous but include no analysis. An LP edited by H. Yurchenco incorporating her field recordings made in Morocco in the late 1950s[3] includes no musical commentary. My own forthcoming article[4] discusses the music of the songs and mentions the idea of expressive modes, though in very little detail; it should be stressed that Dr. Anahory-Librowicz did not know of this article's existence when preparing her study.

Sephardic wedding songs from the eastern Mediterranean tradition, as opposed to the Moroccan repertoire, which is the subject of this study, have received somewhat more attention from enthnomusicologists. N. Kaufman includes a few transcriptions and commentaries in an overview article on Bulgarian Sephardic music[5] and, more recently, S. Weich-Shahaq, an Israeli ethnomusicologist, has published several articles and an excellent LP of field recordings.[6] It should be noted here that, although the texts of the wedding songs from the two traditions, Moroccan and eastern Mediterranean, have much in common, musically the songs are very different.

Most wedding songs are sung by groups of people, unlike the *romances*, which are usually sung by one person with no instrumental accompaniment. Women, the main bearers of the wedding song tradition, traditionally accompanied these songs with percussion instruments, especially the tambourine or *sonaZa*. They also punctuate the songs with the *barwalá*, the joyful ululation typical of women's singing in the Mediterranean. These are among the aspects of performance practice which rarely, if ever, appear in musical transcriptions, although they are in fact the very aspects which impart a unique North African flavor to these songs, whose musical modes are basically European ones.

This brief commentary is not the place for a full analysis of music of Moroccan Judeo-Spanish wedding songs. At this time, I will simply mention some of the more typical characteristics of the melodies—descending melodic lines, terraced or arched; stepwise motion with wider intervals often filled in by passing tones or other ornamentation; and a melodic range which may reach or even exceed an octave. The same melody may be used for different texts, and the same text may be heard sung to different melodies. This trait, together with the fact that the same melody may be used for songs of other genres such as the *romance* or paraliturgical texts, makes it difficult to establish relationships between the characteristics of the melodies and the expressive modes of the texts. Analysis of the performance practices of the different genres might help to identify such a relationship, but the traditional contexts for the singing of these songs have been greatly altered or have disappeared, although it is still relatively easy to find informants who know a number of wedding songs.

In the musical transcriptions that follow, the complete sung version as collected by Dr. Anahory-Librowicz is given, except for #3. All metronomic markings are approximate. In order to preserve something of the fluidity of the singing, I have not used bar lines. In certain cases, the pitch notation is also approximate, mostly due to intonation problems: 〰️ or 〰️ indicates a glissando; ↓ indicates a note sung flatter than in the tempered scale, and 〰️ indicates a rapid lower mordent of a semitone or less.

#1. NI POR CIEN NAVIOS[7]

I was given two recorded versions of this song. The first, the text of which is discussed in this article, was extremely difficult to transcribe because of intonation problems. The second version, which I have transcribed below, was sung by a man whose has sung a good deal of Western music and is also well-known as a liturgical singer: this background has contributed to both a tendency to sing

strictly within a Western tempered scale and an ornamentation style which draws on liturgical singing for some of its inspiration.

This song is not in the dance rhythm characteristic of most wedding songs. In both recorded versions, it is sung in a rather free, lyrical style, perhaps reflecting something of the nature of the text. The melody is largely stepwise, and the ornamentation accentuates this trait. Before the last phrase there is a dramatic leap of an octave.

#2. ARRELUMBRE + ANSI SE ME ARRIMÓ

These two songs are twinned, a common phenomenon in the Moroccan Judeo-Spanish song repertoire. They are in a minor mode and its relative major. The second song fluctuates between major and minor, as does #5 in this study, a trait common in peninsular traditional songs. In both songs, the melodies are similar but not identical to those transcribed in Larrea, but the first one is totally different from Rubiato's transcription[8]. Both songs are in a dance rhythm and would traditionally be accompanied by the *sonaZa*. This informant favors the glissando,

especially in the first song. In the second song, she varies the figure ♩♪ with

♩♩ and ♪♩. , without impairing the fluidity of her singing.

#3. LA FRAGUA DE LA CASA SANTA + EL ZEJUT DE LOS ABOT

This song is particularly interesting, for it was recorded in Morocco (the others were performed in North or South America) some thirty years ago, when there was still an important Jewish community there. It was difficult to transcribe, as the rendition is heterophonic rather than in true unison and—as it seems not to have been previously published—there are no other versions to compare it

Nº 3. La fragua de la Casa Santa + El zejut de los abot.

with. On the other hand, the fact that it is sung by a group gives some idea of the traditional ambience of the songs.

The melody is in the equivalent of the Western major mode, which is often found in North African music and in the synagogal music of Moroccan Jews. The text of the song is mainly religious, something between a wedding song and a paraliturgical song. An interesting characteristic is the 'bridge' note between the end of one phrase and the beginning of the next (see * in the transcription). This 'connecting note' is common in the Judeo-Spanish song repertoire and in Judeo-Moroccan liturgical music; it creates an impression of circularity and completeness: there is never an 'end'.

As sung by these informants, the form of the song is not symmetrical, but it does eventually stabilize into a regular verse refrain structure. For this reason, I have not transcribed the beginning of the song, but start at line 11.

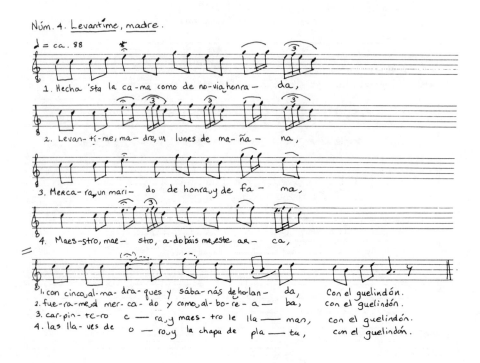

Núm. 4. Levantíme, madre.

1. Hecha 'sta la ca-ma como de no-via honra — da,
2. Levan- tí-me, ma— dre, un lunes de ma-ña — na,
3. Merca- ra un mari— do de honra y de fa — ma,
4. Maes-stro, mae— stro, a-dobáis me este ar — ca,

1. con cinco al-ma- dra-ques y sába-nás de ho lan— da,   Con el guelindón.
2. fue-ra-me al mer- ca-do y como al-bo-re— a — ba,   con el guelindón.
3. car-pin- te-ro   c — ra y maes- tro le lla — man,   con el guelindón.
4. las lla- ves de   o — ro y la chapa de pla — ta,   con el guelindón.

Ton. orig.

#4. LEVANTÍME, MADRE

The melody sung by this informant bears no relation whatsoever to those given for the same text by Larrea and Alvar.[9] Like the other performed by the same informant (#1), it is not sung in a dance rhythm, but in a gentle and lyrical manner. The mode fluctuates between major and minor (see #2). The rhythm is steady, except for the held notes indicated by fermatas (see * in transcription). Because I have not heard or seen this melody elsewhere, it is hard to say whether this is just a characteric of this informant's interpretation. I had the opportunity of asking him about it,[10] and he said he was unaware of having held that note longer.

Num. 5. Jacób y Maẓaltov

#5. JACOB y MAẒALTOV

The informant accompanies herself on the *sonaẒa*, with a simple rhythm as indicated in the transcription punctuated by rests which usually correspond to punctuation in the text. The melody is in the 'Spanish scale' described by

Crivillé[11], with an augmented second in the second half of the melody. This interval, characteristic of the _hijaz kar_ tetrachord of Middle Eastern music, imparts an 'oriental' character to the song, an impression reinforced by the informant's nasal vocal timbre and the rapid, and almost microtonal, ornaments. The limited melodic range suggests an earlier origin for this melody than for the others discussed in this study.

The same melody is used for a brief Passover song, "_Hermana SimHa_," and S. Levy, the performer of #1 and #4 of this study, informs me[12] that it is also used for two liturgical songs, "_LeHa dodi_," a joyous welcome of the Sabbath, and the solemn "_Yitgadal_." Above, I transcribe the beginning of each of the two liturgical songs as sung by Mr. Levy. For them, he sings in a smoother and more ornamented style than he uses for "_Jacob y Mazaltov_" or for "_Hermana SimHa_": again, examination of performance practice reveals musical traits which do not appear in conventional transcriptions and which can only be understood in the traditional social and cultural context of the musical repertoire being studied.

NOTES

1. Manuel Alvar, _Cantos de boda judeo-españoles_ (Madrid: CSIC, 1954).

2. A. Larrea Palacin, _Canciones rituales hispano-judías_ (Madrid: CSIC, 1971).

3. H. Yurchenco, _Ballads, Wedding Songs and Piyyutim of the Sephardic Jews of Tetuan and Tangier_ [sic] _Morocco_ (New York: Ethnic Folkways FE4208, 1983).

4. J. Cohen, "_Ya salió de la mar_"—_Judeo-Spanish Wedding Songs_, in press in E. Koskoff, ed., _Women and Music in Cross-Cultural Perspective_ (New York: Greenwood Press).

5. N. Kaufman, "Muzikalnijat folklor na spanjolskite (sefardskite) evrei v'Bulgaria", _Bulletin de l'Institute de musique_ XII: 231–67 (Sofia, Academie bulgare des sciences, 1967).

6. S. Weich-Shaahaq, _Sephardic Songs from the Balkans_ (LP) (Jerusalem: Hebrew University AMTI 8001, 1980). "The Wedding Songs of the Bulgarian-Sephardi Jews", _Orbis Musicae_ 7:81–107 (Tel Aviv, 1979–80). "Structural Phenomena in the Wedding Songs of Bulgarian Sephardi Jews," _The Sephardi and Oriental Jewish Heritage_, I. Ben Ami, ed. (Jerusalem: Magnes Press, 1982).

7. I have given English versions or summaries of these songs in my translation of Dr. Anahory-Librowicz's article, of which this is the musical commentary.

8. Larrea, op. cit., pp. 72–3; Alvar, op. cit., p. 357.

9. Larrea, 28, 30; Alvar: 363.

10. Interview with Solly Levy, Montreal, April 1986.

11. J. Crivillé i Bargalló, _El folklore musical_ (Madrid: Alianza, 1983), pp. 311–16. Larrea (op. cit., p. 89) transcribes the song without the hijaz kar tetrachord, in a major mode.

12. Interview with Solly Levy, 1985.

Contributors

Oro Anahory-Librowicz is Professor of Spanish at Collège du Vieux-Montréal. Her area of specialization is traditional Judeo-Spanish balladry. Author of many articles and two books, she has lectured at international conferences in North America, Venezuela, Israel, Spain, and Germany. She is also co-founder and director of the musical ensemble Gerineldo, whose goal is the perpetuation and dissemination of Moroccan Judeo-Spanish songs and traditional culture. The group has performed in Israel, Spain, Venezuela, Canada, and the United States.

Issachar Ben Ami is Lecturer on Jewish Folklore at the Hebrew University of Jerusalem. He is the founder of the "Folklore Research Center Studies" series. His research focuses on the traditions of North African Jewry, and he recently became the first Israeli to receive the Interantional Pitre-Salomone Marino Prize for Ethnoanthropological Research for the French edition of his book, *Culte des Saints et Pelerinages Judeo-Musulmans au Maroc.*

Joshua Blau is Max Scholessinger Professor of Arabic at the Hebrew University of Jerusalem.

Judith R. Cohen is currently researching Judeo-Spanish song as a post-doctoral research fellow at the University of Toronto. She is also active as a performer of Judeo-Spanish, medieval, and other musical traditions and is a founding member of the ensemble Gerineldo.

Sandra Messinger Cypess is Professor of Spanish, Latin American Studies, and Comparative Literature at SUNY-Binghamton. She has published extensively on Hispanic women writers and Latin American drama and has contributed chapters to books on diverse topics. She is co-editor of *Women Authors of Modern Hispanic South America: A Bibliography of Literary Criticism and Interpretation* (Scarecrow Press, 1989), and author of *La Malinche in Mexican Literature: From History to Myth* (Univ. of Texas Press, forthcoming).

Paloma Díaz-Mas is Professor of Spanish Literature at the Universidad del Pais Vasco in Spain. She has written many articles on Sephardic Studies, concentrating on elegies and ballads. Her book, *Los sefardies: Historia, lengua y cultura* (Barcelona:

Riopiedras, 1986), has been published in English translation by the University of Chicago Press under the title *Sephardim: The Jews from Spain*.

Jacqueline Genot-Bismuth is holder of the Chair of Ancient and Medieval Judaism at the Sorbonne Nouvelle. She is also the founder and director of the Centre de Recherche sur la culture de l'Israël Ancien et Médiéval. She has participated in many academic conferences and has published numerous articles in specialized international journals.

Matilde Gini de Barnatán is Director of Sephardic programs in Judeo-Spanish for Radio Exterior de España.

David M. Gitlitz is Professor of Spanish at the University of Rhode Island. He served for several years as Dean of Arts and Sciences at SUNY-Binghamton. He has written about stereotyping in the Golden Age Spanish theatre, and the 'new-Christian' agendas of a variety of authors of that period. His current work centers on Crypto-Jewish religious and social customs.

Reginetta Haboucha is Professor of Spanish at Lehman College of CUNY. She has lectured and published extensively in the United States and internationally on the Judeo-Spanish folktale and has received several national grants and fellowships. Her most recent publication is *Types and Motifs of the Judeo-Spanish Folktale* (New York, 1991).

Pier Cesare Ioly Zorattini is Professor of History of Judaism at the University of Udine, Italy. His main interests are the study of the history of Conversos in Italy and of Jewish settlements in the territories of the Republic of Venice during the modern ages. He is publishing all the trials held by the Venetian Inquisition against Jews and Judaizers from 1548 to the end of the seventeenth century.

Isaac Jack Lévy is Professor of Spanish Language and Literature at the University of South Carolina. He has published articles on Hispanic topics, and on the culture, poetry, and folklore of the Sephardim of the Balkans, Turkey, and the Dodecanese Islands. He is now co-authoring a book with Professor Rosemary Lévy Zumwalt on folk religion and folk medicine of the Sephardim of the Ottoman Empire. Among his books are *Prolegomena to the Study of the 'Refranero Sefardí'* (New York: Las Americas, 1969); *And the World Stood Silent: Sephardic Poetry of the Holocaust* (Urbana: Univ. of Illinois Press, 1989); and *Jewish Rhodes: A Lost Culture* (Berkeley: Judah L. Magnes Museum, 1989).

Ze'ev Levy is Professor Emeritus at the University of Haifa. Author of several books, including *Between Yafeth and Shem: The Relationship Between Jewish and General Philosophy* (Hebrew, 1982; English, 1987); *Baruch or Benedict: On Some*

Jewish Aspects of Spinoza's Philosophy (English, 1989); and *David Baumgardt and Ethical Hedonism* (English, 1989).

Carlos Mota is in the Departamento de Filología Española at the Universidad del País Vasco in Spain.

Daniel J. Schroeter is holder of the Melton Chair in Jewish History at the University of Florida. Has published *Merchants of Essaouira: Urban Society and Imperialism in Southwestern Morocco, 1844–1886* (Cambridge Univ. Press, 1988), as well as articles in Morocco, France, Israel, England, and the United States. His research concentrates on the Jews of Morocco.

Helen A. Shepard is Associate Professor of Spanish at Lorain County, Community College in Ohio. She has lived and traveled extensively both in Spain and Portugal, often retracing the past in the ancient streets and synagogues, folklore, and literature of Iberia's Sephardic heritage.

Rachel Simon is currently at Princeton University. Her research focuses on the Middle East and North Africa in the nineteenth and twentieth centuries, concentrating recently on the Jews of Libya. Author of *Libya between Ottomanism and Nationalism* (Berlin: Klaus Schwarz Verlag, 1987) and *Change within Tradition among Jewish Women in Libya (19th–20th Centuries)* (Seattle: Univ. of Washington Press, forthcoming).

Steve Siporin is Associate Professor of English and History at Utah State University. He has also worked as a public folklorist for the states of Iowa, Oregon, and Idaho. He writes on the folklife of Italian Jews, public folklore, and regional folk art in the American West.

Norman A. Stillman is Professor of History and Arabic at SUNY-Binghamton and author of six books and numerous articles. His most recent book, *The Jews of Arab Lands in Modern Times* (Philadelphia: Jewish Publication Society, 1991), is a sequel to his highly acclaimed *The Jews of Arab Lands: A History and Source Book*, by the same publisher in 1979. He is editor of the *AJS Review*, and has received numerous academic honors.

Yedida K. Stillman is Professor of Near Eastern Studies and Chair of the Department of Judaic Studies at SUNY-Binghamton. Recognized as a leading ethnographer of Near Eastern and North African Jewry and as the premier authority on both Islamic and Jewish costume, she is the author of many articles and contributions for such works as the *Encyclopedia of Islam*, the *Dictionary of the Middle Ages*, and the *Dictionary of Art*. She has been guest curator or technical advisor to the Smithsonian Institution, the Museum of International Folk Art, the Jewish Museum, the Diaspora Museum, and the Jewish Museum of Greece. Among her books are *Palestinian Costume and Jewelry* (Albuquerque: Univ. of New Mexico Press, 1979), and *From Southern Morocco to Northern Israel: A Study in the Material Culture of Shelomi* (Haifa Univ. Press, 1982).

Shmuel Trigano is Professor of Sociology at the University of Paris X-Nanterre, Director of the Collège des Etudes Juives of the Alliance Israélite Universelle, and of *Pardès*, a review of Jewish studies. Among his publications are *La récit de la disparue, essai sur l'identité juive* (Gallimard, 1977), *La Nouvelle question juive* (Gallimard, 1979), and *La Demeure oubliée génèse religieuse du politique* (Lieu Commun, 1986).

Eva Alexandra Uchmany is Professor of History at the Universidad Nacional Autónoma de México. She has published several articles on Precolombian and Colonial History and has lectured at universities in Latin America, Spain, Portugal, Israel, India, Japan, and the United States. She is author of *Life between Judaism and Christianity in New Spain: 1580–1606* (Archivo General de la Nación de México, 1991).

Paul Wexler is Professor of Linguistics at Tel-Aviv University. He has published several articles and books on historical, Jewish, and Slavic linguistics. He is co-editor of the *Mediterranean Language Review* and the accompanying *Mediterranean Language and Culture Monograph* series. Among his books are *Explorations in Judeo-Slavic Linguistics* (Leiden, 1987); *Three Heirs to a Judeo-Latin Legacy: Judeo-Ibero-Romance, Yiddish and Rotwelsch* (Wiesbaden, 1988); *Judeo-Romance Linguistics: A Bibliography (Latin, Italo-, Gallo-, Ibero- and Rhaeto-Romance except Castilian)* (New York, 1989); and *The Schizoid Nature of Modern Hebrew: A Slavic Language in Search of a Semitic Past* (Wiesbaden, 1990).

Walter P. Zenner is Professor of Anthropology at SUNY-Albany. His major interests are Middle Eastern culture and the general ramifications of ethnicity.

Zvi Zohar is at both the Shalom Hartman Institute in Jerusalem and the Institute of Contemporary Jewry at Hebrew University.

George K. Zucker is Professor of Spanish at the University of Northern Iowa. He is the compiler of the *International Directory for Sephardic and Oriental Jewish Studies* and translator of *Sephardim: The Jews from Spain* by Paloma Díaz-Mas (Chicago: The Univ. of Chicago Press, 1992).

Rosemary Lévy Zumwalt is Associate Professor of Anthropology at Davidson College. She has published articles on Eskimo mythology and ritual, children's folklore, Sephardic folklore, and history of anthropology and folklore. She is currently co-authoring a book with Isaac Jack Lévy on the folk religion and folk medicine of the Sephardim of the Ottoman Empire. Among her books are *American Folklore Scholarship: A Dialogue of Dissent* (Bloomington: Indiana Univ. Press, 1988); *The Enigma of Arnold van Gennep (1873–1957): Master of French Folklore and Hermit of Bourg-la Reine* (Helsinki: Folklore Fellows Communications, 1988); and *Wealth and Rebellion: Elsie Clews Parsons, Anthropologist and Folklorist* (Urbana: Univ. of Illinois Press, in press).